AGRARIAN STUDIES 4

A NEW STATISTICAL DOMAIN IN INDIA

An Enquiry into Village Panchayat Databases

AGRARIAN STUDIES 4

A NEW STATISTICAL DOMAIN IN INDIA
An Enquiry into Village Panchayat Databases

JUN-ICHI OKABE

APARAJITA BAKSHI

 Tulika Books

Published by

Tulika Books

35 A/1 (ground floor), Shahpur Jat, New Delhi 110 049, India

tulikabooks.wordpress.com

First edition (hardback) 2016

ISBN: 978-93-82381-78-5

Printed at Chaman Offset, New Delhi 110 002

CONTENTS

Foreword   vii

Acknowledgements   xi

Abbreviations   xiv

Glossary   xv

1 Introduction   1

2 Data Required for the Village Panchayat   12

3 Introducing the Two Village Panchayats   59

4 Basic Structure of the Main Data Sources at the Village Level   152

5 A Potential Village-Level Database on the Panchayat   215

6 Potential Databases on Village Panchayat's Jurisdiction   242

7 Potential Village-Level Data for Public Finance   273

8 A Potential Database for Local-Level Planning, with Special
  Reference to the Village Schedule on Basic Statistics   295

9 Conclusion   339

Annexure   347

Bibliography   372

Index   379

FOREWORD

E.M.S. Namboodiripad once observed that, at the Central and State levels, the Indian Constitution as originally drafted gave the people institutions of bourgeois parliamentary democracy; at all levels below that of the State, however, it gave the people the bureaucracy. In other words, while the people had a Constitutional right to vote for their Member of Parliament or their Member of the Legislative Assembly, at the level of the district, administrative block or village, their lives were controlled by unelected officials – the Collector, District Magistrate, Block Development Officer, Patwari or Village Administrative Officer, and the like. Thus, even issues of street lighting in a village, or sanitation and sewage in a hamlet, were issues that had to be raised in elections to Parliament or State Legislatures.

West Bengal was the first State in India to institutionalise local government by elected representatives of the people at the district, Block, and village levels in any meaningful way. In its Statement of Objects and Reasons, the Constitution Seventy-Third Amendment Act of 1992 criticised panchayati raj institutions that had been in existence until that time for not having "acquired the status and dignity of viable and responsive people's bodies," and, in effect, listed the failures of erstwhile panchayats that the West Bengal experience had overcome: that is, "absence of regular elections, prolonged supersessions, insufficient representation of . . . Scheduled Castes, Scheduled Tribes, and women, inadequate devolution of powers, and lack of financial resources" (Government of India 1992). The Amendment went on to list 29 areas in which administrative activity was to be devolved to panchayats, and to envisage the involvement of panchayats in the "preparation of plans for economic development and social justice and for the implementation of development schemes" (*ibid.*).

With the devolution of administrative responsibilities and responsibilities for planning came a new need for statistical data to fulfil the constitutional requirements of local self-government at the district, Block, and village levels. New panchayat-level responsibilities demanded new panchayat-level databases. In this pioneering study, Jun-ichi Okabe and Aparajita Bakshi examine the "new statistical domain" that was created as a result of the Seventy-Third Amendment to the Constitution, concentrating on the socio-economic data needs of village panchayats in the post-devolution era.

The analysis in this book can be located in the context of the literature on local self-government in the post-Independence period, including the discussion around the work of the Balwantrai Mehta Committee, the Committee on Panchayati Raj Institutions chaired by Asoka Mehta, and the movement for Peoples' Planning in Kerala. The authors draw on the critique of Thomas Isaac and Richard Franke (2000, p. 106), who wrote that a "major weakness of the Indian database is its near-total insensitivity to the needs of planning from below."

Two important contributions to the official literature are of immediate concern to the authors. The first is the report of the National Statistical Commission in 2001, which argued that "no standardised system exists for the collection of local-level databases in the country," and, further, that the Indian statistical system "appeared to be crumbling" at its foundations. The second document is the Report on Basic Statistics for Local-Level Development, submitted in 2004 by an Expert Committee of the Planning Commission chaired by Abhijit Sen. The core recommendation of the Committee was that the village panchayat "consolidate, maintain and own village level data" (Central Statistical Organisation 2006, p. 1), and that existing records be validated and used to the extent possible.

A distinctive aspect of the book is that the authors examine in detail the functions of a village panchayat as envisaged in the Constitution, create an anticipatory list of the items of statistical information necessary to fulfil those functions, and then evaluate the actually existing databases in the two villages that they have chosen for detailed case study. The book thus explores micro-level aspects of the databases available at the village panchayat level. Okabe and Bakshi, who conducted their field studies between 2007 and 2011, had benchmark data from the two villages, Warwat Khanderao in Buldhana district, Maharashtra, and Bidyanidhi in Barddhaman district, West Bengal, which had been studied by the Foundation for Agrarian Studies in 2007 and 2005. Household data from Bidyanidhi were also collected by Bakshi in 2005–6.

Since village panchayats are the administrative institutions closest to the people in rural areas, unit-level information on village society is crucial. At present, unit-level records and registers are used primarily for the identification and selection of beneficiaries of public policies and for delivery of services, and not for a broader range of purposes. The authors identify the village panchayat (and sub-panchayat bodies) as being the institutions best suited to correct micro-level discrepancies in administrative records and registers.

An instructive conclusion from the analysis is that, in order to maintain a record-based system of statistical databases, a data-sharing mechanism between the village panchayat and other village-level agencies is indispensable. Village panchayats have to overcome bureaucratic obstacles involved in the division of powers between panchayat institutions and regular departments of State Governments in order to create such a mechanism.

Of particular interest is the Okabe–Bakshi proposal for a People's List – their response to the fact that no register or list exists (or is statutorily required to exist) in any village in India of the persons actually resident in that village.

This book is a new and important contribution to the study of statistical databases of rural India. Chapters 1 and 9 of this book are of interest to any student of economic development, democratic decentralisation, and panchayati raj in India. The intermediate chapters are invaluable as a manual and guide to persons involved in the administration of village panchayats, or concerned with the overlapping territory between Constitutional requirements and administrative practice with regard to panchayat functioning. Chapter 4, for example, is useful for all students of rural statistics.

An important qualification that Okabe and Bakshi make to their argument and analysis is that the reference period of their study is 2005 to 2011. Two important changes have occurred since the end of that reference period. The first is the general weakening after 2011 of local self-government in West Bengal, the State that pioneered panchayati raj. Aparajita Bakshi has written of the subversion of decision-making processes in village panchayats and of the general regression that has occurred in local self-government in rural West Bengal after 2011 (see Bakshi 2011). The second change is the decision of the Government of India to abolish the Planning Commission, a decision that cannot but damage village panchayats' mandate to "prepare plans for economic change and social justice." This institutional change has been accompanied by a curtailment of funds available for social welfare programmes, the very programmes that lie at the core of a village panchayat's administrative and developmental concern.

The relevance of the issues discussed in this book, the innovative method that the authors use to study these issues, and their meticulous handling of the available material and of the data that they have collected mark it as an important departure in the literature on statistical databases and village-level local government in India.

V.K. RAMACHANDRAN
General Editor, Agrarian Studies series

ACKNOWLEDGMENTS

The research presented in this book began as two independent studies initiated by Jun-ichi Okabe and scholars associated with the Foundation for Agrarian Studies (FAS). The first study, by Okabe and V. Surjit, focused on birth records and the Civil Registration System in Warwat Khanderao. The focus of the second study, by Okabe and Aparajita Bakshi, was on data needs for local-level planning and development in West Bengal. These two studies were presented at "Studying Village Economies in India: A Colloquium on Methodology," held in Chalsa in December 2008. The two studies laid the basis for a deeper interest in village-level statistics in India, an interest that led us to the research that culminated in this book.

Niladri Sekhar Dhar carried out large parts of the fieldwork and research for Warwat Khanderao village. The book would not have been possible without contributions by him and V. Surjit.

The people of the two villages – Warwat Khanderao in Buldhana district, Maharashtra, and Raina in Barddhaman district, West Bengal – were our principal instructors and are the principal contributors to this book. They were forthcoming and patient in sharing information with us when we conducted interviews and verified village-level data. We acknowledge the support and guidance given by Gopal Galkar, the *sarpanch* of Warwat Khanderao village panchayat, and Sabyasachi Dey and Madhabilata Dhara, erstwhile *pradhans* of Raina village panchayat. The inputs received from elected officials, the Gram Sevak, Warwat Khanderao village panchayat, the Executive Assistant and other officials in Raina village panchayat, Integrated Child Development Services workers, health workers, school teachers, and revenue officials in the two villages were indispensable to our research.

We are grateful to the Block Development Officers and staff at the Block offices at Raina and Sangrampur, the Raina Block agricultural officer, the staff at Raina Block land and land reforms office, and medical officers and staff at Raina and Paturda primary health centres, for sharing information with us. We also acknowledge the help we received from Anup Shengulwar, Project

Director, DRDA, Buldhana district; Uday Sarkar, *Sabhadipati*, Barddhaman district panchayat (*zilla parishad*); Subrata Chakraborty, Programme Coordinator, Strengthening Rural Decentralisation (SRD) Cell, Panchayat and Rural Development Department, West Bengal; and Rahul Majumder, Consultant, West Bengal State Rural Development Agency (WBSRDA).

We acknowledge the research assistance we received from Navpreet Kaur, Ajay Niture, Rahul Gaikwad, Bharat Patil, and the FAS team. Yoshifumi Usami and Biplab Sarkar made an important contribution to analysing data from village records in Warwat Khanderao. Harshan Teepee and Karan Raut translated documents from Malayalam and Marathi for us.

We appreciate the encouragement we received from Abhijit Sen, Member, Planning Commission, at the Chalsa Colloquium. The work and findings of the Expert Committee on Basic Statistics for Local Level Development (the Abhijit Sen Committee) were an important influence on our work. We also received comments from Pronab Sen, Chairman of the National Statistical Commission. Some of the preliminary research on the project was presented at seminars and discussed with scholars at Yokohama National University and Kobe University in 2009. We are grateful to the participants of the seminars, and the faculty and staff of these universities who facilitated the research visit. An earlier version of this book was presented at a "National Seminar on Statistical Databases in Gram Panchayats" held at the Economic Analysis Unit, Indian Statistical Institute, Bangalore, on November 7, 2013. We are grateful to the participants, particularly T.J. Rao, Abhijit Sen, Pronab Sen, and T.M. Thomas Isaac, for comments. Some of the findings of the book were also presented at the "Tenth Anniversary Conference of the Foundation for Agrarian Studies," Kochi, January 2014. We are grateful to the participants for their comments.

L. Divyabharathi, Shad Naved, and V.K. Ramachandran edited the manuscript.

At different stages of this book, we have had discussions on its subject matter with Venkatesh Athreya, T. Jayaraman, the late Vinayak Gaikwad, K.N. Harilal, Jihei Kaneko, Surjya Kanta Mishra, R. Ramakumar, Vikas Rawal, Daisuke Sakata, P.V. Unnikrishnan, and Yoshifumi Usami.

During the period of this research, one of us (Aparajita Bakshi) was at the Indian Statistical Institute, the Foundation for Agrarian Studies, and the Tata Institute of Social Sciences, and the other (Jun-ichi Okabe) at the Faculty of Economics, Yokohama National University. We are grateful to these institutions for the facilities that were provided to us.

Particular thanks are due to V.K. Ramachandran, Madhura Swaminathan, and the Foundation for Agrarian Studies team for their active support of this project. The book has evolved from fruitful collaboration between Yokohama National University and FAS. V.K. Ramachandran has promoted this study from the outset. He was a constant source of inspiration and guidance for this study.

JUN-ICHI OKABE and APARAJITA BAKSHI
December 2, 2015

ABBREVIATIONS

AAY	*Antyodaya Anna Yojana*
BDO	Block Development Officer
BPL	Below Poverty Line
IAY	*Indira Awaas Yojana*
ICDS	Integrated Child Development Services
IGNOAPS	Indira Gandhi National Old Age Pension Scheme
MSK	*Madhyamik Shiksha Karmasuchi*
NFBS	National Family Benefit Scheme
NREGS	National Rural Employment Guarantee Scheme
PS	*panchayat samiti*
SGRY	*Sampoorna Grameen Rozgar Yojana*
SGSY	*Swarnajayanti Gram Swarozgar Yojana*
SSA	*Sarva Shiksha Abhiyan*
SSK	*Shishu Shiksha Karmasuchi*
TSC	Total Sanitation Campaign
WBSEDCL	West Bengal State Electricity Distribution Company Limited
ZP	*zilla parishad*

GLOSSARY

Aam Admi Bima Yojana: Government of India insurance scheme that provides death and disability cover to persons in the age group 18 to 59 years, in specific occupational groups including rural landless households

Accelerated Irrigation Benefits Programme (AIBP): Government of India programme intended to provide loan assistance to the States to help them complete major and medium irrigation projects that were at an advanced stage of completion

Accelerated Rural Water Supply Programme (ARWSP): Government of India programme to assist States and Union Territories (UTs) to accelerate the pace of coverage of drinking water supplies

anganwadi: village-level child care centre. The Government of India started these in 1975 as part of the Integrated Child Development Services (ICDS) programme. They are established in villages or neighbourhoods, and are expected to provide supplementary nutrition for children, pregnant women, and lactating mothers, and provide pre-school services for children of 3 to 6 years.

Annapurna Yojana: centrally sponsored food security scheme. Under this scheme, persons who are recognised as destitute and are eligible for but do not receive a National Old Age Pension (NOAPS), are to be provided 10 kg of foodgrain a month free of cost.

Antyodaya Anna Yojana (*AAY*): food subsidy programme of the Government of India under which very poor and economically vulnerable families are to receive 25 kg of foodgrain a month at subsidised rates. Beneficiary households receive a separate ration card, the *Antyodaya* card. The programme began in December 2000.

Balika Samriddhi Yojana: centrally sponsored scheme of the Ministry of Women and Child Development whose declared objective is to change negative family and community attitudes towards a girl child at birth and towards her mother. The scheme envisages the provision of a post-birth grant of money for parents of a girl child and scholarships for schoolgoing girls.

Bal Vikas Samiti: Child Development Committee

Bhavishyanidhi Yojana: Provident Fund Scheme

chulha: open stove

Dalit *basti*: hamlet of Scheduled Caste households

dharmasala: resting place or shelter, particularly for pilgrims

ghat: series of steps leading to a water body

---

* This glossary deals with terms as they are used in the context of the present study.

girdawari: record of ownership and tilling (and of harvest inspection) of land maintained by the village revenue officer

gram: village

gram sabha: general body of all members registered in the electoral rolls pertaining to a *gram panchayat*

gram sansad: electoral constituency within a village (*gram*) panchayat. More technically, according to the West Bengal Panchayat Act of 1973, a body consisting of persons registered at any time in the electoral rolls pertaining to a constituency of a village panchayat delimited for the purpose of the preceding general election to the village panchayat.

gram sevak: village development officer

Gram Shiksha Samiti: Village Education Committee

Grameen Swachchhata Vibhag: Rural Sanitation Department

Gram Unnayan Samiti: Village Development Council. An executive body responsible for implementation and monitoring of various schemes at the *gram sansad* level. It comprises elected members to the *gram panchayat*, the opposition candidate obtaining the second highest vote in the preceding *gram panchayat* election, three representatives of non-governmental organisations or community-based organisations, three representatives of active self-help groups with at least two members from women-led self-help groups, one serving or retired Government employee, one serving or retired teacher (all voters of the area), and another 10 members or 1 per cent of the total number of members of the *gram sansad*, whichever is higher (from Government of West Bengal 2007).

haat: rural market

Integrated Child Development Services (ICDS): programme which provides pre-school education and nutrition for children below the age of six, pregnant women, and lactating mothers

Indira Awaas Yojana (*IAY*): rural housing scheme sponsored by the Government of India which provides support for construction and repair of houses for selected poor households in rural areas

jakat tax: type of customs duty

Jawahar Gram Samriddhi Yojana (*JGSY*): development scheme begun in 1989 by the Government of India. Its declared aim is to create "need-based rural infrastructure," and to provide foodgrain and wage employment in rural areas.

kisan mela: farmers' fair

kishan bon: type of fodder

Kishori Shakti Yojana: centrally sponsored scheme of the Ministry of Women and Child Development to "empower adolescent girls in rural India." The scheme is implemented through the Integrated Child Development Services (ICDS).

krishi karmadhyaksha: secretary of Agricultural Committee

krishi sahayak: village agricultural extension official

Madhyamik Shiksha Karmasuchi: programme of the West Bengal State Panchayati Raj Department. It is intended to ensure universal access to schooling and enrolment of all children between 9 and 14 years.

Maharashtra Gramin Paani Parota Yojana: Maharashtra Rural Water Supply Scheme

Mahila Baal Samiti: Woman and Child Committee (in Maharashtra)

Mahila Samriddhi Yojana: microfinance scheme for women

mandi: market

Member of Parliament Local Area Development Scheme (MPLADS): fund that can be used by Members of Parliament for constituency-level development work. Each Member of Parliament is allowed Rs 50 million a year under the scheme.

Mid-Day Meals Programme (MDM): Government of India school meal programme implemented in primary and upper primary government and government-aided schools

mithun: cattle

mouza: revenue village in West Bengal

Nari o Shishu Unnayan Sthayee Samiti: Standing Committee on Woman and Child Development

National Family Benefit Scheme (NFBS): centrally sponsored social security programme to provide one-time financial assistance to a household in the event of the death of a breadwinner

National Old Age Pension Scheme (NOAPS): centrally sponsored social security programme which provides monthly old age pensions to below poverty line individuals aged 60 years and above

National Rural Employment Guarantee Scheme (NREGS): centrally sponsored universal rural wage employment programme launched in 2007 that entitles every rural household to 100 days of wage employment on demand

National Rural Health Mission (NRHM): umbrella programme with the goal of achieving better health outcomes in rural areas

National Social Assistance Programme (NSAP): umbrella programme comprising different pension and social assistance schemes for rural households

Nirmal Gaon Seva: Rural Sanitation Programme

panchayat samiti: second tier of the panchayat system. A *panchayat samiti* is constituted at the level of an administrative Block, which consists of a number of village panchayats.

patwari: village land revenue officer

pradhan: elected chairperson of a village panchayat; also called *sarpanch*

Protibedon: title of the Annual Report of Raina *gram panchayat*

raiyatwari: land revenue administration system in colonial India under which land revenue was directly imposed on cultivators of agricultural land or *raiyat*

Rajiv Gandhi Grameen Vidyutikaran Yojana (*RGGVY*): rural electrification scheme that provides free electricity connections to below poverty line households

Rajiv Gandhi Niwara Yojana: Maharashtra Government home loan scheme for economically weak but above poverty line households

Rural Infrastructure Development Fund (RIDF): fund instituted by the National Bank for Agriculture and Rural Development (NABARD) in 1995–6 with the objective of giving low-cost loans to State Governments and state-owned corporations for the quick completion of projects involving medium and minor irrigation, soil conservation, watershed management, and other forms of rural infrastructure

sajaldhara: drinking water project in Bidyanidhi village, West Bengal

Sampoorna Grameen Rozgar Yojana (SGRY): universal rural employment scheme launched by the Government of India in 2001. Its declared objective was to provide employment and food for the population below the poverty line. The scheme was to be implemented through panchayati raj institutions.

sanchalak: director

sarai: resting place or shelter for travellers

sarpanch: elected chairperson of a village panchayat

Sarva Shiksha Abhiyan (SSA): programme of the Government of India for universalising elementary education

siddha: system of traditional medicine

Shishu Shiksha Karmasuchi: West Bengal State Panchayati Raj Department programme aimed to set up Child Learning Centres in locations where at least twenty children were without access to a primary school or required some special dispensation that was not available in the formal primary schools

Swarnajayanti Gram Swarozgar Yojana (SGSY): micro-credit-based self-employment and livelihood support programme of the Government of India

talathi: village land revenue official

tehsil: land revenue administrative unit below the district

tehsildar: land revenue official at the administrative level of the *tehsil* (or *taluk*), a unit of land revenue administration above the village

Total Sanitation Campaign (TSC): centrally sponsored programme aimed to accelerate sanitation coverage in rural areas, and create awareness about sanitation and health education

upa-pradhan: elected deputy chairperson of a village panchayat

ward *sabha*: general body of all listed voters of an electoral ward within the village panchayat

zamindari: statutory landlordism; system of land tenure introduced by British rule in colonial Bengal

zilla parishad: district panchayat

Chapter 1

INTRODUCTION

1.1 BACKGROUND AND MOTIVATION FOR THE STUDY

A new statistical domain has emerged in rural India as a consequence of the Constitution (Seventy-Third Amendment) Act, 1992, a domain based on the needs and Constitutional functions of the panchayati raj institutions. Our study examines this new statistical domain. We discuss its potential and substance with respect to the village panchayat (*gram panchayat*), which is the lowest level for which elections are held, and is the first stage of data collection and recording.

Village panchayats have become an integral part of rural life in India, and provide the institutional framework for democratic decentralisation.[1] India's Constitution (Seventy-Third Amendment) Act, 1992 is a watershed in the history of democratic decentralisation. It gave Constitutional status and devolved twenty-nine subject functions to the panchayati raj institutions at the village, block, and district levels. It provided mechanisms for regular elections and raising financial resources, and for panchayats to function as institutions of local self-government. It also politically empowered women and "the weaker sections of the population" through reservations. Since the panchayat is the tier of government closest to the citizens and to residents of settlements under it, and thus is in a better position than other tiers to appreciate their immediate concerns, the establishment of panchayats has opened up new ways to expanding the basic capabilities of citizens in rural

---

[1] The *Report of the Administrative Reforms Committee 1958* (Kerala Administrative Reforms Commission 1959, vol. 1, part I) of the Government of Kerala is considered an epoch-making work on the first generation of modern panchayats. The origin of panchayats has been traced back to the British colonial period and even further back to the pre-colonial period (Mathew 1995, pp. 1–3). However, the panchayati raj of the Nehruvian era is often considered the first generation of modern panchayats, which culminated in 1959 in the recommendations of the study team headed by Balwantrai Mehta, giving birth to three tiers of the panchayati raj institutions. The second generation of the modern panchayati raj institutions is said to have started in 1978 when the West Bengal Government gave new life to the State's panchayats on the lines of the Asoka Mehta Committee's recommendations (*ibid.*, pp. 3–9, Committee on Plan Projects 1959, Ministry of Agriculture and Irrigation 1978, Planning Commission 1952, ch. 7, Kashyap 1989, and Crook and Manor 1998).

areas.[2] As a result of the Seventy-Third Amendment, 1992, many new local leaders are presenting themselves on the local political stage in India.

The institutions of local self-government require statistical databases for their own use. This requirement has necessitated systematic, from-below development of databases.[3] The provisions of the Seventy-Third Amendment are such that village panchayats need datasets to serve multiple and basic functions related to self-governance, micro-level planning of various development programmes and their implementation, and information on panchayat finances.

In 2001, the National Statistical Commission under the Chairmanship of C. Rangarajan argued that "even today no standardised system exists for the collection of local level databases in the country."[4] Under the system of centralised planning, there had been little demand for local-level databases.[5] In the preceding three decades, various working groups, study groups and committees had done a large amount of work on the subject.[6] The Commission observed, however, that "implementation of these recommendations has not been taken seriously."[7]

---

[2] On capabilities and representation, see Sen (1992) and Marx (1959), pp. 28–49. The Second Administrative Reforms Commission (2007, p. 8) stated that "Improving the quality of life of citizens by providing them civic amenities has been the basic function of local governments ever since their inception and it continues to be so even today. Local governments are ideally suited to provide services like water supply, solid waste management, sanitation, etc., as they are closer to the people and in a better position to appreciate their concerns and even economic principles state that such services are best provided at the level of government closest to the people. However, the performance of a large number of local bodies on this front has generally been unsatisfactory."

[3] National Statistical Commission (2001, para 9.2.17).

[4] *Ibid.*, para 9.2.21. Isaac and Franke (2000, p. 106) note that, "major weakness of the Indian database is its near total insensitivity to the requirements of planning from below."

[5] The National Statistical Commission (2001, para 9.2.17) argues that "as there was little or no local level planning for provision of public goods and facilities, there seemed to be little or no need or demand for local level databases." In this regard, Isaac and Franke (2000, p. 106) note: "The data management practices and institutions in the country were evolved to suit the requirements of highly centralised systems of administration and planning. Indeed, most of the national level data are ultimately collected from the localities. But the centralised systems of planning and governance do not require that these data be made available in printed form at the local level."

[6] National Statistical Commission 2001, para 9.2.21. For work done previously, see Central Statistical Organisation (2014, pp. 6–10). On the District Information System of the National Informatics Centre (DISNIC) Programme, see DISNIC Programme Division (2005).

[7] National Statistical Commission (2001, para 9.2.21).

The statistical data sources available at the grass roots are primarily administrative records and census-type surveys.[8] Large-scale sample surveys, highly sophisticated in India, do not necessarily fulfil data requirements at the local level, since these usually provide estimates at the national and State levels.[9] Most of the socio-economic data in India used for purposes of planning and development (except for agricultural statistics) are derived from national sample surveys. This may have weakened the systems of generating statistical data from administrative records. The National Statistical Commission aimed at stemming the deterioration in Indian administrative statistics at the farthest end of the government system.[10] The Commission argued that

> over the years, the Administrative Statistical System has been deteriorating and has now almost collapsed in certain sectors. The deterioration had taken place at its very roots namely, at the very first stage of collection and recording of data, and has been reported so far in four sectors: agriculture, labour, industry and commerce. The foundation on which the entire edifice of Administrative Statistical System was built appears to be crumbling, pulling down the whole system and paralysing a large part of the Indian Statistical System. This indisputably is the major problem facing the Indian Statistical System today.[11]

Accordingly, the Commission recommended that a committee of experts be constituted to look into all aspects of the development of basic statistics for local-level development and to suggest a minimum list of variables on which data needed to be collected.[12] In keeping with this recommendation, the Ministry of Statistics and Programme Implementation constituted, in December 2002, an Expert Committee under the chairmanship of S. P. Gupta to review the existing system at local levels and recommend an appropriate

---

[8] "The main sources of statistics in India as elsewhere are: (a) Administrative Statistics – generally collected by State Governments, consisting of statutory administrative returns and data derived as a by-product of general administration; and (b) other important sources namely, censuses and sample surveys" (*ibid.*, para 14.3.1).

[9] *Ibid.*, para 9.2.22. However, to support decentralised planning, the Planning Commission considered the generation of "a local statistical system by increasing the sample size of National Sample Surveys so that interpretation is possible at least at the level of the Block, if not the village" (Planning Commission 2008a, p. 227). Keeping in mind decentralized planning through the panchayati raj institutions, the International Institute for Population Sciences sponsored by the Ministry of Health and Family Welfare undertakes the District Level Household and Facility Survey (International Institute for Population Sciences 2010).

[10] "The recommendations on individual subjects in the Report aim at stemming the deterioration in the Administrative Statistical System and to improve it over time" (National Statistical Commission 2001, para. 2.12.1).

[11] *Ibid.*, para. 14.3.10.

[12] *Ibid.*, para. 9.2.22.

system for the regular collection of data on a set of core variables for local-level development. With the reconstitution of the Planning Commission in June 2004, Abhijit Sen became the chairman of the committee and completed its work and submitted a comprehensive report on *Basic Statistics for Local Level Development*.[13] The Committee reviewed the efforts made previously and provided a conceptual framework for developing a system of compilation of statistics, one originating from the panchayati raj institutions in the rural sector. Furthermore, the Expert Committee developed a Village Schedule and tested it through pilot studies. Subsequently, in 2009, the Ministry of Statistics and Programme Implementation launched a large-scale pilot scheme for Basic Statistics on Local Level Development to identify data sources in thirty-two States and Union Territories.[14]

The essential recommendation made by this Expert Committee was that "the Gram Panchayat should consolidate, maintain and own village level data."[15] It suggested that the village panchayat (*gram panchayat*) should take responsibility for reorganising and maintaining such records at the village level.[16] In its emphasis on village-level data sources, the recommendation was a simple one but a landmark in the era of democratic decentralisation in rural India. The Committee's recommendation that the village panchayat should "consolidate, maintain and own village level data" identified, in effect, a new statistical domain, one that opens a new area for debate, discussion, and study.[17] The recommendation itself was based on the finding that in almost all States and Union Territories various types of village-level data are regularly collected by local-level functionaries — such as the village development officer (*gram sevak*), health worker (e.g. Auxiliary Nursing Midwife), revenue officials (*patwari*), school teachers, Integrated Child Development Services (*anganwadi*) workers, the village headman, knowledgeable persons, and others — and maintained in their respective registers or records.[18] At

---

[13] Central Statistical Organisation (2006).

[14] Central Statistics Office (2011) and (2014). Initially, small-scale pilot studies were conducted by the Expert Committee on Basic Statistics from 2003 to 2005 in Haryana, Gujarat, Karnataka, Kerala, Meghalaya, West Bengal, Bihar, Tamil Nadu, and Tripura (Central Statistical Organisation 2006, pp. 8ff.).

[15] Central Statistical Organisation (2006, p. 1).

[16] *Ibid.*, p. 2.

[17] The Planning Commission (2008b, p. 16) points out that "the key to the new approach is to link up data collection with the panchayats."

[18] Central Statistical Organisation (2013, pp. 3–4) and (2014, pp. 131–2). "The High Power Expert Committee headed by Abhijit Sen, Member of the Planning Commission, in its report on basic statistics for local level development has provided a conceptual framework for

present, such village-level databases available with the panchayati raj institutions cannot be properly utilised because they are scattered, there is lack of coordination among the agencies responsible for them, the format and itemised details of different sources are inconsistent, and updating and maintaining the data has been irregular.[19]

Based on these findings, the expert committee drafted a framework for Village Schedules (chapter 6) that contained a minimum number of selected variables on which data were to be collected, compiled, aggregated, and transmitted to the district level. The point here is that such village-level data exist before the information is filled up in the Village Schedule. A set of data sources presumably exists in the village along with the data items of the Village Schedule. The Schedule is merely a framework for compiling statistics that have already been collected by local-level functionaries.[20]

Thus, the view of the Expert Committee on village-level data sources is in striking contrast to that of the National Statistical Commission. While the Commission raised serious concern over the degeneration of records maintained by government staff, village land revenue officials, village

---

developing a system of compilation of statistics originating from PRIs in rural sector. It is based on the finding that PRIs in almost all States/UTs have comprehensive repertoire of essential and basic information on desired parameters and have access to sources of these information particulars" (Central Statistical Office 2011, p. A-1).

[19] As the *Basic Statistics on Local Level Development* report (Central Statistical Organisation 2006, p. 19) points out, even the village directory information in the District Census Handbook has been "collected by Census Officers from the records of the villages maintained by the various village functionaries, e.g. Health worker, Auxillary Nurse Midwife, child care centre (*anganwadi*), *chowkidar*, village head (*pradhan*), village revenue officer (*patwari*) etc. The village-wise information available in District Census Handbook contains most of the critical indicators required for local level planning. Since the Census data are available after a gap of 10 years, there is need to update the village directory on annual basis . . . The State governments have to update the census information on an annual basis so that year-wise information on all the basic parameters of village is available for local level planning." Thus, the Village Schedule provided by the *Basic Statistics* report is to be updated annually. In this respect, the Village Schedule can be considered a sort of updated version of the village directory information in the District Census Handbook.

[20] The Village Schedules provide even source codes to be recorded in each item of information as under: Panchayat: 01, *anganwadi* worker: 02, Health worker (ANM/FHW/MHW etc.): 03, *Patwari* (Land Records): 04, Village Headman: 05, Local School: 06, Local Doctor: 07, PHC/Sub-Centre/Hospital: 08, Knowledgeable Person(s)/Others (Female: 09, Male: 10). Using these source codes, the Central Statistical Office (2011, p. 27) presented statistics on major data sources for each item of information for selected States and UTs. But, as mentioned later, source codes in the Village Schedules have some problems.

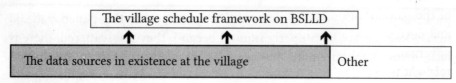

Figure 1

development officers, and primary-school teachers at the village level,[21] the Expert Committee, in the spirit of democratic decentralisation, saw potential in some of the existing village-level records in rural India.[22]

Since village-level databases are neglected by data users, there has been little discussion of these data sources, their quality, and usefulness. With rare exceptions, such as discussions in Kerala in the context of the State's people's planning campaign,[23] there has been little enquiry into the quality and usefulness of village-level data sources that exist in parallel to the Village Schedule. Such an enquiry would require a comprehensive discussion on databases generated as by-products of village-level administrative requirements as well as databases generated from the official censuses. In order to empower the village panchayats after the Seventy-Third Amendment, these village-level databases must be a subject of discussion and debate. In this context, this book comprehensively discusses the new statistical domain that has emerged in rural India after the Seventy-Third Amendment.

1.2 METHODOLOGY AND ORGANISATION

Without an outline of the village panchayats' data needs we cannot evaluate this new statistical domain. In this study, we assess the data needs of panchayats on the basis of the provisions of the Constitution (Seventy-Third Amendment) Act, 1992. Chapter 2 describes and classifies the data needs

---

[21] National Statistical Commission (2001, para. 14.6.1–14.6.4).

[22] Isaac and Franke (2000, p. 110) raise a difficult question: "In many places the secondary data collected from the field offices did not tally with the published statistics of the block and district levels. Were the higher tiers of the local bodies to use data aggregated from below or the aggregate statistics published by official sources? It was agreed that while gram panchayats and municipalities would rely mostly on locally collected data, the higher tiers would use official statistics as far as possible unless there was sufficient justification to modify them."

[23] In Kerala, the matter was discussed during the people's campaign for the Ninth Five Year Plan. The people's campaign initiated a process of planning from below in which local bodies could draw up local plans and development schemes to meet local needs. As part of this exercise, data sources available with and owned by the local bodies that could be used for local-level planning were identified (State Planning Board, Government of Kerala 1996).

of the panchayat on the assumption that State Governments will legislate and devolve powers (whether or not they have actually done so) of self-governance and development to panchayats as provided by the Act. The relevant provisions are Article 40 in Part IV (Directive Principles of State Policy), all Articles in Part IX (Panchayats), the Eleventh Schedule related to Article 243 G, and Article 243 ZD in Part IX A (Municipalities) of the Constitution. Therefore, the scope or boundaries of our study are slightly different from those of the *Basic Statistics on Local Level Development* report. We have identified the panchayat's data needs on the basis of the Constitutional requirements as a whole, whereas the report identified these data needs on the basis of its terms of reference, i.e., "for use in micro-level planning of various developmental programmes."[24]

We have examined the issue of panchayat-level databases in general as well as in two villages, in Maharashtra and West Bengal respectively, both studied previously by the Foundation for Agrarian Studies.[25] The first case study is of Warwat Khanderao village panchayat in Buldhana district, Maharashtra. The second case study is of Raina village panchayat in West Bengal and Bidyanidhi village in the jurisdiction of the Raina village panchayat. The Foundation conducted census-type socio-economic surveys in these two villages in 2007 and 2005, respectively. In chapter 3, we give the background of the evolution of the new statistical domain in both village panchayats. In chapter 4, we describe the village-level data sources that exist and those that are actually maintained by the village panchayats and their satellite agencies. In chapters 5, 6, 7, and 8 we describe the village-level databases that are required by village panchayats, and by panchayati raj institutions as a whole, in the post-Seventy-Third Amendment regime. In particular, we discuss data on the panchayat itself (chapter 5), the People's List (chapter 6), and data connected with public finance (chapter 7). We also evaluate the Village Schedule on Basic Statistics (chapter 8). Further, we present certain issues regarding the scope for new data that go beyond the proposed Village Schedule on Basic Statistics.

For an analytical discussion of the utility of village panchayat-level databases, we need a clear idea of specific operational and activity-related responsibilities of the village panchayat. Without information on its functional domain,

---

[24] Central Statistical Organisation (2006, p. A-1).
[25] Available on the Foundation for Agrarian Studies' website: http://www.agrarianstudies.org/, viewed on November 30, 2014.

we cannot even know what the village panchayat is doing. Without such information, it is not possible to discuss the usefulness of any databases. Therefore, we used as reference the information available on Activity Mapping – the delineation of functions for each level of the panchayats by unbundling their activities into smaller units of work and re-assigning these units to different levels of the panchayati raj institutions – as proposed by the State and Central Governments.[26] We also interviewed panchayat officials about Activity Mapping at the village panchayat level.

While this study deals exclusively with village-level data sources, it discusses not only their usefulness in the village panchayat or sub-panchayat bodies, but also their usefulness for panchayati raj institutions at large. Data generated at the village-level sometimes moves upward for use at the Block or district level.

However, since the study focuses almost exclusively on panchayat and village-level data, data used for medium- and large-scale projects are beyond its scope. For example, data on roads for connectivity between Blocks and the district, and data on medium- and large-scale community centres can be collected or recorded directly, independently of the villages, by an upper tier of the panchayati raj institutions. Such data are not considered here since this enquiry is limited to village-level data sources. This is a methodological limitation of our study.

Within the jurisdiction of the above-mentioned village panchayats, we identified village-level data s3ources that may fulfil the provisions of the Constitution (Seventy-Third Amendment) Act, 1992. We also assessed their quality and usefulness. The status of data sources at the point of collection and recording was a focal point of this study. Both the *Basic Statistics on Local Level Development* report and the National Statistical Commission have stressed the need to "pay attention to data collection in all its dimensions."[27] We looked into data sources at their "very roots, namely, at the very first

---

[26] Second Administrative Reforms Commission (2007, p. 147).

[27] The National Statistical Commission (2001, para. 2.1.1) states that "collection of numerical data for the purpose of understanding the behaviour of various socio-economic variables has a long history. The origin of the term 'statistics' is associated with this concept, which is to describe the state. Of course, statistics, as a scientific discipline, goes beyond enumeration. Statistical inference is an important part of the discipline. However, inference will be fruitless, if the basic data are faulty or inaccurate or unreliable. That is why we have to pay attention to data collection in all its dimensions." For decades, indeed, world statisticians, including the National Statistical Commission, have shed light on the process of collection and recording

stage of collection and recording of data."[28] With rare exceptions, such as the study material for the people's planning campaign in Kerala, there was not even a comprehensive list of village-level data sources that exist for a panchayat area in India.[29] Therefore, we visited each village panchayat and conducted interviews at the panchayat offices and other agencies in the jurisdiction of the village panchayats about data sources and their uses at the panchayat or village level. We started the interviews using the simplified Village Schedule on Basic Statistics as a questionnaire. As a follow-up, we added to the questionnaire a few items regarding the additional data needs identified in chapter 2. We also visited the Block-level offices of the respective village panchayats in order to interview them about village-level data sources. Panchayat officials helped us collect and check various documents and data used in the village panchayat's functioning.

Since census-type household surveys had already been conducted in Warwat Khanderao and Bidyanidhi by the Foundation for Agrarian Studies, we used household data from the surveys as a point of reference. This enabled us to assess the quality of some data items available in the village and carry out micro-discrepancy analyses of the data sources.[30]

Apart from the official Census data, most data generated in the panchayat area, as will be seen later, are by-products of the administrative requirements of the panchayats themselves or of other satellite State Government agencies. There has been no intensive discussion of the quality and usefulness of these data.[31] Therefore, along with the official Census data, databases generated as by-products of village-level administrative requirements are the main point of discussion in the new statistical domain. These by-product data are fundamentally different from data generated by the Census of India and official sample surveys. Under the Census Act, 1948, the filled-up Census schedules are absolutely confidential. Similar confidentiality rules apply to

---

of data in order to assess the "data quality." As for "data quality," see Elvers and Rosén (1997), Laliberté, Grünewald, and Probst (2004).

[28] National Statistical Commission (2001, para. 14.3.10).

[29] Bakshi and Okabe (2008) give a comprehensive list of village-level data sources that exist for the Raina village panchayat area.

[30] Organisation for Economic Cooperation and Development (2002, p. 53): "Discrepancy analysis can be carried out at micro as well as macro level. For example, data for individual persons or enterprises, retrieved from tax files or from other administrations, can be compared with data from surveys." See the well-known pioneering work conducted over an area under the then Singur Health Centre in West Bengal (Chandrasekar C. and Deming W. E., 1949).

[31] Bakshi and Okabe (2008) look into details of this issue in the West Bengal case studies.

official sample surveys. Thus, village panchayats and other Government offices cannot use household or individual records from the Census of India or official sample surveys for administrative purposes (although aggregative data at the village or higher administrative levels are available and may be used). At the same time, the unit-level records generated from administrative requirements are ready for aggregation, but are primarily used as such in the identification and selection of targets of various public policies. The administrative functions of village panchayats require unit-level information on households and individuals. Such information, which cannot be obtained from the Census of India, has to be acquired from other administrative records available with the village panchayat. Therefore, this study deals not only with aggregate data generated as by-products of administrative requirements, but also with unit-level data (such as list of households, persons, events, facilities or establishments, plots, and so on) for administrative requirements. We have explored some household lists available with the village panchayats, such as the Integrated Child Development Services registers and Below Poverty Line Census data in our analysis.

There are at least two important reasons for studying unit-level data. First, the status and quality of unit-level data have direct consequences for the quality of aggregate data generated from them. Secondly, unit-level information on the village society is of utmost importance for the village panchayat, which is the administrative unit closest to the residents of the village. Village panchayat and village council members require unit-level data in order to carry out the tasks of public administration that are within their respective jurisdictions.

Policy decisions will have to be taken with regard to the persons and functionaries to whom access to unit-level data, for administrative purposes, is granted.[32] The particular focus of this study, however, is the potential use of such unit-level data.

As these unit-level databases are ready to aggregate "statistics" and direct bases of "statistics,"[33] we deal with them as a part of the "statistical databases" under consideration.

---

[32] The problem here is not only who in the village may have access to the unit-level database, but also whether the State and Central Governments should have direct access to all such databases.

[33] In principle, however, "administrative registers" can be processed into anonymous "statistical registers" before they are transferred to the statistical office to produce statistics. See Thygesen (1995), United Nations Economic Commission for Europe (2007).

We use the term "administrative statistics" broadly, and in addition to the unit-level data, we discuss financial accounting data (aggregate data on recorded transactions). Accounting data is often not a matter of concern for the official statistician. But it is not appropriate to exclude accounting data from administrative records when we study the overall panchayat statistical records, since accounting data are an integral part of the village panchayat's record system. We will also deal with them as a part of the "statistical database."

This study covers the period from April 2005 to March 2011, with some follow-up surveys conducted after 2011. Therefore, we will not discuss in chapter 4 details of many issues regarding the Socio-Economic and Caste Census and the National Population Register as these surveys were conducted in and after 2011.

As the reference period of our study is 2005–11, in West Bengal it covers the period during which the Left Front Government, led by the Communist Party of India (Marxist), was in office. There was a shift in the political regime in West Bengal in 2011, with the Trinamool Congress forming the government. This shift has had implications for the panchayati raj system in the State.[34] The reference period of the study covers two successive governments at the Centre, the United Progressive Alliance, i.e., UPA-I (2004–9) and UPA-II (2009–14) led by the Congress Party. In 2014, the Bharatiya Janata Party-led National Democratic Alliance assumed power at the Centre. Many government schemes and programmes implemented at the village-level were changed, revamped, and renamed during the study period and thereafter. In this book we discuss government programmes that were operating at the time of the study and retain the names of the schemes that were used at that time, even though the names and schemes may have changed since then.

---

[34] Bakshi (2011).

Chapter 2

DATA REQUIRED FOR THE VILLAGE PANCHAYAT

2.1 THE SCOPE OF DATA NEEDS

Although a new statistical domain is emerging in rural India, the nature of panchayats' data needs has not yet been comprehensively investigated. Keeping in view the recommendation by the Rangarajan Commission (now the National Statistical Commission), the terms of reference of the *Basic Statistics for Local Level Development* report was "the development of a system of regular collection of data on a set of core variables/indicators, which should be compiled and aggregated at local levels for use in micro-level planning of various developmental programmes."[1] These data needs are crucial to the decentralisation initiated by the Seventy-Third Amendment because powers and responsibilities of panchayats are provided in the Amendment with respect to "the preparation of plans for economic development and social justice," and "the implementation of schemes for economic development and social justice" (Article 243G of the Constitution).

However, the scope of data needs and items of information identified by the *Basic Statistics for Local Level Development* report are somewhat limited and exclude some important information. For example, the Eleventh Central Finance Commission and subsequent Central Finance Commissions have repeatedly called for the creation of databases on finances of local bodies[2]

---

[1] "The National Statistical Commission (NSC) . . . had recommended the development of a system of regular collection of data on a set of core variables/indicators, which should be compiled and aggregated at local levels for use in micro-level planning of various developmental programmes. NSC had further recommended for setting up of a committee of experts to look into all aspects related to development of local-level indicators" (Central Statistical Organisation 2006, p. A-1).

[2] Eleventh Finance Commission (2000, pp. 78–9) notes: "There is no mechanism for collection of data on the revenue and expenditure of the various tiers/levels of the rural/urban local bodies at a centralised place where it could be compiled, processed and made available for use. In the absence of any reliable financial/budgetary data, no realistic assessment of the needs of the panchayats and municipalities for basic civic and developmental functions can be made nor can any information be generated on the flow of funds to the local bodies for the implementation of various schemes for economic development and social justice. We are, therefore, of the view that a database on the finances of the panchayats and municipalities needs to be developed at

and the maintenance of accounts at the village panchayat level[3] for the post-Seventy-Third Amendment regime.[4] In fact, the Central Finance Commissions have repeatedly allocated grants, inter alia, for the creation of a database on the finances of panchayati raj institutions.[5] Indeed, the Constitution (Seventy-Third Amendment) Act, 1992 provides for the maintenance of accounts by panchayats (Article 243J of the Constitution). The Third State Finance Commission of West Bengal claimed that "the information system should be part of the general statistical information system necessary for planning and delivering public services."[6] At the village we found that the core of a village panchayat's record system was maintained to track the allocation and expenditure of funds and to assess the progress of different schemes. Nevertheless, the Village Schedule on Basic Statistics for Local Level Development (see section 8.1 of chapter 8) does not include a data item about the financial condition of the respective village panchayat.

To take another example, the Self-Evaluation Schedule for Panchayats in West Bengal contained data items about the status of the village council (*gram sabha*) and panchayat personnel, of village-panchayat buildings and facilities, and of activities of the village panchayat and village assembly (*gram sansads*).[7] In fact, the Seventy-Third Amendment includes provisions to enable panchayats to function as democratic institutions of self-government (Article 243G of the Constitution). However, the Village Schedule on Basic

---

the District, State and Central Government levels and be easily accessible by computerising it and linking it through V-SAT." Thus the Eleventh Finance Commission highlighted the need for a district-level database about finances. However, the Thirteenth Finance Commission (2009, p. 165) argues that "accurate data on the financial performance of local bodies are best obtained from accounts of the local bodies themselves." Therefore, the village panchayat or the sub-panchayat-level database on finances is also required.

[3] Twelfth Finance Commission (2004, p. 154): "It is, therefore, imperative that high priority should be accorded to creation of database and maintenance of accounts at the grass-roots level."

[4] Thirteenth Finance Commission (2009, p. 165): "Much has been said by the earlier Finance Commissions on this important subject. Despite this, little improvement has been noted in the situation."

[5] Eleventh Finance Commission (2000, pp. 78–80). However, as the Twelfth Finance Commission (2004, pp. 153–4) indicated, "the EFC allocated Rs 200 crores for creation of database by local bodies, but only Rs 93 crores could be utilised, as per information received from the Ministry of Finance. Out of the allocation of Rs 483 crores for maintenance of accounts, only Rs 113 crores was utilised. The total utilisation has, thus, been hardly 30 per cent of the allocation. While the reasons for such gross under-utilization are far from clear, there is no doubt that the data quality at the grass-roots level is poor."

[6] Third State Finance Commission of West Bengal (2008, p. 35).

[7] Government of West Bengal (2008).

Statistics does not contain data items of this nature on the panchayat itself.

This study attempts to broaden the scope of discussion of data needs under the decentralisation initiated by the Seventy-Third Amendment, by taking into account the provisions of the Amendment itself. We have interpreted the data needs on the assumption that State Governments will legislate and devolve powers of self-government and development to panchayats in the manner envisaged in the Constitution. According to Article 243G of the Constitution:

> Subject to the provisions of this Constitution, the Legislature of a State may, by law, endow the panchayats with such powers and authority as may be necessary to enable them to function as institutions of self-government and such law may contain provisions for the devolution of powers and responsibilities upon panchayats at the appropriate level, subject to such conditions as may be specified therein.

Here, the word "may" implies that the powers and authority given to panchayati raj institutions (PRIs) are at the discretion of State Governments, and are a matter of political debate in the Legislature of each State.[8] Although State governments may or may not legislate and devolve powers of self-governance and development to panchayats as described in the Seventy-Third Amendment, in this enquiry we discuss the data needs of panchayats on the assumption that they do so.

Amitava Mukherjee has discussed, from the outset of the Seventy-Third Amendment regime, panchayats' data needs based on the assumption that "the State government would legislate and devolve powers of self-governance and development to the panchayati raj institutions at both the district and sub-district levels."[9] He stated that panchayats' data needs, based on a reading of provisions from Articles 243 to 243O of the Constitution, would revolve around three basic functions: (i) to assess the resource base of the economy, raising of resources, and auditing resource use (see Articles 243H to 243J of the Constitution); (ii) to prepare plans for economic development and social justice, implementation of schemes for economic development and social justice, and expending the resources raised (see

---

[8] Mukherjee (1994, p. 145) writes, "In the worst case scenario of the panchayats being unable to function for want of supplementary legislation and/or rules (the Indian Statute Book is replete with laws which could not be implemented in the absence of rules/states laws necessary for giving effect to the law), then there is no need to generate a database."
[9] *Ibid.*, p. 146.

Article 243G and the Eleventh Schedule added to the Constitution); and (iii) to govern at the appropriate level as democratically elected governments at the district and sub-district levels (see Articles 243A to 243D and 243K of the Constitution). In this way the data needs of panchayats should relate to their basic functions as stipulated in the Seventy-Third Amendment. Here, function (i) is related to public finance of panchayats; function (ii) is mainly related to panchayat-level planning and its implementation; and, function (iii) is related to the self-governance of panchayats. The "micro-level planning of various developmental programmes," that is, function (ii), is just one component of these three functions. From this viewpoint, we can see that the *Basic Statistics for Local Level Development* report has dealt primarily with function (ii) above, and has not elaborated on data needs in relation to functions (i) and (iii).

Indicators adopted in the Self-Evaluation Schedule for Panchayats in West Bengal were widely discussed among people engaged in panchayat activities. "Draft formats were circulated among all panchayats for obtaining suggestions and workshops were organised in all the districts for proper appreciation of the exercise and how to take up the same objectively."[10] This Schedule contained numerous indicators of institutional aspects of panchayats, such as self-governance and public finance.[11]

In order to facilitate self-assessment by each panchayat, the West Bengal Panchayats and Rural Development Department started preparation of a Self-Evaluation Schedule from 2006–7. This schedule was specific to West Bengal, and its purpose was not the same as that of the Village Schedule of Basic Statistics. The panchayats received financial incentives from the State Government based on their self-assessment scores,[12] whereas the main purpose of the Village Schedule of Basic Statistics was to collect basic data. The Self-Evaluation Schedule nevertheless points to important areas for which data are required by panchayat functionaries to empower the institution. The subjects covered in the Schedule are illustrated in Table 2.1.

In addition to the basic information, this schedule contained indicators of economic and social development, especially in the sectors of education,

---

[10] Panchayats and Rural Development Department, Government of West Bengal (2007, p. 27).
[11] Department of Panchayats and Rural Development, Government of West Bengal (2008b).
[12] Each panchayat has to make a self-assessment and assign scores for the different indicators specified in this Schedule. Panchayats receive financial incentives from the State government based on this evaluation.

Table 2.1 *List of subjects in Self-Evaluation Schedule, Village Panchayat, West Bengal*

Introduction (village panchayat at a glance)

A. Institutional functioning and good governance

   1. Peoples' participation in village panchayat's activities
   2. Participation of the members in the functioning of village panchayat
   3. Services delivered by village panchayat
   4. Village panchayat building and office management
   5. Village panchayat information management & disposing system
      (a) Register related
      (b) Are the following lists available at the village panchayat office for public viewing?
      (c) Regarding right to information
   6. Transparency in village panchayat's work
   7. Education
   8. Public health
      (a) Health services
      (b) Drinking water & sanitation
      (c) Women and child development
   9. Pro-poor activities
   10. Development of economic and social infrastructure
   11. Housing
   12. Disaster preparedness
   13. Social security

B. Mobilisation of revenue and utilisation of resources

   14. Issues regarding bye-laws of village panchayat
   15. Issues regarding village panchayat plan and budget
   16. Own-source revenue
   17. Financial management
   18. Audit
   19. Fund utilisation
   20. Provision for sending utilisation certificates and report returns
   21. Natural resource utilisation

Source: Gram Panchayater Abasthaner Mulyayaner Pratibedan, 2006–7.

public health, and pro-poor activities. However, it also contained indicators of institutional aspects of panchayats such as self-governance and public finance. In this respect, firstly, it contained indicators covering "institutional functioning and good governance" that were primarily focused on subjects of self-governance, such as peoples' participation in panchayat activities, transparency in panchayat work, and its administrative infrastructure. Secondly, the schedule contained indicators covering "mobilisation of revenue and utilisation of resources" that were focused on issues of public finance, such as the panchayat's budget, its audit, its own source of revenue and inflow of funds utilised by the panchayat.

The *Manual for Integrated District Planning*, provided by the Planning Commission in the context of district planning, outlines the data required for panchayati raj institutions as follows:

Basic facts of the district, including natural resources
Geographical area, terrain, agro-climatic conditions, flora and fauna, land use, water availability, geology, minerals, demographic data, types of habitation, households and families, social structure, occupations and way of life, etc.

Infrastructure and services for the public
Transport and communication network, irrigation and water supply, electricity and fuel supply, housing and basic amenities, drainage and sanitation, food supply and nutrition services, health delivery system, schooling and education, employment and self-employment, farm sector development, industry and trade, technical training and skill development, professional education, etc. Verification of physical assets, both community and individual assets, undertaken at each local government level.

Data on important indicators and assessment of development
Life expectancy at birth, maternal mortality, neonatal and infant mortality, child mortality, immunisation, malnutrition, acquired disabilities, morbidity and linked mortality, literacy, mean years of schooling, average educational attainment, age at marriage, family planning, gainful employability and employment, economic status with regard to the poverty line, access to adequate housing and basic amenities, standards of living, social security, fulfilment of civic rights, etc.

The local administrative set-up
The number and statistics regarding rural and urban local government (panchayats, urban local bodies, autonomous councils etc.), line departments

attached to local government, state line department offices, missions and other parastatals operating in the district.

Financial information

District government budget allocations source-wise and sector-wise, actual receipt and expenditure in previous years, pattern of resource distribution among local government, own revenues of local governments, district credit plans, major corporate investment details, investments by self-help groups (SHGs), and micro-finance institutions (MFIs).

New areas for accelerated growth; potential "lead sectors"

New areas of economic growth such as new industries, corporate investments, tourism, agricultural diversification.[13]

This dataset includes some data regarding institutional aspects such as "financial information" and "the local administrative set-up" that are outside the scope of the Village Schedule of Basic Statistics.

Assuming that panchayats are empowered as envisaged by the Seventy-Third Amendment, their data needs can be categorised as follows:

1. data required for self-governance (data needs I),
2. data required for public finance (data needs II), and
3. data required for micro-level planning of various developmental programmes and their implementation (data needs III)

These three categories of data needs are, in practice, closely interrelated. The same data can sometimes be used for different categories of data needs. However, each category deserves to be analysed separately in order to discuss multiple aspects of the new statistical domain. We will elaborate on them in the following sections.

2.2 DATA NEEDS I: DATA REQUIRED FOR SELF-GOVERNANCE

The Constitution of India envisaged self-governance by village panchayats before the enactment of the Seventy-Third Amendment: "The State shall take steps to organise village panchayats and endow them with such powers and authority as may be necessary to enable them to function as units of self-government" (Article 40). The Seventy-Third Amendment provides for self-governance for panchayati raj institutions as a whole:

---

[13] Planning Commission (2008b, pp. 57–8).

"There shall be constituted in every State, panchayats at the village, intermediate and district levels in accordance with the provisions of this Part" (Article 243B); "The Legislature of a State may, by law, endow the panchayats with such powers and authority as may be necessary to enable them to function as institutions of self-government" (Article 243G).

The provisions in Articles 243A to 243D and 243K define panchayats as democratically elected governments. With the enactment of the Seventy-Third Amendment, panchayats were empowered as democratic "institutions of self-government," which have evolved from being just a development organisation at the local level into a political institution.[14] In the context of democratic decentralisation, data needs for self-governance reflect the requirements of the new statistical domain. Data needs for self-governance are classified into two parts – for the panchayat itself and for its object domain.

2.2.1 Data on the Panchayat

For the sake of democratic self-governance, panchayat needs to be transparent in its working as a public sector institution. The core data on the panchayat itself comprises data on the panchayat as a political entity and its functions.[15]

2.2.1.1 Documents for the Village Council
The Seventy-Third Amendment envisages that panchayats are governed democratically, and that people participate in the panchayat's activities

---

[14] Mathew (1995, p. 9). However, the political situation in and around a panchayat can be sometimes strained due to the social structure and the historical background. Before Constitutional support was established, as Mathew (*ibid.*, p. 7) argues, "evidence suggests that there was a deliberate plan by bureaucracy, local vested interests and their elected representatives in the state legislatures and in the Parliament to cripple and eventually discard panchayati raj, because its ascendancy was feared." Also see Ministry of Agriculture and Irrigation (1978, pp. 5–6). Further, Mathew (1995, p. 8) writes, "Politicians would not like to see the erosion of their power by a breed of new, local leadership. Thus it is legitimate to conclude that a combination of bureaucracy, commercial interests, the professional middle class, the police and political elite "ganged up" against democratic decentralization."

[15] As will be seen in section 2.2.2, the object domain of the panchayat is a geographically defined jurisdiction with a special focus on its functional domain. Therefore, the functioning of the panchayat will not only determine the panchayat itself, but also shape the panchayat's object domain. Its functioning creates an essential link between the panchayat itself and the panchayat's object domain. However, the panchayat's object domain is, in a sense, external to the panchayat. The panchayat may discover not-yet-known administrative needs beyond its ongoing functioning. Its functioning may also generate an unexpected impact (or "outcome") on the local society.

(Article 243A). The panchayat is a democratically elected form of government through which new leaders appear on the local political stage.[16] The State Election Commission supervises all elections to panchayats. This external agency prepares the electoral rolls (Article 243K). The electoral rolls are also an essential record for the panchayat's regular activities because the village council is a body consisting of all eligible voters. Even the quorum for the village council meetings is prescribed in relation to the number of its members. The village council requires records for its meetings, such as an attendance register and a minutes book. The West Bengal Self-Evaluation Schedule for Panchayats, for example, requested data on the number of voters (according to the electoral roll), frequency of village council meetings, and even the attendance rate at these meetings.

In addition to the information on the village council, information on panchayat activities, especially information on the functioning of subcommittees under the panchayat, needs to be in the public domain. The village council entrusts powers to the subcommittees with respect to certain subjects or schemes. The West Bengal Self-Evaluation Schedule, for example, requested details of the functioning of subcommittees (*upa-samitis*) and village development committees (*gram unnayan samitis*).

2.2.1.2 Data for the Panchayat's Functional Domain

Data on how the panchayat is functioning is absolutely necessary for its self-governance. First, under decentralisation, a panchayat must perform the devolved functions, for which it needs data. Secondly, under democratic decentralisation the panchayat has to disclose, in part,[17] the data in order to fulfil the democratic procedures of its self-governance. The panchayat's functioning – both current and future – is required to be transparent according to the democratic procedures of self-governance. In order to participate in the panchayat's activities, it is necessary to have access to the database on its functioning. The Panchayat Acts in two States (Section 8 of the Bombay Village Panchayats Act, 1958, and Section 18 of the West Bengal Panchayati Raj Act, 1973) direct the village panchayats to prepare village council reports, showing work done under different projects, programmes, or schemes.

The panchayat needs data pertaining to its functional domain. Its functional

---

[16] See G. Kumar (2006).

[17] Policy decisions will have to be taken with regard to the persons and functionaries to whom access to such data, for administrative purposes, is granted.

domain is broadly defined as "economic development and social justice as may be entrusted to them including those in relation to the matters listed in the Eleventh Schedule" (Article 243G). Schedule XI of the Constitution identifies twenty-nine subjects as a functional domain to be devolved to the panchayati raj institutions:

1. Agriculture, including agricultural extension
2. Land improvement, implementation of land reforms, land consolidation, and soil conservation
3. Minor irrigation, water management and watershed development
4. Animal husbandry, dairying, and poultry
5. Fisheries
6. Social forestry and farm forestry
7. Minor forest produce
8. Small-scale industries, including food-processing industries
9. Village and cottage industries, such as Khadi
10. Housing
11. Drinking water
12. Fuel and fodder
13. Roads, culverts, bridges, ferries, waterways, and other means of communication
14. Rural electrification, including distribution of electricity
15. Non-conventional energy sources
16. Poverty-alleviation programme
17. Education, including primary and secondary schools
18. Technical training and vocational education
19. Adult and non-formal education
20. Libraries
21. Cultural activities
22. Markets and fairs
23. Health and sanitation, including hospitals, primary-health centres and dispensaries
24. Family welfare
25. Women and child development
26. Social welfare, including welfare of the handicapped and mentally retarded
27. Welfare of the weaker sections, and, in particular, of the Scheduled Castes and the Scheduled Tribes
28. Public distribution system
29. Maintenance of community assets

Modifying the classification suggested in the *Manual for Integrated District Planning*, we can summarise the functional domain as follows:[18]

A. Primary sector: 1, 2, 3, 4, 5, 6, 7, 12
B. Education: 17, 18, 19, 20, 21
C. Health and child development: 23, 24, 25
D. Poverty alleviation and social welfare: 10, 16, 26, 27, 28
E. Infrastructure: 11, 13, 14, 15, 29
F. Industry and commerce: 8, 9, 22

However, this is just a list of "subjects" that State governments may transfer to panchayats. It does not provide specific operational and activity-related responsibilities of each tier of the panchayati raj institutions. The functions assigned to each tier with respect to different subjects are unclear.[19] Without clear delineation of functions for each tier, "it is not possible to devise a workable devolution scheme for the local bodies."[20]

In this light, the Second Administrative Reforms Commission of India called for an "Activity Mapping" exercise prescribed for each State government.[21] Activity Mapping means "unbundling subjects into smaller units of work and thereafter assigning these units to different levels of government."[22] According to the Commission, these unbundled subjects may be classified under five categories: "(i) Setting standards, (ii) Planning, (iii) Asset creation,

---

[18] Planning Commission (2008b, p. 115). According to the *Manual for Integrated District Planning*, the twenty-nine subjects in Schedule XI can be roughly classified into six categories, that is, "Primary Sector" (1, 2, 3, 4, 5, 6, 7, 12), "Education" (17, 18, 19, 20, 21), "Health" (23, 24, 25), "Poverty" (10, 16, 26, 27, 28), "Infrastructure" (11, 13, 14, 15, 29), and "Economic development" (8, 9, 22).

[19] The Second Administrative Reforms Commission (2007, p. 49) observes: "The difference between a subject and a function remains as a major hiatus between local-level activity and local governance." The Third State Finance Commission of West Bengal (2008, p. 21) also states that "a general devolution of functions to panchayati raj institutions (PRIs) will hardly serve the purpose."

[20] Second Administrative Reforms Commission (2007, pp. 137–8). The Commission (*ibid.*) notes that "In order to make devolution functional, the matters listed in the Eleventh Schedule of the Constitution need to be broken down into discrete activities, because it may not be appropriate to transfer all the activities within a broad function or a subject to the panchayati raj institutions. The State Government may retain some activities at a macro level. For example, in primary education, activities like designing syllabi, maintaining standards, preparation of textbooks, etc. would have to be with the State Government, while tasks concerning management of schools may be with the village panchayat or district council."

[21] Second Administrative Reforms Commission (2007, p. 149).

[22] *Ibid.*, p. 146.

(iv) Implementation and Management, and (v) Monitoring and Evaluation."[23]

Once the subjects are unbundled, each of them is to be assigned to panchayats, at which tier they could be most efficiently handled.[24] The Commission noted,

> Factors such as economy of scale, externality, equity and heterogeneity will play a major role in this process. Economies of scale tend to push the service towards higher levels of government. Conversely, if some activity is scale neutral in implementation, it may be preferable to push it down to the lowest level for implementation.[25]

On the basis of Activity Mapping, the functions of each level of the panchayat was to become clearly delineated.[26]

However, in most States the progress in specifying the functions of different tiers of local government within a given subject has been very slow.[27] Such delay is considered to be one of the serious hindrances to decentralisation

[23] *Ibid.*

[24] The Second Administrative Reforms Commission (*ibid.*, pp. 146–7) recommends the following key principles for the devolution exercise:
There should be exclusive functional jurisdiction or an independent sphere of action for each level of the panchayat. The State Government should not exercise any control over this sphere, except giving general guidance. If any activity within this sphere is presently performed by any line department of the State Government, then that department should cease to perform the activity after devolution.
There may be spheres of activity where the State Government and the panchayats would work as equal partners.
There may also be a sphere where panchayati raj institutions would act as agencies for implementing Union or State Government schemes/programmes (The difference between the partnership mode and agency mode of functioning is that the scope of independence in discharging responsibility is more in the former case compared to the latter).

[25] *Ibid.*, p. 147.

[26] Activity Mapping cannot be operationalised without links with financial and administrative requirements. The Commission recommends that funds and functionaries should be devolved upon Activity Mapping (*ibid.*, p. 353).

[27] *Ibid.*, p. 45. "The progress in delineation of functions of the different tiers of local governments in a given subject matter has been very slow . . . Due to the persistent efforts of the Ministry of Panchayati Raj in the last three years, detailed "Activity Mapping" of different tiers of local governments have been undertaken in all the States . . . However, the exercise continues to be partial and prolonged. The draft activity mapping lists have not been approved by the State Governments in some cases . . . Even where activity mapping has been approved, parallel action to enable local governments to exercise the functions has not been taken. The existing government departments with their executive orders and instructions, parallel government bodies like District Rural Development Agencies (DRDAs) and the continuance of statutory bodies (as regards water, electricity, etc.) without any change, prevent the local governments from exercising the so called transferred functions" (*ibid.*, p. 45).

in rural India.[28] The Second Administrative Reforms Commission observed that almost all the states have chosen to assign functions to the panchayati raj institutions not through statute, but by delegated legislation in the form of rules or executive orders.[29] Furthermore, Activity Mapping on the ground is often different from what was envisaged in the Acts and rules. Functions assigned to panchayats in the Acts sometimes exist only on the statute book. For assessing the situation on the ground, the best method is to conduct interview of panchayat officials on what may be called "de facto Activity Mapping." The panchayat officials usually have a clear idea of what responsibilities are actually assigned to them on the ground. As will be seen in chapter 3 (section 3.3.7), we conducted these interviews in each of the selected villages.

No standard model of Activity Mapping to date has stood the test of application in diverse situations.[30] The Ministry of Rural Development of the Central Government appointed a Task Force on devolution of powers and functions to panchayati raj institutions, 2001. In its report it suggested a guideline for Activity Mapping as "a broad framework of devolution."[31] We can also use this guideline for Activity Mapping to discuss data needs of each tier of the panchayats. The Ministry of Panchayati Raj of the Central Government also suggested that Activity Mapping in Kerala could be a reliable point of reference.[32] However, since the Seventy-Third Amendment leaves considerable scope for State-to-State variation, instances of Activity Mapping are diverse in each State.[33]

While Activity Mapping proposed by the Second Administrative Reforms Commission was meant "to ensure that panchayats at all levels function as institutions of self-government rather than as implementing agencies,"[34] the existing Activity Mapping is sometimes considered as an assignment of functions "to perform tasks on behalf of the State primarily as an agent

---

[28] "Activity mapping has been one of the major action points identified for urgent attention by the states" (Oommen 2008, p. 7).

[29] Second Administrative Reforms Commission (2007, p. 138).

[30] "In the absence of a model that stood the best of application in diverse situations, only a broad framework of devolution can be suggested" (Ministry of Rural Development 2001, paragraph 3.5.3).

[31] Ibid., pp. 15, 47–93.

[32] "The detailed Activity Map prepared by Kerala State could be a good reference point for the Activity Mapping" (Ministry of Panchayati Raj 2011, p. 21).

[33] Second Administrative Reforms Commission (2007, pp. 138–45).

[34] Ibid., p. 146.

of the Government."[35] As these tasks are allocated from above by the line departments, Activity Mapping exercises in different states have essentially remained top-down and bureaucratic.[36] Nevertheless, we will interpret Activity Mapping in its original sense as defined by the Second Administrative Reforms Commission: Activity Mapping delineates the functional domain for panchayats not merely to act as implementing agencies of the State government,[37] but also to act as institutions of self-government. It addresses their functional domain in order "to respond to the need-based demands of the people and acquire more responsibilities of their own for realisation of such demands, stemming from the local needs and aspirations."[38]

Data for the panchayat's functional domain are a set of data for functions delineated by Activity Mapping. This means that the data must be shared with the panchayat's own functionaries, its satellite agencies as well as agencies working outside the panchayati raj system but in the panchayat's functional domain. The latter include outside agencies under the control of line departments, such as the Auxiliary Nurse Midwives (ANM), the Integrated Child Development Services workers, child-care centre (*anganwadi*) workers, revenue officials (*patwari*), school teachers, etc. As will be mentioned later in section 2.3, the panchayat may coordinate between them in order to establish data-sharing mechanisms.

Data for the panchayat's functioning should not necessarily mean "statistics" or "estimation." Unit-level data (such as lists of households, persons, events, facilities or establishments, plots or areas and so on) may be preferable

---

[35] Panchayats and Rural Development Department, Government of West Bengal (2009, p. 14).
[36] Second Administrative Reforms Commission (2007, p. 369). In this context, the Panchayats and Rural Development Department, Government of West Bengal (2009, p. 13) provided the *Roadmap for the Panchayats of the State* not merely "for devolution of responsibilities by the various departments of the State Government through the conventional exercise of activity mapping and assigning responsibilities from above through either legislative or executive route but also the roadmap for developing various capacities within the panchayats so as to respond to the need-based demands of the people and acquire more responsibilities of their own for realization of such demands, stemming from the local needs and aspirations." The Department recognised that "devolution through activity mapping provides certain space to the panchayat bodies, which were so far occupied by the Government, but the experience shows that much space in the development matrix is available beyond that occupied by the Government and a proactive panchayat may tread on such spaces uncharted so far, provided they have the capacity to do so."
[37] Panchayats and Rural Development Department, Government of West Bengal (*ibid.*, p. 13) regards it as "the conventional exercise of activity mapping."
[38] *Ibid.*, p. 13.

depending on the concerned function. Where a function requires unit-level data, a list of certain units would be required. For example, a list of children born in a particular year can be used not only to compute the number of children or the birth rate of the village-panchayat area, but also to notify the concerned parents that their child may be admitted to school.

2.2.1.3 Data on Personnel and Assets of the Panchayat

Official records for panchayat personnel, including elected panchayat representatives and their administrative staff, need to be disclosed. These data reflect the basic human resource of the panchayat's general administration. The Right to Information Act, 2005, facilitates such disclosure of information. The West Bengal Self-Evaluation Schedule for Panchayats, for example, requested data on personnel in the panchayat. The Panchayat and Rural Development Department of West Bengal included capacity building for its panchayat functionaries in its roadmap.[39] Furthermore, information on infrastructure of the panchayat's general administration is supposed to be transparent.[40] Data on all facilities of the village panchayat are required not only for managing revenue resources, but also for maintaining them properly. The tax system for the panchayat's assets may be simple and focused for operational convenience, but the data on maintenance of such assets need to be exhaustive.

2.2.2 Data on the Panchayat's Jurisdiction for Strengthening Self-Governance

The object domain of the panchayat's governance is defined by its geographical area and its functional domain. Since the object of local governance is a region within the nation, the panchayat's object domain, first, is its geographically defined jurisdiction. No government can be ignorant of its jurisdiction. A jurisdiction delineates regional boundaries of local society in relation to its inhabitants. Therefore, data on the panchayat's jurisdiction must include data on the local society in question. Unlike data on the panchayat alone, the data on jurisdiction includes not only the public sector, but also the private

---

[39] Ibid., p. 54.

[40] In fact the subcommittees (Upa-samitis) in West Bengal have been given powers to inspect immovable property of the village panchayat (Section 32A of the West Bengal Panchayati Raj Act, 1973). The subcommittee members may "call for any information, return, statement, account or report from the office of the village panchayat and enter on and inspect any immovable property of the village panchayat or inspect any work in progress connected with the functions and duties of the subcommittee."

sector located within the panchayat's area of jurisdiction. The panchayat may regulate or even intervene in the private sector as far as its functional domain is concerned.

The panchayat's function assumes a certain object domain. Its functioning is obviously not self-contained. Its object domain is more or less external to the panchayat for the following reasons:

1. The panchayat may discover unknown administrative needs as an object domain. It may find its new functional domain "to respond to the need-based demands of the people and acquire more responsibilities of their own for realisation of such demands, stemming from the local needs and aspirations."[41] The panchayat may even find unrecorded administrative needs in its current functional domain.
2. The panchayat may also find an unexpected impact (or "outcome") on its object domain through its functioning. The impact (or outcome) of a public activity is often distinguished sharply from the direct result of that activity because the relation between activity and outcome is usually not simple.

Indeed, examining the registers or records generated by the panchayat and its satellite agencies, we often found unrecorded values in the object domain with respect to its functioning. These were obviously external to the panchayat. For example, there was widespread discontent in village panchayats regarding the Below Poverty Line (BPL) list generated from the BPL Census 2002 (also referred to as the Rural Household Survey in West Bengal) because some poor households were excluded and some non-poor households were included in the list. Therefore, while some of these village panchayats had independently conducted a house-to-house re-survey to revise the BPL list, many discrepancies were not amended. Even the expert group set up by the Ministry of Rural Development of the Central Government admitted that the number of errors of exclusion and inclusion in the BPL Census 2002 remained above acceptable limits.[42] In this example, the panchayat found an unrecorded object domain of the panchayat – eligible BPL households excluded in the BPL list, based on knowledge among the village people or their house-to-house re-survey.

[41] *Ibid.*, p. 13.
[42] Ministry of Rural Development (2009, p. 20).

Table 2.2 *Level of birth registration, India and states, 1985–2011* in per cent

All India/State/Union Territory	Level of birth registration (%)									
	1985	1995	2000	2005	2006	2007	2008	2009	2010	2011
All India	39	55	56.2	62.5	69	74.5	76.4	81.3	82	83.6
States										
Andhra Pradesh	26.9	34.4	58.1	61	73.4	77.4	77.5	76.3	79.1	79.8
Arunachal Pradesh	19.7	66.3	84.8	73.9	100	100	100	100	100	100
Assam	–	–	38.7	71.2	74.6	76.8	78.5	82.1	100	85.8
Bihar	20	18.7	3.7	16.9	20.3	26.2	31.6	45	46.6	59.8
Chhattisgarh	–	–	62.3	63.3	64.1	62.4	46.8	49.4	51.8	55.1
Goa	105.2	120.6	100	100	100	97.9	100	95	100	92.6
Gujarat	62.1	96.3	88.8	89.5	96.6	97.9	100	100	100	100
Haryana	60.8	73.4	76.4	84.3	90.8	91.6	95.9	96	97.1	100
Himachal Pradesh	57.9	71.7	94.1	100	100	100	100	100	100	100
Jammu & Kashmir	46.4	–	68.1	64.8	66.5	66	68.2	68.7	68.4	69.9
Jharkhand	–	–	19	32.9	37	44.7	52.3	51.6	56.2	60.7
Karnataka	40.4	86.5	87.9	87.6	92.2	92	94.6	94.5	94.6	98.9
Kerala	94.8	101.7	100	100	100	100	100	100	100	100
Madhya Pradesh	46.3	50.8	40.6	53.3	65.2	72.9	84.3	83.1	82.3	86.5
Maharashtra	64.7	80.3	91.1	85.9	88.1	91.5	100	100	100	100
Manipur	7.5	14	46.9	72	80	77.2	70.7	72.2	57.2	81.2
Meghalaya	–	44.5	72.2	100	100	100	100	100	100	100
Mizoram	–	–	100	100	100	100	100	100	100	100
Nagaland	60.9	–	–	100	100	100	100	100	100	100
Orissa	47.6	58.6	81.8	85.3	88.3	88.7	87.8	87.6	92.4	95.6
Punjab	74.2	92.4	92.2	100	100	100	100	100	100	100
Rajasthan	16.4	23.7	35	65.3	81.5	83.2	85.9	92.4	97.4	96.7
Sikkim	–	24.4	80	95.8	97.5	93.9	88.4	87.6	77.8	79.3
Tamil Nadu	67.7	90.3	93.5	100	99.7	100	99.4	97.3	99.8	100
Tripura	41.7	108.9	93.6	100	100	89.1	97.8	100	75.8	85.9
Uttar Pradesh	13.6	40.6	37.7	35.3	45.3	61.6	58	73.5	69.6	64.9
Uttarakhand	–	–	–	61.5	57.4	66	65.4	69.1	71.6	77.5
West Bengal	–	64.3	97.2	97	97.9	97.3	98.9	88.2	86.7	100

Table 2.2 (*extended*)

All India/State/ Union Territory	Level of birth registration (%)									
	1985	1995	2000	2005	2006	2007	2008	2009	2010	2011
Union Territories										
Andaman & Nicobar Islands	73.3	128.1	94.4	86.9	91.7	87	79.2	76.8	76.5	97.6
Chandigarh	112.7	126.6	100	100	100	100	100	100	100	100
Dadra & Nagar Haveli	48.6	85.9	84.1	79.4	82.6	80.6	79.8	83.5	69	73.1
Daman & Diu	· 96.4	148.7	100	98.3	99.6	99.3	99	87.9	81.8	91.2
Delhi	85.3	116	100	100	100	100	100	100	100	100
Lakshadweep	93.7	86.5	86.7	76.6	73.9	68.2	77.3	59.4	62.9	76.8
Pondicherry	182.9·	198.8	100	100	100	100	100	100	100	100

Notes: (i) The level of birth registration is defined as the percentage of registered births to births estimated through the Sample Registration System (SRS).

(ii) The level of registration in 1985 and 1995 exceeds 100.0% in some States/Union Territories because the people from the neighbouring areas outside these States/Union registered in these States/Union Territories. In SRS, such births are accounted at the place of usual residences of the mother. Union Territories come here to avail of better medical facilities, and due to the de facto method of registration, all such births get registered.

(iii) The level of registration in 2000 and after is 100.0%, if it exceeds 100%.

(iv) not available

Source: For the estimate for 1985 and 1995, Registrar General, India. For the details, see Office of the Registrar General, India (1998). For the estimate for 2000 and after, see Office of the Registrar General, India (2009, p. 29).

Another example, as will be mentioned in chapter 6 (section 6.7), is the Civil Registration System (CRS), which will clearly illustrate the distinction between the panchayat's functioning as such and the object domain of the function of a system. The number of unregistered births in the CRS is still substantially high in rural India. Table 2.1 reveals the coverage of CRS in the States and Union Territories. The all-India level of birth registration in 2011 was 83.6 per cent even more than 40 years after the enactment of the Registration of Births and Deaths Act in 1969. The Office of the Registrar General states that "the level of registration for births has recorded sharp exponential increase after 2005 and has shown consistent improvement over the years."[43] The level of birth registration in Maharashtra and West Bengal is estimated to be 100 per cent in 2011, where the village development officer or the elected head (*pradhan*) of the village panchayat work as the Registrar/Sub-Registrar. However, according to the 2005–6 National Family Health Survey, the all-India percentage of children under the age of five years whose births were registered with the CRS was 41.1. The same was 34.8 per cent in rural India.[44] These figures are much lower than the estimates furnished by the Office of the Registrar General and Census Commissioner.

Our analysis of village data also reveals lower registration of births in Warwat Khanderao (see section 6.7 in chapter 6). A majority of unregistered children in Warwat Khanderao belonged to what are called the "weaker sections of society," such as children from Muslim households. In addition, children were often not registered at their village panchayat of residence, but at other village panchayats or local bodies.

As birth registration is "a fundamental human right and an essential means of protecting a child's right to an identity,"[45] all children living in the area of the panchayat's jurisdiction are considered within its object domain. In spite of this, village panchayats keep unregistered children outside the coverage of CRS. They are an unrecorded object domain for the village panchayat. Unrecorded births may be for two reasons: firstly, some children are not registered in the CRS. Secondly, some children are not registered with the village panchayat of residence but registered in the CRS elsewhere, outside the panchayat of their area of residence. These children are, in principle, non-existent to their nearest village panchayat. They are, so to speak, marginalised in birth-registration process of the CRS. They are, in other words, external to the functioning of the CRS in the village panchayat. Birth registration through CRS covers only a part of the panchayat's object domain, as illustrated in Figure 2.1 by a disc under the cone. The cone's base does not cover the total area of the disc. Outside CRS coverage, as noted above, there are a number of unregistered births, which are external to the village panchayat because they are unregistered or are registered outside their village panchayat of residence.

---

[43] Office of the Registrar General (2009). The Office of the Registrar General, India, states that "the level of registration of births in the country is highly erratic even after more than 40 years of enactment of the Registration of Births and Deaths Act, 1969."
[44] International Institute for Population Sciences (2007, pp. 45–7).
[45] UNICEF (2005). "Birth registration, the official recording of the birth of a child by the government, is a fundamental human right and an essential means of protecting a child's right to an identity."

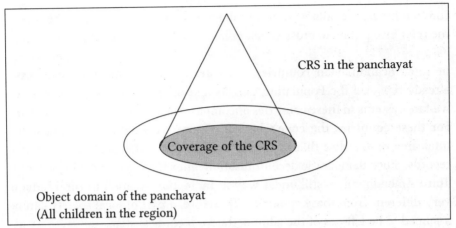

Figure 2.1 Panchayat and the Local Society in CRS
Note: CRS = Civil Registration System.

In this way, data on the panchayat itself should be distinguished from data on its object domain. Similarly, the administrative registers or records on the panchayat's functioning should be distinguished from data on the object domain of its function. Data on the functioning of the panchayat – registered births of the CRS in this case – can precisely reflect the nature of the panchayat's functioning. However, often the object domain of the panchayat is more or less external to the panchayat itself, as illustrated by Figure 2.1. The administrative registers or records do not always reflect its object domain as a whole. It reflects only a part of the object domain (only 22.3 per cent of all children, in case of the CRS).

In order to explore the object domain that is external to the panchayat itself, the panchayat needs data or information to cross-check the existing registers or records on its own administrative functions. In fact, in order to cross-check the CRS birth registration and to explore the object domain expected to be outside the coverage of the CRS, the panchayat can use other administrative records such as the Integrated Child Development Services (*anganwadi*) child registers, the Population Census or census-type surveys organised by the Central Government such as the Below Poverty Line Census. As will be seen in section 2.3 of this chapter, the panchayat may coordinate with other agencies to check these records against different data sources. In order to cross-check village-level registers or records, a data-sharing mechanism with other panchayat agencies will often be required.

The panchayat can also use common knowledge among villagers. As will be seen in chapters 4, 6, and 8, some types of information on the village community were available to most villagers.[46] This knowledge can be one of the reference points to cross-check village-level records.

In some Scandinavian countries,[47] register-based statistical systems have already replaced the Population Census and other statistical surveys, since welfare systems in these countries encompass the entire lifespans of citizens. For these countries the cone's base in Figure 2.1 would cover almost the total area of the disc thanks to the wide range of detailed administrative records. Since democratic decentralisation, after the passage of the Seventy-Third Amendment, is still under way in India, the situation in rural India is very different from these countries. Therefore, a part of local society can be assumed to be left out of the administrative records system.

Data on the panchayat's jurisdiction is not necessarily restricted to "statistics" or "estimation." Unit-level data on village society is of utmost importance for the village panchayat, which is the administrative unit closest to the village residents. Unit-level data (such as lists of households, persons, events, facilities or establishments, plots or areas) may be preferable, depending on the function to be reviewed.

2.2.2.1 Comprehensive List of People Residing in the Panchayat's Jurisdiction

People living in the panchayat's jurisdiction are not only the most important object domain, but also the main actors of the panchayat. This is precisely the point of "self-governance." The panchayat is expected to become a people-oriented local government working through popular participation. Database on area residents, therefore, is an integral part of the panchayat databases.

Village-level population data on an aggregate basis from the Census of India are available with the village panchayat with some time lag. Aggregate data on people living in the village are essential as statistics on the panchayat's jurisdiction. At present, however, a comprehensive list of people is not available with the panchayat's office. There is no official list of each and every resident living under the jurisdiction of Indian local bodies (such as panchayats and municipalities). Unit-level population records gathered by the Census of India are not available. The Census is conducted as per the provisions of the Census Act, 1948, which, on the one hand, places a legal obligation upon the public to cooperate and give truthful answers and, on

---

[46] Bakshi and Okabe (2011, pp. 24–5, 27).
[47] See Thygesen (1995) and United Nations Economic Commission for Europe (2007).

the other, guarantees confidentiality of information to individuals. Therefore, unit-level household or individual data from the Census cannot be used for administrative purposes.

Without a comprehensive list of residents in its jurisdiction, however, the panchayat's public policies would be inefficient or discretionary, and less objective. Thus, the panchayat requires not only aggregate data but also unit-level records for data retrieval. In section 6.6 of chapter 6, we will discuss a comprehensive People's List, i.e. a list of every individual and household in the jurisdiction of the panchayat.

2.2.2.2 Records as By-products of Routine Tasks for Self-Governance

As "institutions of self-government," panchayats need to keep track of changes in places under their jurisdiction. Incidents or events occurring in local society and the progress of schemes executed in the village must be recorded by the village panchayat or its satellite agencies. Some records as by-products of such routine tasks are dynamic in nature. They keep track of facts at the time of occurrence. Such records include registers of births and deaths, records of migration, records of public health and child care in the village, and of work done by the panchayat. Although this dynamic information is recorded for the operational use of the panchayat's functions, some of this information, such as information in the birth and death registers, is indispensable in lending a dynamic aspect to the panchayat's functions.

The panchayat's satellite agencies under the control of line departments – the Auxiliary Nurse Midwives (ANM), revenue officials, school teachers, and Integrated Child Development Services (ICDS) (*anganwadi*) workers – often work in its functional domain although independently of the panchayati raj set up. As will be mentioned in section 2.3 below, the panchayat can coordinate them as departmental liaison officers of the panchayat to keep track of facts and data for self-governance structure.

2.2.2.3 Shift of Requirement of the Recording Principle

Even when a record appears to be available with the village panchayat, its recording structure may not be accurately related to the people living within the geographical area of the panchayat's jurisdiction and thus not support self-governance, which causes considerable difficulty in data use.

There are two aspects of this difficulty. The first is that the geographical boundaries of the administrative jurisdiction of the line department agencies may be different from that of the panchayat, so that village-level data cannot be taken from the records maintained by these agencies.[48] Even if this problem does not arise, a second issue emerges: the village-level records may be not properly related to people resident there. For example, the Civil Registration System (CRS) determines the place of birth registration regardless of whether or not it occurs in the village of the mother's usual residence. Thus, the recording structure of the CRS is not oriented to only children resident in the panchayat's jurisdiction, which causes considerable difficulty in data use. As another example, the revenue official's existing land records are not entirely coincident with landholders resident in the village panchayat's jurisdiction. While a land record includes information on those landholders who live outside the village but own plots in it, the same land record does not include information on those landholders who live in the village but own plots outside it. In this way, the ideal requirements for village-level records in the post-Seventy-Third Amendment regime have shifted to a new type of record documenting focused on the place of usual residence of the people concerned. This new type of record is entirely related to people resident in the village panchayat and suits a people-oriented self-governance.

2.3 Data Needs IA: Data for Managing Transition to Constitutional Devolution

The enactment of the Seventy-Third Amendment envisages the panchayat transforming from just a development organisation at the local level into a political institution. The emphasis has, therefore, shifted from the bureaucracy to political elements.

Panchayats are not yet fully empowered for self-governance, leading to jurisdictional duality between them and the line departments.[49] Substantial resources flow from the Centre to the States through centrally-sponsored schemes. Major centrally-sponsored schemes include the Mahatma Gandhi National Rural Employment Guarantee Scheme (MGNREGS), *Pradhan Mantri Gram Sadak Yojana* (*PMGSY*), *Indira Awaas Yojana* (*IAY*), National Social Assistance Programme (NSAP), National Rural Health Mission (NRHM), Integrated Child Development Services (ICDS), Accelerated Rural Water Supply Programme (ARWSP), Mid-Day Meals Programme (MDM), *Sarva Shiksha Abhiyan* (*SSA*), Accelerated Irrigation Benefits Programme

---

[48] The Central Statistics Office (2014, pp. 139–40, 142, 196–202) looks into this issue.
[49] Planning Commission (2008b, p. 53).

(AIBP), and *Rajiv Gandhi Grameen Vidyutikaran Yojana* (RGGVY)[50] which have been implemented in rural areas. Consequently, State plans tend to be an aggregation of State line departments' plans, which, in turn, tailor their plans to fit the resources available under centrally-sponsored schemes. In a sense, rural India is becoming a domain over which the Central, State and panchayat governments are struggling for hegemony. As the Second Administrative Reforms Commission put it, "confusion, unnecessary duplication, inefficiency, wastage of funds, poor outputs and outcomes are the result of this organisational jungle."[51]

Each of these schemes gives detailed prescriptions for planning, its implementation, and monitoring processes, but these are not all in tune with each other. Most schemes envisage a line department-sponsored hierarchy that has a separate decision-making system for resource allocation and project execution, independent of the panchayati raj set up.[52] The *Manual for Integrated District Planning* notes:

> Several departments have also set up societies or missions, often under directions by the Central or State governments, to plan and execute development projects in areas which are in the functional domain of local governments, using funds provided by the Central or State governments or donor funds. Such institutions are termed parallel because they have a separate decision-making system for resource allocation and project execution, independent of the panchayati raj set up. These parallel bodies comprise of bureaucrats, elected representatives, and even non-officials and community representatives. They have considerable autonomy, flexible procedures and function in isolation, directly reporting to the State government, and sometimes to the Central government.[53]

The Thirteenth Central Finance Commission suggested that all parallel bodies operating in areas earmarked for local bodies (panchayats and municipalities) by XI and XII Schedules added to Articles 243G and 243W of the Constitution be abolished and that funds flow directly to local bodies through the State government.[54] In some States, however, the task of Constitutional devolution

---

[50] The *Rajiv Gandhi Grameen Vidyutikaran Yojana* (RGGVY) was renamed Deendayal Upadhyaya Gram Jyoti Yojana (DDGJY) in 2014.
[51] Second Administrative Reforms Commission (2007, p. 45).
[52] Planning Commission (2008b, pp. 5–6).
[53] *Ibid.*, pp. 54–5.
[54] Thirteenth Finance Commission (2009, p. 171). According to the Twelfth Finance Commission (2004, p. 145), some State Finance Commissions claim a transfer of the centrally-sponsored schemes along with funds and functionaries to the State government/local bodies.

of functions to the panchayats is considered incomplete. In such States, panchayats still function as agents of line departments. The institutional mechanisms of the Central and State schemes and programmes continue to bypass and ignore panchayats or, at best, seek only a cursory and token linkage. Most of the Central and State schemes and programmes envisage a role for the District Collector to organise them at the district level. Once the plans are approved, implementation is again entrusted to the line departments, with, at best, advisory committees set up at the district, intermediate or village level. In other States, however, panchayats are considered relatively more empowered and have considerable control over the line departments.[55]

Although the position and scope of panchayats varies widely across states, relationships between line departments and panchayats have been changing. These changes can be considered a transition to the constitutional devolution to panchayats.[56] In order to manage this transition, panchayats have to know and coordinate these outside agencies – the Central and State line departments and other agencies – working in the functional domain of the panchayats and still working independently of the panchayati raj set up.[57] In this transition to Constitutional devolution, panchayats cannot achieve true self-governance without information on such outside agencies working in their functional domain.

For this reason, the *Manual for Integrated District Planning* (2008) provided by the Planning Commission recommends that local government should

[55] Planning Commission (2008b, pp. 6, 54).

[56] Panchayats and Rural Development Department, Government of West Bengal (2009, pp. 13–14). "The West Bengal Panchayat Act will be amended appropriately through which specific responsibilities shall be assigned to those bodies in this regard. While such assignment shall endow the panchayats with exclusive powers and responsibilities in certain fields of activities, there will be areas where the panchayat will be assigned authorities running concurrently with that of the State Government. The latter assignments shall not immediately reduce the responsibility of the State Government but shall at the same time encourage the panchayats to be more proactive in many areas, sometimes independently and sometimes in collaboration with the State Government drawing liberally from its knowledge bank, technical or otherwise. One can argue that those are not exclusive functions but concurrent jurisdiction of the panchayats in taking up those activities. The considered view of the State Government is that in the present context it is more logical, pragmatic, and productive to provide concurrent jurisdictions in certain areas, which will help the panchayats to acquire adequate capacities in voluntarily taking up those activities or utilising the infrastructure and expertise of the government machinery on suitable occasions; the State Government shall in due course provide exclusive responsibilities as and when the same will be necessary and appropriate."

[57] Planning Commission (2008b, p. 77).

undertake a census of all schemes entrusted to the Central and State line departments and other agencies, stating their broad goals and major outcomes.[58] The *Manual* terms this exercise the "scheme census," and recommends that "details ought to be logged about the local government jurisdictions in which they operate."[59] Thus, panchayat-level databases should contain a detailed sector-wise list of current Central and State schemes and programmes. At the least this information should include:

(1) information on all sector-wise public activities of the outside agencies – the Central and State line departments and other agencies – working in the panchayat's territory, that is, information on all Central and State schemes and programmes being carried out in that territory; and

(2) information on the part of the public activities listed above that which fall in the panchayat's functional domain, that is, information on Central and State schemes and programmes being carried out in the panchayat's jurisdiction within the scope and responsibility of that panchayat.

The information in (1) is required to place the panchayat's functional domain in relation to all the public activities in that territory. This includes not only the information in (2), but also information on public activities dealing with matters not devolved to the panchayat concerning electricity distribution, or certain agricultural activities, etc., being carried out in that territory.

As the line departments' agencies work independently of panchayats, they generate and maintain their own databases independently of panchayats.[60] The latter may coordinate with such outside agencies to share data with them. For example, village panchayats may be required to coordinate Integrated Child Development Services (*anganwadi*) workers and Auxiliary Nurse Midwives to establish a data-sharing mechanism with records maintained by them, as is the case in West Bengal. As will be discussed later, such a data-sharing mechanism with outside agencies is crucial for panchayats to develop a village-level statistical database.

---

[58] *Ibid.*, p. 59.

[59] *Ibid.*, p. 55, 76–7.

[60] Isaac and Franke (2000, pp. 106–7) write: "The administrative offices of line departments in every locality act as independent units related to only to their respective department hierarchies. The information available in the files and registers of each department would be sufficient for its own day-to-day operations and not require information from other departments. But the comprehensive area plan, which the People's Planning is attempting to draw up, required comprehensive database for every locality."

Therefore, we can see that data for managing Constitutional devolution to panchayats is required for self-governance of panchayat (data needs I). More specifically, data on line departments and other agencies working in the panchayat's jurisdiction and still working independently of the panchayat raj system are required, especially to practise Constitutional devolution. Within data needs I, this special component can be identified as data needs IA.

2.4 DATA NEEDS II: DATA REQUIRED FOR PUBLIC FINANCE

Data required for public finance under fiscal decentralisation is based on Articles 243H, 243I, 280(3)(bb), and 243J of the Constitution. The State government may "by law, make provisions with respect to the maintenance of accounts by the panchayats and the auditing of such accounts" (Article 243J). The State government may

> by law, (a) authorise a panchayat to levy, collect and appropriate taxes, duties, tolls and fees; (b) assign to a panchayat taxes, duties, tolls and fees levied and collected by the State government; (c) provide for making grants-in-aid to the panchayats from the Consolidated Fund of the State; and (d) provide for constitution of Funds for crediting all moneys received, respectively, by or on behalf of the panchayats and also for the withdrawal of such money therefrom (Article 243H).

The State government must constitute a State Finance Commission to review the financial position of the panchayats and to make recommendations as to the "principles" that should govern assistance to panchayats from the State Government in the form of revenue sharing, revenue assignments and grants-in-aid. The Central Finance Commission also makes recommendations as to "the measures needed to augment the Consolidated Fund of a State to supplement the resources of the panchayats in the State on the basis of the recommendations made by the Finance Commission of the State" [Articles 243(3)(bb)].

Financial management can be considered as a particular element of the panchayat's overall functional domain as already described in section 2.2.1.2.

2.4.1 Accounting Data

The core of the dataset of the panchayat's public finance (Data Needs II) is accounting data on revenue and expenditure. Accounting data is of particular importance for the working of panchayats. In the context of fiscal

Data Required for the Village Panchayat

decentralisation, own-source revenues and "untied" funds on its revenue side of the account become the basis for assessing financial autonomy in the post-Seventy-Third Amendment regime. The expenditure side of the account reflects the functioning of the panchayat and its administrative needs. However, the quality of accounting data at the village level is inadequate in most States.[61] The Central Finance Commissions in their reports have repeatedly noted these shortcomings.[62] The Thirteenth Central Finance Commission noted:

> Ten years have elapsed since the 11th Central Finance Commission (FC-XI) underlined the need for maintaining a database as well as up-to-date accounts and made a provision for supporting State Governments in addressing these shortcomings. Five years have elapsed since 12th Central Finance Commission (FC-XII) highlighted similar inadequacies and made similar recommendations. Much has been said by the earlier Finance Commissions on this important subject. Despite this, little improvement has been noted in the situation.[63]

The Thirteenth Central Finance Commission focused on the accounting data maintained by the local bodies and stated that "accurate data on the financial performance of local bodies are best obtained from accounts of the local bodies themselves, apart from the budget documents of the State Governments."[64]

---

[61] Twelfth Finance Commission (2004, p. 154). The Thirteenth Finance Commission (2009, p. 165) also points that, "The data provided varied in quality across State Governments. While some State Governments furnished good quality data, most of them provided data which was sparse, and frequently inconsistent with the data furnished to earlier Finance Commissions. Despite considerable follow-up as well as an attempt to give the State Governments an opportunity to confirm the data submitted by them, significant problems remain with the quality of data supplied to us by State Governments."

[62] Oommen (2008, pp. 135–6). He observes, "In fact, neither the local body, nor state directorate of panchayats or municipalities, nor local fund audit, or accountant general of the state, or, the Reserve Bank of India, or the central statistical organization, or the ministry of panchayati raj, or ministry of urban development, or the planning commission have consistent fiscal data on local bodies. Many State Finance Commissions (SFCs) have attempted to gather data from the thousands of panchayati raj institutions (PRIs) and hundreds of urban local bodies (ULBs). The first SFC of Andhra Pradesh, Assam, Himachal Pradesh, Karnataka, Madhya Pradesh, Uttarakhand, Uttar Pradesh and the second SFC of Andhra Pradesh, Assam, Karnataka, Kerala, Madhya Pradesh, Uttarakhand, Uttar Pradesh are clear cases. However, data presented in these reports cannot be compared with other sources" (*ibid.*, p. 135).

[63] Thirteenth Finance Commission (2009, p. 165).

[64] *Ibid.*, p. 168. To demonstrate compliance with the conditionality for financial data imposed by the Thirteenth Finance Commission, a State government has to certify that the accounting systems as recommended have been introduced in all rural and urban local bodies (Thirteenth Finance Commission 2009, p. 178).

There are many reasons for the poor quality of accounting data at the panchayat level. The Eleventh Central Finance Commission stated that panchayats, at the village and sometimes also at the intermediate levels, do not have exclusive staff for maintaining accounts. "Most village-level panchayats do not have any staff except for a full or a part-time Secretary because of financial constraints. It would, therefore, be rather too much to expect a village panchayat to have a trained person dedicated exclusively to manage accounts."[65] More importantly, unclear Activity Mapping for each level of the panchayat's functions confuses financial devolution and results in degeneration of accounts maintained by the panchayats. The devolution of funds to panchayats at different levels has to be patterned on the applicable Activity Mapping. Conversely, no Activity Mapping can be operationalised without a link to financial requirements.[66]

Based on the Eleventh Finance Commission's recommendations the formats for the preparation of budget and accounts and database on finances of panchayati raj institutions were prescribed by the Comptroller and Auditor General of India in 2002.[67] The Comptroller and Auditor General and the Ministry of Panchayati Raj finalised a Model Panchayat Accounting System – the Simplified Accounting System – in 2009. This new accounting system uses a simplified cash-based system (with provision to shift to accrual accounting), along with the list of codes for functions, programmes and activities capturing receipts and expenditure in respect to all twenty-nine subjects mentioned in Schedule XI of the Constitution.[68]

2.4.2 Auditing

Needless to say, the panchayat-level accounting data has to be properly prepared before auditing. An inferior accounting system would hinder auditing in that panchayat.[69] In the process of audit in 18 district panchayats (*zilla parishads*), 151 Block-Level Committees and 3,214 village panchayats during 2008–9, the Examiner of Local Accounts of West Bengal found that 29 Block-level committees and 28 village panchayats did not prepare their

---

[65] *Ibid.*, pp. 77–8.
[66] Second Administrative Reforms Commission (2007, p. 353).
[67] Eleventh Finance Commission (2000, p. 77).
[68] Comptroller and Auditor General and Ministry of Panchayati Raj (2009). These new accounting formats are to be synchronised and linked to the scheme of classification in Central and State government accounts, making it amenable to computerisation and building of a database for the generation of all-India data and effective monitoring.
[69] Eleventh Finance Commission (2000, p. 77).

accounts in the prescribed format. According to the Comptroller and Auditor General, 17 out of the 80 selected village panchayats in Maharashtra had not submitted 65 annual accounts for 2003–08 to the village council for approval.[70] The Comptroller and Auditor General pointed out that "this . . . shows lack of proper control and supervision of village panchayats (*gram panchayat* – GP) by higher officials like Block Development Officer (BDO) of Block-level committee (*panchayat samiti* – PS) and Chief Executive Officer (CEO) of district panchayats (*zilla parishad* – ZP)."[71] People's trust in panchayats would decline if panchayats are not accountable for their financial management.[72] The Thirteenth Central Finance Commission recommended that the State government should entrust the Comptroller and Auditor General with technical guidance and supervision (TGS) over proper maintenance of accounts and audit of all three tiers of panchayats in the State.[73] A comprehensive audit of the accounts is to be undertaken at the village council, at the Block-level committee-level (Block *sansad*) and at the district panchayat level (*zilla sansad*). The statutory or internal audit report can be discussed in these meetings.

2.4.3 OWN-SOURCE REVENUES (OSR)

The State government may authorise panchayats to levy, collect, and appropriate taxes, duties, tolls and fees in the post-Seventy-Third-Amendment regime. There are two categories in the revenue of panchayats: own-source revenue and other revenue. The panchayat's own-source revenue comprises own-tax-revenue and own-non-tax-revenue. The own-source revenue is important for panchayats to ensure their fiscal autonomy since they have the authority to use their own-source revenues. In many States, however, the size of own-source revenue is considerably limited in relation to the total revenue of panchayati raj institutions.[74]

[70] Comptroller and Auditor General (2008, p. 37).
[71] *Ibid.*, pp. 38–40.
[72] Rai, Nambiar, Paul, Singh, and Sahni (2001, pp. 181–2). For example, the *Maharashtra State Development Report* (Planning Commission 2007, p. 250) mentions that "The major challenge that the panchayati raj institutions (PRIs) in the state face is the corruption at various levels, which is the common practice in many states. Instances of misappropriation of funds by village panchayat heads, panchayat secretaries often appear in the local newspapers."
[73] Thirteenth Finance Commission (2009, p. 178).
[74] The Twelfth Finance Commission (2004, p. 147) suggests that "the share of own revenues of the panchayats (all tiers) was 6.40 per cent of their total revenues for the period 1998–9 to 2002–3 which is a definite improvement over 4.17 per cent estimated for the period 1990–1 to 1997–8 but is still low." However, the Thirteenth Finance Commission does not rely on such data. It further states, "There are significant discontinuities in data relating to revenue and

There is a broad consensus that local governments should concentrate on immobile and residence-based taxes.[75] At present, the major own-tax source for the village panchayat is the property tax levied in many States.[76] The revenue from property tax depends upon: (a) enumeration of properties in the tax register; (b) the collection rate; (c) the assessment and valuation system; (d) the extent of exemptions; and (e) the level of tax rate.[77] In order to assess and collect property tax, therefore, a property tax register is required. A census-type survey such as the Population Census can be used as a reference point to estimate the tax base. Similarly, a list of persons liable to pay tax is required to gather other own-source revenues.

Agricultural lands are core productive assets in rural areas which makes them the obvious basis for taxation. In fact, the Eleventh Central Finance Commission stated that "in many States, land revenue has either been abolished or land holdings up to a certain size have been exempted. However, taxes on land/farm income in some form may be levied to strengthen the resource base of the local bodies."[78] Revenue yield from taxes on land is negligible at present. As suggested by Indira Rajaraman, one reason for this is that taxation of agriculture confronts "an information vacuum" in India, one that is impossible to overcome when attempted at levels higher than the local government.[79] Land records will be required for the land-based tax system of panchayats on agriculture.[80]

---

expenditure of local bodies submitted by State Governments to Eleventh Finance Commission (FC-XI), Twelfth Finance Commission (FC-XII), and to this Commission. These discrepancies detract from the credibility of the data. Unfortunately, successive Finance Commissions, including our own, have been unable to independently verify the data provided on local bodies" (Thirteenth Finance Commission 2009, p. 165).

[75] Oommen (2008, p. 4).

[76] Yu Sasaki (2005) compares village panchayats in Madhya Pradesh and Tamil Nadu in terms of their capacities for collecting house tax or property tax. As a result of her enquiry, it was found that "village panchayats in Madhya Pradesh hardly collect tax while their counterparts in Tamil Nadu show a very high level of collection. . . . Ironically, therefore, it appears in the Tamil Nadu case in particular that the members of the centralised State administration play a constructive and supportive role in securing accountability of village panchayats as well as improving the performance of panchayati raj institutions."

[77] Thirteenth Finance Commission (2009, p. 162).

[78] Eleventh Finance Commission (2000, p. 75).

[79] Rajaraman (2003, p. 3). She argues that the transfer of the right to levy taxes on agriculture from the State government to the panchayats, with jurisdictional retention, will give panchayats a stake in raising revenue yields, and thus lead to revenue additionality in the Indian fiscal system as a whole, aggregating across all levels of government (ibid., p. 159).

[80] "A number of existing Acts including the CAs need to be amended. For example, a simple Constitutional amendment reserving Agricultural Income Tax to panchayats would yield

Panchayats may also prepare an assessment list for non-tax revenue. Common property resources such as public facilities, village land and forests can be sources of resource mobilisation for the panchayats.[81]

2.4.4 Allocation of Funds between the State and Panchayats

Usually the own-source revenue generated by panchayats falls far short of their requirements. Tax allocated to local bodies yields less revenue than taxes that have a national or State-wide base. This asymmetry between the local bodies' taxation power and the responsibility to fulfil their functional requirements necessitates the transfer of funds from the higher tiers to the local government either through untied grants, or through a share in other State taxes, or as part of various development schemes. A considerable number of funding streams is thus reaching the panchayats from the Central and State governments.

The grants allocated for centrally-sponsored schemes and State Governments' special purpose programmes are usually tied to predetermined objectives, leaving little room for the local government's own priorities. Therefore, untied fund-transfer from higher tiers of government to panchayati raj institutions is required in the post-Seventy-Third Amendment regime. This is based on two points of thinking: first, panchayats seek financial autonomy from Central and State Governments in this regime. Fund allocation through untied funds can ensure financial autonomy for the panchayats. The panchayati raj institutions can take care of their local priorities using untied funds.[82] Secondly, regional disparities draw special attention in this regime.[83] Financial equalisation among poorer and richer local governments is necessary. "The protection of financially weaker local authorities calls for the institution of financial equalisation procedures or equivalent measures which are designed to compensate for the effects of the unequal distribution of

---

enough money resulting in minimal financial dependence of panchayats on higher level governments. According to the Directorate of Economics and Statistics, Department of Agriculture & Co-operation, the total foodgrain production in India in 1996–7 was 199.3 million tonnes. Even a simple levy of 5 paise per kilogram will bring to the panchayats a sum of Rs 996.5 crore. This amount is almost equal to the total yearly grants to all the panchayats under the Seventy-Third Amendment as recommended by the Tenth Finance Commission. If we include plantation crops, oilseeds, etc. under this proposed basket of agricultural tax, the said amount will be about Rs 10,000 crore" (Rai, Nambiar, Paul, Singh, and Sahni 2001, p. 171).

[81] Panchayats and Rural Development Department, Government of West Bengal (2007, p.116).
[82] Second Administrative Reforms Commission (2007, pp. 160–1).
[83] *Ibid.*, p. 160.

potential sources of finance and of the financial burden they must support."[84]

The inter-governmental financial adjustment system has been adopted by many countries since the First World War for the purpose of reducing regional disparity among local governments. As there are many ways to accomplish this, inter-governmental financial adjustment systems differ from country to country. India has created a necessary condition for State–local inter-governmental financial adjustment by the institution of State Finance Commissions through the Seventy-Third and Seventy-Fourth Constitutional Amendments [Articles 243I, 243Y, 280(3)(bb), and 280(3)(c)].[85] The Central Finance Commissions have also made recommendations about State–local inter-governmental financial adjustment, along with their recommendations about "the measures needed to augment the Consolidated Fund of a State to supplement the resources of the panchayats in the State" [Articles 280(3)(bb), 280(3)(c)].

Fiscal transfer requires a principle and formulas for fund allocation among local bodies. In order to fulfil such an inter-governmental financial adjustment, formulas based on a "normative approach" – an approach using certain prescribed formulas – is envisaged for India. The Central Finance Commissions state that it should neither be forecast based on historical trends, nor be amenable to negotiation.[86]

Such a principle and formulas have already been used for grants allocation for the centrally-sponsored schemes. The Gadgil Formula has been used with some modifications to allocate Plan grants and loans to the States for financing their development programmes under the Five Year Plan and Annual Plans. The Gadgil Formula consisted of several proxy indicators for each State, such as its population, per capita income and tax effort.

---

[84] The "European Charter of Local Self-Government" (Council of Europe 1985), Article 9 states: "Local authorities shall be entitled, within national economic policy, to adequate financial resources of their own, of which they may dispose freely within the framework of their powers" (para. 2); "The protection of financially weaker local authorities calls for the institution of financial equalization procedures or equivalent measures which are designed to correct the effects of the unequal distribution of potential sources of finance and of the financial burden they must support" (para. 5).

[85] The Twelfth Finance Commission (2004, pp. 149–51, 159–60) argues that State Finance Commissions have not worked properly in most of the States. Oommen (2008, p. 9) argues that "the State Finance Commissions have not performed their onerous tasks satisfactorily."

[86] Twelfth Finance Commission (2004, pp. 140, 159).

The Thirteenth Central Finance Commission also recommended a normative approach and estimated the State-wide allocation of grants-in-aid aimed at panchayati raj institutions using the following formula with factors and weights:

Criterion	Weight (in per cent)
Population	50
Area	10
Distance from highest per capita sectoral income	10
Index of devolution	15
SC/ST's proportion in the population	10
Finance Commission (FC) local body grants utilisation index	5
Total	100

This formula requires the State-level data on each criterion.[87]

In principle, the inter-governmental financial adjustment aims at financing a gap between administrative needs and financial capability (such as tax-collection capability). In fact, the Eleventh Central Finance Commission has recommended strengthening the normative approach as follows:

> In deciding what would be the appropriate sums to be paid to States as grants-in-aid, the (Central) Finance Commission (FC) assesses the "need" of each State after taking into account what they can raise on their own by exercising the tax powers available with them.[88]

[87] Thirteenth Finance Commission (2009, pp. 176–7). The 2001 Census data is available for working out Population and "SC/ST proportion in the population." In computing the income distance criterion, the Commission uses the average per capita comparable Gross State Domestic Product (GSDP) from the primary sector, derived on the basis of comparable GSDP figures supplied by the Central Statistical Organisation (CSO). "Index of devolution" and "FC local body grants utilization index" are derived from the finance accounts. The amounts devolved to local bodies in the finance accounts are aggregated. "FC local body grants utilization index" is based on the level of draw down of the Twelfth Finance Commission funds in the past. Although the Thirteenth Finance Commission was inclined to use an "index of decentralization" as a parameter for devolution, it did not use it due to serious data constraints (Twelfth Finance Commission 2004, pp. 165–6, 175). The Twelfth Finance Commission used an "index of deprivation" to take into account minimum needs of the population on the basis of the 2001 Census data regarding drinking water and sanitation, but the Thirteenth Finance Commission does not use it because the corresponding data in 2001 Census is out of date in 2009. The Thirteenth Central Finance Commission (2010, p. 175) "[is] strongly inclined to use the revenue effort criteria," but does not do so because data on financial performance do not appear credible for the Commission, as mentioned before.
[88] Eleventh Finance Commission (2000, p. 15).

Thus, ideally speaking, proxy indicators should reflect both administrative needs and financial capability in order to allow for any resource gap in the inter-governmental financial adjustment. The above formula recommended by the Thirteenth Central Finance Commission could not incorporate proxy indicators of financial capability due to the unreliability of the available data. The absence of data on financial capability makes it impossible to assess the gap between financial capability and administrative needs. Proxy indicators such as population, area, distance from highest per capita sectoral income and the SC/ST proportion in the population can reflect administrative needs to a certain degree, but they are still considered insufficient. In fact, the Commission failed to incorporate an "index of deprivation" in the formula, which can reflect the minimum needs of the population. A wide variety of data can be used to estimate the multiple facets of administrative needs.[89]

An "index of devolution" – amounts devolved to local bodies in the finance accounts of the State governments (under sub-heads 196, 197, and 198 under applicable major heads in the non-Plan category) – and "Finance Commission (FC) local body grants utilisation index" – percentage of amounts drawn from the grants awarded by the Twelfth Central Finance Commission – is a kind of incentive index aimed at encouraging State governments to decentralise further.[90] However, such incentive indices are based on a different principle from the financial equalisation principle for local governments. Incentive measures may indeed be useful in the transition to fiscal decentralisation, but they can sometimes end up increasing financial disparities and creating horizontal imbalances among local governments.

The Central Finance Commission recommended that State Finance Commissions also adopt the normative approach, particularly for fund allocation among panchayati raj institutions.[91] Some State Finance Commissions, such as in West Bengal, provided a principle and formulas for fund allocation for panchayati raj institutions, as will be seen later.

These formulas for fund allocation at the district, intermediate, and village

[89] Thirteenth Finance Commission (2009, p. 175).
[90] Ibid., pp. 176-7.
[91] Twelfth Finance Commission (2004, pp. 149–50). "A careful scrutiny of the State Finance Commission (SFC) reports reveals that few SFCs have followed this approach. This has made it impossible for us to adopt the reports as the basis for our recommendations. We strongly recommend that in future, all SFCs including those which are already set up but are yet to submit their recommendations, follow the above procedure so as to enable the central finance commission to do full justice to its constitutional mandate" (Ibid., p. 150).

levels for panchayats require data for each level. However, obtaining reliable data of such kind is far more difficult at the sub-State level than at the State level. In fact, most of the State Finance Commissions do not have accurate information on the finances of their local bodies.[92] The Twelfth Central Finance Commission suggested:

> A proper accounting system has to be put in place at the grass-roots level to facilitate realistic assessment of the needs of the panchayats and municipalities for basic civic and developmental functions. Resource gap estimation for core services is central to the process of a fiscal transfer that would encourage equalisation. The absence of data necessary for a rational determination of the gap between the cost of service delivery and the capacity to raise resources makes the task of recommending measures for achieving equalisation of services almost impossible.[93]

Thus reliable financial data together with rich data closely related to administrative needs are needed to rectify horizontal imbalances arising in inter-governmental fiscal relations. Ideally, such data should reflect inter-jurisdictional disparities in economic and fiscal capacities due to differences in resource endowments, historical developments, and even social disabilities of the residents.[94] However, as many Central and State Finance Commissions have reiterated, data for such purposes at the grass-roots level is lacking.[95]

Therefore, data required for panchayat-level public finance includes not only accounting data, but also other kinds of data closely related to revenue bases and administrative needs. That is why the Third State Finance Commission of West Bengal claimed that financial data "should be part of the general statistical information system necessary for planning and delivering public services."[96]

[92] Oommen (2008, p. 135), and Twelfth Finance Commission (2004, p. 154).
[93] Twelfth Finance Commission (2004, p. 154).
[94] Oommen (2008, p. 4).
[95] The Japan International Cooperation Agency's Study Team and Japanese experts on local public finance faced the same data constraint in the course of studying ways of improving the Internal Revenue Allotment (IRA) System in the Philippines. "Another major constraint of the study is that it has not been able to calculate as meticulously as it desired the financial needs and potential revenue-raising capacities of the target Local Government Units (LGUs) under sample survey. Consequently, the study is short of estimating the financial shortages of LGUs. . . . It is hoped that the data is gathered sufficiently and properly at the local level and managed systematically at the national level. As barangays are basal units of local government, collecting the barangay data systematically should be an idea worth considering" Japan International Cooperation Agency (2008, pp. 181–2).
[96] Third State Finance Commission of West Bengal (2008, p. 35).

2.4.5 Separate Budget Window

It is necessary for a panchayat to know how much money is allocated to it by the State Government. However, the linkage of accounting data between the State and panchayats is ambiguous in most States. The accounting system in most States does not adequately reflect the State–panchayat fiscal relationship. In these States, neither budget documents nor finance accounts depict expenditure incurred by the panchayati raj institutions by means of detailed heads and object heads.[97] Therefore it is essential that some kind of budget separation be made so that panchayats can get an idea of the budget that their expenditure must match. This can be achieved through a series of steps, commencing with the creation of a "Local Government Sector Budget Window" in the budget of State governments, and ending with each local government getting a clear communication about its budget.[98] In this regard, Kerala is the only State whose budget is disaggregated to the level of each local government.[99] In Kerala a separate document indicating local government-wise allotments has been annexed to the State budget.

The Thirteenth Central Finance Commission called for such a budget separation at the State and district levels, and recommended that all States adopt a standardised accounting framework and codification pattern consistent with the uniform Model Panchayat Accounting System uniformly prescribed by the Comptroller and Auditor General.[100]

2.4.6 Funding Streams of Agencies Other Than Panchayats

It is necessary for a panchayat to know of all the funding streams spent by outside agencies working within its jurisdiction. According to the *Manual for Integrated District Planning* (2008), all funding streams entering the jurisdiction of a local government belong to three broad areas:[101]

---

[97] "Any assistance given by the State Governments to panchayati raj institutions (PRIs) is presently booked as a lump sum under the minor heads 196, 197 & 198 which appear in the budget documents as well as in the finance accounts of the State Governments. However, neither the budget documents nor the finance accounts of most State Governments depict the details relating to the expenditure incurred by the PRIs on detailed heads and object heads. Further, it is not possible to determine the corresponding expenditure incurred by the PRIs as they do not maintain similar accounts that could capture these details" (Thirteenth Finance Commission 2009, p. 168).

[98] Planning Commission (2008, p. 36).

[99] Planning Commission (2008b, p. 36).

[100] Thirteenth Finance Commission (2009, pp. 167–8).

[101] Planning Commission (2008b, pp. 37–8).

(a) Funds that are clearly devolved to the local government and are either deposited in its account, or released only on instructions from the funding authorities. These usually comprise of: (i) Central Finance Commission grants, (ii) State Finance Commission grants and tax assignments, (iii) programmes explicitly implemented by panchayats, such as the Mahatma Gandhi National Rural Employment Guarantee Scheme and Backward Regions Grant Fund, and (iv) own-revenues of panchayats.

(b) Funds spent by user groups and local government subcommittees with a large measure of autonomy, such as (i) National Rural Health Mission funds spent by the Village Health Committee, (ii) Sarva Shiksha Abhiyan funds spent by the Village Education Committee, (iii) watershed development funds spent by watershed committees, (iv) drinking water and sanitation funds spent by the Village Water and Sanitation Committee.

(c) Funds spent within local government jurisdiction by departments dealing with matters not devolved to the local government, e.g. irrigation, electricity distribution, agricultural activities that are not devolved, etc.

In the transition to constitutional devolution, a "scheme census" is again required with respect to information on fund allocation for each scheme entrusted to external agencies.

2.5 DATA NEEDS III: DATA REQUIRED FOR LOCAL PLANNING AND ITS IMPLEMENTATION

The Legislature of a State may devolve powers and responsibilities upon panchayats at the appropriate level with respect to "the preparation of plans for economic development and social justice," and "the implementation of schemes for economic development and social justice" (Article 243G). Data are required for such local planning and its implementation (data needs III).

Local planning and its implementation presuppose good self-governance in the panchayat's functional domain with well-delineated Activity Mapping as described in section 2.2.1.2. The planning exercise as such constitutes an element of the panchayat's overall functional domain. The functional domain may include the planning exercise as one of its unbundled activities.[102] However, the planning exercise is a special function that is feasible only for a functional domain with a high degree of autonomy. It is impossible

---

[102] The Second Administrative Reforms Commission (2007, p. 146) classified activities to be unbundled in the Activity Mapping as follows: "(i) Setting standards, (ii) Planning, (iii) Asset creation, (iv) Implementation and Management, and (v) Monitoring and Evaluation."

in a functional domain where the panchayat cannot have its own vision or initiative. If the panchayat acts strictly as a delivery unit of administrative services provided by line departments and is not autonomous in the functional domain, it may fulfil its function but not as part of planning exercise.

2.5.1 Empirical Grounding for the Vision

According to the *Manual for Integrated District Planning* provided by the Planning Commission, the planning exercise includes gathering relevant data, analysing it to identify public needs and issues, setting priorities with respect to solutions, determining solutions, matching the set priorities to available budgets, defining processes of implementation, and setting targets. Panchayats also need to monitor the execution of prepared plans. This means monitoring not only the progress (or "output") of the schemes, but also the impact (or "outcome") of plans on the local society.

Every plan starts with and is based upon a vision.[103] That is why the planning exercise is impossible in a functional domain where the panchayat does not have its own vision or initiative. For democratic decentralisation in the post-Seventy-Third Amendment regime, this vision must be formulated through intensive participation of the people and stakeholders. It cannot be prepared in isolation.[104]

The *Manual for Integrated District Planning* uses the term "envisioning" to refer to this democratic process of planning.[105] This vision must have "a strong empirical grounding provided through rigorous compilation and analysis of baseline data, which needs to be as institutionalised and strong as the planning system itself."[106] A set of such baseline data is illustrated in section 2.1 above. Based on such a comprehensive database, various assessments are made

> highlighting any significant features of development or lack of development, also focusing on progress and shortfalls, and gaps in outcomes in implementing the previous plan, spillover works and funds required for their completion.[107]

The dataset "for use in micro-level planning of various developmental

---

[103] *Ibid.*, p. 13.
[104] *Ibid.*, p. 65.
[105] *Ibid.*
[106] *Ibid.*, p. 13. This exercise is referred to as "stock-taking report" in the *Manual.* Also, *ibid.*, pp. 57–8.
[107] *Ibid.*, p. 57.

programmes"[108] that was identified by the *Basic Statistics for Local Level Development* report was also a minimum set of such baseline data.

The panchayats below the district level, at the intermediate and village levels, also have planning processes, which need a strong informational basis provided through a dataset to build a clear understanding of the local area.[109] This dataset must be disaggregated to the relevant scale for use by the panchayats.[110] According to the *Manual for Integrated District Planning*, the village panchayat's planning process comprises the following steps: [111]

(a) Identification of issues by village council and ward council, based on the vision of the panchayat.
(b) Determination of solutions by working groups and standing committees of the village panchayats.
(c) Prioritisation of solutions and fund allocation by standing committees of village panchayats, resulting in the preparation of the first village panchayat plan draft.
(d) Reconsideration of the plan draft in the second village council meeting.
(e) Finalisation of sectoral plans by standing committees/working groups.
(f) Finalisation of village panchayat plan at a full meeting of the panchayat.

However, the *Manual* notes:

> In some States, where decentralisation and empowerment of panchayats has proceeded quite far, the envisioning process would touch every village panchayat and sub-panchayat body. However, in others, for practical reasons, envisioning might have to be confined to the intermediate level, because village panchayats have not been empowered enough.[112]

2.5.2 District Planning Committee

Article 243ZD of the Constitution envisages that District Planning Committees are constituted in every State to consolidate the plans prepared by the district's panchayats and municipalities and to prepare a draft development plan for the entire district. In preparing the development plan, the District Planning Committee is required to consider matters of common interest

---

[108] Central Statistical Organisation (2006, p. A-1).
[109] *Ibid.*, p. 81.
[110] *Ibid.*, p. 13. It can be noted on GIS/Data grids (*ibid.*, p. 61).
[111] *Ibid.*, p. 81.
[112] *Ibid.*, pp. 65–6.

between panchayats and municipalities, including spatial planning, sharing water and other physical and natural resources, integrated development of infrastructure, and environmental conservation.[113]

For this planning exercise, the *Manual for Integrated District Planning* recommends:

> The District Planning Committee must have the capacity to organise the compilation of essential data for each local government, monitor its progress by measuring outcomes on important sectors and provide feedback to them. This will require close coordination between local governments and the District Planning Committee. The District Planning Committee should possess the skills to guide local bodies to develop and manage their own data bases and to utilise data for a well directed planning and implementation effort.[114]

However, District Planning Committees have yet to come into their own in most States. Even in States that have constituted District Planning Committees, their roles are often markedly different from what is expected of them under the Constitution.[115] According to the *Manual for Integrated District Planning*:

---

[113] *Ibid.*, p. 21. The *Manual for Integrated District Planning* calls for Activity Mapping for the District Planning Committees and states that "For District Planning Committees to perform meaningfully, it is necessary that their precise roles are made clear through formal government orders. An activity mapping for District Planning Committees would include:
  a) providing overall leadership to the district planning process;
  b) leading the district visioning exercise;
  c) setting district priorities on the basis of consensus among local governments, line departments, civil society, academia, and other stakeholders in development;
  d) during the process of consolidation, review plans of local governments and development departments particularly to ensure that these address the district vision as a whole and are free of overlapping and duplication;
  e) perform the central role in the preparation of the Potential Linked Credit Plan (PLCP) for the district, with the support of National Bank for Agricultural and Rural Development (NABARD);
  f) oversee the participative planning process of the district development plan, to ensure that timelines are followed;
  g) after the plan is approved, to review implementation progress with local governments, line departments and other implementing agencies and planning units; and
  h) oversee capacity-development of staff and elected representatives of local governments and line department staff regarding decentralised planning and implementation."
[114] *Ibid.*, p. 25.
[115] "However, in the 15 years that have elapsed since the enactment of the 74th Amendment, District Planning Committees have yet to come into their own in most states. As of date, five states have not constituted District Planning Committees in accordance with the constitutional provision. Moreover, in states that have constituted District Planning Committees, the roles

One of the key reasons why District Planning Committees have generally not been able to prepare draft development plans for the district as a whole is because they are usually not adequately equipped to lead the process of district planning. Consequently, at best, District Planning Committees perform as committees that meet occasionally to hurriedly endorse, without adequate appreciation, a "plan" or plans prepared by departmental officials.[116]

To give a specific example, the Third State Finance Commission of West Bengal noted:

In the prevailing circumstances, District Planning Committees (DPCs) in West Bengal have failed in the mandatory responsibility of preparing the District Plan scientifically. A disparate set of schemes stitched together without proper integration have been put into volumes and labelled now as District Plans in all the districts. Terms like integrated District Plan, consolidation of schemes, comprehensive plan etc. are being loosely used in most of the instruction manuals, plan guidelines, Government orders and training materials without conceptual clarity or operational directions. Of course, one cannot blame the DPCs for such conditions as, in addition to the primary deficiency in respect of devolution, they do not have adequate expertise and office support for effective functioning and as such, they cannot facilitate the preparation of the District Plans by ensuring the participation of official experts, elected members of local bodies, non-official experts nominated by the State Government and the local bodies and also individual and voluntary groups interested in joining the planning process.[117]

The Third State Finance Commission of West Bengal added:

It is worth mentioning in this connection that the same situation was prevailing in Kerala a few years back. Kerala has, however, changed the position now. Apart from the steps taken to clarify the devolution of functions, allocation of resources, etc., the State has strengthened the DPCs by associating them with experts from various sources – technical people from the departments, colleges, universities and various institutes including NGOs working on development and related activities.[118]

---

performed by them are often markedly different from what is expected of them under the Constitution" (Planning Commission 2008b, p. 21).

[116] *Ibid.*, p. 21.
[117] Third State Finance Commission of West Bengal (2008, pp. 131–2).
[118] *Ibid.*, p. 132.

2.5.3 Planning Exercise below the District Level

Articles 243G and 243ZD also envisage draft plans prepared by the panchayats below the district level.

The planning exercise of a certain tier of the panchayati raj institutions has to be carried out within its functional domain provided by Activity Mapping, i.e., delineation of the functions of each level of the panchayat. Besides, as mentioned above, the panchayat requires enough autonomous space in its functional domain to have its own vision to carry out the planning exercise. As mentioned in section 2.2.1.2, however, the progress of devolution of powers and responsibilities to the panchayats at various levels is poor and uneven in many States. In some States, functional assignments to panchayats are still not clear, or orders in this direction remain on paper and have not been implemented. As will be seen in chapter 8, section 8.3.1, the possibility of planning at the village panchayat-level was limited when autonomy in its functional domain is substantially limited.

2.5.4 Data Required for Implementing a Line Department's Plan

The data required to implement a plan prescribed by line departments is fundamentally different from data required for the "envisioning" exercise for the panchayat to plan its own initiatives. In practise, most panchayats continue to be treated as agencies of the State or the Central governments for implementing prescribed schemes.[119] The major role of the panchayat remains largely confined to the delivery mechanism for programmes of the State and the Central governments. Its own initiatives are not of a high order. In such a case, the panchayat has little authority to envision plans for holistic development.[120] The panchayat may only define a process of implementing the plan provided by other agencies. As the plan prescribed by line departments is tied to predetermined objectives, data needs for its implementation accordingly have a narrow scope.

Nevertheless, certain government schemes such as the Mahatma Gandhi National Rural Employment Guarantee Scheme and *Swarnjayanti Gram Swarozgar Yojana* (now revamped as National Rural Livelihoods Mission) leave considerable scope for setting out the priorities of individual panchayats. Therefore, even when panchayats act as mere implementing agencies, they

---

[119] Second Administrative Reforms Commission (2007, p. 8).
[120] Panchayats and Rural Development Department (2009, p. 11).

may sometimes get some autonomy in the functional domain. We discuss this further in chapter 8, section 8.3.

2.5.5 Planning Exercise in the Move Towards Constitutional Devolution

In the spirit of Constitutional devolution of powers, panchayats cannot adequately prepare plans without information on outside agencies that are working in their functional domain. The Second Administrative Reforms Commission stated:

> Even where Activity Mapping has been approved, parallel action to enable local governments to exercise their functions has not been taken. The existing government departments with their executive orders and instructions, parallel government bodies like District Rural Development Agencies (DRDAs) and the continuance of statutory bodies (as regards water, electricity, etc.) without any change, prevent the local governments from exercising the so-called transferred functions.[121]

Therefore, a widespread coordination is required for planning exercises among panchayats at the district, intermediate and village levels, along with the Central and State line departments and other agencies.[122] As a result, plans prepared by panchayats in the move towards Constitutional devolution will include, in any case, elements of implementing schemes of other line departments.

2.5.6 Data Needs Identified by the Basic Statistics for Local Level Development Report

Based on the terms of reference of the *Basic Statistics for Local Level Development* report, the Village Schedule on Basic Statistics can be considered a result of efforts to identify data "for use in micro-level planning of various developmental programmes."[123] The framework provided by the *Basic Statistics* report was developed on the basis of a review of efforts already made by groups and committees. In addition, extensive pilot studies,

---

[121] Second Administrative Reforms Commission (2007, p. 45).

[122] The Planning Commission (2008b, p. 54) states that "typically, in a good decentralised district planning exercise, each planning unit, namely panchayats, at the district, intermediate and village levels, municipalities, line departments and parastatals would prepare a plan for execution of each of their functions and responsibilities after wide ranging consultations."

[123] However, the relationship between data items of the Village Schedule and the above twenty-nine functions are not explicitly defined by the *Basic Statistics for Local Level Development* report.

including the large-scale pilot scheme launched by the Ministry of Statistics and Programme Implementation since 2008, have been conducted repeatedly to test and modify the Village Schedule. In the course of the pilot studies, feedback from different States was sought on data sources, availability of data for different items of information, problems in data compilation, etc. Therefore, the Village Schedule is at present the highest achievement in efforts to pursue data requirement for micro-level planning and its implementation in rural India (Data Needs III). It will be examined in detail in section 4.3.5.1 in chapter 4 and section 8.1 in chapter 8.

However, for the planning exercise the panchayat may supplement the Village Schedule data with other secondary data from the village, which will be discussed in section 8.4 in chapter 8.

Several core statistical databases can be used as baseline data for local planning exercises. The Census of India, including the population enumeration data, the house-listing and housing data, and the non-Census village-level amenities data (Village Directory) is indisputably a core statistical database for micro-level planning and its implementation in rural India. The Below Poverty Line Censuses (and the Socio-Economic and Caste Census, 2011) are also core databases that provide panchayats with digitised unit-level data on households and persons. These databases cover essential aspects of local development. Nevertheless, they do not systematically cover all aspects of data requirements for micro-level planning and its implementation in rural India.

2.5.7 Micro-Level Planning on the Basis of List of Residents

While aggregate data are very important for the upper-level administrative institutions such as the district- or State-level administrative bodies in order to have a large-scale view, disaggregated or unit-level data are of relatively high importance at the grass-root level. Unit-level data on residents and facilities is sometimes essential for a village panchayat to formulate and implement development programmes. Unit-level records on residents are essential for the village panchayat and its subordinate bodies to identify and select targets of local planning and its implementation. Unit-level data of each facility with information on its quality is essential to formulate programmes to develop village infrastructure.

A list of residents – the People's List – will be discussed in section 6.6 in chapter

6. Without a comprehensive list of residents, the panchayat cannot perform and implement micro-level planning with objectivity and accountability.

2.6 CONCLUSIONS ON DATA NEEDS OF PANCHAYATS

In this chapter we have identified data needs of the panchayats under the decentralisation initiative of the Constitution (Seventy-Third Amendment) Act, 1992, by taking into account the provisions of the Amendment itself. We have interpreted the data needs on the assumption that State governments will legislate and devolve powers of self-governance and development to the panchayats in the manner envisaged in the Constitution. Therefore, the paradigm of our study is slightly different from that of the *Basic Statistics for Local Level Development* report. We have identified the panchayat's data needs on the basis of the Constitutional requirement as a whole, whereas the *Basic Statistics* report identifies these on the basis of its terms of reference, that is, "for use in micro-level planning of various developmental programmes."[124] In this chapter, the data needs of panchayats, assuming that power is actually devolved to them, have been identified as follows:

1. Data needs I: This category covers data required for self-governance. Within this category, a special component can be identified, that is:
   Data needs IA: This covers data required for managing the process of devolution as envisaged in the Constitution.
   In addition, in practice, data generated or used by line departments and other agencies working in the panchayat's jurisdiction, independent of the panchayati raj system are required by the panchayats, especially to manage devolution of powers.
2. Data needs II: This category covers data required for matters of public finance.
3. Data needs III: This category covers data required for micro-level planning (and plan implementation) for economic development and social justice.

These data needs, in practice, are closely interrelated. Data required for matters of panchayat-level public finance (Data Needs II) are closely related to self-governance of the panchayat (Data Needs I). Public finance of the panchayat can be considered as just a monetary aspect of its self-governance. Public finance is interrelated with the preparation of the panchayat's plan and its implementation (Data Needs III). The panchayat's expenditure is often assessed in relation to its planning for economic development and social

---

[124] Central Statistical Organisation (2006, p. A-1).

justice. Conversely, a comprehensive database to build a vision for planning requires a description of all financial resources available to the panchayat in order to match the budget with its plan.[125]

The same data are often used for different data needs. For example, the panchayat's self-governance requires various data on its jurisdiction. Such data sometimes overlap with data required for micro-level planning and its implementation, or data required for assessing own-source revenues. Nevertheless, each of these sets of data has its own definition and deserves separate consideration. We shall examine the multiple aspects of these data needs in the new statistical domain and discuss them one by one.

For further analytical study of data needs of panchayats, we have to look into the functions assigned to each tier of the panchayati raj institutions in relation to various data uses. For this analysis, clear information on Activity Mapping – i.e., delineating the functions of each level of the panchayat on the basis of unbundling of subjects in Schedule XI of the Constitution into smaller units of work – is required. However, as the Seventy-Third Amendment leaves considerable scope for inter-State variations, we will have to discuss Activity Mapping in the specific contexts of two States that we have chosen for our study.

[125] Oommen (2008, p. 2).

Chapter 3

INTRODUCING THE TWO VILLAGE PANCHAYATS

3.1 PROFILE OF THE TWO PANCHAYATS AND THEIR VILLAGES

In order to study the new statistical domain, we conducted case studies in two villages. The first was Warwat Khanderao village panchayat in Maharashtra. The second was Raina village panchayat in West Bengal, and Bidyanidhi village which was in the jurisdiction of the Raina panchayat. Warwat Khanderao is located in a traditionally *raiyatwari* area. This village was studied by the Foundation for Agrarian Studies in 2007 as part of the Project on Agrarian Relations in India (PARI). Raina village panchayat is located in a former *zamindari* and post-land reform area. Bidyanidhi village, one of thirteen villages (*mouzas*) in the jurisdiction of the Raina village panchayat was studied in 2005 as part of a land and credit survey ("Landlessness and Debt in Rural West Bengal") conducted by V. K. Ramachandran, Vikas Rawal, and others.

3.1.1 Profile of Warwat Khanderao Village and Panchayat

Warwat Khanderao village was part of the Sangrampur *tehsil* of Buldhana district in the State of Maharashtra. The nearest town, Shegaon, is 20km from the village and is connected by road. The village had no Primary Health Centre or other medical facilities.

During the 2007 PARI survey, the village was home to 250 households; the village population was 1308. There were 99 females per 100 males. There were 130 children in the village who were 5 years of age or younger. The Census of India recorded the village population as 1479 in 2011. About 8 per cent of the population belonged to the Scheduled Castes.

The proportion of literate persons in the population above the age of 7 years was 94 per cent among males and 81 per cent among females in 2011. The village had a primary school and a middle school that offered education up to class 7. At the authors' time of first field visit for this study in 2009, the village had one Integrated Child Development Services (ICDS) centre (*anganwadi*).

The ICDS centre was bifurcated in 2011. In 2011, the total enrolment was 69 (31 boys and 38 girls) in the first ICDS centre, and was 67 (36 boys and 31 girls) in the second centre. The village depended on agriculture, with 93 per cent of workers employed in the agricultural sector (Census of India 2011). Within the agricultural work force, 59 per cent of workers were cultivators and 34 per cent were agricultural labourers. The shares of non-agricultural labourers and salaried employees in the work-force were negligible.

Table 3.1 *Distribution of population by caste and sex, Warwat Khanderao, 2007 in numbers and per cent*

Caste/religious group	Number			As percentage of total population		
	Females	Males	All	Females	Males	All
Scheduled Caste	57	57	114	8.7	8.7	8.7
Other Backward Class	308	325	633	47.2	49.5	48.4
Muslim	163	158	321	25	24.1	24.5
Nomadic tribe	124	116	240	19	17.7	18.3
Total	652	656	1308	100	100	100

Source: FAS survey data, 2007.

Table 3.2 *Profile of Warwat Khanderao village panchayat, Buldhana district, Maharashtra, 2011*

Total population		1479
Scheduled Castes (as percentage of total population)		8.1
Scheduled Tribes (as percentage of total population)		0.1
Literacy rate (7 years and above) (in per cent)	All	87.3
	Male	93.6
	Female	80.7
Work participation rate (percentage of workers in total population)	All	52.3
	Male	59.8
	Female	44.5
Cultivators (as percentage of total workers)		58.7
Agricultural labourers (as percentage of total workers)		34.4
Household industry (as percentage of total workers)		0.8
Other workers (as percentage of total workers)		6.9

Source: Census of India 2011.

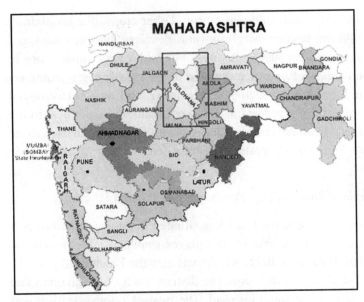

Figure 3.1 *Location of Buldhana district, Maharashtra*

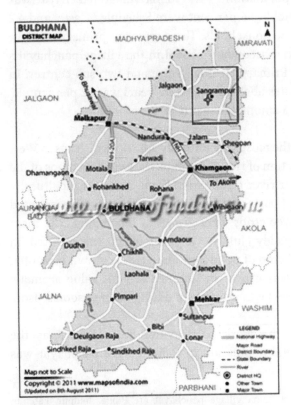

Figure 3.2 *Location of Sangrampur tehsil,*
Buldhana district, Maharashtra

In 2007, the major crop cultivated was cotton. Other crops, like groundnut, sunflower, green gram, sesame, sorghum (*jowar*), maize, pulses, wheat, red gram, and black gram were also cultivated, but had a very small share in the gross cropped area. Cotton was cultivated in the kharif season (summer/monsoon), from June–July to October–November, and was intercropped mainly with green gram and red gram. A few cultivators raised wheat in the rabi season (winter), from November–December to February. There was no irrigation in the village and cultivation was rain-fed.

3.1.2 Profile of Raina Village Panchayat and Bidyanidhi Village

Raina village panchayat in Raina I Block is situated in the southeastern part of Bardhaman district. It consists of 13 villages (*mouzas*).[1] The panchayat office was situated in Rayna village, which was also the Block headquarters. Rayna was located 25 kilometres from the district town of Bardhaman and was well connected to the town by road. The nearest railway station was also Bardhaman. The total population of the Raina village panchayat was 15,569 in 2011. Of all households, 36 per cent were Scheduled Caste, and 4.2 per cent were Scheduled Tribe households. There were ten primary schools, one secondary and one higher secondary school in the village panchayat's jurisdiction. There was one Primary Health Centre and two sub-centres. In 2011, the proportion of literates above the age of 7 years was 82 per cent, 87 per cent among males and 76 among females (Census of India).

Bardhaman district is one of the most agriculturally advanced districts in West Bengal, leading in the production of rice and potato, the two main crops of the State. Bound by the Damodar river on the east, Raina was an agriculturally advanced area and significant parts of the area of the panchayat are irrigated by canals and tubewells. Three crops were grown in this region. The main crop was monsoon (*aman*) paddy (July to October), which was rain-fed. In the irrigated tracts, a second crop of potato or oilseeds was grown in winter, or a short duration paddy was grown in summer. A high value aromatic variety of paddy (*Gobindo-bhog*) was also grown during the monsoon season.

According to Census data, the work participation rate, defined as the proportion of workers in total population in Raina village panchayat was

---

[1] The villages (*mouzas*) under the Raina village panchayat are Pipila, Ibidpur, Fatepur, Bidyanidhi, Hakrishnapur, Bokra, Birampur, Rayna, Raynagar, Jot Rajaram, Bishwesharbati, and Maheshbati.

Table 3.3 *Distribution of population by caste and sex, Bidyanidhi village in Raina village panchayat, West Bengal, 2005* in numbers and per cent

Caste/religious group	Number			As percentage of total population		
	Female	Male	Total	Female	Male	Total
Scheduled Caste	169	157	326	51.4	47.6	49.5
Muslim	58	61	119	17.6	18.5	18.1
Other	102	112	214	31.0	33.9	32.5
All	329	330	659	100	100	100

Source: FAS survey data, 2005.

Table 3.4 *Profile of Raina village panchayat, Bardhaman district, West Bengal, 2011*

Total population		15,569
Scheduled Castes (as percentage of total population)		36.2
Scheduled Tribes (as percentage of total population)		4.2
Literacy rate (7 years and above) (in per cent)	All	81.9
	Male	87.2
	Female	76.3
Work participation rate (Percentage of workers in total population)	All	41.0
	Male	62.8
	Female	18.6
Cultivators (as percentage of total workers)		10.8
Agricultural labourers (as percentage of total workers)		43.7
Household industry (as percentage of total workers)		4.6
Other workers (as percentage of total workers)		40.9

Source: Census of India, 2011.

41 per cent – 63 per cent among men and 19 per cent among women. In 2011, only 11 per cent of all workers were cultivators and 44 per cent were agricultural labourers. A sizeable section of the work force was engaged in non-agricultural activities.

The studies by the Foundation for Agrarian Studies (FAS) were conducted in Bidyanidhi village in Raina village panchayat. Bidyanidhi is about 4 km from the Raina village panchayat office. The village was located 2 km off the main road that connects Rayna to the district town of Bardhaman. An all-weather road connected the village to the main road. The population of Bidyanidhi

Figure 3.3 *Location of Bardhaman district in West Bengal*

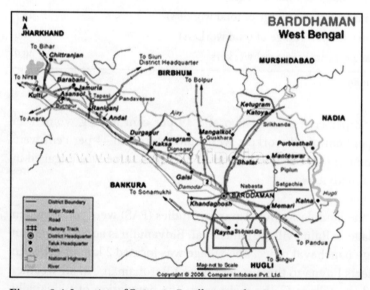

Figure 3.4 *Location of Raina in Bardhaman district*

was 659 at the time of the survey in 2005. Scheduled Castes constituted 50 per cent of the population and 18 per cent of the population were Muslims. There was one Integrated Child Development Services (*anganwadi*) centre and one primary school in Bidyanidhi. During our visit to the village, the total enrolment in the Shishu Siksha Kendra (Children's Education Centre) (for children aged 3 to 6 years) was 22 and 60 children under the age of 6 were registered at the *anganwadi* centre. Forty children were enrolled in the primary school, which had two classrooms and two teachers.

3.2. EVOLUTION OF PANCHAYATI RAJ IN MAHARASHTRA AND WEST BENGAL

Maharashtra had a strong legislative tradition with regard to panchayats even before the enactment of the Seventy-Third Amendment in 1992. The Bombay Village Panchayats Act 1958 stipulated the duties, responsibilities, and powers of the village panchayat. The foundations of panchayati raj in Maharashtra were laid in 1960 by its first chief minister Y.B. Chavan, who envisaged that the newly formed State would follow a form of democratic socialism. The State government appointed the V.P. Naik Committee in 1960. The Naik Committee recommended a three-tier panchayati raj structure, as did the Balwantrai Mehta Committee. But unlike the latter, the Naik Committee suggested that the district panchayats be all-powerful in the panchayati raj hierarchy.[2] It recommended the devolution of powers of taxation and disbursement of development funds to the district panchayats. Thereafter, the Maharashtra Zilla Parishad and Panchayat Samiti Act, 1961, was enacted. As village panchayats had already been in existence under the Bombay Village Panchayats Act, 1958, the three-tier panchayati raj system was introduced in the State, with the village panchayat at the bottom, the Block-level committee in between, and the district panchayat at the top.[3] The first elections for the Block-level committees and district panchayats were held in 1962.

In 1974, the State Government, placing emphasis on the district as a basic unit of planning and development, established District Planning and Development Councils (DPDC). Under the Seventy-Fourth Amendment, the DPDCs were dissolved in 1999. However, the Maharashtra State Development Report stated that the District Planning Committee, as per the provision prescribed

---

[2] "Village council" or "*gram sabha*", "village panchayat" or "*gram panchayat*", "district council" and "district panchayat" or *zilla parishad* are used interchangeably in this book.
[3] See Planning Commission (2007), and Matthew and Institute of Social Sciences (2000).

under Article 243ZD (1) of the Constitution, had not been constituted like in West Bengal and other states.[4]

West Bengal had a long tradition of rural local self-government. Under the British, *Chowkidari panchayats* were set up in 1870 in groups of villages, mainly for the maintenance of law and order. In 1885, with the coming of the Bengal Local Self-government Act, a system of District Boards, sub-divisional Local Boards and Union Committees of village clusters was set up. The Royal Commission on Decentralisation (1907–9) recommended a little more autonomy for the local self-government institutions and the Bengal Village Self-government Act, 1919 was passed, merging the *Chowkidari* Union and the Union Committee in the newly created Union Board at the village level. This set-up lasted until the 1950s.[5]

The West Bengal Panchayat Act of 1957 established a two-tier panchayat system at the village and union (village cluster) levels. On the basis of the recommendations of the Balwant Rai Mehta Committee, the West Bengal Zilla Parishads Act, 1963, added two tiers at the block and district levels, thus creating a four-tier structure of district panchayats, regional councils (*anchalik parishad*), regional panchayats (*anchal panchayat*) and village panchayats in the State. A further initiative was taken to frame a consolidated piece of legislation, which became the West Bengal Panchayat Act, 1973, paving the way for a three-tier system with the district panchayat at the district level, Block-level committee at the Block level, and village panchayat at the cluster of villages (*anchal*) level.

However, the major thrust for decentralisation in West Bengal was initiated by the Left Front government that assumed office in 1978. The first elections at all three tiers under the 1973 Act were held in June 1978 and since then panchayat general elections have been held every five years. The Left Front government viewed the panchayati raj institutions as central to their vision of an "alternative approach to development" that focused on redistribution with growth. The primary tactical approach to achieve such development was democratic decentralisation of the power structure through panchayats and municipal bodies. This involved the formation of planning committees headed by elected representatives at the district level and below, in order to prepare, implement, and monitor plans at the local level. Thus decentralisation

---

[4] Planning Commission (2007), p. 247.
[5] This section draws from Mishra, Surjyakanta (1991), *An Alternative Approach to Development: Land Reforms and Panchayats*.

of planning for development took root in West Bengal much before the Seventy-Third and Seventy-Fourth Amendments.

3.3 ASPECTS OF PANCHAYATI RAJ INSTITUTIONS IN MAHARASHTRA AND WEST BENGAL UNDER THE SEVENTY-THIRD AMENDMENT, 1992

3.3.1 State Governments and Panchayati Raj Institutions

In accordance with the Seventy-Third Amendment, 1992, Legislatures of both States, by law, endow panchayati raj institutions with such powers and authority as to function as institutions of self-government. In Maharashtra, the Bombay Village Panchayats Act, 1958, and the Maharashtra Zilla Parishad and Panchayat Samiti Act, 1961 were amended. At the State level, the Panchayati Raj and Rural Development Department (RDD) is headed by a Secretary. The West Bengal Panchayati Raj Act, 1973 was amended. At the State level the Panchayat and Rural Development Department was headed by a Principal Secretary who exercises administrative control over the PRIs.

Even the devolution of functions listed in the Bombay Village Panchayats Act, 1958, and Maharashtra Zilla Parishad and Panchayat Samiti Act, 1961, is still controversial. In a meeting of all departmental Secretaries in the State on June 5, 2005, "it was considered that it would not be feasible to devolve subjects/functions such as land improvement, land consolidation, dairy development, small industries, rural electrification, including distribution of electricity and public distribution system, listed in Schedule XI."[6] The Government of Maharashtra argued this notwithstanding the fact that some of them were already covered by the Schedules in the Acts of 1958 and 1961.

The Panchayats and Rural Development Department in West Bengal reformed the panchayat system and supported its development with a special focus on poverty alleviation.[7] A roadmap for panchayats in West Bengal was provided

---

[6] Chander (2008, pp. 9–10).

[7] The Panchayats and Rural Development Department listed need-based reforms as follows: (a) *gram sansad* at village level, Block *sansad* at Block-level committee level and *zilla sansad* at district panchayat level, (b) district panchayat at each district panchayat headed by the leader of the opposition, (c) Village development committee at the *gram sansad* level, (d) institutional involvement of opposition members in the Standing Committees of District councils and Block-level committees and in the Finance and Planning subcommittee of the *gram panchayat*, (e) determination of principles of subsidiarity for each tier of panchayats, (f) mapping of activities to be performed by three-tier panchayats falling under 28 subjects (out of 29) listed in the Eleventh Schedule of the Constitution of India, (g) empowering the Standing Committees and subcommittees to prepare and implement their own work plan and budget,

by the same department, and its annual administrative reports were available in the public domain.[8] Even a critical review by the State Finance Commission of West Bengal of the panchayat system was available.[9] However, similar efforts were not available in the public domain in Maharashtra at the time of this study.

3.3.2 Geographical Coverage of Panchayati Raj Institutions at Each Level

As shown in Table 3.5, the two States were similar in their rural population: 61,556,074 in Maharashtra and 62,183,113 in West Bengal, according to the Census of India, 2011. The number of inhabited villages in the two States were also similar: 40,959 in Maharashtra and 37,469 in West Bengal in 2011. However, their respective panchayats' geographical coverage of population and villages at each level is quite different. Village panchayats in Maharashtra cover around 2,000 inhabitants, whereas those in West Bengal cover more than 17,000 on average. This occurs because village panchayats in Maharashtra usually cover only one or two villages, whereas those in West Bengal are usually based on a cluster of villages. This indicates a fundamental difference in the characteristics of village panchayats in the two States. The function of the village panchayats will vary according to its scale. For this reason, in our analysis, we sometimes compare the Warwat Khanderao panchayat with the Raina panchayat and at other times with Bidyanidhi village in the jurisdiction of the Raina panchayat.

The jurisdiction of the Warwat Khanderao panchayat in Maharashtra was identical to the Census village "Warwat Khanderao." Since the panchayat covered only one village, the total population of the panchayat was only 1308 (PARI survey data 2007). Although this village had three wards as constituencies to elect panchayat representatives (or members), these wards

---

(h) opening panchayat Window in the State Budget by Departments that have substantial flow of funds to panchayats, (i) annual self-evaluation of all the three-tier panchayat bodies through score-based schedules for assessment of their performances and providing incentive grants to the best performing village panchayat in each Block, to the best performing Block-level committee in each district and to the best performing district panchayat in the State separately under two heads – (1) institutional functioning and good governance; and (2) mobilisation of revenue and utilisation of resources on the basis of validated scores of self-evaluation, and (j) double-entry system of accounting for all the three-tier panchayats (Panchayats and Rural Development Department, Government of West Bengal 2009b).

[8] Panchayats and Rural Development Department, Government of West Bengal (2007, p. 49) and (2008a, pp. 48–9).

[9] Third State Finance Commission of West Bengal (2008).

Table 3.5 *Number of panchayats at each level*

	Maharashtra	West Bengal	All India
District panchayats	33	18	589
Intermediate panchayats	352	333	6,321
Village panchayats	27,907	3,351	238,955
Rural population (Census of India 2011)	61,556,047	62,183,113	742,490,639
Rural population per village panchayat	2,206	18,557	3,107

Source: Census of India (2011).

neither had an independent function in the panchayati raj system nor did they have an independent representative body.

However, the total population under the Raina panchayat was as high as 14,967 (Census of India 2001). The territory of the Raina panchayat consisted of 13 Census villages (*mouzas*). The panchayat consisted of 12 village assembly established in 1992 as constituencies in the panchayat. The village assembly was not merely a constituency for election, but also had independent roles and functions. A village development committee was formed at the village assembly-level. The village development committee had several powers and responsibilities, including identification and implementation of schemes and selection of beneficiaries. The village panchayat could not ignore or refuse to act upon any recommendation of a village assembly relating to prioritisation of any list of beneficiaries or schemes or programmes if it related to the jurisdiction of the village assembly The village assembly could also record its objection to any action of the elected head or any other member of the panchayat for failing to implement any development scheme or without popular participation. Thus, each village assembly in the Raina panchayat area was an independent political unit. Bidyanidhi village was one such village assembly.

The three-tier system – the panchayat system at the village, intermediate and district levels – was common to the panchayati raj institutions in the two States. The provision that "there shall be constituted in every State, panchayats at the village, intermediate and district levels" (Article 243B[1] of the Constitution) is a mandatory provision of the Seventy-Third Amendment.[10] It cannot differ across States. However, the provisions in the

---

[10] However, "notwithstanding anything in clause (1), panchayats at the intermediate level may not be constituted in a State having a population not exceeding twenty lakhs" (Article 243B[2])].

Constitution for the devolution of powers and responsibilities to panchayati raj institutions are recommendatory, not mandatory. It is at the State Legislature's discretion that powers and responsibilities "may be" given to panchayati raj institutions.[11]

3.3.3 Elected Panchayat Representatives at Each Level

All the seats in a panchayat "shall be" filled by persons chosen by direct election from territorial constituencies in the panchayat area (Article 243C[2]). It is a mandatory provision for the State governments and so cannot differ across States.[12] It is also a mandatory directive to the State governments that "all elections to the panchayats shall be vested in a State Election Commission consisting of a State Election Commissioner to be appointed by the Governor" (Article 243K[2]).

As shown in Table 3.6, there are more elected panchayat representatives in Maharashtra than in West Bengal. The ratio of population to panchayat representative was 249:1 in Maharashtra and 1166:1 in West Bengal. Compared to the district panchayat, the intermediate panchayat, i.e., the Block-level committee was given a smaller role in Maharashtra. "In the overall structure of panchayati raj in the State, Block-level committee is given a negligible role. It acts almost like an agency of the district panchayat for all practical purposes."[13]

Table 3.6 *Number of elected panchayat representatives at each level*

	Maharashtra	West Bengal
District panchayats/*zilla parishads* (ZP)	1,951	721
Intermediate panchayats/Block-level committee	3,902	8,483
Village panchayats/gram panchayat (GP)	223,857	49,545
Ratio of population to elected representatives at village panchayat level	8.0	15.3
Ratio of population to village panchayat representatives	249	1,166

Sources: Directorate of Economics & Statistics, Government of Maharashtra (2010), Panchayat and Rural Development Department, Government of West Bengal (2008).

[11] Third State Finance Commission of West Bengal (2008, pp. 19–20).
[12] It is also a mandatory provision in the Constitution (Article 243E[1]) that "every panchayat, unless sooner dissolved under any law for the time being in force, shall continue for five years from the date appointed for its first meeting and no longer."
[13] Planning Commission (2007, p. 247).

The State Election Commission in Maharashtra was established in 1994. Village panchayats in Maharashtra consisted of no fewer than 7 and no more than 17 members (depending upon the population) elected from wards. The intermediate panchayats (*panchayat samitis*) consisted of all directly elected members from electoral colleges in the Block for which each electoral division is divided into two electoral colleges. The district panchayats (*zilla parishads*) were constituted of Councillors directly elected on the basis of universal adult franchise from electoral divisions in the district.

The State Election Commission was constituted in West Bengal in 1995. Village panchayats in West Bengal consisted of no fewer than 5 and no more than 25 members elected from village assembly. The intermediate panchayats consisted of directly elected members not exceeding 3 from each village panchayat. The district panchayat consisted of directly elected members representing two from each intermediate panchayat.

Reservation of seats in a panchayat is a mandatory provision of the Seventy-Third Amendment (Article 243D). In both States, one-third of the seats in the village panchayat (*gram panchayat*), intermediate panchayat (*panchayat samiti*) and district panchayat (*zilla parishad*) have to be reserved for women (including reserved seats for Scheduled-Caste and Scheduled-Tribe women). Reservations for Scheduled Castes and Scheduled Tribes were provided in the State Acts in proportion to their population within the total population. Maharashtra also provided for 27 per cent reservation for the Other Backward Classes.

In both States, the chairman and deputy chairman of each level of the panchayati raj institutions were elected from the directly elected members. The administrative staff in charge of each level support them. At the village-panchayat level, the key posts, panchayat head (*sarpanch)* and Deputy

Table 3.7 *Number of elected representatives at the village panchayat level,* on March 31, 2008

		General	SC	ST	Total	Women
Maharashtra	Total no.	172,370	24,624	26,863	223,857	75,148
	Percentage	77.00	10.99	12.00	100.00	33.56
West Bengal	Total no.	31,425	14,492	3,628	49,545	18,150
	Percentage	63.42	29.25	7.32	100.00	36.63

Source: Ministry of Rural Development (2011–2), Section 9: Panchayati Raj.

sarpanch (*upa-sarpanch*), were elected from amongst the elected members for a five-year term in Maharashtra. In West Bengal, the elected head of village panchayat (*pradhan*) and Deputy *pradhan* (*upa-pradhan*) were elected from amongst the elected members for a five-year term. As a result, many local leaders are appearing on the political stage in both States.

3.3.4 Administrative Staff of the Panchayat

Each level of the panchayati raj institutions in the two States has its own administrative staff. However, as far as the village panchayat level administration is concerned, we found an obvious manpower shortage in the Warwat Khanderao panchayat.

At the village panchayat level, the village development officer serves as the administrative staff in Maharashtra. The Bombay Village Panchayats Act, 1958, provides for the appointment of a panchayat secretary for a group of panchayats based on the size and population of the villages. The expenditure on salaries of village panchayat employees is to be borne equally by the State Government and the concerned panchayat.

Warwat Khanderao panchayat faced a shortage of administrators. It did not have any permanent staff apart from the panchayat secretary. A parent of a child unregistered in the Civil Registration System told us that the panchayat secretary (also the official Registrar) was not at the panchayat office every day. The panchayat secretary stayed at Warwat Khanderao only two days in a week. He exercised jurisdiction over three villages. The panchayat hired a peon to help in the panchayat secretary's administrative work.

In West Bengal, the permanent staff such as the Executive Assistant, Job Assistant (*Nirman sahayak*), Secretary, Assistants (*sahayak*) and the panchayat workers (*karmi*) served as administrative staff for the panchayat. Funds were provided by the State government for establishment costs, including salaries and pensions of the panchayat employees. The village assembly, a sub-panchayat body in West Bengal, did not have its own administrative staff.

3.3.5 Coordination between the Panchayat and Line Departments

Apart from the panchayat's administrative staff, there were some village-level functionaries under the line departments; they included the Integrated Child Development Services (*anganwadi*) workers, Auxiliary Nurse Midwives

(ANM), health supervisors, and local school teachers. There was also a land-revenue official's office in Warwat Khanderao, as Maharashtra is a part of the temporarily-settled or *raiyatwari* areas where a land-revenue official collects and revises village-level land records annually. Instead of a Revenue official there was a Revenue Inspector in Raina who maintained land records.

According to the amendment made in the Bombay Village Panchayats Act (No. 3 and No. 27 of 2003), all officials working at the village level and non-government organisations fall under the control of the village panchayat. Unless exempted by the village council, all government, semi-government and panchayat employees are required to attend the council meetings. The village council has disciplinary control over the government, semi-government and panchayat employees working in the village. It shall report to the concerned Block Development Officer any irregularities committed by any employee. Therefore, the village-level functionaries in Warwat Khanderao were statutorily under the control of the panchayat.

However, there was no institutional mechanism to coordinate the officials' activities except for personal effort by the panchayat head or panchayat members. The only village-level functionaries for which there existed a coordination mechanism were the ICDS (*anganwadi*) workers. The Warwat Khanderao village panchayat had subcommittees (such as the Woman and Child Committee (*Mahila Bal Samiti*) and the Child Development Committee (*Bal Vikas Samiti*)) to coordinate activities of the ICDS workers but they were, at the time of the survey, not functional. Before 2008, the Village Education (*Gram Shiksha*) Committee was formed at Warwat Khandrao as a subcommittee with the panchayat head as its president. However, under the Right to Education Act, 2009, the concept and formation of the Village Education (*Gram Shiksha*) Committee was scrapped.

The *Basic Statistics for Local Level Development* report points out in its pilot survey in Maharashtra that these outside agencies "send periodical reports to their respective controlling officers and there is no formal arrangement for sharing the information with the panchayat and it has no role in monitoring the activities of these functionaries." The Committee states:

> There are no formal data sharing mechanisms between different agencies working at village panchayat, tehsil or district levels. In fact there are multiple lines of control and reporting mechanisms. In the case of revenue officials, the line of reporting is from village officer (*Talati*) to the Circle Officer, Tehsildar

and District Collector. The channels of reporting in the case of different functionaries at the village panchayat, Block development office and District panchayat office are through the respective line of control of the respective departments. The reports being received by different departments are generally not being integrated at any stage.[14]

Although the coordination mechanism between the panchayat and line departments was not strong in Warwat Khanderao, the Block Development Officer (BDO) was expected to coordinate activities of line departments. According to our interview with the BDO of Sangrampur, Buldhana district, Maharashtra,[15] several extension officers ("sector planning officers") at the block are to report to the BDO on the planning and implementation of schemes of other departments (such as health, education, agriculture, animal husbandry). However, according to the BDO, while the BDO was the executive officer for all matters related to the panchayat, the revenue-collection officer (*tehsildar*) was the Programme Officer in charge of all programmes under the Ministry of Rural Development. Thus, the power of the BDO was limited.

Among these multiple lines of control, a line of hierarchy of revenue officials – *patwari*, *tehsildar* and District Collector under the Revenue Department – had the most sweeping administrative powers in Maharashtra. At the sub-district level in Maharashtra, there are two overlapping administrative units: the block and the *tehsil*. The block is the development administrative unit, while *tehsil* is the revenue administrative unit. The BDO represents the Block-level administration and the *tehsildar* represents the *tehsil*-level administration. Unlike West Bengal, where the administrative duties of the Block Land and Land Reform Officer are restricted to the areas of land reform and land revenue, *tehsildars* in Maharashtra wield greater administrative powers.[16]

Thus, coordination between the panchayat and its functionaries with different

---

[14] Central Statistical Organisation (2006, p. 25). For example, "Though the jurisdiction of the Block Development Office is the same as Tehsil, both the Block Development Officer and the Tehsildar have two different Offices."

[15] Interview conducted at the Block Development Office of Sangrampur on April 25, 2014.

[16] Gazetteers Department, Government of Maharashtra (n.d.): "In addition to the duties mentioned above, the Tehsildar is responsible to the Collector and the Sub-Divisional Officer whom he has to keep constantly informed of all political happenings, outbreak of epidemics and other matters in the area within his jurisdiction. He generally helps or guides the officers of other departments in the execution of their respective duties in so far as his tehsil is concerned. He is responsible for holding the cattle census. The Tehsildar is also expected to propagate co-operative principles in his tehsil. The Tehsildar's position in relation to the tehsil officers of other departments, e.g. the station officers of the Police Department, the Sub-

line departments was weak in rural Maharashtra. Since a strong coordination mechanism was not institutionalised in the Warwat Khanderao panchayat, the personal efforts of the panchayat head who had an ability to coordinate and knew the situation well, were indispensable.

There was a coordination mechanism in West Bengal between village-level activities and different line departments. A regular panchayat meeting of functionaries, known as the "Fourth Saturday Meeting," was institutionalised.[17] Members of the panchayat subcommittee (*upa-samiti*) on Education and Public Heath, functionaries of the Health and Family Welfare Department, field-level functionaries of the Integrated Child Development Services programme under the Women and Child Development and Social Welfare Department, and representatives of self-help groups met on the fourth Saturday of every month to review issues pertaining to public health. The meeting ensured close coordination between the ICDS supervisor, the ANM, the Health Supervisor and panchayat officials.[18]

The convergence of the *Swarnajayanti Gram Swarozgar Yojana* with the Mahatma Gandhi National Rural Employment Guarantee Scheme (MGNREGS) was also present in West Bengal, with the assistance of Self-Help Groups (SHGs) for improving the implementation of the MGNREGS.[19]

3.3.6 Village Councils (Gram Sabhas)

The village council is a body of persons registered in the electoral roll of a village within the panchayat's jurisdiction.[20] "A village council (*gram*

Registrar, the Range Forest Officer, Medical Officer, Postmaster, etc., is not definable. Though they are not subordinate to him they are grouped round him and are expected to help and co-operate with him in their spheres . . . Though the Tehsildar is not expected to work directly for local bodies he is usually the principal source of the Collector's information about them."

[17] Panchayats and Rural Development Department, Government of West Bengal (2007, p. 49) and (2008a, pp. 48–9).

[18] Chakrabarti, Chattopadhyay, and Nath (2011) give warning against the weakening of coordination between the panchayats and line departments. "In West Bengal, a state in eastern India, where the panchayats were revitalised before the constitutional amendment, the initial years were marked by strong coordination between the panchayats and other departments, especially land and agriculture, making West Bengal a "model" case for the panchayats. However, where service delivery through the panchayats has been criticised in recent years, the disjuncture between panchayats and the line departments is a cause for alarm."

[19] Panchayats and Rural Development Department, Government of West Bengal (2009a, pp. 95–7).

[20] Article 243 of the Constitution.

sabha) may exercise such powers and perform such functions at the village level as the Legislature of a State may, by law, provide" (Article 243A). This provision of the Constitution is not mandatory for the State governments.[21] It is at the discretion of the Legislature of each State. Powers and functions of village councils may be different between the States. The State governments can limit the role of village councils.[22] However, they are statutorily given extensive powers in Maharashtra and West Bengal. Each village council in the two States has several standing committees. In addition, village council in West Bengal had village assembly under them. Each village assembly had a village development committee as its executive committee.

Village councils in Maharashtra enjoy extensive powers under Section 7 of the Bombay Village Panchayats Act, 1958, as amended in 2003. Six meetings of the village council must be held every year. At least 15 per cent of its members or 100 persons, whichever is less, shall constitute a quorum for the meeting. Unlike in West Bengal, in Maharashtra it is mandatory to convene the women members of the village council (the Village *mahila sabha* meeting) before every regular meeting of the village council. A panchayat is required to obtain permission of the village council for any expenditure on development. The latter is also authorised to approve the social or economic development plan or any projects to be implemented by the panchayat. The village council has the power to select beneficiaries for individual beneficiary schemes of the State or the Central government.

In Maharashtra, all officials working at the village level and in non-government organisations have been statutorily brought under the control of the village panchayat. Unless exempted by the village council, all the government, semi-government and panchayat employees are required to attend the meetings of the village council. The village council in Maharashtra may constitute subcommittees for issues under Article 49 of the Bombay Village Panchayats Act, 1958. For example, the following committees were formed in the Warwat Khanderao village panchayat in 2009.[23] Two panchayat members are members of each committee.

---

[21] However, it is a Directive Principle of State Policy in India that "The State shall take steps to organise village panchayats and endow them with such powers and authority as may be necessary to enable them to function as units of self-government" (Article 40 of the Constitution).
[22] "The State Governments have taken full advantage of this "non-mandatory" nature of the Constitutional provision. Devolution . . . has generally remained weak in most of the States, as a result" (Third State Finance Commission of West Bengal 2008, pp. 19–20).
[23] This information was collected from the panchayat head in 2009. After the implementation of

(a) Tantamukti Committee (to resolve disputes among villagers)[24]
(b) Dakshyata Committee (monitors ration shops in the village)
(c) Shiksha Committee (to take care of educational issues in the village)
(d) Bal Vikas Samiti (to look after children's welfare in the village)
(e) Swachchhta Samiti (to look after sanitation and hygiene)

These subcommittees did not always function. For example, the panchayat head, child care workers and some parents of students belonged to the Child Development Committee, and they are supposed to meet every three months, but this committee's meetings, according to the panchayat head, were not held in Warwat Khanderao.[25]

In West Bengal, the quorum for meetings of the village council is one-twentieth of the total electorate. Without the quorum, the meeting is to be adjourned and the adjourned meeting reconvened after seven days; the quorum is not required for a re-convened meeting of the village council.

West Bengal had a legislated system of standing committees at each panchayat level that ensured that all decisions were taken collectively. As for the village panchayat, the following subcommittees (*upa-samitis*) were constituted:

(i) Finance and Planning (*Artha O Parikalpana*)
(ii) Agriculture and Animal Resources Development (*Krishi O Pranisampad Bikas*)
(iii) Education and Public Health (*Siksha O Janasasthya*)
(iv) Women & Child Development and Social Welfare (*Nari, Sishu Unnayan O Samaj Kalyan*)
(v) Industries and Infrastructure (*Shilpa O Parikathama*)

Each committee had a convener selected from the panchayat members. The panchayat elected head of village panchayat and the deputy *pradhan* could

---

the Right to Education Act, the Education Committee may have changed to conform to the Act.
[24] This committee is formed under the *Mahatma Gandhi Tanta Mukti Gaon Mohim* (Dispute-Free Village Scheme) of the Maharashtra Government.
[25] "However, it was evident during the study that the committee system is quite weak and unable to take decisions, hence the decision making processes in the village, is dominated by panchayat head (*Sarpanch*) and village development officer in combination" (Deshpande and D'Souza 2009, p. 47). "The representation in committees is more symbolic than substantial, as most of the members of the committees were not able to describe their duties, role and responsibilities" (*ibid.*, p. 48). The Watershed Organisation Trust conducted a study of the functioning of the panchayati raj institutions in twelve villages, three each in the regions of north Maharashtra, Vidarbha, Marathwada, and western Maharashtra during 2007.

convene the Finance and Planning Committee. Subcommittees had wide-ranging powers, which included preparing proposals for execution of a scheme within the budgetary provisions of the village panchayat. The village head was not to sanction any funds for a scheme, programme or project without considering the views of the members of the subcommittees to whom powers were delegated by the village panchayat with respect to that scheme, programme or project. The subcommittees were authorised to call for information and inspect immovable property of the village panchayat or any work in progress.

The sub-village-panchayat level body in West Bengal, the village assembly, was established in 1992, and had several powers as an independent political unit. Two meetings of the village assembly in a year were mandatory – an annual meeting in May and the half-yearly meeting in November. For annual and half-yearly meetings of village assemblies, an attendance of ten per cent of the electors pertaining to the constituency formed the quorum. In its absence, the meeting would be adjourned and reconvened seven days later. Attendance of five per cent of the electors was necessary for the quorum.

The recommendations of the village assembly were placed before the village council for consideration and approval. The decisions of the village assembly on the priority lists of beneficiaries and development schemes within the village assembly-area were final and could not be questioned even by the village panchayat, unless they violated the law or specific government orders.

Provision was made for the constitution of the village development committee through the 2003 amendment of the Panchayat Act for strengthening decentralisation. A village assembly constituted a village development committee as an executive committee with jurisdiction over its area. The village development committee was responsible for ensuring public participation in implementation and equitable distribution of the benefits of rural development programmes within its jurisdiction. These committees were entrusted with preparing village-level plans of the village assembly, which was the basis of the village panchayat's plan and also to be implemented by the village assembly. The village panchayat cannot ignore or refuse to act upon any recommendation of a village assembly relating to prioritisation of any list of beneficiaries, schemes or programmes. The village development committee comprised an elected member or members from the village assembly; the opposition candidate being the one obtaining the second-highest number of votes in the previous village panchayat election; three representatives of

NGOs/CBOs; three representatives of active SHGs, with at least two members from women-led self-help groups; one serving or retired Government employee; one serving or retired teacher (all being voters of the area, so members of the village assembly); and another ten members or one per cent of the total number of members of the village assembly, whichever was higher.

3.3.7 Activity Mapping: Devolution of Functions to Panchayati Raj Institutions

As mentioned previously, devolution of functions to the panchayati raj institutions is at the discretion of the Legislature of each State. The Constitutional provisions regarding functional devolution are not mandatory. As far as the two States are concerned, most of the subjects included in Schedule XI of the Constitution have been legislatively devolved to the three levels of panchayats through their Acts.[26] Some administrative staff of the Block Development Officer (BDO) and the village panchayat in the two States attempted Activity Mapping – unbundling these subjects into smaller units of work and thereafter assigning these units to different levels of government to delineate their functional domains.[27] However, the actual status of Activity Mapping on the ground is substantially different in the two States.

According to the second Administrative Reforms Commission, there has not been much progress on Activity Mapping in Maharashtra as of November 2006.[28] However, functional devolution from the State government to the panchayati raj institutions was once done in Maharashtra under the Bombay Village Panchayats Act, 1958, and the Maharashtra Zilla Parishad and Panchayat Samiti Act, 1961. Almost all the subjects (other than Non-Conventional Energy Sources) under Schedule XI of the Constitution have already been covered within the Schedules of the Acts of 1958 and 1961.[29] Delineation of functions assigned to each level of the panchayats is provided for in the following Schedules:

[26] However, "15. Non-conventional Energy Sources" has been omitted from the Bombay Village Panchayats Act, 1958, and the Maharashtra Zilla Parishad and Panchayat Samiti Act, 1961.

[27] Second Administrative Reforms Commission (2007, p. 146).

[28] *Ibid.*, p. 142.

[29] The Comptroller and Auditor General of India (2008, pp. 4–5) states: "However, as of March 2009, the State Government had transferred only 214 schemes pertaining to 15 functions to the panchayati rural institutions and 3.53 lakh functionaries had been transferred to perform the functions of district panchayats. Out of 214 schemes, 78 schemes with 15171 functionaries and 16 schemes without functionaries had been transferred (November 2000 to September 2002) after the 73rd constitutional amendment."

(i) Functions to the village panchayat are given in Schedule I (Village List) of the Bombay Village Panchayats Act, 1958 (Section 45).

(ii) Functions assigned to the Block-level committee are provided in Schedule II of the Maharashtra Zilla Parishad and Panchayat Samiti Act, 1961 (Section 100).

(iii) Functions assigned to the *zilla parishad* are provided in Schedule I of the Maharashtra Zilla Parishad and Panchayat Samiti Act, 1961 (Section 101).

Since they pre-date Schedule XI, the categorisation of assigned subjects in the Schedules of the Acts of 1958 and 1961 is different from that of Schedule XI. However, Activity Mapping is considered de facto legislation in Maharashtra. In fact, the panchayat secretary of Warwat Khanderao showed us the statute book of the Act of 1958 when we asked him about Activity Mapping. Schedule I (Village List) of the Bombay Village Panchayats Act, 1958 (Section 45) is given in full in the appendix to this book. In addition to the subjects of activities in Schedule I (Village List), a water supply scheme was added to the duties of the panchayat in 1981 (Section 45 of the Bombay Village Panchayats Act, 1958).

Nevertheless, the devolution of functions listed in the Bombay Village Panchayats Act, 1958 and Maharashtra Zilla Parishad and Panchayat Samiti Act, 1961 is still controversial. As mentioned previously, it was reviewed by the Chief Secretary, Government of Maharashtra, in a meeting of all departmental Secretaries on June 5, 2005, and as a result of the meeting "it was considered that it would not be feasible to devolve subjects/functions, such as land improvement, land consolidation, dairy development, small industries, rural electrification, including distribution of electricity and public distribution system, listed in Schedule XI."[30] The Government of Maharashtra argued so, notwithstanding the fact that some functions have already been covered by the Schedules in the Acts of 1958 and 1961. For example, items such as "assistance in implementation of land reforms schemes" have been listed under the head "Agriculture" in the Schedule (Village List) of the Act of 1958. In addition, according to the Maharashtra State Development Report, many schemes are only partially transferred to the panchayati raj institutions:

"The Line Departments and District Rural Development Agencies continue to have major control over the planning and implementation of the schemes. The PRIs mostly act as the delivery units."[31]

[30] Chander (2008, pp. 9–10).
[31] Planning Commission (2007, p. 251).

The situation on the ground in Warwat Khanderao village was somewhat different from that envisaged in the Village List. We conducted an interview in the village about each function of the village panchayat.[32] We asked about the actual status of activities assigned to Warwat Khanderao village panchayat. We used the village panchayat level activities in the Activity Mapping of West Bengal (Table 3.1.1 in the appendix) as a point of reference because it followed almost the same categorisation of subjects as listed in Schedule XI of the Constitution. The result of the interviews was as follows.[33]

With regard to subject 1 ("Agriculture, including agricultural extension" in Schedule XI of the Constitution), subsidised pesticides and machines were distributed by the Block-level committee. They were distributed on the basis of recommendation of Block-level committee or district panchayat members. After preparing the list the Block-level committee informed the village panchayat, and then the former distributed them to the people in the list. Crop estimation for the Block-level committee was done by the revenue officials, panchayat secretary, village head and "Police Patel." The Agricultural Coordinator (*Krishi Sahayak*) from the State Agriculture Department signed the documents, and the village panchayat forwarded the document to the *tehsildar*.

With regard to subject 2 ("Land improvement, soil conservation and land reform"), vested land or other land was distributed by the *tehsildar*. The village panchayat sometimes gave its suggestions.

With regard to subject 3 ("Minor irrigation, water management and watershed development"), (for all matters of minor irrigation, the village panchayat was responsible for the basic formalities such as filling forms and attaching documents. These documents were then sent to the Block-level committee, which forwarded them to the District Collector. The rest of the work was done by the office of the District Collector. For watershed development, the Watershed Area Committee (*Panlot Kshetra* Committee) worked under the village panchayat and the Agricultural Science Centre (*Krishi Vigyan Kendra*). The Agricultural Science Centre selected the village. Work such as making *bunds* for controlling water and watershed management were done under this scheme and payment was made by the Village Watershed Committee.

[32] Interview at Warwat Khanderao on August 18–22, 2011.
[33] Where no information comparable to a subject in the Activity Mapping of West Bengal is found, we do not include the subject in our discussion. Hence some subject numbers are missing in our discussion in this section.

The Watershed Committee was elected by the village panchayat and then approved by the village council. The Committee for Accounts (*Lekha Samiti*) prepared the budget for maintaining *bunds*, watersheds and the like. The work was supervised by the Agricultural Science Centre.

With regard to subject 4 ("Animal husbandry, dairying and poultry"), beneficiaries of schemes were identified by the *tehsildar*. People applied for funds under the scheme to the *tehsildar*, who chose the beneficiary and gave responsibility for distribution to a separate agency such as the veterinarian, who distributed benefits on the basis of the number of animals owned by each beneficiary. The Block-level committee sometimes prepared the notice. A drum-beater made the announcement.

With regard to subject 10 ("Rural housing"), the village panchayat sent the Block-level committee the list of people who did not have houses. The Block-level committee selected the beneficiaries of the *Indira Awaas Yojana* from this list. There were 171 buildings in the village. The *Indira Awaas Yojana* houses were allotted to those people who reported not having a house in the Below Poverty Line Census survey.

With regard to subject 11 ("Drinking water"), all responsibilities rested with the village panchayat. The village panchayat decided the beneficiaries of the Drinking Water Scheme (*Paani Parota Yojana*). There was an accountant for the scheme. The engineer gave an estimate of expenses and submitted it to the Committee for Accounts (*Lekha Samiti*), which then decided on the budget.

With regard to subject 13 ("Roads, culverts, etc."), connectivity within the panchayat's area of jurisdiction was assigned to the village panchayat, which had to mobilise funds and then list the work to be done.

With regard to subject 14 ("Rural electrification, including distribution of electricity"), all responsibilities rested with the Maharashtra State Electricity Board.

With regard to subject 16 ("Poverty alleviation programme"), according to the panchayat head, the village panchayat only filled the forms. All rights rested with the Block-level committee.

With regard to subject 17 ("Education, including primary and secondary schools"), the School Management Committee monitored schools and the improvement of school infrastructure was the responsibility of the village panchayat until 2010. It has been given to the School Management Committee after 2010.

With regard to subject 20 ("Libraries"), a charitable trust owned the village library. The trust had a committee to deal with this matter.

With regard to subject 22 ("Markets and fairs"), the village panchayat had the authority to control fairs and weekly markets. In fact, a fair (*mela*) tax and licence fee for weekly village markets (*haat* and *bazaars)* were charged. The village panchayat collected fees from shop owners as professional tax.

With regard to subject 23 ("Health and sanitation, including hospitals, primary health centres and dispensaries"), the State Sanitation Scheme was implemented by the village panchayat, which prepared the priority list. The Warwat Khanderao village panchayat was also an implementing agency for the Rural Sanitation Department (*Grameen Swachchhta Vibhag)* of the Central Government. Households which reported not having a toilet in the Below Poverty Line Census, were given Rs 2200 under this scheme.

With regard to subjects 24 ("Family welfare") and 26 ("Social welfare, including welfare of the handicapped and mentally retarded"), the village panchayat was again responsible only for the basic formalities such as filling forms and attaching documents, and the rest was done by the Block-level committee. The National Maternity Benefit Scheme (NMBS) was implemented by the Primary Health Centre under the Public Health Department. The Indira Gandhi National Old Age Pension Scheme (IGNOAPS) was implemented by the revenue officials under the *tehsildar.* The *Sanjay Gandhi Niradhar Anudhan Yojna* and the National Family Benefit Scheme (NFBS) were implemented by the *tehsildar.*

With regard to subject 25 ("Women and child development"), there was a committee of the village panchayat (Woman and Child Committee) to mobilise social support against female discrimination. The committee discussed and resolved matters related to women and child welfare. The organisation of self-help groups was done by NGOs, and the village panchayat was responsible for constructing Integrated Child Development Services (*anganwadi*) centres and coordinating their activities.

With regard to subject 27 (Welfare of the weaker sections, and in particular, of the Scheduled Castes and the Scheduled Tribes"), the village panchayat had no specific role in the implementation of schemes for the Scheduled Caste and Scheduled Tribe categories. There were subsidies for buying small tractors for people in these categories, but these are implemented by the District council.

With regard to subject 28 ("Public distribution system"), the village panchayat was responsible for identification of beneficiaries of food-related schemes such as *Antyodaya* and *Annapurna*. The village panchayat's subcommittee, Dakshata Committee, distributed ration cards. Along with the Food Supply Officer, it attended to complaints regarding supply through the Public Distribution System.

With regard to subject 29 ("Maintenance of community assets"), the village panchayat had responsibilities for them as long as they were the panchayat's assets.

In this way, the Activity Mapping provided for in Schedule I (Village List) of the Bombay Village Panchayats Act, 1958 was *de jure* Activity Mapping, and the situation on the ground as revealed in our interview was somewhat different from that envisaged in the Village List. As argued by the panchayat head, some responsibilities of the Warwat Khanderao village panchayat were only basic formalities, such as filling forms. Central and State schemes had only a cursory and token linkage with the Warwat Khanderao village panchayat, as the panchayat did not have any major responsibility in these schemes. The actual status of activities assigned would be the *de facto* Activity Mapping in Maharashtra.

As seen above, the panchayat's authority to carry out village-level schemes was not as great as the authority provided for in the Village List. Moreover, the panchayat head complained that the State Government was slowly taking rights away from village panchayats and giving them to Block-level committees. Such action cannot always be explained by advantage of size, even though the scale of Warwat Khanderao village panchayat is much smaller than village panchayats in West Bengal. Some functions not devolved to Warwat Khanderao village panchayat in Maharashtra were assigned to the sub-panchayat bodies, i.e. village assemblies, in West Bengal. For example, beneficiary selection for the *Indira Awaas Yojana* was made through village assemblies in West Bengal, while the final decisions were made by the Block-level committee for Warwat Khanderao village panchayat in Maharashtra.

To take another example, functions actually assigned to the village panchayat to discharge responsibilities of "1. Agriculture" in Schedule XI were quite limited, compared with functions statutorily assigned to the village panchayat for "Agriculture" in the Village List of the Bombay Village Panchayats Act, 1958, which included activities such as "making arrangements for co-operative management of lands and other resources in the village, organisation of collective co-operative farming," and "improvement of agriculture (including provision of implements and stores) and establishment of model agricultural farms." The functions indicated in the Village List are the duties only "so far as the village fund at its disposal will allow" (Section 45 of the Act). Therefore, some of them are mentioned only in the statute book.

Based on the West Bengal Panchayat Act, 1973, and its Amendment Act, 1994, the State Government devolved all twenty-nine functions listed in Schedule XI of the Constitution to the three levels of panchayats. The functional transfer to different levels of the panchayat bodies was clarified through an Activity Mapping exercise.[34]

In West Bengal the focus of development activities shifted towards the village panchayat level in the process of decentralisation.[35] Activities assigned to panchayats in West Bengal were more plentiful than those in Maharashtra. According to Activity Mapping in West Bengal, as shown in Table 3.1.1 in the appendix, functions assigned to panchayats in the State were as follows.[36]

With regard to subject 1 ("Agriculture, including agricultural extension") in Schedule XI of the Constitution, beneficiary selection for distribution of mini-kits, seeds, equipment at subsidised prices, awareness campaigns among farmers, and the estimation of need-based requirement of seeds for the management of agrifarm, are all functions assigned to village panchayats. In Raina, whenever the Agricultural Department distributed mini-kits, fertilizers, seeds and other benefits, it informed the village panchayat, specifying the number of beneficiaries to be selected from each village panchayat or

[34] Executive order No. 6102/PN/O/dated 7. 11. 2005, and No. 3969/PN/O/dated 25. 07. 2006, and No. 4769/PN/O/ dated 29. 10. 2007. However, the Third State Finance Commission of West Bengal (2008, pp. 21–2) criticised that all sixteen Departments have not issued formal notifications published in the official gazette as required for functional transfers under section 207B of the West Bengal Panchayat (Amendment) Act, 1994, arguing that "even this limited effort has not been translated into action."

[35] Third State Finance Commission of West Bengal (2008, p. 134).

[36] Third State Finance Commission of West Bengal (2008), Annexure XII: "Activity Mapping worked out by the Panchayats and Rural Development Department."

village assembly. The village panchayats informed the village assembly. The beneficiaries were selected by the the village development committees.

With regard to subject 2 ("Land improvement, soil conservation and land reform"), the identification of beneficiaries of programmes to distribute vested land to the landless was a function assigned to village panchayats. In Raina, the village development committees identified projects in the Action Plans for land improvement, based on which the village panchayat prepared estimates and sent a project proposal to the Block which, in its turn, approved the budget and sent funds to the village panchayat. The village panchayat implemented the project. For land reform, the Block Land and Land Reform Office declared vested land. The village development committee selected beneficiaries for granting title deed.

With regard to subject 3 ("Minor irrigation, water management and watershed development"), the functions assigned to panchayats were: identification of locations for projects and beneficiaries for the development of minor irrigation systems, construction of percolation tanks, field channels within the panchayat area, maintaining minor irrigation schemes concerning deep tubewells and clusters of shallow tubewells, and collecting water charges through user committees for new projects handed over to panchayati raj institutions.

With regard to subject 4 ("Animal husbandry, dairying and poultry") the following functions were assigned to village panchayats: beneficiary selection for animal husbandry, dairy and poultry schemes, breed upgradation through distribution of improved variety of birds/small animals to farmers, providing hatcheries, vaccination of animals against epidemics, and the execution of artificial insemination with the help of *prani bandhu* at a fixed price – were all functions assigned to the village panchayats.

With regard to subject 5 ("Fisheries"), the functions given to village panchayats were the identification of beneficiaries and their ponds/open-cast pits, identification and selection of derelict/semi-derelict tanks, the supply of lime and mini-kits, and improvement of tanks for pisciculture.

With regard to subject 6 ("Social forestry and farm forestry"), the establishment of nurseries for the supply of samplings and seedlings and the selection of sites for plantation and execution of work through self-help groups/village development committees were the functions assigned to the village panchayats.

With regard to subject 7 ("Minor forest produce"), functions assigned to village panchayats included the maintenance of social forestry through self-help groups/village development committees, and the distribution of sale proceeds to self-help groups/village development.

With regard to subject 8 ("Small-scale industries, including food processing industries"), the identification of micro-enterprises/entrepreneurs was a function assigned to the village panchayats.

With regard to subject 9 ("Khadi, village and cottage industries"), group formation and selection of activities for development of micro-enterprise, identification of training need for skill-development training and of its beneficiaries, motivation of rural artisans, and the organisation of awareness camps at the panchayat level to assist in accessing credit from financial institutions by artisans were the functions assigned to the village panchayats.

With regard to subject 10 ("Rural housing"), the functions assigned to the village panchayats included beneficiary selection in village assembly meetings for housing schemes and the distribution of funds to individuals. In Raina, the *Indira Awaas Yojana* beneficiaries were selected from the Below Poverty Line Census survey list.

With regard to subject 11 ("Drinking water"), identification of schemes and locations, the construction of wells, tanks, tubewells (ordinary handpump), and the repair of tubewells and periodical chlorination of open wells and disinfection of tube wells were functions assigned to the panchayats. In Raina, the village development committees mobilised people to participate in the *Sajaldhara* (Drinking water project in Bidyanidhi village, West Bengal) scheme. The households benefitting from the scheme had to pay 10 per cent of the total cost of installation of the drinking-water tank and pipelines. Once a location was selected, the construction agency undertook project planning and construction work. The panchayat monitored the project but had no direct responsibilities.

With regard to subject 12 ("Fuel and fodder"), the panchayat had the functions of awareness generation and wide publicity for the promotion of biogas plants, augmenting fodder production through the distribution of mini-kits, seeds and manure to farmers, and giving field demonstration to farmers.

With regard to subject 13 ("Roads, culverts, bridges, ferries, waterways and other means of communication"), construction and upgradation of roads/ culverts (not exceeding Rs 200,000) for connectivity between villages within the panchayat area were functions assigned to the village panchayat.

With regard to subject 14 ("Rural electrification, including distribution of electricity"), the functions assigned to village panchayat were: (a) the issuing certificates by the headman for electrification of villages; (b) mobilisation of consumers through authorised franchisees of the West Bengal State Electricity Board for connectivity to households; (c) awareness generation regarding efficient management of energy; and (d) demonstration of energy-saving devices in the panchayat office.

With regard to subject 15 ("Non-conventional energy sources"), the functions to the village panchayat were the identification of potential consumers of alternative sources of energy, and organising awareness camps for harnessing alternative sources of energy including biofuel.

With regard to subject 16 ("Poverty alleviation programmes"), the panchayat was given the tasks of: (a) planning and implementing works/schemes under the *Sampoorna Grameen Rozgar Yojana* (Universal Rural Employment Programme) not exceeding Rs 200,000; (b) preparing a list of prospective workers, distribution of job cards, planning and implementing works under the Rural Employment Guarantee Scheme; (c) identifying and selecting beneficiaries for the *Indira Awaas Yojana* through the village assembly and handing over funds to beneficiaries; (d) identifying beneficiaries for the National Old Age Pension Scheme through the village assembly and handing over the pension to each beneficiary; (e) identifying beneficiaries under the National Family Benefit Scheme through the village assembly, recommending names to the Block-level committees, releasing funds to beneficiaries through "account payee" cheques; and (f) holding awareness camps and motivating people for building sanitary toilets; listing names for construction of toilets and handing it over to the Sanitary Mart; meeting with teachers and members of the Village Education Committee for school sanitation.

With regard to subject 17 ("Education, including primary and secondary schools"), the panchayat had to: (a) identify hamlets without schools for opening *Sishu Siksha Karmasuchi* (SSK)/*Madhyamik Siksha Karmasuchi* (MSK) and sending proposals to the Block-level committee, (b) constructions related to SSK/MSK through own-fund/*Sampoorna Grameen Rozgar Yojana* (Universal Rural Employment Programme)/Untied funds/local contributions and funds received from the Block-level committee, and (c) supervise the attendance of teachers and students, the quality of midday meals, and distribution of books.

With regard to subject 19 ("Adult and non-formal education"), the functions assigned to panchayat were: (a) publicity and supervision of Adult High Schools to impart education up to the middle-level to interested adult learners who were not enrolled in a formal school; and (b) regular contact with literates and neo-literates for attendance in Continuing Education Centres.

With regard to subject 20 ("Libraries"), the functions assigned to a village panchayat were: (a) the establishment and maintenance of libraries and reading rooms and supervision of the activities of Rural Libraries/ Community Library-cum-Information Centre (CLIC); and (b) sending copies of guidelines/booklets for all development programmes, the Annual Report/ Budget/Annual Plan of the village panchayat, and information on social issues to Rural Libraries/CLIC for the general information of the public.

With regard to subject 21 ("Cultural activities"), the functions assigned to the village panchayat were: (a) wide publicity/campaigns and selection of venue, (b) selection of venue for folk festivals and identification of participants; and (c) distribution of entry tickets/passes for film shows.

With regard to subject 22 ("Markets and fairs"), the functions assigned were: (a) the management of village markets (*haats/bazaars*) transferred to the panchayat; and (b) construction and regulation of markets, holding and regulating fairs, village markets and exhibition of local produce, local handicrafts/home industries.

With regard to subject 23 ("Health and sanitation, including hospitals, primary health centres and dispensaries"), the village panchayat's functions included: (a) the maintenance of sub-centres; (b) local purchase of non-medical items required by the sub-centers as may be authorised by the Health and Family Welfare Department; (c) involving Self-Help Groups in monitoring community health; and (d) disease surveillance to pre-empt outbreaks, and preventive measures against the spread of communicable diseases.

With regard to subject 24 ("Family welfare"), the village panchayat's functions included: (a) the mobilisation of people for universal immunisation, including the Pulse Polio programme; (b) promoting planned-family norms and practices to assist people in adopting family-planning measures through efficient functioning of the sub-centres; and (c) holding awareness camps for family planning and sterilisation.

With regard to subject 25 ("Women and child development") and partly with regard to subject 27 ("Welfare of the weaker sections, and in particular, of the Scheduled Castes and the Scheduled Tribes"), the panchayat had the following functions: (a) awareness generation in villages to motivate parents for pre-school education and immunisation of their children; (b) the formation of self-help groups, (c) recommendation of sites for and construction of Integrated Child Development Services (ICDS) (*anganwadi*) centres; and (d) convergence of ICDS activities and reporting the functioning of ICDS centres in the convergence meeting at the village-panchayat level.[37]

With regard to subject 26 ("Social welfare, including welfare of the handi-capped and mentally retarded"), the village panchayat's functions were: (a) identifying beneficiaries for *Kishori Shakti Yojana* and pension schemes; (b) issuing Below Poverty Line certificates for beneficiaries of the *Balika Sam riddhi Yojana*; and (c) identifying beneficiaries and collecting subscriptions for the Provident Fund for Landless Agricultural Labourers.

With regard to subject 28 ("Public distribution system"), its functions were: (a) identifying and selecting beneficiaries for the distribution of Below Poverty Line cards, *Antyodaya* cards and *Annapurna* cards; (b) monitoring distribution of foodgrains from modified ration (MR) shops to the beneficiaries; and (c) providing certificates confirming procurement of paddy from the farmers at the Minimum Support Price (MSP).

With regard to subject 29 ("Maintenance of community assets"), the village panchayat's functions were: (a) maintenance of community assets such as public tanks, *ghats*, channels, reservoirs, wells, streets, drains, culverts, lamp posts etc.; (b) construction and maintenance of resting place for travellers and pilgrims, rest houses, cattle sheds, cart stands, and protection and repair of buildings or other property vested in it; (c) to acquire, hold and dispose of immovable property with the approval of the State Government; and (d) fixing and collecting toll and fees as charges for use.

---

[37] These activities are mapped separately to the subject of "Women and Child Development" and of "Welfare of the women and children" in Activity Mapping in West Bengal. (See Third State Finance Commission of West Bengal [2008], Annexure XII).

Similarly, activities were assigned to the Block-level committees and district panchayats according to this Activity Mapping, as shown in Table 3.1.1, appended to this chapter.

The executive assistant of the Raina village panchayat knew of the Activity Mapping of West Bengal. The Block Development Officer of Raina I Block was aware of Activity Mapping and the demarcation of duties between the Block office and panchayati raj institutions based on the subsidarity rule. However, he said that there was some overlap in the actual execution of duties between the two bodies. Such encroachments into each other's responsibilities happened sometimes due to actual administrative needs and mutual cooperation, and sometimes because of conscious violations by officers of both bodies.[38]

As the State Finance Commission of West Bengal noted, executive orders with respect to Activity Mapping were not published in the official gazette,[39] even though the devolution of funds for panchayats' needs was patterned on Activity Mapping that officially applied to them. In addition, the scope of existing Activity Mapping was still limited even in West Bengal. The Panchayats and Rural Development Department of West Bengal observed that devolution by most line departments had not yet been sufficiently carried out:

> The panchayats in the meantime gained deeper roots in rural society and started influencing decisions of the line departments in respect of their activities, which was supervised by the various *Sthayee Samitis* (Standing Committees) of the upper and the middle tiers of the panchayats. However, there has been little formal devolution by most of the departments.[40]

As shown in Tables 3.1.1 and Table 3.1.2 (in the appendix to this chapter), the scope of Activity Mapping in West Bengal was less than that of the Activity Mapping suggested by the Task Force of the Ministry of Rural Development of the Central Government on Devolution of Powers and Functions upon Panchayati Raj Institutions.[41] Although assigned activities shown in Table 3.1.2 are solely for subject 1, i.e., "Agriculture, including agricultural extension," as per Schedule XI of the Constitution, the functions assigned to different panchayat tiers in West Bengal were far from adequate compared to

---

[38] Interview at Raina in February 2011.
[39] Third State Finance Commission of West Bengal (2008, pp. 21–2).
[40] Panchayats and Rural Development Department, Government of West Bengal (2009, p. 10).
[41] Ministry of Rural Development (2001, pp. 47–9).

the functions in the Activity Mapping suggested by the Task Force. The same holds true for subjects other than "Agriculture."[42]

Unlike the Second Administrative Reforms Commission, the Panchayats and Rural Development Department of West Bengal considered Activity Mapping an assignment of functions "to perform tasks on behalf of the State primarily as an agent of the Government."[43] In fact, as observed above, major functions assigned to the village panchayat were related to the implementation of schemes, such as the identification of beneficiaries, location selection, or mobilisation of people for Central or State schemes. In contrast, the Panchayats and Rural Development Department provided a "roadmap for developing various capacities within the panchayats so as to respond to the need-based demands of the people and acquire more responsibilities of their own for the realisation of such demands, stemming from local needs and aspirations."[44]

3.3.8 The Functional Domain of Village Panchayats

The Second Administrative Reforms Commission states: [45]

The spirit behind the proposed scheme for decentralisation of rural governance as envisaged in the 73rd Amendment is reflected in Article 243G and the Eleventh Schedule of the Constitution which seek to establish panchayats as self-governing institutions entrusted with the preparation and implementation of plans for economic development and social justice. However, as observed earlier, in most parts of the country the intent of Article 243G has been ignored by denying autonomous space to local bodies. Panchayats continue to function within the framework of what may be called a "permissive functional domain," since very limited functional areas have been withdrawn from the line departments of State Governments and transferred to local bodies. Only minor

---

[42] In this circumstance the Panchayat and Rural Development Department of West Bengal (2009, pp. 13–4) had to suggest a concept of "concurrent jurisdictions" in certain areas for panchayats and the State Government. "One can argue that those are not exclusive functions but concurrent jurisdiction of the panchayats in taking up those activities. The considered views of the State Government is that in the present context it is more logical, pragmatic and productive to provide concurrent jurisdictions in certain areas, which will help the panchayats to acquire adequate capacities in voluntarily taking up those activities or utilising the infrastructure and expertise of the government machinery on suitable occasions; the State Government shall in due course provide exclusive responsibilities as and when the same will be necessary and appropriate."

[43] *Ibid.*, p. 14.

[44] *Ibid.*, p. 13.

[45] Second Administrative Reforms Commission (2007, p. 137).

civic functions have been exclusively assigned to the local self-government bodies. All the other so-called development functions assigned to the different tiers of panchayats are actually dealt with by the line departments of State Governments or parastatals. Resources as well as staff also remain under the control of the State Government. Therefore, effective devolution of functions as envisaged in the Constitution has not taken place.

Autonomous space in the functional domain of village panchayats was narrower in Maharashtra than those in West Bengal. Village panchayats in Maharashtra continued to function within a "permissive functional domain" for several reasons. First, the panchayati raj institutions in Maharashtra acted as agents of the State or the Central government for implementation of their schemes. Even the chairman of each District Planning Committee was a "guardian minister" (*palak mantri*) appointed by the Maharashtra State Government. The District Rural Development Agencies (DRDAs) – district-level development execution and monitoring agencies through which Central Government funds were transferred and routed under centrally-sponsored schemes – continued to control these schemes. Second, a hierarchy of revenue officials – *patwari, tehsildar*, and the District Collector under the Revenue Department – had extensive administrative powers in Maharashtra. Third, within the panchayati raj institutions, village panchayats had limited authority over development schemes. Moreover, as observed by the panchayat head of Warwat Khanderao, the State Government was slowly taking away rights from the the village panchayat and giving more rights to Block-level committees.[46] In fact, except for schemes for drinking water, roads and culverts, sanitation, Integrated Child Development Services, public distribution, and the Mahatma Gandhi National Rural Employment Guarantee Scheme, most schemes in Warwat Khanderao were implemented by other agencies such as the line departments, *tehsildar*, Block-level committees and the the district panchayat.

The panchayat head of Warwat Khanderao complained that the village panchayat only filled out forms for poverty-alleviation and social welfare schemes which were handled by the Block-level committee. According to the panchayat head, the village panchayat had no specific role in the implementation of schemes for the Scheduled Castes and Tribes.[47] As far as Warwat Khanderao is concerned, self-help groups under the *Swarnajayanti Gram Swarozgar Yojana* (*SGSY*) were organised by non-governmental

[46] Interview with the panchayat head at Warwat Khanderao on August 18–22, 2011.
[47] *Ibid.*

organisations. The Block-level committee implemented the *SGSY* for Warwat Khanderao. The village panchayat did not have a deep commitment to activities of the self-help groups. Subsidised pesticides and machines for agriculture were distributed by the Agricultural Department and the Block-level committee. For schemes concerning minor irrigation, the village panchayat was responsible only for the basic formalities such as filling out forms, but the rest of the work is done by the office of the District Collector.

The *Indira Awaas Yojana* (IAY) was implemented by the Block-level committee as well. The Indira Gandhi National Old Age Pension Scheme (IGNOAPS) was implemented by the revenue official under the *tehsildar*'s supervision. The *Sanjay Gandhi Niradhar Yojana* (SGNY) and the National Family Benefit Scheme (NFBS) were also primarily implemented by the *tehsildar*. In this way, the *tehsildar* generally helped or guided the officers of other departments in the execution of their respective duties as far as his *tehsil* is concerned. The village panchayat only put forward wish lists of beneficiaries for schemes such as the IAY and the SGNY.

The Warwat Khanderao village panchayat assisted and oversaw the functioning of Integrated Child Development Services centres, *Shishu Siksha Kendras*, primary and upper-primary schools. There was a committee of the village panchayat (the Woman and Child Committee) to hear issues related to women's and child welfare.[48] However, the village panchayat as such was not directly involved in the funding and administration of these schemes. The improvement of school infrastructure was the panchayat's responsibility until 2010, but it now rests with the School Management Committee.

At present, autonomous spaces in the functional domain of the Warwat Khanderao village panchayat were limited to schemes for drinking water, roads and culverts, sanitation, Integrated Child Development Services, public distribution, and the MGNREGS. The scheme for drinking water (*paani parota yojana*) was directly implemented by the Warwat Khanderao village panchayat. The village panchayat determined the beneficiaries. According to the panchayat head, under the scheme called the Maharashtra Rural Water Supply Scheme (*Maharashtra Gramin Paani Parota Yojana*), two big water tanks of 18,000 litre capacity were constructed in the village. The village panchayat also owned a tubewell and 110 households were given connection

---

[48] According to the panchayat head, the Woman and Child Committee does not function properly (Interviewed in October 2013).

from it. A tank of 5,000 litre capacity was also filled with this tubewell. Eight general taps were installed. The schemes for connectivity between villages within the panchayat area were also carried out under the responsibility of the village panchayat. It allocated funds and then listed the work to be done. The State Sanitation Scheme was also implemented by the village panchayat, which prepared the priority list. The construction of the Integrated Child Development Services centre was a function assigned to the panchayat. It was responsible for identifying beneficiaries of the *Antyodaya* and *Annapurna* schemes. The panchayat's *Dakshata* Committee distributed ration cards to each beneficiary. The Warwat Khanderao village panchayat certainly acted as an implementing agency for the MGNREGS, but, as will be seen later, the Scheme was not functional in Warwat Khanderao, partly because the wages under its provisions were lower than those of agricultural work in this area.

As in Maharashtra, village panchayats in West Bengal acted as implementing agencies of the State and the Centre. However, the scope of the functional domain of panchayats in West Bengal was not as limited as in Maharashtra. Among the panchayati raj institutions in West Bengal, the focus of development activities was placed on the village panchayat. Numerous schemes were directly implemented by village panchayats in the State. The village panchayat could set their own priorities with respect to development schemes. In addition, panchayats in West Bengal and their village assemblies had some important means to mobilise their communities using government schemes such as the MGNREGA and SGSY. Although such schemes are tied to predetermined objectives provided by the Central Government, they leave considerable scope for the priorities of each village panchayat.

According to the West Bengal Panchayats and Rural Development Department:

> In implementation of these programmes, the role of panchayats to all intents and purposes actually transcends a mere agency function. Because of nearness to the people, they can select the right nature of schemes that will not only generate employment but create durable assets for society for sustained development and for improvement of quality of life of the people. Besides, the panchayats are best placed to select the proper group of beneficiaries for the related schemes and programmes with special emphasis on disadvantaged groups of the community. [49]

---

[49] Panchayats and Rural Development Department, Government of West Bengal (2009b, p. 14).

The schemes implemented by village panchayats in West Bengal were *Sampoorna Grameen Rozgar Yojana* (SGRY), Mahatma Gandhi National Rural Employment Gurantee Scheme,[50] *Indira Awaas Yojana*, Indira Gandhi National Old Age Pension Scheme (IGNOAPS), Provident Fund for Landless Agricultural Labourers (PROFLAL), National Maternal Benefit Scheme (NMBS) and the State Sanitation Programme (SSP). In each of these schemes, the village panchayat received funds for its implementation from Government agencies. The village panchayat was also responsible for maintaining financial accounts for such schemes.

The village panchayat also oversaw the implementation of certain other schemes, though it was not directly involved in their funding and administration. It assisted in the formation and functioning of self-help groups under the SGSY, worked with the Health and Family Welfare Department to implement programmes under the National Rural Health Mission, and oversaw the functioning of Integrated Child Development Services (ICDS) centres, Child Learning Centres and primary and upper-primary schools.

The village panchayat took the initiative with respect to the convergence of public health activities. Panchayats in West Bengal tried to arrange monthly meetings of their health-related functionaries in order to discuss their activities and problems. In other words, the Fourth Saturday Meeting was held at the village panchayat office with the ICDS supervisor, Auxiliary Nurse Midwife and health supervisor, representatives of self-help groups, and panchayat officials.

The village development committee was responsible for implementation and monitoring schemes at the village assembly level. As mentioned before, whenever the Agricultural Department distributed mini-kits, fertilizers, seeds and other benefits, it informed the village panchayat, specifying the number of beneficiaries to select from each panchayat or village assembly. When the village panchayat informed the village assembly of it, the village development committee of each village assembly selected the beneficiaries.

The village development committee also mobilised people to participate in the drinking water (*sajaldhara*) scheme. The households that benefitted from

---

[50] The village panchayat receives grant from the Institutional Strengthening of Gram Panchayat (ISGP) scheme in order to construct community infrastructure and buildings that cannot be otherwise constructed under the NREGS. The Scheme has become functional from 2010–1.

the drinking water scheme had to pay ten per cent of the cost of installation of a drinking water tank and pipelines. Once a location was selected by the committee, the construction agency undertook project-planning and construction.

As was not the case in Warwat Khanderao, poverty alleviation was a core activity for the Raina village panchayat. Poverty alleviation has traditionally been a core activity of panchayats in West Bengal.[51] As shown in Table 3.13, 40.2 per cent of the total schematic fund for the panchayati raj institutions in West Bengal was spent on poverty alleviation in 2007–8. Panchayats in West Bengal stood in sharp contrast with Maharashtra, where the expenditure incurred on poverty alleviation was relatively low.[52]

Besides, village panchayats in West Bengal and its village assembly could utilise certain schemes such as the MGNREGS and the SGSY as measures to mobilise their communities.

With respect to the MGNREGS, the village panchayat was the most important unit of local government since it had the responsibility to prepare a development plan and maintain a shelf of possible works to be taken up under the Scheme as and when demand for work arises. According to section 16 of the National Rural Employment Guarantee Act, 2005:

(1) The village panchayat (*gram panchayat*) shall be responsible for identification of the projects in the village panchayat area to be taken up under a Scheme as per the recommendations of the village council and the Ward council and for executing and supervising such works.

(2) A village panchayat may take up any project under a Scheme within the area of the village panchayat as may be sanctioned by the Programme Officer.

(3) Every village panchayat shall, after considering the recommendations of the village council and the ward council (ward *sabhas*), prepare a development plan and maintain a shelf of possible works to be taken up under the Scheme as and when demand for work arises.

(4) The village panchayat shall forward its proposals for the development projects including the order of priority between different works to the Programme Officer for scrutiny and preliminary approval prior to the commencement of the year in which it is proposed to be executed.

---

[51] Panchayat and Rural Development Department, Government of West Bengal (2009, p. 9).
[52] Interview with the panchayat head at Warwat Khanderao on August 18–22, 2011.

Under this scheme, the village panchayat can identify the projects in the panchayat area to be taken up under a scheme and can prepare a development plan, considering the recommendations of the village council and the ward council. In this way, the MGNREGS leaves scope for the priorities of each panchayat. The Raina village panchayat could mobilise its community on the basis of this development plan. On the other hand, in Warwat Khanderao, the MGNREGS scheme was not functional.

The Raina village panchayat and its village assembly assisted in the formation and functioning of self-help groups under the SGSY. The convergence of SGSY with MGNREGS was also pursued in West Bengal, relying on the assistance of self-help groups for MGNREGS.[53] In contrast, the Warwat Khanderao village panchayat did not have a strong commitment to self-help groups' activities since the latter were organised by non-governmental organisations.

Although panchayats in West Bengal were implementing agencies of the State and the Centre like panchayats in Maharashtra, the scope of their functional domain was broader than in Maharashtra. Schemes such as SGRY, MGNREGS, IAY, IGNOAPS, PROFLAL, NMBS and the State Sanitation Programme were implemented by the panchayats themselves in West Bengal. As far as Raina village panchayat was concerned, we found some autonomous space available for its activities. Nevertheless, the devolution of functions by most of the line departments had not yet been carried out sufficiently even in West Bengal.[54]

3.3.9 The Financial Position of Panchayati Raj Institutions

The panchayati raj institutions receive development grants from the State and Central Governments. The State Government releases grants to the district panchayats, which then finance the Block-level committees and the village panchayats. The finances of the district panchayats comprise self-raised resources like taxes, fees, cess on land revenue, and assigned revenues and grants from the State and Central Governments.

Although different sources indicate different figures for the income and expenditure of the panchayati raj institutions,[55] the Comptroller and Auditor

[53] Panchayats and Rural Development Department, Government of West Bengal (2009b, pp. 95–7).
[54] Panchayats and Rural Development Department, Government of West Bengal (2009b, p. 10); *ibid.* (2008a, pp. 13–14); Third State Finance Commission of West Bengal (2008, pp. 19–26).
[55] As mentioned before, the State Finance Commissions have repeatedly indicated in their

General of India uses data furnished by the Rural Development Department, Government of Maharashtra (Table 3.8). According to this data source, the scale of funds for the panchayati raj institutions was larger in Maharashtra than West Bengal. The total funds received by district panchayats in Maharashtra alone was many times higher than the total funds received in West Bengal panchayati raj institutions as a whole (see Table 3.11).

The government grant-in-aid constituted about 96 per cent of the district panchayats' total revenue in Maharashtra. It is reported that the share of government grants in relation to the total revenue has increased noticeably. The share of the own-source of revenue (OSR) at the district panchayat level was less than 2 per cent of the total revenue in 2007–8. A large capital receipt by district panchayats was also a salient feature in Maharashtra.

The Block-level committee did not have independent sources of revenue as it is not considered a corporate body. It received block grants from the State Government through the district panchayat. Its accounts were incorporated in the district panchayat's account.

According to the data from the Directorate of Economics and Statistics, Maharashtra,[56] the average income of each village panchayat in Buldhana district was about Rs 500,000 (more than Rs 400,000 which is an average for the State)[57] which included government grants as well as grants from the district panchayats and Block-level committees. As shown in Table 3.9, the share

Table 3.8 *Receipts and expenditures of district councils in Maharashtra* in Rs ten million

Year	Receipts						Expenditure		
	Own revenue*	Govern- ment grants	Other rev- enue	Total revenue	Capital receipts	Total receipts	Revenue	Capital	Total
2006–7	144	7,784	188	8,116	2,691	10,807	8,161	2,314	10,475
2007–8	161	8,246	183	8,590	2,521	11,111	8,494	1,923	10,417

Notes: (i) * excludes opening balance
(ii) Information furnished by the Rural Development Department (RDD).
Source: Comptroller and Auditor General (2008, p. 5).

---

reports low quality of accounting data in most States (Twelfth Finance Commission 2004, p. 154). This is discussed at length in section 7.1, chapter 7.

[56] Directorate of Economics and Statistics, Government of Maharashtra (2010, pp. 636–7).
[57] As shown in Table 3.5, the number of village panchayats is 27,907 in Maharashtra.

of own-source of revenue in total receipt of panchayats was quite large in Maharashtra: as much as 46 per cent of the total receipt in 2007–8. Tax receipt of Rs 4,820 million for panchayats in Maharashtra was much larger than receipt of Rs 707 million from own-source for panchayats in West Bengal (see Table 3.12). On the one hand, the per capita own-source revenue from village panchayats was much larger in Maharashtra than West Bengal, considering that the two States have almost the same rural population (see Table 3.5). On the other hand, about 40 per cent of the total receipts of the village panchayats in Maharashtra came from grants from the State and Central Governments.

The grants allocated for centrally-sponsored schemes and special purpose programmes of the State Governments usually had predetermined objectives, leaving little scope for the priorities of the village panchayat. The large own-source revenue enabled the panchayat to autonomously develop and implement programmes focused on specific local problems, not often addressed by programmes from above (i.e. from the Centre and the State). In Maharashtra's panchayats, own-source revenue met half the expenditure on salaries of employees. The expenditure on salaries of its employees was borne equally by the State Government and the concerned village panchayat. In the Warwat Khanderao village panchayat, besides salaries of workers and officials, expenses for sewage cleaning and electricity bills were paid by funds from own-source revenue.

The village panchayat's large own-source revenue reflected an aspect of its self-governance. Panchayats in Maharashtra had high potential for their self-governance in terms of their own-source of revenue, although the devolution of functions to them was substantially limited as mentioned in section 3.9.

As shown in Table 3.10, most of the expenditure of the district panchayats in Maharashtra was on education. The highest expenditure by village panchayats in the State was for public works, health and sanitation, and administration.[58] The expenditures incurred by village panchayats for poverty alleviation and social security were low. In fact, according to the panchayat head of Warwat Khanderao, the village panchayat's responsibility for poverty alleviation was limited.[59]

The total expenditure by district panchayats in Maharashtra (2007–8) was

---

[58] Planning Commission (2007, p. 250).
[59] Interview conducted at Warwat Khanderao on August 18–22, 2011.

Table 3.9 *Receipts and expenditures of village panchayats in Maharashtra* in Rs ten million

Year	Receipts					Expenditure
	Government grants	Taxes	Contri- butions	Other receipts	Total receipts	
2006–07	376	430	113	71	990	938
2007–08	377	482	131	69	1,059	1,075

Note: Figures furnished by Rural Development Department (August 2009). These figures exclude opening balance.
Source: Comptroller and Auditor General (2008, p. 7).

Table 3.10 *Expenditures of village and district panchayats in Maharashtra* in Rs ten million

Components	Village panchayats' expenditure		District panchayats' expenditure	
	2006–7	2007–8	2006–7	2007–8
Administration	154	179	576	610
Health and sanitation	241	250	947	965
Public works	352	423	591	692
Education	20	25	3,638	3,917
Irrigation	–	–	239	211
Agriculture	–	–	92	128
Social welfare	44	42	735	700
Public lighting	47	50	–	–
Animal husbandry	–	–	115	123
Forests	–	–	7	6
Other expenditure	80	106	1,221	1,142
Capital expenditure	–	–	2,314	1,923
Total	938	1075	10,475	10,417

Note: These figures are as furnished by RDD of the Maharashtra Government.
Source: Comptroller and Auditor General (2008, p. 8–9).

Rs 10,417 crore (or 104,170 million), whereas the total expenditure by village panchayats was only Rs 1,075 crore (10,750 million). This shows that more resources were allocated in Maharashtra to the district level than to the village panchayat level.

The revenue receipts of panchayati raj institutions in West Bengal comprise receipts from their own sources, their assigned revenue (a small amount of State-tax share, such as from Entertainment Tax, Profession Tax, etc.), and grants-in-aid from the State and Central Governments.[60]

Although different sources cite different figures for the income and expenditure of the panchayati raj institutions, the Examiner of Local Accounts, West Bengal, provides data on receipts and expenditures of these institutions during 2008–9 as shown in Table 3.11.[61] According to this data source, only about 3.7 per cent of total revenues of panchayati raj institutions was derived from own-source of revenue and 96.3 per cent came from grants, of which 64.6 per cent came from the Central Government and 31.7 per cent from the State Government. Therefore, the panchayati raj institutions in West Bengal were overwhelmingly dependent on grants from the Central and State Governments. The share of own-source revenue in their total receipts was quite small in West Bengal.

From 2002–3 to 2008–9, the State government grants to panchayati raj institutions increased 191 per cent and the Central grants increased 418 per cent. Although own-source-revenue collection also increased 218 per cent during this period, it constituted a very small portion of the total revenues.[62]

In West Bengal, own-source revenue for village panchayats was from tax and non-tax sources, while own-source revenue for Block-level committees and

Table 3.11 *Receipts and expenditures of panchayati raj institutions in West Bengal during 2008–9* in Rs ten million

Receipts		Expenditure	
Central funds	2,303.85	Salary and allowance	293.03
State funds	1,131.87	Schemes	2,527.43
Own funds	130.97	SFC and TFC	360.93
		Other	150.85
Total	3,566.69	Total	3,332.24

Notes: SFC = State Finance Commission Fund, TFC = Twelfth Finance Commission Fund.
Source: Examiner of Local Accounts, West Bengal.

[60] Third State Finance Commission of West Bengal (2008, p. 31).
[61] As mentioned before, the Central Finance Commissions have repeatedly indicated in their reports low quality of accounting data in most States (Twelfth Finance Commission 2004, p. 154).
[62] Examiner of Local Accounts, West Bengal (2009, p. 8).

district panchayats was only from non-tax sources. The latter did not have taxation powers in West Bengal. Village panchayat could collect taxes on land and buildings.

District panchayats took Rural Infrastructure Development Fund (RIDF) loans for some medium-sized rural programmes. The loan liabilities, including interest payments, were, however, borne by the State Government.[63]

The respective financial positions of the three panchayati raj tiers are depicted in Table 3.12. Table 3.12 reveals that relatively greater resources were allocated in West Bengal to village panchayats than to the district panchayats. It contrasts sharply with Maharashtra where greater resources were allocated to the district-level institutions. A total of Rs 2,099 crores (20,990 million) were allocated to the village panchayat level in West Bengal as compared to Rs 1,059 (10,590 million) in Maharashtra. Further, the average income of each village panchayat in West Bengal was about Rs 8 mllion in 2008–9, which was much higher than in Maharashtra.[64] The scale of finance of each village panchayat in West Bengal was financially much larger than in Maharashtra.

Table 3.12 also reveals that the share of own-source revenue in total receipts of village panchayats was quite small in West Bengal.[65] It was only 2.6 per cent of total receipts in West Bengal, unlike in Maharashtra where the share of own-source revenue was as much as 46 per cent of total receipts.[66] In Maharashtra, the share of own-source revenue in total receipts of district panchayats was small, but it was quite large at the village panchayat level.

A small share of own-source revenue in receipts and an overdependence on grants restrict the autonomy of village panchayats with respect to the use

---

[63] Third State Finance Commission of West Bengal (2008, p. 31).

[64] As shown in Table 3.5, the number of village panchayats is 3,239 in West Bengal.

[65] According to the *Annual Reports* of the Panchayats and Rural Development Department of West Bengal (2008a, pp. 106–7), the per capita own-source revenue from three-tier panchayats is Rs 18.65 and that from village panchayats is Rs 10.13 for the years 2007–08. However, the Third State Finance Commission of West Bengal (2008, p. 30) suggests that the per capita collection of own revenue may be much less than what has been shown in the Annual Reports of the Department, although the collection has increased, indeed, in all the districts.

[66] Rao and Rao (2008), National Institute of Public Finance and Policy, New Delhi, have shown large-scale variations in inter-State performances in this regard. The own-source-revenue primary-sector GSDP ratio in 2002–3 varied from 1.48 per cent in Kerala and 1.10 per cent in Maharashtra to 0.07 per cent in West Bengal.

Table 3.12 *Financial position of district councils, Block-level committees, and village panchayats in West Bengal 2008–9* in Rs ten million

Heads	Receipts				Total expenditure
	ZPs	PSs	GPs	Total	
(A) Grants:					
(i) Salary and allowances grant	31.93	21.66	214.73	268.32	293.04
(ii) Schematic fund	404.02	162.55	2,183.49	2,750.06	2,527.43
(iii) Other grants	108.94	77.33	231.07	417.34	390.56
(A) Total grants	544.89	261.54	2,629.29	3,435.72	3,211.03
(B) Own source	39.51	20.72	70.74	130.97	121.21
Total (A+B)	584.40	282.26	2,700.03	3,566.69	3,332.24

Notes: ZP = district council (*zilla parishad*), PS = Block committee (*panchayat samiti*), GP = village panchayat (*gram panchayat*).
Source: Examiner of Local Accounts West Bengal.

of funds. The grants allocated for centrally-sponsored schemes and special purpose programmes of State Governments are customarily utilised strictly following the rules or guidelines framed by the Central or State governments. However, "Other Grants"[67] in Table 3.12 include "untied funds" – funds that do not impose any specific rules regarding their utilisation on the spending agency[68] – such as the Twelfth Finance Commission Fund and the Second State Finance Commission Fund, etc.[69] These untied funds could enable village panchayats to prioritise activities that reflect local needs and preferences, not covered by programmes initiated from above (Centre and State). The share of "Other Grants" in total receipts of village panchayats was 8.6 per cent in 2007–8.

In West Bengal, "Salary and Allowance Grants" were provided by the State Government for meeting establishment costs, including salaries and pensions

---

[67] "Other Grants" for village panchayats (Rs 2310.7 million) in Table 3.12 include the Twelfth Finance Commission Fund (Rs 1525.2 million) and the Second State Finance Commission Fund (Rs 723 million) (Panchayats and Rural Development Department, Government of West Bengal 2007, p. 125).

[68] Dongre *et al.* (2011, p. 1). The Third State Finance Commission of West Bengal (2008, p. 5) stated that "The Commission feels that the idea behind the concept of 'untied' fund allocation to LSGs still remains somewhat unclear to its beneficiaries."

[69] In addition, selected village panchayats received untied funds under the "Strengthening Rural Decentralisation" (SRD) programme supported by the Department for International Development (DFID), United Kingdom. Village panchayats, in turn, devolved the SRD untied funds to the village development committees.

of panchayat employees, while in Maharashtra half of that cost was incurred by the panchayat's own-source revenue.

It is difficult to obtain data on expenditure by the three tiers of the panchayati raj system.[70] According to information from a Panchayat Accounts and Audit Officer at the Block Development Office in Raina, there was no standardised format to give a detailed breakdown of expenditure in their accounting system. The Examiner of Local Accounts, West Bengal, presented in its report data on expenditure of the fund for development schemes (Table 3.13). Table 3.13 shows that the panchayati raj institutions spent most of the funds for development schemes on poverty alleviation and rural housing. Expenditures incurred under these two sectors ranged from 68 to 82 per cent of all scheme expenditures from 2006–7 to 2008–9.

Thus, we can compare the financial position of panchayati raj institutions (village panchayats, in particular) in the two States as follows:

Table 3.13 *Sector-wise receipts and expenditures of the scheme fund as per records of the Panchayats and Rural Development Department, Government of West Bengal in Rs ten million*

Name of sector	2006–7		2007–8		2008–9	
	Receipts	Expenditure	Receipts	Expenditure	Receipts	Expenditure
Poverty alleviation	706.88	841.8	1,190.48	1,177.58	1,104.94	1,016.71
Social security Health and family welfare	265.52	129.42 3	351.71	323.09	503.78	481.03
Backward-area development	–	–	266.35	127.04	183	125.2
Development of natural resources	10.95	6.34	1.51	7.68	15.75	1.97
Rural development	44.44	44.44	73.57	73.31	91.17	90.05
Rural roads	3.96	3.96	5.94	5.94	5.99	5.67
Rural housing	274.14	280.51	344.24	269.83	702.92	701.97
Education	31.87	31.87	106.59	106.59	90.76	90.76
Other sectors	–	–	0.17	–	0.16	0.91
Total expenditure	1,341.73	1,369.38	2,460.81	2,137.64	2,750.06	2,527.44

Source: Examiner of Local Accounts West Bengal.

[70] Third State Finance Commission of West Bengal (2008, p. 32).

(i) The scale of funds received by the panchayati raj institutions as a whole was considerably larger in Maharashtra than in West Bengal. Even receipts of panchayats solely at the district-level in Maharashtra were as much as Rs 1,11,110 million in 2007–8, whereas total receipts of all three panchayat tiers in West Bengal in the same period was only Rs 33,430 million. The financial resources of panchayati raj institutions as a whole were much larger in Maharashtra than West Bengal.

(ii) Greater resources were allocated to panchayati raj institutions at the district-level in Maharashtra. In contrast, more resources were allocated at the village panchayat level in West Bengal: a total of Rs 20,990 million in West Bengal and a total of Rs 10,590 million in Maharashtra. In fact, for the untied fund allocation, the State Finance Commission of West Bengal has provided the principle to calculate inter-panchayati raj shares of 12:18:70 for district panchayats, Block-level committees and village panchayats. The Commission states that "there is a growing shift in the focus of development activities towards the GP level under the evolving decentralised planning environment."[71] This was in striking contrast to the situation in Maharashtra.

(iii) The financial scale of each village panchayat was much larger in West Bengal than in Maharashtra. The average income of each village panchayat in West Bengal was about Rs 8 million, whereas the average income of each village panchayat in Maharashtra was less than Rs 0.4 million.

(iv) The share of own-source revenue in total receipts of village panchayats was 46 per cent in Maharashtra, while in West Bengal it was only 2.6 per cent. The large own-source revenue for village panchayats in Maharashtra reveals their high potential for self-governance, although the devolution of functions to them was limited.

(v) Village panchayats and panchayati raj institutions in West Bengal were overwhelmingly dependent on grants from the Central and State Governments. However, these grants include "untied funds" such as the Twelfth Finance Commission Fund and the Second State Finance Commission Fund.

(vi) Alleviating poverty was a core activity of the panchayats in West Bengal.[72] This is in contrast to Maharasthra's village panchayats, where less was spent on poverty alleviation.

---

[71] Third State Finance Commission of West Bengal (2008, p. 134).
[72] Panchayats and Rural Development Department, Government of West Bengal (2009, p. 9).

3.3.10 Financial Management in Panchayati Raj Institutions

Article 243 of the Constitution states: "The Legislature of a State may, by law, make provisions with respect to the maintenance of accounts by the panchayats and the auditing of such accounts." Internal and statutory audits are carried out for panchayati raj institutions in the two States. However, some weaknesses in financial management have been pointed out by auditors in both States.

The Chief Auditor, Local Fund Accounts (CALFA), Maharashtra, has acted as the statutory auditor in accordance with provisions of the Bombay Local Fund Audit Act, 1930, the Maharashtra Village Panchayat (Audit of Accounts) Rules, 1961, and the Bombay Village Panchayats Act, 1958. The Comptroller and Auditor General (CAG) of India also conducts audits of district panchayats and Block-level committees under Section 14 of the Comptroller & Auditor General of India's (Duties, Powers and Conditions of Services) Act, 1971, and under Section 142A of the Maharashtra Zilla Parishad and Panchayat Samiti Act, 1961. During the audit of Block-level committees, audits are also conducted on selected village panchayats under a Block-level committee.[73]

Each district panchayat in Maharashtra had a financial management system not only for itself but also for the Block-level committees and village panchayats under it. Under the provisions of Section 136 (2) of the Maharashtra Zilla Parishad and Panchayat Samiti Act, 1961, the Block Development Officers forward the accounts approved by the Block-level committees to the district panchayats and these form part of the district panchayats' accounts. Under provisions of Section 62(4) of the Bombay Village Panchayats Act, 1958, the village development officer of the village panchayats are required to prepare annual accounts of the village panchayats. The approved accounts are to be forwarded to the concerned district panchayat. The annual account of the Warwat Khanderao village panchayat is consolidated at the Block-level and

[73] The Comptroller and Auditor General (2008, p. 20) conducted a performance audit in Maharashtra between December 2008 and May 2009. Panchayats were selected by random sampling method. That is, there are 33 district panchayat (ZP), 351 Block-level committees (PS), and 27909 village panchayats (GP) in the State. Out of 33 ZPs, eight ZPs (Akola, Chandrapur, Jalna, Nasik, Ratnagiri, Satara, Thane, and Yavatmal) representing at least one ZP from each of the six regions (Amravati, Aurangabad, Nasik, Mumbai/Thane, Nagpur, and Pune) in the State, alongwith sixteen PSs (Balapur, Chiplun, Chimur, Deola, Jalna, Karad, Mahabaleshwar, Murbad, Murtizapur, Nasik, Partur, Pusad, Ratnagiri, Vasai, Wani, and Warora), and eighty GPs were selected by random sampling method for the performance audit covering the period from 2003–4 to 2007–8. The performance audit conducted between December 2008 and May 2009 involved scrutiny of records maintained in the department, selected.

audited annually by the Local Fund Audit Department and by the Comptroller and Auditor General once every three years.[74] The Block Development Officer has an annual account in the Maharashtra State Gram Panchayat Annual Report. The abstracts of the approved accounts of all three tiers are prepared by the Chief Accounts and Finance Officer (CAFO) at the district level and forwarded to the Chief Auditor, Local Fund Accounts (CALFA) for auditing, certification and publication in the Maharashtra Government Gazette.[75]

However, the Comptroller and Auditor General observes some weakness in the financial management of panchayati raj institutions in Maharashtra. The findings of the Comptroller and Auditor General reveal problems with the internal control of financial management not only at the village panchayat level, but also at higher panchayati raj levels. The Comptroller and Auditor General found arrears in finalisation of accounts by the district panchayats and certification thereof by the CALFA. According to the Comptroller and Auditor General, "it was observed from the information collected (August 2009) from CALFA that out of the 33 ZPs (*zilla parishad* or district panchayats) except Akola, Bhandara, Kolhapur, Pune, Sangli, Satara and Solapur, all others had not finalised their accounts for 2007–8. Arrears in finalisation of accounts by the ZPs and certification thereof by the CALFA ranged from one to four years."[76] The Comptroller and Auditor General states that "arrears in finalisation and publication of accounts is indicative of inefficient internal controls" and "absence of a proper management information system and the increasing arrears in finalisation and publication of accounts are fraught with the risk of misappropriations and other irregularities."[77]

The Auditing authority further observes that not all district panchayats and Block-level committees reconcile their cash book balances with bank balances.[78] Non-reconciliation of cash book balances with bank balances

---

[74] Interview at the Block Development Office of Sangrampur on April 25, 2014.

[75] Comptroller and Auditor General (2008, pp. 9–10).

[76] *Ibid.*, p. 10. "However, information regarding the status of publication of the ZPs' accounts made available by the Government indicated arrears of one to three years in publication of annual accounts of ZPs, although procedure for ensuring timely finalisation and publication of the accounts had been prescribed."

[77] *Ibid.*, pp. 10–1. The Comptroller and Auditor General (2008, p. 23) observed "from records of two ZPs [Chandrapur ZP and Yavatmal ZP] that there were delay ranging between six and 22 months in compilation of accounts whereas there were delays ranging from seven months to 23 months in publishing of annual accounts by three ZPs [Akola ZP, Chandrapur ZP, and Yavatmal ZP] during 2003–4 to 2007–8."

[78] *Ibid.*, pp. 33–4. "Scrutiny of records revealed that reconciliation of cash book balances with bank balances as on 31 March 2008 was not carried out by ZP Thane and four selected

reveals the poor quality of some of the accounts even at the higher panchayati raj tiers.

It further claims that "accumulation of huge funds with the ZPs need to be examined."[79] According to its report, scrutiny of records of eight test-checked district panchayats revealed that unspent grants under an agency scheme amounting to Rs 972.9 million, as on 31 March 2008, were not refunded to the Government. "Audit has noticed many cases of failure to refund unspent balances leading to huge blocking of public money for no purpose."[80] Upon further scrutiny of the records the Comptroller and Auditor General found that a surplus fund of Rs 5923.3 million was accumulated in the same eight district panchayats.[81]

Unlike the funds received by district panchayats in the State budget, it is difficult to incorporate centrally-sponsored schemes' funds in the district panchayats' accounts because these funds are received by the Block-level committees directly from the District Rural Development Agencies (DRDA). The Auditor points out problems in Maharashtra in the flow of funds through the DRDA for schemes such as the *Indira Awaas Yojana* and *Rajiv Gandhi Gandhi Niwara Yojana*.[82]

PSs for the period 2003–8. As a result, the difference of Rs 122 million between Cash Book and Bank Pass Books remained unreconciled as of March 2008" (*Ibid.*, p. 34). "Fraud and embezzlement cannot be ruled out due to non-reconciliation of balances between cash book and bank accounts. The facts were accepted (September 2009) by the Government and they stated that instructions were issued in August 2009" (*Ibid.*, p. 34). The Maharashtra State Development Report mentioned that "The major challenge that the PRIs in the state face is the corruption at various levels, which is a common practice in many states. Instances of misappropriation of funds by village heads, panchayat secretary often appear in the local newspapers. However, the recent initiatives of the government to empower the village council (*gram sabha*) by recalling panchayat representatives under certain circumstances, in response to social crusader Anna Hazare's demand, may check such incidents. Moreover, the wider anti-corruption movement initiated by Anna Hazare and his campaign for the people's right to information could generate effective and vigilant public opinion against the individuals and groups involved in such practices" (Planning Commission 2007, pp. 250–1).

[79] Comptroller and Auditor General (2008, p. 42).

[80] *Ibid.*, p. 32.

[81] Thirteenth Finance Commission (2009, p. 423). The Thirteenth Finance Commission summarises the major recommendations of the State Finance Commissions. It states that there is no information ("no data available") on the State Finance Commission Report in Maharashtra. According to the staff of the library at the Mantralaya, Mumbai, the report "is not in the public domain."

[82] Comptroller and Auditor General (2008, p. 23).

As a result, different sources indicate different figures on the district panchayats' expenditures. The expenditure of Rs 1,04,170 million during 2007–8 (Table 3.8) was based on the figures adopted from the Rural Development Department of Maharashtra. However, on the basis of the information received from all district panchayats for 2007–8, the Comptroller and Auditor General noticed that these may have incurred an expenditure of Rs 1,23,290 million (Rs 4,834.4 million on their own schemes, Rs 1,02,894.3 million on transferred schemes by the State Government, and Rs 15,560.6 million on schemes funded by other agencies).[83]

The Comptroller and Auditor General also observed problems at the village panchayat level concerning internal control over financial management. According to the Auditing authority, 17 out of 80 selected village panchayats had not submitted 65 annual accounts for 2003–8 to the village council for approval, and none of the selected 80 village panchayats had submitted their annual accounts to the district panchayats for 2003–8.[84] The Comptroller and Auditor General indicates that the accounts and related records are often not properly maintained by panchayats in Maharashtra. This scrutiny of records revealed that 70 out of a test-checked 80 village panchayats did not maintain Forms 3 to 27 required in the Bombay Village Panchayats (Budget and Accounts) Rule, 1959. The Audit Report states that "this also shows lack of proper control and supervision of GPs by higher officials like BDO of PS and CEO [Chief Executive Officer] of ZP."[85]

The village panchayats prepared budgets only for work that can be done with their own resources. However, the Central and State schemes implemented directly by village panchayats were substantially limited in Maharashtra. The village panchayat was not responsible for maintaining annual accounts for the schemes not directly implemented by it. Therefore, as far as the Warwat Khanderao village panchayat was concerned, the annual account in the "Annual Budget Report on Gram Panchayats in Maharashtra" provided little information on grants from the State and Central Governments. Accounting data for the Central and State schemes, implemented within the village panchayat's jurisdiction, constituted an information vacuum in the panchayat's financial management.

[83] *Ibid.*, p. 9. Expenditure figures are furnished by the Rural Development Department of the State Government and vary from the figures given in the Economic Survey of Maharashtra (*ibid.*, p. 5).
[84] *Ibid.*, p. 37.
[85] *Ibid.*, pp. 38–40.

A test-checking of cash books of six village panchayats from three district panchayats by the Comptroller and Auditor General revealed that the cash books were not always maintained during 2003–8. The Auditor observed that village panchayats were making huge cash payments in violation of all codal instructions.[86]

The Examiner of Local Accounts (ELA), West Bengal has been the statutory auditor for examining accounts of all the district panchayats and Block-level committees since 1980. In 2003, the ELA of West Bengal was appointed as the statutory auditor for examining accounts of all the village panchayats; since then the ELA has audited their accounts every year.

The Panchayat Accounts and Audit Officer posted in each Block examines accounts and undertakes an internal audit of all village panchayats within the Block in every quarter. The Samiti Audit and Accounts Officer posted in each subdivision examines the accounts and audits all Block-level committees within the subdivision every quarter. The Comptroller and Auditor General also observes problems at the village panchayat level concerning internal control over financial management. According to their report, 17 out of 80 village panchayats selected for audit had not submitted 65 annual accounts for 2003–8 to the village council for approval, and none of the selected 80 village panchayats had submitted their annual accounts to the district panchayats for 2003–8 (the footnote 86 gives the reference for the report). The Regional Accounts and Audit Officer posted in each Division examines the accounts and conducts an internal audit of all district panchayats within the Division every quarter.

Unlike the Warwat Khanderao village panchayat, the Raina village panchayat provided accounting data for many grants from the State and Central Governments. The latter was responsible for maintaining financial accounts for numerous schemes for which the panchayat receives funds from Government agencies (e.g., the *Sampoorna Grameen Rozgar Yojana*, MGNREGS, IAY, IGNOAPS, PROFLAL, National Maternal Benefit Scheme, and the State Sanitation Programme). Unlike the Warwat Khanderao village panchayat, the Raina village panchayat also provided information on "untied funds" such as the Central and State Finance Commission Funds.

---

[86] *Ibid.*, p. 37. "According to Rule 5(A) of the BVP [Bombay Village Panchayats], (Budget & Accounts) Rules, 1959, payment of any sum in excess of Rs 500 out of the village fund shall be made by cheque signed by the panchayat head and Secretary of the village panchayat."

However, both the State Finance Commission and the ELA, West Bengal, were concerned about the poor financial management of panchayati raj institutions in West Bengal. In the audit of 18 district panchayats, 151 Block-level committees and 3,214 village panchayats in the State during 2008–9, the ELA found that the internal audit of Bankura and Bardhaman district panchayats, 67 Block-level committees and 1,252 village panchayats was not conducted for periods ranging from one to five years.[87] The ELA found that 29 Block-level committees and 28 village panchayats did not prepare the account in the prescribed format. The ELA also found that 735 panchayati raj institutions did not maintain the Demand and Collection Register, 1039 did not maintain the Appropriation Register, 1589 did not maintain the Advance Register, and 2,059 did not maintain the Works Register.[88] This is indicative of inefficient internal controls in some of the panchayati raj institutions in West Bengal. The ELA found in its audit scrutiny that in the Jalpaiguri district panchayat, 17 Block-level committees and 85 village panchayats did not reconcile the difference between the cash book and the pass book balances of Banks and Treasuries as on March 31, 2008.[89]

Consequently, the Third State Finance Commission of West Bengal suggested that "the accounts keeping by all the three tiers are not in order."[90] Both the State Finance Commission and the ELA of the State point out differences between the allocation of funds in the State Budget and their actual release, and between the actual release and their utilisation (Table 3.14). According to the ELA, the Panchayats and Rural Development Department of West

Table 3.14 *West Bengal budget allocation of funds, actually released and utilised* in Rs ten million

	State budget allocation	Actually released	Utilisation
2006–7	1,272.65	1,233.95	787.60
2007–8	2,168.93	1,880.77	980.72
2008–9	2,048.07	1,830.89	1,687.89

Source: Examiner of Local Accounts West Bengal.

[87] Examiner of Local Accounts, West Bengal (2009, pp. 17, 19, 20).
[88] Examiner of Local Accounts West Bengal (2009, pp. 19, 85–6).
[89] The Third State Finance Commission of West Bengal (2008, p. 109) indicates that "Considerable amounts are found to have remained unreconciled between the Cash Book and the Pass Book every month leaving the risk of misappropriation of funds going undetected."
[90] *Ibid.*, p. 33. The Commission states: "The analysis vindicates the evidence adduced by the Auditors and Examiner of Local Accounts before the Commission."

Bengal was requested to explain the shortfall in allocation and utilisation but no reply had been received.[91] The Third State Finance Commission of West Bengal claims that "large amounts of specific purpose funds remain unutilised for years altogether."[92]

3.3.11 State Finance Commission (SFC)

Article 243I(1) of the Constitution states that the Governor of a State shall constitute a Finance Commission to review the financial position of the panchayats. It is a mandatory provision of the Seventy-Third Amendment Act, 1992.

The first State Finance Commission (SFC) in Maharashtra was established in April 1994 and its report was submitted in November 1996. The Second SFC was established in May 1999 and its report was submitted in October 2002. The Third SFC was set up in 2005 and submitted its report in June 2006. According to the Comptroller and Auditor General, the report was presented

---

[91] Examiner of Local Accounts, West Bengal (2009, pp. 19, 7–8). The Third State Finance Commission of West Bengal (2008, p. 32) argues that "Apparently, the difference is on account of the facts that P & RD Department has shown less releases in respect of some schemes and has not included funds released on account of pensionary benefits."

[92] Third State Finance Commission of West Bengal (2008, p. 109). This Commission, in the course of interaction with the ELA of the State, found the following issues with regard to financial accountability of local bodies in West Bengal:

  (i) Village panchayats prepare receipts and payments accounts under the single accounting system, while Block-level committees and district panchayats under the double entry system. Supporting vouchers, ledgers, etc. are however not maintained properly;

  (ii) Basic registers like Asset Registers, Works Register are not maintained and as such it is not possible to know whether the same works are being done again;

  (iii) Diversion of funds is very common: often out of compulsion, and late receipt of guidelines;

  (iv) Most of the village panchayats cannot collect revenue because there is no employee for tax collection. Demand and Collection registers are not maintained properly;

  (v) Substantial funds are spent by the panchayati raj institutions without budget preparation/provision;

  (vi) Considerable amounts are found to have remained unreconciled between the Cash Book and the Pass Book every month, leaving the risk of misappropriation of funds going undetected;

  (vii) Irregularities in selection of beneficiaries, irregular engagement of contractors, irregular payments etc. are some of the problems;

  (viii) Large amount of specific purpose funds remain unutilised for years together; and

  (ix) Capacity building of employees should be given importance.

Most points listed above are also pointed out in the audit of selected panchayati raj institutions in Maharashtra conducted by the Comptroller and Auditor General.

to the Maharashtra legislature in December 2013.[93] However, details of recommendations and reports of the Third SFC were not available in the public domain.[94]

The first State Finance Commission (SFC) of West Bengal was appointed in May 1994 and its report was submitted in November 1995. All the recommendations of the SFC were accepted by the West Bengal Government. The second SFC was set up in July 2000 and its report was submitted in February 2002. The State Government accepted most of the recommendations. The third SFC was set up in February 2006 and its report was submitted in October 2008. All of these reports were available in the public domain.

3.3.12 Planning in Panchayati Raj Institutions

As mentioned before, the devolution of powers and responsibilities upon panchayats at each level with respect to planning and implementation of schemes for economic development and social justice is at the discretion of the Legislature of a State (Article 243G). Therefore, devolution may vary across States.

The District Planning Committees in both States were not considered functional. In particular, the committees in Maharashtra were not constituted as they should be under the Seventy-Third Amendment.[95] As for planning at the village panchayat level, the authority of the panchayat to carry out planning exercises was considerably more limited in Maharashtra than in West Bengal. Although the village panchayats in both States act as implementing agencies of the State or the Centre, their autonomy was not as limited in West Bengal as in Maharashtra.

As mentioned before, Article 243ZD of the Constitution envisages that District Planning Committees (DPCs) be constituted in every State at the district level to consolidate the plans prepared by the villages and towns in the district. Each DPC prepares a draft Development Plan of the district with regard to matters of common interest between the panchayats and the

---

[93] Comptroller and Auditor General (2014).
[94] The Thirteenth Finance Commission (2010, p. 423) summarises the major recommendations of the State Finance Commissions. It states that there is no information ("data not available") on recommendations of the State Finance Commission of Maharashtra. We were unable to obtain the report.
[95] Planning Commission 2007, p. 247).

municipalities, such as spatial planning, sharing of water and other physical and natural resources, and integrated development of infrastructure and environmental conservation.

However, according to the Maharashtra State Development Report, "the District Planning Committees (DPCs) as per the provision prescribed under Article 243 ZD(1) of the Constitution have not yet been constituted like that of Karnataka, West Bengal, Kerala, Madhya Pradesh and many other states."[96] In Maharashtra, the Department of Rural Development and Panchayati Raj was under the State's Ministry of Rural Development. A cabinet minister of the State Government was appointed "guardian minister" (*palak mantri*) for each district, who had to oversee the implementation of all schemes and programmes in the district. The same person was the chairman of the DPC. The DPC comprised the Guardian Minister, the Project Director and selected member of the district panchayats. The District Rural Development Agency had not been abolished and prepared plans for schemes and programmes under its jurisdiction. Therefore, the Maharashtra State Development Report stated that "the Line Departments and District Rural Development Agencies (DRDAs) continue to have major control over the planning and implementation of the schemes. The PRIs mostly act as the delivery units."[97]

At the Block level, there were several extension officers for different programmes and departments (e.g. for agriculture, industry, and statistics). These extension officers were given additional charges such as that of "sector planning officer." A sector, in this case, refers to a geographical area comprising ten to fifteen villages. The sector planning officer was responsible for all planning activities for each scheme/programme (of the Ministry of Rural Development) in that sector, with the help of the village development officer. Block-level engineers/technical officers provided technical support to the sector planning officer. Planning and implementation of schemes of other departments (such as health, education, agriculture, and animal husbandry) were done by the relevant department officials. The sector planning officers reported them to the Block Development Officer and the District Planning Committee.

However, according to the Block Development Officer (BDO) of Sangrampur, the powers of the position are limited. The BDO represents the Block-level

---

[96] *Ibid.*
[97] *Ibid.*, p. 251.

administration and the *tehsildar* represents the *tehsil*-level administration. The BDO was the executive officer for all matters related to the panchayats, while the *tehsildar* was the Programme Officer for all programmes under the Ministry of Rural Development.

On the basis of Activity Mapping, the village panchayat can prepare its own plan. Indeed, "Preparation of plans for the development of the village" is included in Schedule I (Village List) of the Bombay Village Panchayats Act, 1958. Section 8(1) of the Bombay Village Panchayats Act, 1958, stipulates:

> The first meeting of the village council (*gram sabha*) in every financial year shall be held within two months from the commencement of that year, and the *panchayat* shall place before such meeting – (i) the annual statement of accounts; (ii) the report of the administration of the preceding financial year; (iii) the development and other programme of work proposed for the current financial year; (iv) the last audit note and replies (if any) made thereto; (v) any other matter which the Standing Committee, Block-level committee or Chief Executive or any officer authorised by the Standing Committee or Block-level committee in this behalf, requires to be placed before such meeting.

Here "the development and other programme of work proposed for the current financial year" is comparable, to some extent, to the "annual plan" provided in Section 19 of the West Bengal Panchayati Raj Act, 1973.

In principle, the village panchayat can appoint subcommittees. Article 49 of the Bombay Village Panchayats Act, 1958, states:

> A panchayat may from among its members, constitute committees for the purpose of exercising such powers, and discharging such duties and performing such functions as may be delegated or assigned to them by the panchayat, and may appoint any member or a committee of members to enquire into and report on any matter referred to them.

However, the authority of village panchayats in Maharashtra to carry out planning exercises was circumscribed. As far as the Warwat Khanderao village panchayat was concerned, the scope of autonomy in the panchayat's functional domain in Maharashtra was significantly less than in West Bengal. As described in section 3.8, the Warwat Khanderao village panchayat continued to function within the "permissive functional domain." The line departments and the District Rural Development Agencies controlled the planning exercises, and, furthermore, a hierarchy of revenue officials (*patwari, tehsildar* and District Collector under the Revenue Department) had extensive administrative powers in Maharashtra. The village panchayat did not demonstrate initiative for rural development except for schemes for drinking water, sanitation, ICDS, MGNREGS, and public distribution. The village panchayat prepared wish lists of beneficiaries for schemes such as the IAY and the *Sanjay Gandhi Niradhar Yojana* but it acted as an agency of the Block-level committee or the State or Central governments for implementation of schemes. Capabilities of the village council for the planning exercise were quite restricted in this regard. Therefore, it is difficult for the village panchayat to have a holistic vision of development in planning.

In West Bengal, the District Planning Committees (DPCs) were constituted in conformity with the West Bengal District Planning Committee Rules, 1994, based on Article 243 ZD of the Constitution. The DPCs' Plan was considered independent of the State Plan and was not integrated with the latter. As mentioned before, the District Rural Development Agencies (DRDAs) were reportedly merged with the district panchayats in April 2000 and their resources, facilities, and manpower are available to the panchayati raj institutions.

However, the ELA of West Bengal found that Bardhaman district, in which the Raina village panchayat lies, prepared draft Development Plans for 2005–6, 2007–8, and 2008-9, which were duly accepted by the DPC, but no draft Development Plan was prepared for 2003–4, 2004–5, and 2006–7.[98] Moreover, the district did not prepare the statement showing the annual execution of the prepared plan.

The Third State Finance Commission of West Bengal argued that "DPCs in West Bengal have failed in the mandatory responsibility of preparing the District Plan scientifically." The Commission stated:

> a disparate set of schemes stitched together without proper integration have been put into volumes and labeled now as District Plans in all the districts. The terms like integrated District Plan, consolidation of schemes, and comprehensive plan are being loosely used in most of the instruction manuals,

[98] However, the Examiner of Local Accounts, West Bengal (2009, pp. 11–2) points out that functioning of (DPCs) is not necessarily effective. The ELA found, for example, that the Bardhaman district prepared draft Development Plans (DPs) for the years 2005–6, 2007–8, and 2008–9, which were duly accepted by the DPC but no draft DP was prepared for the years 2003–4, 2004–5, and 2006–7, and did not prepare the statement showing annual execution of plan prepared.

plan guidelines, Government orders and training materials without conceptual clarity or operational directions.[99]

According to the Commission, one reason for this failure is that Activity Mapping, on which the devolution of funds to each local body was to be patterned, does not clearly define functions, and activities for each tier of panchayats in West Bengal.[100] Executive orders with respect to Activity Mapping are not published in the official gazette. Hence panchayats do not clearly know their roles and responsibilities, which is a prerequisite for effective planning. Another reason is that the DPCs in West Bengal do not have the expertise and office support that they need to function properly.[101] Therefore, the Commission urgently recommended the rejuvenation of the DPCs in West Bengal, and stated that "West Bengal may, perhaps, review the situation and draw upon the benefit of Kerala's experience for rejuvenation of the DPC and the District Plan."[102]

The West Bengal Panchayat Act authorises all tiers of panchayati raj institutions to prepare annual and five-year plans. The West Bengal Panchayati Raj Act, 1973, envisages that:

---

[99] Third State Finance Commission of West Bengal (2008, pp. 131–2). The Commission noted that "one cannot blame the DPCs for such conditions as, in addition to the primary deficiency in respect of devolution, they do not have adequate expertise and office support for effective functioning," and that "West Bengal may, perhaps, review the situation and draw upon the benefit of Kerala's experience for rejuvenation of the DPC and the District Plan" (*Ibid.*, p. 132).

[100] *Ibid.*, p. 130. "The panchayat plans should refer to the assigned Functions/Activities. Unfortunately, such assignment of functions with appropriate division of sub-functions and sub-activities (Activity Mapping) has not been done by the State Government as yet, as discussed. The panchayats at all the three tiers, therefore, do not know what their specific responsibilities are. They do not know exactly what role they are to play in respect of Primary Education, Primary Health Care, Water Supply, and so on. Along with the functions, the finance is also not known."

[101] *Ibid.*, pp. 127–32. "DPCs . . . cannot facilitate the preparation of the District Plans by ensuring the participation of official experts, elected members of local bodies, non-official experts nominated by the State Government and the local bodies and also individual and voluntary groups interested in joining the planning process." (*ibid.*, p. 132) "It is worth mentioning in this connection that the same situation was prevailing in Kerala a few years back. Kerala has, however, changed the position now. Apart from the steps taken to clarify the devolution of functions, allocation of resources etc., the State has strengthened the DPCs by associating them with experts from various sources – technical people from the departments, colleges, universities, and various institutes including NGOs working on development and related activities."

[102] *Ibid.*, p. 132.

A village panchayat shall function as a unit of self-government and, in order to achieve economic development and secure social justice for all, shall, subject to such conditions as may be prescribed or such directions as may be given by the State Government, –

(a) prepare a development plan for the five-year term of the office of the members and revise and update it as and when necessary with regard to the resources available;

(b) prepare an annual plan for each year by the month of October of the preceding year for development of human resources, infrastructure and civic amenities in the area;

(c) implement schemes for economic development and social justice as may be drawn up by, or entrusted upon it. (Section 19)

Further, village panchayats in West Bengal adopted a bottom-up style of planning. In the decentralisation process the focus of development activities in West Bengal shifted towards the village panchayat or sub-panchayat (village assembly) level.[103] The Raina village panchayat prepared an Action Plan each year for implementation in the succeeding financial year and the preparation of the Action Plan began at the village assembly-level general meetings (in November). The people attending the meeting made an assessment of the work that needs to be done in that year in the village and an Action Plan was drawn up for each village assembly based on these demands. The panchayat received all Action Plans from the village assembly to prepare the panchayat's Action Plan. The village development committees may assist the village assembly "in the preparation and implementation of its prospective plan for five years and annual plan" (Section 74) for achieving economic development and social justice. As mentioned before, the village panchayat could not omit or refuse to act upon any recommendation of a village assembly relating to prioritisation of any list of beneficiaries, schemes or programmes in so far as it relates to the village assembly.

At the sub-panchayat level, therefore, the village development committees were entrusted with the preparation of village-level plans ("Action Plan") of the village assembly, which was the basis of the panchayat plan. The village development committee was also responsible for the implementation and monitoring of schemes at the village assembly level. Village panchayats devolved a part of the funds to the village development committees for implementation of different developmental programmes. The implementation

[103] *Ibid.*, p. 134.

of the Annual Action Plan was assessed at the village assembly meeting. In this way the West Bengal State Government engaged in a bottom-up style planning exercise with a special focus on village panchayats and their village assembly. In fact, the Panchayats and Rural Development Department of West Bengal, with the support of the Department for International Development (DFID), Government of the United Kingdom, intended to upscale this planning process under the Programme for Strengthening Rural Decentralisation (SRD).[104] Thus, village assembly-plan-based panchayat planning, the panchayat-plan based Block-level-committee planning and, the Block-level-committee-plan-based district panchayat planning were pursued in West Bengal.

Village panchayats in West Bengal and their village assemblies were also implementing schemes of the State and the Centre as in Maharashtra. Most of the projects that could be taken up under the different types of schemes and funds were specified by the funding authority of the State or the Centre. Even the Panchayat and Rural Development Department of West Bengal recognised that panchayats in West Bengal "perform tasks on behalf of the State primarily as an agent of the Government."[105] Nevertheless, the village panchayat's authority in West Bengal to carry out planning exercises was not as restricted as in Maharashtra. As mentioned in section 3.8, the Raina village panchayat had some autonomy with regard to poverty alleviation, the MGNREGA schemes, and SHG activities. The village panchayat also had some autonomous space of functioning through its initiative for the convergence of public health-related activities.

However, most of the line departments have not adequately devolved functions in West Bengal. The Panchayat and Rural Development Department of West Bengal had a "Roadmap for developing various capacities within the panchayats so as to respond to the need-based demands of the people and acquire more responsibilities of their own for realisation of such demands, stemming from the local needs and aspirations."[106] In order to follow up on this roadmap and prepare a plan, village panchayats in West Bengal need a vision of holistic development.

---

[104] Barr, Basavraj, Girdwood, Harnmeijer, Mukherjee, Prakash, Thornton, ITAD with KIT, and Verulam Consultants (2007).
[105] Panchayats and Rural Development Department, Government of West Bengal (2009b, p. 14).
[106] *Ibid.*, p. 13.

CONCLUSION

The legislative framework for panchayati raj institutions in Maharashtra and West Bengal were similar since they had to meet the constitutional requirements of the Seventy-Third and Seventy-Fourth Amendments. However, the actual functioning of the panchayati raj institutions in the two States differed in several respects. In our attempt to understand the functioning of village panchayats in two States, we selected two village panchayats for a case study. In this chapter, we have presented a profile of the panchayats and discussed some of the differences in institutional mechanisms and structures in the two panchayats, with the help of secondary material available and extensive interviews conducted at the two panchayats. The major differences that have emerged from our discussion are as follows:

(i) The scale of village panchayats: The geographical area, number of villages and population under the jurisdiction of each panchayat were very different in the two states. A village panchayat in Maharashtra usually covers only one or two villages, and a population of roughly 1000. The geographical boundary of the Warwat Khanderao village panchayat is identical to the Census and revenue village of Warwat Khanderao. In contrast, a village panchayat in West Bengal covers a cluster of villages. Therefore, a village panchayat in West Bengal consists of many Census/revenue villages, or "*mouzas*." The population covered by a village panchayat is much larger in West Bengal, roughly 10,000. The village panchayats are subdivided into electoral wards or "village assembly." The average number of voters in the village assembly was 752 in 2006–7. The electoral wards may coincide with the village boundaries, but larger villages may be divided into several electoral wards.

(ii) The land revenue systems were traditionally different. A large part of bureaucratic administrative structures in India originate from the colonial revenue-collection system. Maharashtra is part of the erstwhile temporarily settled or *raiyatwari* (*ryotwari*) areas that were cadastrally surveyed, and where a land revenue officer collects and revises village-level land records annually. On the other hand, West Bengal is part of the erstwhile permanently settled or *zamindari* areas that were cadastrally surveyed, but where no village-level agency exists for assessment and collection of land revenue. The revenue administrative officials have greater administrative powers and responsibilities in Maharashtra than their counterparts in the Land and Land Reforms Department in West Bengal. Panchayats in Maharashtra receive a share of the land revenue collected by the land revenue department. This is not the case in West Bengal. Also, the revenue administrative officials in Maharashtra had extensive powers and responsibilities in domains other than land-revenue assessment and collection.

(iii) The Maharashtra State Government has traditionally placed emphasis on districts as basic units of planning and development. In fact, generous amounts of resources are allocated to the district panchayats in Maharashtra. More resources were allocated to the village panchayat level in West Bengal than in Maharashtra.

(iv) Coordination mechanisms between the panchayat and different line department functionaries was weak in rural Maharashtra. There was, however, some coordination in West Bengal between the panchayat and line departments for the implementation of certain schemes and programmes, such as an interlinked health and child care system among the village panchayat, the ICDS centre, and the Block Primary Health Centre.

(v) Functional domains for each level of the panchayat, Activity Mappings were substantially different between the two States.

(vi) The District Planning Committees (DPCs) in both States were not sufficiently functional. In particular, the DPCs in Maharashtra were not operating as per the requirements of the Seventy-Third Amendment Act, 1992. A cabinet minister of the Maharashtra State Government was appointed as the "guardian minister" (*palak mantri*) for each district and was the chairman of the DPC. Line departments and District Rural Development Agencies (DRDAs) continued to have the major control over DPCs in Maharashtra.

(vii) The village panchayat's authority to carry out planning exercises was more limited in Maharashtra than in West Bengal. Panchayats in West Bengal had more autonomy in the functional domain than in Maharashtra.

(viii) Poverty alleviation was traditionally a core activity of the panchayats of West Bengal. In Maharashtra, however, poverty alleviation was not necessarily the aim of the panchayat's expenditures.

APPENDIX 3.1

SCHEDULE I (VILLAGE LIST) OF THE BOMBAY VILLAGE PANCHAYATS ACT, 1958
(SECTION 45)

Subjects of activities including development activities

Agriculture
1. Making arrangement for cooperative management of lands and other resources in village; organisation of collective cooperative farming
2. Improvement of agriculture (including provision of implements and stores) and establishment of model agricultural farms
3. Bringing under cultivation waste and fallow lands vested by Government in the panchayats
4. Reclamation of wasteland and bringing wastelands under cultivation with the prior permission of the State Government
5. Establishment and maintenance of nurseries for production of improved seeds and encouraging their use
6. Crop experiments
7. Crop protection
8. Ensuring conservation of manurial resources; preparing compost and sale of manure
9. Securing minimum standards of cultivation in the village with a view to increasing agricultural production
10. Assistance in the implementation of land reform schemes
11. Establishment of granaries

Animal Husbandry
12. Improvement of cattle and cattle breeding and general care of livestock

Forests
13. Raising, preservation, improvement and regulation of the use of village forests and grazing lands, including lands assigned under section 28 of the Indian Forests Act, 1927

Social Welfare
14. Relief of the crippled, destitute and the sick
15. Promotion of social and moral welfare of the village, including promotion of prohibition, the removal of untouchability, amelioration

of the condition of backward classes, eradication of corruption, and the discouragement of gambling and useless litigation

16. Women's and Children's organisation and welfare.

Education

17. Spread of education
18. Other educational and cultural objects[107]
    18-A. (Maintenance and Repairs of Primary School Buildings)[108] vesting for the time being in the district committee (*zilla parishad*)
19. Provision of equipment and playgrounds for schools
20. Adult literacy centres, libraries and reading rooms
21. Rural Insurance

Medicine and Public Health

22. Providing medical relief
23. Maternity and child welfare
24. Preservation and improvement of public health
25. Taking of measures to prevent outbreak, spread or recurrence of any infectious disease
26. Encouragement of human and animal vaccination
27. Regulation by licensing or otherwise of tea, coffee and milk shops
28. Construction and maintenance or control of slaughterhouses
29. Cleansing of public roads, drains, *bunds*, tanks, and wells (other than tanks and wells used for irrigation), and other public places or works
30. Reclaiming of unhealthy localities
31. Removal of rubbish heaps, jungles, growth, prickly pears, filling in of disused wells, insanitary ponds, pools, ditches, pits or hollows, prevention of water-logging in irrigated areas and other improvements in sanitary conditions
32. Construction and maintenance of public latrines
33. Sanitation, conservation, prevention and abatement of nuisance and disposal of unclaimed corpses and animal carcasses
34. * * * *[109]
35. Excavation, cleansing and maintenance of ponds for the supply of water to animals.

---

[107] Entry 18-A was inserted in 1971.
[108] These words were substituted for the words "which may be vesting in the *Zilla Parishad* or Block-level committee" in 1977.
[109] Entry 34 was deleted in 1997.

36. Management and control of bathing or washing *ghats* which are not managed by any authority.
37. Provision, maintenance and regulation of burning and burial grounds

Building and Communications

38. Maintenance and regulation of the use of public buildings, tanks and wells (other than tanks and wells used for irrigation) vesting in or under the control of the panchayats.
39. Removal of obstructions and projections in public streets or places and in sites, not being private property, which are open to the public, whether such sites are vested in the panchayat or belong to Government[110] [removal of unauthorised cultivation of any crop on any grazing land or any other land not being private property]
40. Construction, maintenance and repair of public roads, drains, *bunds* and bridges:
    provided that, if the roads, drains, *bunds*, and bridges vest in any other public
    authority such works shall not be undertaken without the consent of the authority
41. Planting of trees along roads, in marketplaces and other public places and their maintenance and preservation
42. Provision and maintenance of playgrounds, public parks, and camping grounds
43. Construction and maintenance of *dharmasalas*
44. Extension of village sites and regulation of buildings in accordance with such principles as may be prescribed
45. Lighting of the village

Irrigation

46. Minor irrigation

Industries and Cottage Industries

47. Promotion, improvement and encouragement of cottage and village industries

Cooperation

48. Organisation of credit societies and multi-purpose cooperative societies

---

[110] These words were added in 1970.

49. Promotion of cooperative farming.

Self-Defence and Village Defence
50. Watch and ward of the village: provided that the cost of watch and ward shall be levied and recovered by the panchayat from such person in the village, and in such manner, as may be prescribed
51. Village Volunteer Force and Defence Labour Bank
52. Rendering assistance in extinguishing fires and protecting life and property when fire occurs
53. Regulating, checking and abating of offensive or dangerous trades or practices

General Administration
54. Preparation, maintenance, and upkeep of panchayat records
55. Numbering of premises
56. Registration of births, deaths and marriages in such a manner and in such form as may be laid down by the Government by general or special order in this behalf
57. Collection of land revenue (when entrusted by the State Government under section 169)[111]
58. Maintenance of village records relating to land revenue in such manner and in such form as may be prescribed from time to time by or under any law relating to land revenue
59. Preparation of plans for the development of the village
60. Drawing up of programmes for increasing the output of agriculture and non-agricultural produce in the village
61. Preparation of the statement showing requirement of supplies and finances needed for carrying out rural development schemes
62. Establishment, control and management of cattle pounds
63. Destruction of stray and ownerless dogs and pigs
64. Disposal of unclaimed cattle
65. Construction and maintenance of houses for the conservancy staff of the panchayat
66. Reporting to proper authorities village complaints which are not disposable by the panchayat
67. Making surveys
68. Acting as a channel through which assistance given by the Central or State Governments for any purpose may reach the village

---

[111] These words were substituted for the words "to the extent provided under" in 1965.

69. Establishment, maintenance and regulation of fairs, pilgrimages and festivals

70. Establishment and maintenance of markets, provided no market shall be established without prior permission of the district panchayat.

71. Control of fairs, *bazaars*, tonga stands and car stands

72. Establishment and maintenance of warehouses

73. Establishment and maintenance of works or the provision of employment in time of scarcity.[112] [73-A. Provision of employment to needy local persons seeking manual work under any scheme for employment guarantee undertaken or adopted by, or transferred to, the panchayat]

74. Preparation of statistics of unemployment

75. Assistance to residents when any natural calamity occurs

76. Organising voluntary labour for community works and works for the uplift of the village

77. Opening fair price shops

78. Control of cattle stands, threshing floors, grazing grounds and community lands.

79.[113] Securing[or continuing][114] postal facilities of experimental post offices in the village by providing for payment of non-refundable contribution to the Posts and Telegraphs Department, wherever necessary]

---

[112] Entry 73-A was added in 1970.
[113] Entry 79 was added in 1969.
[114] These words were inserted in 1970.

Table 3.1.1 *Activity Mapping in West Bengal*

Activity Mapping (since redrafted) worked out by the Panchayats and Rural Development Department's status of devolution of functions to different tiers of panchayats [Executive Order No. 6102/PN/O/ dated 07.11.2005 and No. 3969/PN/O/ dated 25.07.2006 and No. 4769/PN/O/ dated 29.10.2007]

Item No.	Subject (as per Schedule XI)	Activities	Activities of district committee	Activities of Block-level committees	Activities of village panchayat
1.	Agriculture, including agricultural extension	1. Distribution of mini-kits, seeds, bio-fertilizer at subsidised price	1. Sub-allotment of mini-kits, seeds, bio-fertilizer (at subsidised price) to intermediate panchayat (panchayat samiti - PS) for distribution among farmers	1. Fix target for distribution of mini-kits, seeds, bio-fertilizer (at subsidised price) to village panchayats	1. Beneficiary selection for distribution of mini-kits, seeds, equipment at subsidised prices
		2. Distribution of agricultural equipment	2. Fix target for each PS for distribution of agricultural equipment	2. Monitor proper and timely distribution of agricultural equipment on the basis of technical possibilities and field situation	
		3. Awareness campaign and wide publicity among farmers 4. Management of Agrifarm			3. Awareness campaign and wide publicity among farmers 4. Estimation of need-based requirement of seeds
2.	Land improvement, implementation of land reforms, land consolidation and soil conservation	1. Watershed Development Programme/Hariyali scheme covering soil conservation, irrigation, afforestation, etc.			
		2. Distribution of vested lands to the landless	2. Distribution of vested lands to the landless	2. (i) Pre-distribution survey of undistributed agri-land	2. Identification of beneficiary for distribution of vested land

Table 3.1.1 *(continued) Activity Mapping in West Bengal*

Item No.	Subject (as per Schedule XI)	Activities	Activities of district committee	Activities of Block-level committees	Activities of village panchayat
3.	Minor irrigation, water management and watershed development.	1. Development of Minor Irrigation system		and preparation of a priority list of beneficiaries (ii) Distribution of patta to landless people	1. Identification of locations for projects and beneficiaries
				1. Seeking technical vetting of Executive Engineers through district council (ZP) for Minor Irrigation schemes beyond the competence of intermediate panchayat (PS) and joint supervision / monitoring of schemes	
		2. Construction of tanks and field channels			2. Construction of percolation tanks, field channels within the village panchayat
		3. Management of deep tubewells and cluster of shallow tubewells			3. Maintaining Minor Irrigation schemes, collecting water charges through User Committee for new projects handed over to PRIs
		4. Watershed Development Programme		4. Watershed Development Programme/ Hariyali Scheme	

Table 3.1.1 *(continued) Activity Mapping in West Bengal*

Item No.	Subject (as per Schedule XI)	Activities	Activities of district committee	Activities of Block-level committees	Activities of village panchayat
4.	Animal husbandry, dairying and poultry	1. To identify beneficiaries of different animal husbandry, dairy and poultry schemes.			1. Beneficiary selection for different schemes
		2. Breed upgrading through distribution of improved variety livestock	2. Distribution of improved variety of livestock to Blocks	2. Collection of improved variety of livestock from District Farm and determining scale of distribution to panchayats	2. Distribution of improved variety birds/small animals to farmers
		3. Rearing of birds and small animals: family scheme and individual scheme			3. Providing facility for hatching
		4. Vaccination programme	4. Drawing up action plan for vaccination programme for the district	4. Monitoring of the situation to prevent outbreak of epidemic	4. Vaccination of animals against epidemic
		5. Artificial Insemination programme	5. Action plan for Artificial Insemination programme for the district	5. Monitoring of Artificial Insemination programme; identifying problem areas and covering gap	5. Execution of Artificial Insemination with the help of Prani Bandhu at fixed price
5.	Fisheries	1. Identification of beneficiaries, ponds, derelict, semi-derelict tanks		1. Approval of beneficiaries, ponds, open-cast pits, derelict/semi-derelict tanks for pisciculture	1. (i) Identification of beneficiaries and their ponds and open-cast pits (ii) Identification and selection of derelict/semi-derelict tanks

Table 3.1.1 (*continued*) *Activity Mapping in West Bengal*

Item No.	Subject (as per Schedule XI)	Activities	Activities of district committee	Activities of Block-level committees	Activities of village panchayat
		2. Organising training and awareness camps	2. Action plan for all sorts of training and awareness camps in consultation with the Asst. Director of Fisheries	2. Organisation of training and selection of training venue	2. Holding awareness camps
		3. Distribution of mini-kits			
		3. Helping fish farmers to access credit from financial institutions	3. Allocation of funds and components for Blocks in kind	3. Credit access to fish farmers from financial institutions	3. Supply of lime and mini-kits
		4. Improvement of tanks for fish cultivation		4. Excavation of tanks	4. Improvement of tanks for pisciculture
6.	Social forestry and farm forestry	1. To establish nurseries for the supply of saplings and seedlings			1. To establish nurseries for supply of saplings and seedlings
		2. Execution of social forestry projects in waste-lands and roadsides			2. Selection of sites for plantation and execution of the work through self-help groups/village development committees
		3. Establishing Progeny Nursery		3. Establishing Progeny Nursery for fruit-bearing trees	
7.	Minor forest produce	1. Maintenance of social forestry through self-help		1. Distribution of inputs for microenterprise like sal-leaf	1. Maintenance of Social Forestry through self-help

Table 3.1.1 (continued) *Activity Mapping in West Bengal*

Item No.	Subject (as per Schedule XI)	Activities	Activities of district committee	Activities of Block-level committees	Activities of village panchayat
		groups/village development committees for livelihood		plate-making, saplings of fruit trees and providing assistance for income-generating activities	groups/village development committees
		2. Distribution of sale proceeds to self-help groups/village development committees			2. From sale proceeds the panchayat will get a share to recoup actual expenditure. The balance amount will go to self-help groups/village development committees for livelihood
8	Small-scale industries, including food processing industries.	1. Development of small enterprises and entrepreneurs 2. Skill development training programmes 3. Organising credit facility	1. Organisation of entrepreneur development programmes 2. Organising skill development training program 3. Coordination between entrepreneurs and financial institutions for credit linkage	1. Selection of trainees/venue for training programmes 2. Selection of entrepreneurs for training 3. Developing microenterprise/self-enterprise with bank credit	1. Identification of microenterprise/entrepreneurs
9.	Khadi, village and cottage industries	1. Identification of beneficiaries and forming groups 2. To arrange training for	1. Action plan for development of microenterprise	1. Selection of trainees/venue for skill development training programme	1. Group formation and selection of activities 2. Identification of training

Table 3.1.1 (*continued*) Activity Mapping in West Bengal

Item No.	Subject (as per Schedule XI)	Activities	Activities of district committee	Activities of Block-level committees	Activities of village panchayat
		skill development/ upgradation of artisans 3. Motivation of artisans 4. To assist in accessing credit from financial institutions by artisans		4. Accessing credit from financial institutions	need for skill development training and beneficiaries 3. Motivation of rural artisans 4. Organisation of awareness camps at the panchayat level
10.	Rural housing	1. Beneficiary selection for housing schemes 2. Financial assistance to beneficiaries 3. Monitoring and supervision		3. Monitoring and supervision	1. Beneficiary selection in the meetings of the rural ward (*gram sansad*) 2. Distribution of funds to individuals
11.	Drinking water	1. Identification of schemes, locations 2. Formulation of projects and schemes 3. Technical approval of schemes	2. Formulating major water supply schemes (piped water supply) 3. Technical approval of schemes beyond the competence of Block-level committees	2. Selection of location and beneficiaries for pipe-water schemes in consultation with village panchayats 3. Seeking technical approval from district panchayat for projects beyond the competence of Block-level committees	1. Identification of schemes and locations

Table 3.1.1 (continued) *Activity Mapping in West Bengal*

Item No.	Subject (as per Schedule XI)	Activities	Activities of district committee	Activities of Block-level committees	Activities of village panchayat
		4. Execution of schemes	4. Execution of schemes beyond the competence of Block-level committees	4. Execution of schemes (e.g. DTW/Mark-II/Tara Hand Pump) beyond the competence of village panchayats	4. Construction of wells, tanks, tubewells (ordinary hand pump)
		5. Maintenance and periodical disinfection		5. Handing over schemes to panchayats/User Committees for day-to-day maintenance	5. Repair of tubewells and periodical chlorination of open wells and disinfection of tubewells
12.	Fuel and fodder	1. Promotion of biogas-plant training in the construction of smokeless chulhas.		1. To provide assistance and supervision in construction of biogas plants	1. Awareness generation and wide publicity
		2. Augmentation of fodder production through distribution of mini-kits, sale of seeds, Kishan Bon, fodder demonstration etc.	2. (i) Fixing scale of distribution of minikit, seeds, manure per block; (ii) Policy decision on purchase of seeds and sub-allotment of fund to different Blocks	2. (i) Supply of mini-kits to different panchayats and fixing scale of distribution of mini-kits per village panchayat; (ii) Monitoring and supervising distribution of mini-kits and sale of seeds to farmers	2. (i) Distribution of mini-kits, seeds, manure to farmers; (ii) Field demonstration to farmers
13.	Roads, culverts, bridges, ferries, waterways and	Planning, construction, upgrading roads, culverts: 1. For connectivity between	1. Constructing and upgra-		

Table 3.1.1 (*continued*) Activity Mapping in West Bengal

Item No.	Subject (as per Schedule XI)	Activities	Activities of district committee	Activities of Block-level committees	Activities of village panchayat
	other means of communication	Blocks and district roads	ding roads/culverts exceeding Rs 10 lakhs	2. Constructing and upgrading roads/culverts amounting to Rs 2 to 10 lakhs	3. Constructing and upgrading roads, culverts, not exceeding Rs 2 lakhs
		2. For connectivity within Block and between village panchayats			
		3.Connectivity between villages within the panchayat (WBM and earthen roads)			
		4. Bridges	4. Construction of bridges		
4.	Rural electrification, including distribution of electricity	1. Issuing certificates regarding electrification of villages (mouzas)			1. Issuing certificates by village head for electrification of villages (mouzas)
		2. Preparation of a master plan for linking different villages(mouzas) with the network	2. Preparation of a master plan for linking different villages (mouzas) with the West Bengal State Electricity Distribution Company Limited (WBSEDCL) network	2. To ensure coordinated efforts between panchayat and other Deptartments in respect of development of electricity infrastructure	
		3. Mobilising consumers		3. Organising workshops/ seminars at Block level for awareness generation	3. Mobilising consumers through authorised franchisees of WBSEB (self-help groups) for connectivity to households
		4. Identification of graded	4. Identification of suitable		

Table 3.1.1 (*continued*) *Activity Mapping in West Bengal*

Item No.	Subject (as per Schedule XI)	Activities	Activities of district committee	Activities of Block-level committees	Activities of village panchayat
		self-help groups	graded self-help groups through DRDC and Standing Committee on Woman and Child Development (Nari O Sishu Unnayan Sthayee Samiti) and capacity-building of self-help groups for working as franchisees of West Bengal State Electricity Distribution Company Limited (WBSEDCL)		
		5. Energy management		5. Demonstration of energy saving devices in Block-level committee office	5. Awareness generation regarding efficient management of energy
		6. Energy saving devices and demonstration of models			6. Demonstration of energy-saving devices in the village-panchayat office
		7. Monitoring constitution of Licensing Board in the district for issuing licences	7. Monitoring constitution of Licensing Board in the district for issuing licences		
15.	Non-conventional energy sources	1. Identification of potential consumers			1. Identification of potential consumers of alternative sources of energy
		2. Technical and financial assistance for installation		2. Extending technical and financial assistance for	

Table 3.1.1 (*continued*) *Activity Mapping in West Bengal*

Item No.	Subject (as per Schedule XI)	Activities	Activities of district committee	Activities of Block-level committees	Activities of village panchayat
		of biogas in potential households 3. Development of demonstration models of biogas 4. Development of energy parks 5. Awareness generation for harnessing alternative sources of energy, including biofuel	4. Development of energy parks for demonstration of alternative sources of energy and biofuel 5. Organising workshops/seminars to emphasise the need of harnessing alternative sources of energy	installation of biogas in potential households 3. Development of demonstration models of biogas, alternative sources of energy and biofuel for publicity	5. Organising awareness camps for harnessing alternative sources of energy, including biofuel
16.	Poverty alleviation programmes	Planning, beneficiary selection and implementation of (a)SGRY, (b)REGS, (c)SGSY, (d)IAY, (e)IGNOAPS, (f)NFBS, (g)Total Sanitation Campaign (TSC), etc.	1. Planning and implementation of works/schemes under SGRY exceeding Rs 10 lakhs 2. To inform State Government for giving unemployment assistance under REGS; receipt of funds from State Government and allotment of funds to BDOs, sending	1. Planning and implementation of works/schemes under SGRY between Rs 2 lakhs and 10 lakhs 2. Approval of action plan and schemes under REGS	1. Planning and implementation of works/schemes under SGRY not exceeding Rs 2 lakhs 2. Preparing list of prospective workers, distribution of job cards, planning and implementation for works under REGS

Table 3.1.1 (continued) Activity Mapping in West Bengal

Item No.	Subject (as per Schedule XI)	Activities	Activities of district committee	Activities of Block-level committees	Activities of village panchayat
			Utilisation Certificates to State Government 3. To allot funds under IAY to panchayats to ensure expenditure of 3% of funds for handicapped persons and sending compiled report of fund utilisation to State Government	3. Monitoring and supervision of IAY programme, collection of report and UC from all panchayats and sending to district panchayats	3. Identification and selection of beneficiaries for IAY through village assembly; handing over funds to beneficiaries
				4. Approval of names of pensioners under IGNOAPS received from the village panchayat	4. Identification of beneficiaries for IGNOAPS through village assembly and disbursing pension to each beneficiary
				5. Sending names of beneficiaries under NFBS to Sub-Divisional Officer for approval	5. Identification of beneficiaries under NFBS through village assembly; recommending names to Block-level committee; releasing fund to beneficiaries through 'account payee' cheques
			6. Releasing funds to Block-level committees for capacity building, organising	6. Selection of NGOs for running Sanitary Marts and organising awareness	6. Awareness camps and motivating people for sanitary toilets; listing of names for

Table 3.1.1 (continued) *Activity Mapping in West Bengal*

Item No.	Subject (as per Schedule XI)	Activities	Activities of district committee	Activities of Block-level committees	Activities of village panchayat
			Sanitary Marts and awareness campaigns	camps through NGOs/Clubs/voluntary organisations for total sanitation	toilet construction and handing over it to Sanitary Mart. Meeting with teachers & members of village education committee for school sanitation
17.	Education, including primary and secondary schools	1. Identification of school-less hamlets (mouzas) 2. Organising alternative school education: Sishu Siksha Karmasuchi (SSK) and Madhyamik Siksha Karmasuchi (MSK); improvement of school infrastructure, e.g. buildings, toilet, kitchen, etc. 3. Information collection/ supervision/ monitoring through EMIS and District Information System for Education	1. Identification of school-less hamlets (mouzas) in district for preparation of status report 2. Preparation of action plan for organising SSK/MSK in district 3. Supervision/monitoring and report collection through District Information System for Education	1. Collection of proposals for new SSK/MSK from panchayats and sending the plan to district panchayat for approval 2. Construction of SSK/MSK from SGRY/RIDF/Untied funds/own-source revenue, etc. 3. Collection of information through EMIS and District Information System for Education and analysis of information	1. Identification of school-less hamlets (mouzas) for opening SSK/MSK and sending proposals to Block-level committee 2. Construction of SSK/MSK through own fund/SGRY/ Untied funds/local contributions and funds received from Block-level committee 3. To supervise attendance of teachers and students, quality of midday meals, distribution of books

Table 3.1.1 (*continued*) *Activity Mapping in West Bengal*

Item No.	Subject (as per Schedule XI)	Activities	Activities of district committee	Activities of Block-level committees	Activities of village panchayat
		4. Fund release for teachers' salary	4. Release of fund for salary of teachers of SSK/MSK		
18.	Adult and non-formal education	1. To impart education up to Madhyamik level to interested adult learners not enrolled in schools	1. Consideration of proposal for opening of new Adult High School. (To be forwarded to the MEE Department with recommendation or otherwise)	1. Publicity and Supervision of Adult High Schools.	1. Publicity and Supervision of Adult High Schools
		2. Monitoring and supervision of Continuing Education Centres	2. Planning, Monitoring and Supervision by the Zilla Saksharata Samiti	2. Monitoring and supervision of Continuing Education Centres	2. Regular contact with Literates/Neo-literates for attendance at Continuing Education Centres
19.	Libraries	1. Establishment and maintenance of libraries and reading rooms and supervision of activities of Rural Libraries	1. Supervision of activities of District Libraries	1. Supervision of activities of Sponsored Libraries	1. Establishment and maintenance of libraries and reading rooms and supervision of activities of Rural Libraries/ CLIC
		2. Dissemination of information on Rural Development Programmes, social issues, locally available resources, functioning of PRIs	2. Sending information to District Library: (i) copies of guidelines/booklets for all development programmes (ii) Annual Report/Budget/Annual Plan of district	2. Sending information to Sponsored Library: (i) copies of guidelines/booklets for all development programmes (ii) copy of Annual Report/Budget/Annual Plan of Block-	2. Sending copies of guidelines/booklets for all development programmes, Annual Report/Budget/Annual Plan of village panchayat and information on social issues to

Table 3.1.1 *(continued) Activity Mapping in West Bengal*

Item No.	Subject (as per Schedule XI)	Activities	Activities of district committee	Activities of Block-level committees	Activities of village panchayat
		3. Disbursing salaries to organisers of CLIC 4. Audit of CLIC by Panchayat Audit and Accounts Officer	panchayat (iii) information on social issues	level committee (iii) information on social issues 3. Disbursing salaries to organisers of CLIC 4. Audit of CLIC by Panchayat Audit and Accounts Officer	Rural Library/CLIC for general information of public
20.	Cultural activities	1. Celebration of red-letter days 2. Organising folk festivals 3. Workshops on Tagore songs, Nazrul songs, and folksongs 4. Selection of films for each Block	1. Selection of Blocks and release of funds 2. Selection of themes for folk festivals 3. Supply of musical instruments and selection of teachers 4. Contact with cinema hall owners and fixing time for film shows	1. Liaison with village panchayats for organising programmes/campaigns 2. Selection of village panchayat for organising folk festivals and providing infrastructural support 4. Contact with schools for publicity among students	1. Wide publicity/campaigns and selection of venues 2. Selection of venues for festivals and identification of participants 4. Distribution of entry tickets/cards
21.	Markets and fairs	1. Management of village markets up to an area of 5 acres.	1. Management of village markets transferred to district panchayat by State Government	1. Management of village markets transferred to Block-level committee by State Government	1. Management of village markets transferred to village panchayats by State Government

Table 3.1.1 *(continued) Activity Mapping in West Bengal*

Item No.	Subject (as per Schedule XI)	Activities	Activities of district committee	Activities of Block-level committees	Activities of village panchayat
		2. To provide licences to hold fairs or	2. Issuing licences to hold fairs		
		3. To issue licence for hat or market		3. To issue licences for establishing markets	
		4. To hold village markets and fairs	4. Acquire and maintain village markets		4. Construction and regulation of markets, holding and regulation of fairs, village markets and exhibition of local produce and products of local handicrafts/home industries
22.	Health and sanitation, including hospitals, Primary Health Centres and dispensaries	1. Maintenance of sub-centres, Bureau of Primary Health Care, Primary Health Centres, District Hospital		1. Maintenance of Bureau of Primary Health Care and Primary Health Centres	1. Maintenance of sub-centres
		2. Procuring materials and their distribution	2. Lifting of materials from State Headquarters and supply to different Blocks	2. Local Purchase of non-medical items required by the Primary Health Centres and Bureaus of Primary Health Care as may be authorised by Health and Family Welfare Department	2. Local Purchase of non-medical items required by the sub-centres as may be authorised by Health and Family Welfare Department
		3. Monitoring and supervision of service delivery system	3. Compilation of reports and returns from Block-level and analysis for	3. Compilation of monthly reports from sub-centers and village panchayats, and	3. Involving Self-Help Groups in monitoring community health

Table 3.1.1 *(continued) Activity Mapping in West Bengal*

Item No.	Subject (as per Schedule XI)	Activities	Activities of district committee	Activities of Block-level committees	Activities of village panchayat
		4. Involving community in promotive and preventive health-care management	monitoring crucial public health indicators 4. Developing Information, Education and Communication materials	analysis for monitoring crucial public health indicators 4. Planning and organisation for Information, Education and Communication activities	4. Disease surveillance to pre-empt outbreak, preventive measures against spread of communicable diseases
23.	Family welfare	1. Universal immunisation including Pulse Polio programme	1. Fund allotment, monitoring and supervision of immunisation programme, including Pulse Polio programme	1. Implementation of immunisation programme	1. Mobilisation of people for immunisation
		2. To assist people in adopting family planning measures through efficient functioning of sub-centres and supervision of health workers' work.	2. Development of infrastructure for institutional delivery	2. Promotion of institutional delivery	2. Promoting planned family norms and practices
		3. Organisation of sterilisation camps	3. Organising sterilisation camps for eligible couples		3. Awareness camps for family planning and sterilisation
		4. Training of traditional birth attendants (dais)		4. Organising training of traditional birth attendants (dais)	
24.	Women and Child Development	1. Mobilising social support against social evils discriminating against women	1. Selection of beneficiaries for non-institutional care of children up to 18 years	1. Recommendation of beneficiaries for non-institutional care of children up to 18 years	1. Awareness generation in villages to motivate parents for pre-school education and

Table 3.1.1 (continued) Activity Mapping in West Bengal

Item No.	Subject (as per Schedule XI)	Activities	Activities of district committee	Activities of Block-level committees	Activities of village panchayat
		2. Formation of self-help groups	2. Monitoring formation of self-help groups, providing financial assistance and creating marketing support for self-help groups	2. Formation of self-help groups and providing training for key activities and group management	immunisation of their children 2. Formation of self-help groups
25.	Social Welfare	1. Identification of beneficiaries for Social Welfare Schemes 2. Issue of Below Poverty Line certificates for Balika Sambriddhi Yojana 3. Identification of beneficiaries for PROFLAL (Provident Fund for Landless Agricultural Labourers)	3. Sanction and allotment of fund for payment to beneficiaries	1. Recommendation of names of beneficiaries for pension schemes to the District Magistrate for approval 3. Maintenance of PROFLAL accounts and payment of money on maturity of scheme or death of beneficiary	1. Identifying beneficiaries for Kishori Shakti Yojana and pension schemes 2. Issuing Below Poverty Line certificates for beneficiaries of Balika Sambriddhi Yojana 3. Identification of PROFLAL beneficiaries and collection of subscriptions
26.	Welfare of women and children	1. Construction of anganwadi Centres 2. Monitoring and supervision	2. Monitoring and	1. Supervision of construction of anganwadi Centers	1. Recommendation of sites for anganwadi Centers and construction of anganwadi Centres 2. Convergence of ICDS

Table 3.1.1 (*continued*) *Activity Mapping in West Bengal*

Item No.	Subject (as per Schedule XI)	Activities	Activities of district committee	Activities of Block-level committees	Activities of village panchayat
		of programmes and convergence of Integrated Child Development Services activities	supervision of anganwadi centres and convergence of activities		activities and reporting of functioning of anganwadi centres in the convergence meeting at the village-panchayat level
27.	Public distribution system	1. Identification of beneficiaries of Antyodaya and Annapurna schemes	1. Approval of beneficiary list	1. Preparation of list of beneficiaries for Below Poverty Line cards	1. Identification and selection of beneficiaries for distribution of Below Poverty Line cards, Antyodaya cards and Annapurna cards
		2. Lifting of food grains from Food Corporation of India	2. Monitoring lifting of food grains from Food Corporation of India	2. Monitoring distribution of food grains to MR dealers	2. Monitoring distribution of food grains from MR shops to beneficiaries
		3. Distribution of ration cards		3. Monitoring preparation and distribution of ration cards	
		4. Selection of Farmers' Cooperative Societies		4. Selection of Farmers' Co-operative Societies for purchase of paddy	4. Providing certificates confirming procurement of paddy from farmers at Minimum Support Price (MSP)
		5. Fixing targets for each rice mill	5. Fixing targets for each rice mill		
		6. Milling of paddy and storing of rice	6. Monitoring milling of paddy and storing of rice in godowns		

Table 3.1.1 (*continued*) *Activity Mapping in West Bengal*

Item No.	Subject (as per Schedule XI)	Activities	Activities of district committee	Activities of Block-level committees	Activities of village panchayat
28.	Maintenance of community assets	1. Development and maintenance of public assets, such as buildings, shopping centres, passenger sheds, bathing ghats, ferry ghats, tanks, community centres, auditoria, playground etc.	1. Manage or maintain any institution for promotion of livelihood, education, health, communication, tourism or public utility works, including auditoria, dispensaries, diagnostic clinics, bus-stands, guest houses, eco-parks constructed by it or vested in it for control and management	1. Management and maintenance of any institution for promotion of livelihood, education, health, communication, tourism or public utility works, including village markets, auditoria, bus-stands, eco-parks, guest houses constructed by it or vested in it for control and management	1. Maintenance of community assets such as public tanks, ghats, public channels, reservoirs, wells, streets, drains, culverts, lamp posts etc.
		2. Construction and maintenance of public assets	2. Management of road side land		2. Construction and maintenance of resting places for travellers and pilgrims, rest houses, cattle sheds, cart stands, and protection and repair of buildings or other property vested in it
		3. Fixing and collecting rents/user charges	3. Fixing and collecting toll, fees, rates as user charges	3. Fixing and collecting tolls, fees, rates as user charges	3. Fixing and collecting tolls, fees, rates as user charges

Source: Third State Finance Commission of West Bengal (2008, Annexure XII).

Table 3.1.2 *Activity Mapping for "Agriculture" as suggested by the Task Force on Devolution of Powers and Functions upon Panchayati Raj Institutions*

Item-1	Activity	Distribution of functions		
		District panchayat (zilla panchayat)	Intermediate panchayat (panchayat samiti)	Village panchayat (gram panchayat)
Agriculture, including agricultural extension.	1. Increasing agricultural, horticultural and vegetable production.	(i) To develop necessary agricultural infrastructure	(i) To help in crop yield estimation through maintaining links with various agencies and village panchayats/farmers	(i) Estimation of crop yield and maintaining a data base
		(ii) To prepare a comprehensive crop plan	(ii) To advise suitable cropping system based on location-specific characteristics.	(ii) To assist in preparation of a crop plan
		(iii) To develop and maintain a data base for cropping pattern, land use and inputs use for planning	(iii) To assist DP in organising farmers' fairs, Kisan mela, etc.	(iii) To assist in advising farmers about remunerative crop activities and crop diversification
		(iv) To maintain inventory of technological options	(iv) To organise on-farm verification trials and demonstration of new technologies	(iv) To assist in identifying progressive farmers for adoption and diffusion of new technologies
		(v) To propagate adoption of new technologies	(v) Reporting and initiating action plan for different items	(v) To help in providing custom hiring services for plant protection equipment and farm implements
		(vi) To organise farmers' (kisan) melas, fairs and	(vi) To coordinate activities of field-level extension	(vi) To generate awareness in use of organic vermiculture, etc.

Table 3.1.2 (continued)

Item-1	Activity	District panchayat (zilla panchayat)	Distribution of functions Intermediate panchayat (panchayat samiti)	Village panchayat (gram panchayat)
		(vii) To arrange awards to best progressive farmers (viii) To protect bio-diversity and promote profitable crop technologies	workers and officials (vii) To act as a link between DP and village panchayats for transfer of knowledge and technologies	exhibitions
	2. Assessment and distribution	(i) To prepare a consolidated plan for input requirement of inputs (ii) To acquire and arrange distribution of inputs in time (iii) To improve adequate storage facilities for inputs (iv) To monitor distribution of quality inputs	(i) Assessing inputs needs for village panchayats and forwarding consolidated request to DPs (ii) Ensuring timely availability of required inputs to village panchayats (iii) Arranging storage and transport facilities for inputs (iv) Close monitoring of the inputs delivery system	(i) To assist in assessing needs of various inputs such as seeds, fertilizers, pesticides. (ii) To assist in timely distribution of adequate inputs to farmers
	3. Credit support	(i) Preparing a credit plan	(i) To assist in preparing credit plans	(i) To assist in assessing credit needs of various groups of

Table 3.1.2 (continued)

Item-1	Activity	Distribution of functions		
		District panchayat (zilla panchayat)	Intermediate panchayat (panchayat samiti)	Village panchayat (gram panchayat)
		(ii) Ensuring timely credit availability and linkage between agricultural development and credit institutions, and monitoring credit mobilisation	(ii) Ensuring timely credit from formal institutions	farmers and crops. (ii) Exercising social control and regulating interest areas and recovery of loans from formal and informal credit institutions.
		(iii) Help in strengthening cooperative credit institutions	(iii) Monitoring credit delivery system.	(iii) Help in formation of self-help groups
	4. Extension support	(i) To maintain linkage with research and training organisations and agriculture departments	(i) to monitor the visit of extension workers to village farms.	(i) Identifying suitable plots for conducting soil and demonstration
		(ii) to ensure regular visits of extension staff and to help in disseminating new technologies	(ii) To prepare plans for visiting extension workers and monitor their work.	(ii) Selecting farmers for participating in farmers' (kisan) melas and training.
		(iii) To ensure regular training of extension officials for updating their knowledge of advancements in technologies.	(iii) To advise and identify extension officials for training	
			(iv) To assist scientists in identifying local problems for designing their research work	

Table 3.1.2 (continued)

Item-1 Activity	Distribution of functions		
	District panchayat (zilla panchayat)	Intermediate panchayat (panchayat samiti)	Village panchayat (gram panchayat)
		relevant to local needs. (v) Ensuring better linkages between farmers and extension staff.	
5. Soil Testing	(i) To establish soil-testing laboratories and own it (ii) To monitor soil-testing work	(i) To monitor soil-testing work (ii) To help in identifying locations for soil-testing work (iii) To help farmers for improvement of soil fertility as per soil-testing results	(i) To assist technical experts in conducting soil tests (ii) To help in giving feedback from soil-testing to farmers. (iii) Selection of beneficiaries for relief of Natural calamities and undertaking distribution of assistance.
6. Post-harvest management	(i) To establish and improve storage facilities (ii) To develop marketing infrastructure at suitable locations (iii) Monitoring regulated marketing (iv) To control private traders	(i) Maintenance of godowns (ii) To organise Market Committees and maintain market yards (iii) Regular market charges and ensure correct weights and measures (iv) Ensuring quick sale of pro-	(i) To help in organising farmers for group sale in bulk (ii) To assist in increased awareness about better storage facilities for seeds and foodgrains

Table 3.1.2 (*continued*)

Item-1	Activity	Distribution of functions		
		District panchayat (*zilla panchayat*)	Intermediate panchayat (*panchayat samiti*)	Village panchayat (*gram panchayat*)
		from exploiting farmers (v) To ensure correct weights and measures (vi) Supervision of crop insurance facility	ducts and payment to farmers	
	7. Risk management	(i) To assess losses due to natural calamities and formulate rehabilitation plans (ii) To monitor and supervise relief operations (iii) To arrange crop insurance schemes and coordination among insurance agencies (iv) Preparation of contingency agricultural plans.	(i) To estimate crop losses and report of action (ii) To monitor relief operations (iii) To help in identifying farmers for crop insurance schemes (iv) To assist in providing benefits from crop insurance schemes.	(i) Reporting of losses due to natural calamities and rehabilitation requirements (ii) To supervise relief operations and distribution of materials (iii) To motivate farmers for using crop insurance schemes. (iv) To assist in the implementation of contingency plan.

Source: Ministry of Rural Development (2001).

Chapter 4

BASIC STRUCTURE OF THE MAIN DATA SOURCES
AT THE VILLAGE LEVEL

This chapter describes the existing status of the main data sources in the two village panchayats during the period of our analysis. The reference period of this chapter is from April 2005 to March 2011. We discuss the kinds of village-level data that exist, and are maintained by the village panchayats and other agencies. In the villages we can observe the very roots of the panchayat statistical system, that is, the first stage of collection and recording of panchayat-level statistical data.

4.1 Basic Structure of Statistical Data Sources at the Village Level

We have tried to identify possible village-level data sources to serve the data needs discussed in chapter 2. As the National Statistical Commission noted, "the main sources of statistics in India, as elsewhere, are (a) administrative records – generally consisting of statutory administrative returns and data derived as a by-product of general administration; and (b) other important sources, namely, censuses and sample surveys."[1] Indeed this dichotomy is quite universal. For example, the Organisation for Economic Cooperation and Development states, "There are two basic mechanisms for collecting economic data. They are, access to data already being collected for administrative purposes, and direct survey by the statistical office."[2]

However, this dichotomy was not so clear at the village level. There were some data sources of an intermediate type between administrative records and typical census type-surveys. As will be seen later, some administrative records, such as the Integrated Child Development Services village survey register, were established and regularly updated through census-type survey operations. Some census-type surveys, such as the Below Poverty Line (BPL) Census, were used by the panchayati raj institutions for administrative purposes such as BPL-household identification. In this way, most data

---

[1] National Statistical Commission (2001), para. 14.3.1.
[2] Organisation for Economic Cooperation and Development (OECD) (2002, p. 105). Here, the OECD (2002, p. 106) adds, "Here, the term survey is assumed to include a census as a particular type of survey in which all units are in the sample."

generated and used in the panchayat areas were a by-product of the administrative requirements of the panchayats themselves or other satellite State-government agencies.

Therefore, we classify these data sources according to their relation to the village panchayat in terms of data generation and ownership. That is to say, they could be classified according to whether or not they were generated inside the village panchayat system, where they were generated (if outside the village panchayat system) and how far would they came under the village panchayat's control. Consequently, in the villages, we sometimes found administrative records that had been generated from census-type surveys.

Nevertheless, the Population Census is different from administrative records. It is organised exclusively for statistical purposes by the Central Government. More importantly, it is conducted as per the provisions of the Census Act, 1948, which places a legal obligation upon the public to cooperate and give truthful answers on the one hand, and guarantees confidentiality of their information on the other. Under the Census Act, respondents have less reason to deliberately misreport. The statistical office, however, must guarantee that information on each household is kept strictly confidential and is not used for administrative purposes.

Similarly, official sample surveys are also different from administrative records. The Eleventh Five-Year Plan of the Planning Commission once considered "generat[ing] a local statistical system by increasing the sample size of National Sample Surveys so that interpretation is possible at least at the level of the Block, if not the village."[3] However, the Block-level National Sample Survey has not yet been conducted.[4] In principle, sample surveys can be carried out below the district level by the Central or State Government, or the panchayati raj institutions, but estimation at the level of smaller geographical units would require a larger sample size and/or more complex sample designs.

Thus, the main sources of data at and below the village panchayat level can be classified as follows:

[3] Planning Commission (2008a, p. 227).
[4] Keeping in mind decentralised planning through the panchayati raj institutions, the International Institute for Population Sciences (2010) sponsored by the Ministry of Health and Family Welfare undertook the District Level Household and Facility Survey. Apart from it, Chaudhuri and Gupta (2009) analysed district-wide National Sample Survey data.

1. Registers and records collected and maintained by the village panchayat
2. Census-type surveys independently conducted by the panchayati raj institutions (at the Raina village panchayat in West Bengal, and not in the Warwat Khanderao panchayat in Maharashtra)
3. Registers and records collected and maintained by other village-level agencies, such as:
   a. Village Integrated Child Development Services (or *anganwadi*) registers
   b. Village school registers
   c. Records at the Primary Health Centre
   d. Revenue official records (in Warwat Khanderao), or records at the Block land and land reform office (in Raina)
   e. Others
4. Census-type surveys organised by Central or State Government, such as:
   a. the BPL Census, including the Rural Household Survey (RHS)
   b. the Census of India
   c. Others

In addition to the data sources described above, there were administrative reports concerning the village panchayats and/or the villages. These reports were compiled primarily from secondary data, the original sources of which are listed above in items 1 to 4. The administrative reports were submitted to the Block- or district-level offices and sometimes to the State or Central Governments. The information in these reports was usually not collected by conducting household-to-household, facility-to-facility or plot-to-plot surveys. It was usually gathered from the records already maintained by village-level functionaries, otherwise from the subjective assessment of knowledgeable persons in the village.[5] Such administrative reports were as follows:

5. Administrative reports of the village panchayat, such as:
   a. the Village Schedule
   b. Village-level amenities data (Village Directory data) in the District Census Handbook
   c. the Self-Evaluation Schedule (at Raina only)
   d. Others

---

[5] In the large-scale pilot scheme on Basic Statistics conducted in 2009, many items in the Village Schedule were recorded by knowledgeable persons in the village panchayat. However, there was no validation check on such data (Central Statistics Office 2011, D:3).

4.2 IDENTIFYING THE DATA SOURCES

We have identified the above data sources through interviews using a questionnaire, and by means of follow-up studies after the interviews. In India, no comprehensive list of village-level data sources is available in the panchayat area.[6] Thus, we started the interview with the village panchayat, using main data items extracted from the Village Schedule on Basic Statistics for Local Level Development as a questionnaire, and then adding a few follow-up items regarding the Data Needs I, IA and II to the questionnaire.

The main data items in the Village Schedules provided by the *Basic Statistics for Local Level Development* report include:

(a) Availability of basic facilities in the village. Information on assets available in the village, viz. number of factories, business establishments, bridges, declared forest area, orchards, roads, etc.

(b) Distance of the village from the nearest such facilities

(c) Demographic status of villagers, including population, births, deaths, morbidity, migration, marriages, etc.

(d) Educational status of the villagers

(e) Land utilisation statistics

(f) Data on livestock and poultry

(g) Number of market outlets

(h) Employment status of the villagers[7]

We used these data items as a checklist for the initial stage of our interviews. Keeping in mind the Indian statistical system described by the National Statistical Commission, we discussed sources for the above data at the grass-roots level with the local people. The status of information available at the Warwat Khanderao village panchayat and the Raina village panchayat is shown in Tables 4.1 and 4.2.[8]

[6] In Kerala, one-third of the State's 1997 plan budget was earmarked for local government. In the preparation of local plans, a need arose for a comprehensive database for local-level planning and monitoring of planned activities. The participatory planning process that was encouraged also increased the human-resource requirements at the local level. In order to cope with the needs of local planning, the Kerala government took several initiatives, which included preparing extensive manuals for listing administrative records and information available at the panchayats that could be used for planning. See, for instance, Planning Board, Government of Kerala (1996). All efforts in the direction culminated in the Information Kerala Mission (IKM) that sought to computerise all administrative records and systems in local-government bodies in Kerala (Unnikrishnan 2012, and personal communication).

[7] Central Statistical Organisation (2006, pp. 1–2).

[8] Bakshi and Okabe (2008, pp. 24–5).

Table 4.1 *Status of information available at the Warwat Khanderao village panchayat*

Type of information	If records are available at village panchayat	If records are accessible to village panchayat from other source	Source of information	Comments
Basic facilities	No	No		Facilities that are present are common knowledge. The information is available but not recorded. Only properties transferred by Government and district panchayat to the village panchayat are recorded in the Permanent Asset Register (Village Panchayat Register No. 25).
Number of factories	No	No		
Commercial establishments	No			Common knowledge
Bridges and roads	Yes	Yes	Village Panchayat Register No. 26 (Details of Road under Panchayat Jurisdiction) Record at the patwari office	
Forest area and orchards	Yes (in part)	Yes	Village Panchayat registers, Record at the Revenue official office	Village Panchayat Register No. 27
Distance from nearest facilities	No	Yes	Block Development Office	Also common knowledge
Population	Yes	Yes	Census of India	
Birth and death	Yes	Yes	Civil Registration System, monthly reports	ICDS/anganwadi worker reports to panchayat head on the Monthly Progress Report
Morbidity	No	Yes	Auxiliary Nurse Midwife	
Marriages	No	No	ICDS register (in part)	Common knowledge
Migration	No	No		

Table 4.1 (*continued*)

Type of information	If records are available at village panchayat	If records are accessible to village panchayat from other source	Source of information	Comments
Educational status of villagers	No	Yes	School Register	Including private school
Land utilisation statistics	No	Yes	Record at the relevant Revenue department office	
Livestock and Poultry	No	Yes	Livestock Census	Block Development Office
Number of market outlets	No	No		Common knowledge
Employment status of villagers	No	No		

Table 4.2 *Status of information available at the Raina village panchayat*

Type of information	If records are available with the village panchayat	If records are accessible to the village panchayat from other sources	Source of information	Comments
Basic Facilities	No	No		Facilities that are present are of common knowledge. The village panchayat maintains registers of current facilities being constructed. The information is available but not recorded.
Number of factories	No	No		Common knowledge
Commercial establishments	Yes		Village panchayat's tax register	
Bridges and roads	No	No		Location of such facilities are common knowledge, other information may not be available unless

Table 4.2 *(continued)*

Type of information	If records are available with the village panchayat	If records are accessible to the village panchayat from other sources	Source of information	Comments
				constructed by the village panchayat. If constructed by the panchayat, details can be obtained from the Works Register.
Forest area and orchards	No	Yes	Block Land and Land Reforms Office	
Distance from nearest facilities	No	No		Common knowledge
Population	Yes	Yes	Census of India, ICDS household survey register	
Birth and death	Yes	Yes	Panchayat registers, ICDS registers, PHC registers, monthly reports	
Morbidity	Yes		Monthly report of ICDS, ANM and Health supervisor	
Marriages	No	No		ICDS worker records these in her register, but date not recorded.
Migration	No	No		Some information on permanent out-migration can be obtained from ICDS records
Educational status of villagers	Yes	Yes	Panchayat Sanitation Survey 2008 and ICDS household survey	
Land utilisation statistics	No	Yes	Block Land and Land Reforms Office	
Livestock and Poultry	No	Yes	Livestock Census	Household-level records available
Number of market outlets	No	Yes	Common knowledge and village panchayat's tax register	
Employment status of villagers	No	No		Village-survey register has occupation data

We found in this initial stage of the interviews that the village panchayat maintains records for administrative and other purposes, and that a substantial amount of information is available from these records. In addition, certain types of records (for example, the ICDS registers, the school registers, health records at the primary health centre, records at the *patwari* office) are collected and maintained at the village or Block level by official agencies other than the village panchayats. Panchayat officials have access to such records but full sets of records were not available at the panchayat office.

Thus, we visited official agencies other than the village panchayat both at the village and Block levels. We also visited the Block Development Office to validate the information obtained at the village panchayat and through other official agencies. Again, we conducted follow-up studies at the village panchayat and village levels.

Each item of the Village Schedule on Basic Statistics has a column for entering the source codes. For each data item of the Village Schedule, the following source codes are to be entered:

a) Panchayat–01
b) *Anganwadi* worker–02
c) Health worker (ANM/FHW/MHW/etc.)–03
d) Revenue official (Land Records)–04
e) Village Headman–05
f) Local School/Education Officer–06
g) Local Doctor–07
h) PHC/Sub-Centre/Hospital–08
i) Knowledgeable person(s)/Others (Female–09, Male–10)

However, we found that data sources identified using these source codes were unreliable. Using the source codes, the Cross-Sectional Synthesis Report of the pilot scheme conducted by the Central Statistical Organisation (CSO) observed that in the majority of cases, panchayat offices were the primary data source, providing about 50–55 per cent of the data items in the Schedule. In fact, the source code of panchayat-(01) was entered for most items in the Village Schedule of villages in the Raina panchayat area. As the Raina village panchayat was covered by the same pilot scheme conducted by the CSO, we were actually able to have a close look at the filled-up Village Schedule. However, according to the Executive Assistant of the Raina village panchayat, all information for the Schedule was collected by the Integrated Child Development Services (ICDS) workers. However, our discussion with the ICDS worker at Bidyanidhi village in February 2011 revealed that the Basic Statistics pilot survey in the village was conducted by a primary-school teacher at the Birampur Junior High School and a resident of the same village. The Bidyanidhi ICDS worker had conducted the survey for Bogra village. According to her, she had to depend on information from the ICDS worker at Bogra to fill up her schedule. She also obtained information from the panchayat office. Thus, as far as Raina village's cases are concerned, the implication for the source codes filled up in the Schedule was complicated and ambiguous. If a village panchayat asked an ICDS worker to fill in the Village Schedule on the responsibility of the panchayat, someone could well enter in the columns the source code "Panchayat – 01," instead of the source

Table 4.3 *Status of information available at the Warwat Khanderao village panchayat*

Type of information	If records are available with the village panchayat	If records are accessible to the village panchayat from other sources	Source of information	Comments
Electoral Roll	Yes	Yes	Village panchayat	Updated by the District Collector under the supervision of the State Election Commission
Village panch-ayat meeting	Yes		Village panchayat	
Comprehensive list of residents	No	No		The house tax (property tax) resister and the electoral roll are available. The village panchayat does not use APL–BPL list produced by the BPL Census. The village development officer does not depend on the ICDS village-survey register.
Income and expenditure of the village panchayat	Yes		Village-panchayat registers	
Government schemes implemented or monitored by the panchayat	Yes (in part)	Yes	Village panchayat record (in part)	Panchayat head and village development officer have clear knowledge in this regard.

code "*Anganwadi* worker – 02." Consequently, the source code filled up for each data item does not reflect the actual recording of that item. We had to check them independently on the ground.

In addition to these main items in the Village Schedule – items (a) to (h) – we used a few additional items for checking in further interviews related to the Data Needs I, IA and II. As described in chapter 2, the Village Schedule on Basic Statistics primarily aims at Data Needs III (data requirements for micro-level planning). It does not necessarily serve the Data Needs I, IA and

Table 4.4 *Status of information available at the Raina village panchayat*

Type of information	If records are available with the village panchayat	If records are accessible to the village panchayat from other sources	Source of information	Comments
Electoral roll	Yes	Yes	Village panchayat	Updated under the supervision of the State Election Commission
Village panchayat meeting	Yes		Village panchayat registers	
Comprehensive list of residents	Yes	Yes	ICDS registers, BPL census (Rural Household Survey or RHS)	The village panchayat has an APL–BPL list generated by the BPL census (RHS). The village panchayat sometimes depends on the ICDS village-survey register. Unit-level household data of two household surveys conducted in 2007 and 2008 on instruction from the district panchayat to evaluate the rural sanitation scheme
Income and expenditure of the village panchayat	Yes		Village panchayat registers	
Government schemes implemented or monitored by the panchayat	Yes (in part)	Yes	Village panchayat record, in part	Executive Assistant with the village panchayat has clear knowledge on this subject

II. The additional items, which we discussed with the village-panchayat and Block Development Office functionaries in our follow-up studies were:

j) Electoral Roll and village-panchayat meetings
k) Comprehensive list of residents
l) Income and expenditure of the village panchayat
m) Status of property-tax collection
n) Government schemes implemented or monitored by the village panchayat

The status of information available at the Warwat Khanderao and the Raina village panchayats is shown in Tables 4.3 and 4.4.

4.3 STATUS OF EACH DATA SOURCE

4.3.1 Registers and Records Collected and Maintained by the Village Panchayat

The village panchayat maintained various records for administrative and other purposes. These registers and records were maintained to perform self-governance activities or to track the allocation and expenditure of funds and assess the progress of different schemes. Brief descriptions of the registers maintained at the panchayat offices are given in Tables 4.5 and 4.6.

Registers maintained at the Warwat Khanderao village panchayat: At the panchayat head's residence, the village development officer showed us all the registers (presumably brought from the panchayat office) shown in Table 4.5. The panchayat secretary had a booklet that describes the procedures for using the registers. *Item no. 1 Budget* is used each November to prepare the budget for the coming financial year. The village panchayat takes approval from the village council. The supplementary budget can be tabled for approval. Financial transactions can be made after approval from the panchayat subcommittee. Daily income and expenditure are noted in *Item no. 5 Cash-book*. This register is related to the registers of *Item nos. 6 to 24*. All taxable buildings under the panchayat's jurisdiction are recorded in *Item no. 7 General Receipt Book*. All the new buildings constructed in each year, removal of debris of collapsed buildings, any changes in ownership, and types of building are recorded in this register. *Item no. 8 House tax* is a list of all taxable houses in the jurisdiction of the village panchayat. The house tax here is comparable to property tax in West Bengal. The house-tax list includes information on the location of a house, area of the house site, type of house, name of the owner, name of the occupant, and valuation of the house. The village panchayat updates this register every four years. The one we saw was updated in 2005–6. Under the Bombay Village Panchayats Act, 1958, the village development officer issues *Item no. 3 Bill for deposited items* to all the village residents and asks them to pay the tax at the panchayat's office. If people do not adhere to this directive, then the village development officer sends a demand notice to the defaulting households to deposit their house tax. Unpaid taxes are recorded in *Item no. 9 Tax demand-collection and Balance register*. All house owners in Warwat Khanderao were taxed, regardless of their land ownership. Other tax collections are recorded in *Item no. 10 Tax Collection Receipt Book*. According to the village development officer, tax receipts from water supply (through underground pipes) are also recorded in *Item no. 10*. According to the panchayat head, the water tax is a very important source of revenue for the Warwat Khanderao village panchayat.

The Warwat Khanderao village panchayat did not have a tax list on trade, comparable to *Form 9 Assessment List* in the Raina village panchayat. The village panchayat auctions the right to collect tax from weekly markets held in the village. According to the panchayat head, the highest bid for the right to collect tax from weekly markets was Rs 5000 in 2012, which is also a part of the own-source revenue.

All monthly paid workers and daily wage workers appointed by the village panchayat are recorded in *Item no. 16 Employee Salary Register*, *Item no. 20 Advances and Deposit Register*, and *Item no. 22 Attendance sheet/register*, together with all the details related to their jobs. In Warwat Khanderao, the village panchayat hired a peon, for which the district panchayat and the village panchayat each paid half. The village panchayat also employed daily wage workers for sanitation work.

In 2008, the Twelfth Finance Commission provided a grant of Rs 78,000 to the Warwat Khanderao village panchayat for water supply and sanitation. As a result, the village panchayat spent 60 per cent of that amount on sanitation and water supply, and 40 per cent on the construction of drains. These expenses were recorded in the panchayat's registers. Work done by contractors or workers appointed by the panchayat was recorded in *Item no. 23 Work Estimation/Entry Book*.

All buildings, gutters, public toilets, water supply, wells, tanks, trees, etc.

owned by the village panchayat can be recorded in *Item no. 25 Permanent Asset Register*. Tubewells were recorded in this register. All roads within the panchayat's jurisdiction, with information like length, width and other description of the roads, are recorded in *Item no. 26 Details of Road under GP jurisdiction*. Land from the State government and district panchayat, according to Articles 51 and 56 of the Bombay Village Panchayats Act, 1958, and open space acquired by the panchayat itself, according to Article 55, are recorded in *Item no. 27 Land and Barren Space Register*.

Apart from the registers shown in Table 4.5, the Warwat Khanderao village panchayat had the electoral roll that covers its jurisdiction. The electoral roll

Table 4.5 *List of registers maintained by the Warwat Khanderao village panchayat*

Item no. 1	Budget
Item no. 2	Re-planning
Item no. 3	Bill for deposited items
Item no. 4	Bill for expenditure
Item no. 5	Cash-book
Item no. 6	Classification register
Item no. 7	General receipt book
Item no. 8	House tax
Item no. 9	Tax demand-collection and balance register
Item no. 10	Tax collection receipt book
Item no. 11	Other demand register
Item nos. 12–14	Related to Octroi (do not exist)
Item no. 15	Certificate
Item no. 16	Employee salary register
Item no. 17	Stamp register
Item no. 18	Stock register
Item no. 19	Dead stock register
Item no. 20	Advances and deposit register
Item no. 21	Cash-book for minor amounts
Item no. 22	Attendance sheet/register
Item no. 23	Work estimation/Entry book
Item no. 24	Salary and service register
Item no. 25	Permanent asset register
Item no. 26	Details of roads under village panchayat (*gram panchayat*) jurisdiction
Item no. 27	Land and barren space register

was prepared by the State Election Commission which works outside the panchayati raj system. In Maharashtra, the elections are conducted by the District Collector under the control and supervision of the State Election Commission. At the village-panchayat level, the *patwari* supervises the elections under the control of the State Election Commission.[9] The electoral roll is also essential for the panchayat's usual activities since it is required to call for the village council that consists of persons registered in the electoral roll. The electoral roll contains each voter's identification number, full name, father's name, house number, age, and sex.

The Warwat Khanderao village panchayat maintained the "Monthly meeting attendance register" and "Proceeding book" used for keeping minutes of its meetings. The village panchayat also maintained the Birth and Death register of the Civil Registration System. In rural Maharashtra, the village development officer was officially appointed as a village-level Registrar for the Civil Registration System, although it was actually the office attender who assisted. The latter knew very well about each vital event that has occurred in the past. The village development officer of Warwat Khanderao exercised jurisdiction over three villages, and was in Warwat Khanderao for only two days in a week. The village-level birth and death reports in the Civil Registration System have a legal and a statistical part. The Statistical part, submitted to the District Registrar, contains additional information, such as the mother's place of usual residence, religious affiliation of the family, parents' level of education, parents' occupation, age of the mother at the time of marriage, and the number of live births for the mother.[10] However, as will be seen in section 6.7 in chapter 6, the Civil Registration System determines the place of registration according to the site of the vital events, whether they took place inside the village of the mother's usual residence or not. Since the recording structure of the Civil Registration System is not properly oriented to children resident in the panchayat's jurisdictional area, this added considerable problems to the use of data from this source.

Moreover, the Warwat Khanderao village panchayat had access to registers and records to carry out the schemes of the line departments. Centrally-sponsored schemes under the National Rural Employment Guarantee Act, 2005, are handled by the line department of the Ministry of Rural Development as the Mahatma Gandhi National Rural Employment Guarantee Scheme

---

[9] Interview conducted at the *patwari* office in Warwat Khanderao on August 18–22, 2011.
[10] Office of the Registrar General, India (2001). See also Okabe and Surjit (2012).

(MGNREGS). The MGNREGS aims at the enhancement of livelihood security of rural households by providing at least one hundred days of guaranteed wage employment in every financial year to every household whose adult members volunteer to do unskilled manual work. Workers in families that obtain job cards are entitled to guaranteed employment in public works for up to a hundred days per family in a year.

The village panchayats are the most important units of local government for MGNREGS, since the responsibility of issuing job cards after registering the households and providing employment on demand rests with them. In fact, the Warwat Khanderao village panchayat maintained MGNREGS registers. However, the MGNREGS was not functional in the village when we conducted interviews in 2011 and 2014. According to the panchayat head, the wages paid under this scheme were even lower than the wages of agricultural labourers in and around this village. The panchayat head had asked workers' households to demand work, but the workers were not interested in MGNREGS work for two reasons: it was physically too demanding and the wages were low.[11] There were technical assistants for MGNREGS at the Block level, but not at the village-panchayat level. The register was disclosed on its website by the Management Information System of the MGNREGS of the Ministry of Rural Development. According to the website, 270 households and 627 persons had been registered within the Warwat Khanderao village panchayat under the MGNREGS as of 2012–3. However, only three families obtained employment under this scheme as of 2012–3.

Registers maintained at the Raina village panchayat
In West Bengal, the village panchayat maintained registers and records in the prescribed formats. Table 4.6 gives a list of forms provided in the West Bengal Panchayat (Gram Panchayat Administration) Rules, 2004, and its Amendments, 2006, and West Bengal panchayat (Gram Panchayat Accounts, Audit and Budget) Rules, 2007. Some of these forms are just receipts, certificates or application forms, but some other forms reflect the format for records or registers maintained at the village panchayat. In fact, the Executive Assistant of the Raina village panchayat recognised that the panchayat maintains registers enlisted under the above-stated Rules.

Form 1 to *Form 3* specified under the Gram Panchayat Rules, 2004, are used to

---

[11] Interview with the Sarpanch in Warwat Khanderao in October 2013.

hold panchayat meetings. *Form 2* gives the format for the attendance register and minutes book for panchayat meetings.

Form 36 specified under the Gram Panchayat Rules, 2007 is used for preparing the panchayat's budget. Unlike in Maharashtra, even the village assembly and the subcommittee (*upa-samiti*) of the village panchayat prepare the budget using *Form 34* and *Form 35*. The village development committees have to submit an annual plan to the village panchayat in August each year. Based on these annual plans, the village panchayat prepares and submits its first annual budget to the Block office every October, for the next financial year. The budget is submitted using *Form 36*. In this form, the village panchayat reports actual expenses of the previous year, the approved budget of the current year, and the estimated budget for the coming year. The budget outline is then sent for approval to the Block-level committee. Based on the funds flow till December each year, the panchayat prepares a revised or supplementary budget using *Form 38*. The supplementary budget is sent for approval in February.

Daily income and expenditures are noted in *Form 1 Cash Book for Gram Panchayats* specified under the Gram Panchayat Rules, 2007. *Form 1A* gives the format for cash books for each Programme. The village development committees also have cash books specified in *Form 29*. Half-yearly and annual statement of receipts and payments are to be recorded in *Form 27* and *Form 30*.

The Gram Panchayat Rules, 2004, specify *Form 6 Register for market value of land and building located within the Gram Panchayat*. In this form the following are to be recorded: the holding no./location/address; name of the owner with name of father/mother/husband; name of the occupier/tenant with name of father/mother/husband; total area of land showing built-up and vacant areas; the market value of land; description of the building (i.e. *kutcha/pucca*/one-storey/two-storied/three-storied/multi-storied); use of building for residential/commercial purpose; the market value of the building/construction. All permissions to erect structures or buildings or to make an addition or alteration to an existing structure or building in the panchayat area are to be recorded on *Form 4*. Based on *Form 6* and other forms, assessment lists of persons liable to pay tax on land and buildings within the panchayat area are to be prepared using *Form 9 Assessment List* in order to get approval from the village panchayat and the village assembly. We came across a "Panchayat property tax assessment sheet" at the Raina panchayat office. The name of the landowner or house owner, a description of the property, its current market value, and the tax assessed on each property were the details recorded on this

Table 4.6 *List of registers maintained by the Raina village panchayat*

A. West Bengal Panchayat (Gram Panchayat Administration) Rules, 2004, and its Amendments, 2006

Form 1	Notice of ordinary meeting of village panchayat
Form 1A	Notice of emergent meeting of village panchayat
Form 1B	Notice for requisitioned meeting of the village panchayat by the elected village head
Form 1C	Notice for requisitioned meeting of the village panchayat by the requisitionist members
Form 2	Attendance register and minutes book for panchayat meetings
Form 3	Notice for adjourned meetings of the village panchayat
Form 3A	Report on the work of the panchayat for the year
Form 4	Form of application for permission to erect structures or buildings or to make an addition or alteration to an existing structure or building in a panchayat area
Form 5	Form for appointments
Form 5A	Form for self-declaration on house property
Form 6	Register for market value of land and buildings in the village panchayat
Form 7	Registration certificate for vehicles and/or other equipment
Form 8	Register for registration of vehicle and/or other equipment
Form 9	Assessment list
	Part I List of persons liable to pay tax on land and building within the panchayat area
	Part II List of persons liable to pay registration/renewal fee for running a trade (wholesale or retail) within the panchayat area
	Part III List of persons liable to pay fees for registration of vehicles (not registered under Motor Vehicles Act) within the panchayat area
	Part IV List of institutions/organisations/persons liable to water/lighting/conservancy rate in the panchayat area
	Part V List of enterprises/persons liable to pay registration fees for providing supply of water from deep-tubewell/shallow-tubewell fitted with motor-driven pump sets in the panchayat area
	Part VI List of private enterprises/persons liable to pay fees for displaying of any poster/advertisement/banner/hoarding in any private or public place within the panchayat area
	Part VII List of markets (*haats*) from where fees may be collected on sale of village produce
	Part VIII List of roads/ferries/bridges or other assets or resources from where tolls/fees may be collected
	Part IX List of remunerative assets under the control of the village panchayat
Form 10	Draft assessment list
Form 11	(Trade registration certificate)

B. West Bengal Panchayat (*Gram Panchayat* Accounts, Audit and Budget) Rules, 2007

Form 1	Cash book for the village panchayat
Form 1A	Subsidiary cash book for (each) programme

Form 2	Cheque/draft receipt register
Form 3	Chequebook register
Form 4	Receipts for tax, rates and fees as assessed by the village panchayat
Form 5	Miscellaneous receipt
Form 6	Stock register of receipt books
Form 7	Register for arrears and current demand and collection of taxes
Form 8	Durable stock register
Form 9	Register of assets leased out
Form 10	Acquittance register for honorariums of elected village head / deputy *pradhan* / Director (*Sanchalak*)
Form 11	Acquittance register for pay/allowances of employees
Form 12	Bill for Government grant on account of salary of the employees
Form 13	Utilisation certificate for grant-in-aid from the State Government
Form 14	Register for advance against projects/schemes
Form 15	Appropriation register
Form 16	Programme register
Form 17	Scheme register
Form 18	Muster roll for payment of wages to workers
Form 19	Acknowledgement for receipt of adjustment voucher
Form 20	Register of immovable properties
Form 21	General ledger
Form 22	Register for reccipt of letters
Form 23	Register for issue of letters
Form 24	Stores account register
Form 25	Register of stationery articles
Form 26	Monthly statement of fund position
Form 27	Part I Half-yearly/annual statement of receipts and payments
Form 27	Part II Consolidated statement of receipts and payments of the village panchayat (including all village development committees)
Form 28	Form of certificate
Form 29	Cash book for village development committee
Form 30	Half-yearly/annual statement of receipts and payments of the village development committee (*Gram Unnayan Samiti*)
Form 31	Chequebook Register of the village development committee
Form 32	Project-cum-Scheme register of the village development committee
Form 33	Miscellaneous Receipt of the village development committee
Form 34	Budget of village committee (*gram sansad*) of the village panchayat
Form 35	Budget estimate of subcommittee (*upa-samiti*) of the village panchayat
Form 36	Budget estimate of the village panchayat
Form 37	Notice
Form 38	Supplementary and revised budget estimate for the year of the village panchayat

sheet. In Raina, all house owners in the village were taxed. Even a landless household had to pay a minimum annual tax of Rs 3 per annum.

The *Form 9: Assessment List*s specified in the Amendments of 2006 of the Gram Panchayat Rules, 2004, includes not only persons liable to pay property tax, but also enterprises/persons liable to pay other fees, rates, and tolls. Unpaid taxes are to be recorded in *Form 7: Register for Arrears and Current Demand and Collection of Taxes* in the Gram Panchayat Rules, 2007. All payments of honoraria to elected village head/deputy *pradhan*/Director *(sanchalak)* and wages to other workers are recorded in *Forms 10, 11*, and *18* prescribed in the Gram Panchayat Rules, 2007. Unlike in Maharashtra, for West Bengal village panchayats *Form 16: Programme Register* and *Form 17: Scheme Register* are specified in the Gram Panchayat Rules, 2007. The estimates and expenditures of each programme or scheme are documented in these registers. All *Immovable Properties* owned by village panchayat are recorded in *Form 20: Register of Immovable Properties* prescribed in the Gram Panchayat Rules, 2007. Apart from this, Raina village panchayat had a "Tubewell register" which documented number, type and location of all tubewells installed by the panchayat. Raina village panchayat also had a "Lease of water bodies register" which records water bodies leased out to self-help groups and their periodic earnings. Work done by the village panchayat for the year is reported to the panchayat meeting and the village assembly using *Form 3A* prescribed in the Gram Panchayat Rules, 2004. In relation to this report, Raina village panchayat had a "Works register," which records public works done by the village panchayat under various schemes/allocations (such as *SGRY* and the MP fund), with a description of the work, date of proposal, commencement and completion of the work, proposed and actual expenditure, and benefits accrued.

Apart from registers or forms shown in Table 4.6, Raina village panchayat had the electoral roll covering its jurisdiction. Unlike Warwat Khanderao village panchayat, Raina village panchayat had a ward-wise (village assembly-wise) electoral roll, which provided information on the voter's identification number, name, name of the father/husband, house number, age, and sex.

Although the Civil Registration System is a hierarchy, with the Registrar General of India at the top, the registration of births and deaths in rural West Bengal was devolved from the primary health centre to the panchayati raj institutions in 2003.[12] Therefore, the Raina village panchayat maintained

---

[12] Panchayats and Rural Development, Government of West Bengal (2007, p. 49): "In West

the Birth and Death Registers of the Civil Registration System. However, according to panchayat officials in Raina, the most accurate birth record in the panchayat area was the register maintained by Integrated Child Development Services (*anganwadi*) workers, and not the register of the Civil Registration System.

The Raina village panchayat maintained registers and records to conduct schemes of the line departments. Although the latter still had separate decision-making protocols, the implementation of their schemes was fully or partly devolved to the village panchayats. Therefore, the village panchayat owned registers and records for such schemes.

Although the Provident Fund for Landless Agricultural Labourers (PROFLAL) is a State Government scheme, supported by the Central Government, the Raina village panchayat owned records for the Provident Fund. The West Bengal State Government's pension scheme of PROFLAL, supported by the *Aam Admi Bima Yojana* of the Central Government, provides pension to landless agricultural labourers. The scheme launched by the State Government in 1998 offered benefits to landless agricultural labourers between the ages of 18 and 50.[13] Subscription under the scheme costs Rs 20 per month and the State Government contributes an equal amount until the subscribers are 50 years of age. Upon reaching the age of 50, the accumulated amount along with the usual interest are paid to the subscribers. The scheme is administered by village panchayats at the village level. The village panchayat selects beneficiaries. Eligible persons need to apply to it with documents of the landholdings (obtained from the Block Land and Land Reform Office of Raina I Block). Owners of less than 0.5 acre of land are eligible. There were about 1500 Provident Fund account holders in the Raina village panchayat in 2008. Names of landless agricultural workers, the Provident Fund account numbers, and monthly contributions were recorded for PROFLAL. Notably, this scheme was not implemented in Warwat Khanderao.

Although the Mahatma Gandhi National Rural Employment Guarantee

---

Bengal, the panchayats perform quite a few functions beyond what has been provided in the Eleventh Schedule. Some of those functions like registration of births and deaths have been formally devolved by issuing suitable order [Reference No. HF/O/FW/4C-2/94(1)/174-P dated 19.05.1997 of H & FW Department and No. 4231-PN/O/I/4P-5/03 dated 12.11.2003 of Panchayats & Rural Development Department]."

[13] For pension benefits, the age limit for landless agricultural workers was raised to sixty years in 2010.

Scheme (MGNREGS) is a centrally-sponsored scheme, Raina village panchayat maintained the MGNREGS register. The MGNREGS was functional in Raina village panchayat, unlike Warwat Khanderao. Within Raina village panchayat, 3621 households and 8099 persons were registered under the MGNREGS as of 2012–3. The village panchayat had issued 3621 job cards. Compared to the Warwat Khanderao village panchayat, the proportion of households provided employment under this scheme was significantly higher in Raina village panchayat: 2990 out of 3621 households as of 2012–3. An average of 45 person-days was reportedly provided for each household. In Bidyanidhi village, 306 households and 697 persons were registered. In West Bengal the village development committees were also participating in this scheme in order to mobilise their communities. The MGNREGS had become an important scheme for rural development for the West Bengal panchayats.

4.3.2 Census-type Surveys Conducted Independently by the Panchayati Raj Institutions

Raina village panchayat conducted two household surveys in 2007 and 2008 on the instructions of the district panchayat to evaluate the rural sanitation scheme. In the 2007 survey, information was collected on sanitation and on type of ration card (Above Poverty Line/Below Poverty Line/*Antyodaya Anna Yojana*) owned by a household. In the 2008 survey, information was collected on access to toilets and some socio-economic features of households, such as social group (Scheduled Caste, Scheduled Tribe, Other Backward Class), number of literate members, and educational attainment of the most educated member of the household. Unit-level data from these surveys, which provide information on each household, were available at the Raina panchayat office.

In 2005, the Rural Household Survey (or the Below Poverty Line Census) was conducted in the Raina village panchayat by the Ministry of Rural Development in order to identify households living below the poverty line. There was widespread discontent among the panchayat officials over this survey, as they believed that the data collected, especially the list of households described as being below the poverty line, was inaccurate. The panchayat officials conducted their own census-type survey of all households in the panchayat area and collected information on the same parameters as the Rural Household Survey.[14] The village panchayat reported the discrepancies

---

[14] There was similar discontent in the Warwat Khanderao village panchayat over the Below Poverty Line Census conducted in June 2003. The village development officer conducted a

to the Block officials. Some, but not all of the discrepancies were amended later. This survey data was also available at the panchayat office.

This series of events suggests that the Raina village panchayat could organise and conduct census-type surveys. The alternative Rural Household Survey in Raina shows that this panchayat had the ability and expertise to identify discrepancies in data from surveys conducted by other organisations. Arguments and debate between the village panchayat and other organisations about the accuracy of village data suggest that the quality of village data is really a matter of concern for the village.[15]

4.3.3 Village-level Registers and Records Collected and Maintained by Other Agencies

Numerous registers and records were collected and maintained at the village or Block levels by agencies other than the village panchayats. Some of these outside agencies worked in the functional domain of the panchayati raj institutions, using funds provided by the State or Central Governments or donor funds. Most of these outside agencies envisage a line department-sponsored hierarchy, whose decision-making system for resource allocation and project execution are independent of the panchayati raj system. Such agencies generate and maintain their own databases in addition to those maintained by the village panchayats. Although panchayat officials had access to such records, they did not own the full set of these registers and records at the panchayat office.

4.3.3.1 Village Integrated Child Development Services (Anganwadi) Registers

The Integrated Child Development Services (ICDS) was initiated in India in 1975 with financial and technical assistance from the United Nations Children's Fund (UNICEF) and the World Bank. The ICDS programme offers supplementary feeding facilities for children below the age of six, pregnant women and lactating mothers, pre-school facilities for children aged three to six, maternal and child health care services such as immunisation and vitamin supplements, and nutrition and health education for mothers. The ICDS workers are also known as *anganwadi* workers.

---

house-to-house re-survey in 2006 to revise the Below Poverty Line list. However, as in Raina, some of the discrepancies in Warwat Khanderao were amended later but a large part of the discrepancies was not amended. The survey data was available at the panchayat office.
[15] Bakshi and Okabe (2008, pp. 13–4, 26–7).

The ICDS is one of the major centrally-sponsored schemes with support from the State Government. The ICDS scheme is provided by the line department of the Ministry of Women and Child Development. It has a line of control and reporting mechanisms. It has a separate decision-making system for resource allocation and project execution, independent of the panchayati raj system. However, the ICDS works in the same functional domain of the panchayati raj institutions under subject 25: "Women and child development" as stated in Schedule XI of the Constitution. Therefore, the panchayati raj institutions need to share information and coordinate various matters with the ICDS.

The ICDS or *anganwadi* worker maintained several registers, which were not available at the panchayat office. For example, some of the registers in the Bidyanidhi ICDS centre in Raina village panchayat are described below.[16]

  i) *Child register.* All children in the village in the age group of 0 to 6 years were recorded in this register. The date of birth, age, sex, school enrolment, and monthly body weight of each child were also recorded.
 ii) *Food register for children*: All children in the village in the age group of 7 months to 6 years were recorded in this register. A daily attendance list of children who had food from the ICDS centre was also maintained.
iii) *Food register for pregnant women*: A register similar to item (ii) was maintained for all pregnant women in the village.
 iv) *Pre-school students register.* The names and daily attendance of children in the age-group 3 to 6 enrolled for pre-school education at the ICDS centre were recorded in this register. It did not include children in the village enrolled in other schools.
  v) *Register for pregnant women*: This register recorded the names, month of conception, expected date of delivery, immunisation details, and other details of pregnant women in the village. After delivery, the child's date and place of birth and sex were registered.
 vi) *Growth chart of children (Gradation register):* A growth chart with monthly recordings of height and weight of children in the age group of 3 to 6 years was maintained by the ICDS worker.
vii) *Immunisation register.* The ICDS worker and the Auxiliary Nurse Midwife maintained an immunisation register for new-borns in the village, documenting when and where the vaccinations were administered. When the vaccination was done at a private facility, the ICDS worker recorded the date after verifying the papers.

[16] Bakshi and Okabe (2008, pp. 15–6).

viii) The ICDS centre also maintained registers for stocks, accounts and expenses.

ix) *Village survey register.* The ICDS worker conducted a village household survey every five years. The register allotted a page to each household in the village. The following information on each member of the household can be obtained from the register:

a) Name

b) Relationship with the head of the household

c) Age

d) Sex

e) Educational attainment

f) Whether SC/ST

g) Whether landless/marginal cultivator

h) Occupation

i) Date of birth (of children)

j) Comments: In this column information on deaths, marriages or migrations is recorded, though exact dates are not always available.

Although the village survey register was updated every five years, information on births, deaths, marriages, and migrations was updated regularly. With regard to births and marriages, the names and details of new members were to be recorded in the register. When a new survey was conducted, the households that had divided were recorded separately and households that had migrated were deleted from the register. However, where some household members had moved (for example, a son and his wife and children, but not his parents), details of all members of the undivided household were recorded even when the move was permanent.

Although a Children's Centre (*balwadi*) had started in December 1981, the ICDS was initiated in Warwat Khanderao on November 18, 2000. Therefore, the ICDS records in this village can be traced back to 2000. The establishment of an ICDS centre in Warwat Khanderao was in progress at the time of our survey. On our first visit to the village in 2008, there was only a single ICDS centre in the village and one ICDS (*anganwadi*) worker stayed in the staff room of the primary school. When we returned in 2011, however, a detached permanent ICDS centre building had come up next to the primary school and two ICDS (*anganwadi*) workers had been placed in charge of each jurisdiction in the village. The Warwat Khanderao ICDS centre was divided according to the population and the new ICDS (*anganwadi*) worker maintained all the registers for her jurisdiction. The ICDS (*anganwadi*) worker had been maintaining the village survey register without allotting separate pages for individual households until July 2011. However, the ICDS (*anganwadi*) supervisor had asked her to give a separate page to each household after July 2011 as she had done for each household under her jurisdiction since September 2011. Thus, ICDS records in Warwat Khanderao were becoming similar to those of Bidyanidhi.

The ICDS provides for a child-development committee of which the panchayat head is the president and an ICDS (*anganwadi*) worker is the secretary. However, according to the panchayat head, the committee was not held in Warwat Khanderao, even though the panchayat head, an ICDS (a*ganwadi*) worker and some parents of students were expected to convene this committee every three months. The Woman and Child Committee was a subcommittee constituted by the village panchayat to take up issues related to women and child welfare. According to the panchayat head, in Warwat Khanderao this committee did not function as it should.

Under the Bombay Village Panchayats Act, 1958, as amended in 2003, the village council in Maharashtra has been given extensive disciplinary control over Government, semi-Government and panchayat employees in the village. The panchayat head recognised that the coordination of ICDS activities was to be done by the village panchayat. In fact, the ICDS centre building was constructed on the responsibility of the village panchayat. However, in Warwat Khanderao we did not find a strong coordination mechanism between the village panchayat and the ICDS similar to the coordination mechanism in West Bengal. Neither the child development nor the women and children committee was functional in Warwat Khanderao. Nonetheless, the ICDS (*anganwadi*) workers sometimes worked with the Auxiliary Nurse Midwife to perform functions such as immunising children.

The ICDS (*anganwadi*) workers updated the registers every month, as they had to report to their supervisor. However, when we interviewed the village development officer of Warwat Khanderao, he did not rely on ICDS records. He did not trust their accuracy since these records were informal and meant for operational use. With regard to the birth records, for example, the panchayat secretary suggested that registers in the Civil Registration System were formal records and that they should cover births of every child in the village because birth certificates were required for school admission. However, primary school teachers in the same village said that they accepted birth certificates of the Civil Registration System, say, for only about 10 per cent of the school enrolments.[17] According to a primary school teacher, parents can use many documents to confirm the date of birth of their child at the time of enrolment, such as ICDS (*anganwadi*) records, pre- and post-natal vaccination records of parents and children. If nothing is available, the school records the date of birth as reported by parents.[18] This misunderstanding of the panchayat secretary also suggests a lack of coordination among the village panchayat, ICDS (*anganwadi*) workers, and primary school teachers. There were few data-sharing mechanisms in Maharashtra, as pointed out by the *Basic Statistics for Local Level Development* report.[19] Nevertheless, as will be seen in section 6.6, chapter 6, the ICDS child register was still more accurate than birth records in the Civil Registration System. Other issues regarding accuracy and quality of ICDS records in the specific context of the two village panchayats studied are discussed in section 6.6, chapter 6.

In the West Bengal context, ICDS was initiated in Raina I Block in 1984. The ICDS centre at Bidyanidhi village was established in 1999. Prior to that, a single ICDS centre catered to both Bidyanidhi and Birampur villages. At the time of the survey, there were 18 ICDS centres in Raina village panchayat. The Women, Child Development and Social Welfare subcommittee (*upa-samiti*) of the village panchayat deals with various matters under the ICDS.

In the State there was a comprehensive institutional coordination mechanism between panchayats and the ICDS. The protocol for regular meetings of panchayat-level functionaries, known as the "Fourth Saturday Meeting," had been institutionalised.[20] For public health activities, the members of the subcommittee on Education and Public Health in each village panchayat, representatives of Health and Family Welfare Department, field-level functionaries of ICDS centres of Women and Child Development and Social Welfare Department, along with representatives of self-help groups met on every fourth Saturday of a month. The meeting reviewed delivery of public health services such as immunisation, pre- and post-natal services, registration of births and deaths, and children's nutritional status, with participation of officials of the above-mentioned Departments. Public health services delivered by the panchayat, such as water supply and sanitation, were also reviewed. Important events such as deaths of children and pregnant women,

[17] Okabe and Surjit (2012, p. 81).
[18] Interview at the village primary school conducted on April 26, 2014.
[19] Central Statistical Organisation (2006, p. 25).
[20] Panchayats and Rural Development Department, Government of West Bengal (2008a, pp. 48–9) and (2007, p. 49).

and outbreak of diseases were also monitored and discussed for possible preventive measures or drawing the attention of higher-level officials. This meeting was a platform for convergence of the activities related to self-help groups and panchayati raj institutions.[21]

In Raina, the Block Health Centre, ICDS centre and village panchayat formed an interlinked health-and-childcare system. The Fourth Saturday Meeting was held at the panchayat's office with the ICDS supervisor, the Auxiliary Nurse Midwife and health supervisor and panchayat officials present. A monthly data sheet was prepared, recording the number of births and deaths, reported cases of specific diseases (such as tuberculosis, malaria, HIV-AIDS), status of sanitation, and drinking water supply for the panchayat area. This monthly data sheet was on display at the panchayat's office. On the first Saturday of the month, the liaison officers submitted the data sheet to their respective departments.

This interlinked health-and-childcare system made data sharing among its constitutive agencies possible. For example, at the Fourth Saturday Meeting, data on institutional births were collected from Health Department officials and the number of children born at home was collected from the ICDS (*anganwadi*) worker. The information was combined and compiled at the panchayat's office for preparing the monthly chart. There was no such formal data-sharing mechanism at the Warwat Khanderao village panchayat in Maharashtra.[22]

As will be seen in section 6.6 and 6.7 of chapter 6, the quality of ICDS registers in Bidyanidhi village was remarkably good.[23] The data-sharing mechanism may make it possible to check the reliability of data from different sources.[24]

According to the Child Development Project Officer (CDPO) of Raina I Block, the Education and Health Department uses ICDS data. The village panchayat

---

[21] In Activity Mapping, the convergence of ICDS activities belongs to the functions assigned to the panchayat.

[22] Bakshi and Okabe (2008, p. 26).

[23] According to the Child Development Project Officer (CDPO) at the Raina I Block, "In 95 per cent cases, the *Anganwadi* registers are accurate. The ICDS supervisors and the CDPO check the registers regularly. The ICDS supervisors have to submit a monthly progress report with the CDPO. Any sporadic changes and inconsistencies noticed in these reports are cross-checked" (Interviewed on September 14, 2009).

[24] Bakshi and Okabe (2011, p. 26).

also used information from the ICDS (*anganwadi*) workers to identify beneficiaries for the sanitation programme.[25]

While the National Statistical Commission stated that Civil Registration System has the potential to provide estimates for important events at the local level,[26] the panchayat officials in Raina said that the registers maintained by ICDS (*anganwadi*) workers are the more reliable data source.

4.3.3.2 Village School Registers

In Schedule XI of the Constitution, Subject 17 ("Education, including primary and secondary schools") is in the functional domain of the panchayati raj institutions. Therefore, panchayats should share information with schools to coordinate matters of concern.

The school maintained regular school registers on attendance and performance of each student and registers for staff, accounts, and stocks (inventories such as chairs, tables, etc.). Furthermore, the primary school maintained a register with a list of all children in the village.

In Maharashtra, schools for primary and secondary education were entrusted to the panchayati raj institutions. Before 2008, the school management committee (*Gram Siksha* Committee) was a sub-committee of the village panchayat, with the panchayat head as its president. However, under the Right to Education Act, 2009, only parents of students enrolled in the school can serve as president of the committee. One panchayat member and one *anganwadi* worker also sit on the committee.[27] Since then, the school management committee has been scrapped. According to the panchayat head of Warwat Khanderao, improving school infrastructure had been a responsibility of the village panchayat until 2010, but it was later handed over to the school management committee. In this respect, its authority over primary and secondary education was taken away from the village panchayat.

There was one Urdu-medium primary school, one Marathi-medium upper-primary school, and one Marathi-medium secondary school in the Warwat Khanderao village panchayat. The Marathi-medium upper-primary school

---

[25] Interview with the Child Development Project Officer at the Raina I Block on September 14, 2009.
[26] National Statistical Commission (2001, para. 2.7.8).
[27] At least half of the total members of the School Management Committee must be women (interview at the village primary school in November 2013).

offered instruction till class seven and maintained the school register. It had seven class rooms, seven teachers and two helpers for cooking. It had separate toilets for boys and girls. The school's total enrolment in the academic year of 2008 was 101 for the primary school (for classes one to four) and 84 for the middle school (for classes five to seven). Out of 101 students in the primary school, 27 were from Scheduled Caste families, 23 from Notified Tribes, 31 from the Other Backward Classes, and 20 from the General category.

Apart from the Marathi-medium school, there was one Urdu-medium primary school (Zilla Parishad Urdu Primary School, Warwat Khanderao) that taught students of classes one to four from Muslim families. The Zilla Parishad Urdu Primary School maintained the same school register format as the Marathi-medium school. Students who want to continue their study in the Urdu medium after class four attend the Zilla Parishad Urdu School, Paturda (for classes five to seven), and for further study they can go to a private school either in Paturda or Shegaon. All the Muslim students in the village attend a *madrassa* (called Ziya-ul-Quran) in the morning from 7 a.m. to 8 a.m., and in the evening from 5.30 p.m. to 6.30 p.m. where they study the Quran in Arabic.

The Marathi-medium upper-primary school also maintained a register of all children in the age group of zero to eighteen years, based on an annual house-to-house enquiry. Information in the register was updated every year. The survey was conducted between January and April. The school authority sends somebody to the household in order to ask parents to send their child to school when the child turns six.

The school authorities did not consult ICDS (*anganwadi*) registers for any purpose, but sometimes accept the help of an ICDS (*anganwadi*) worker to conduct a survey. They did not share data or perform a consistency check against ICDS data.

In West Bengal, the responsibility of providing education rests not with the panchayati raj institutions, but with the School Education Department. Every village panchayat in West Bengal has an education and public health subcommittee (*upa-samiti*) to look after this. However, the village education committee (equivalent to the school management committee in Maharashtra) monitors schools.

There were nine Government primary schools, including one Muslim school, three private primary schools, one secondary school and one higher secondary school in the area of the Raina village panchayat. In Bidyanidhi village, there was a village primary school. The school maintained its school register. It taught four classes (one to four), and had two classrooms and two teachers. The school's total enrolment was 40 in the academic year 2008.

Apart from the village primary schools, there were three private primary schools (for classes nursery to four) in the panchayat area. According to panchayat officials, some children from well-off families were sent to the private schools only because these schools teach English better than the village schools. The panchayats knew of these schools, but do not collect any data about them.

The school also maintained a register of all children in the village up to the age of thirteen, based on an annual house-to-house enquiry conducted by the school teachers. The survey was generally conducted between November and December. In the child register, a separate sheet was allotted for each household with children aged thirteen years and below. If there was more than one child in the household, all were recorded on the same sheet. Each year the child's enrolment status was updated, even when the child was not enrolled in the village primary school or ICDS centre. When a child attains the age of five, a green card was sent to the parents to notify them that the child can be admitted to the school in the next academic session.

The teacher at Bidyanidhi primary school informed us that though they prepare this register independently, the ICDS (*anganwadi*) workers help them with the preparation of the register.

4.3.3.3 Records at the Primary Health Centre

In Maharashtra, the function of Medical and Public Health was assigned to village panchayats under the Bombay Village Panchayats Act, 1958. However, there was no primary health centre or any other medical facility within the geographical boundaries of Warwat Khanderao village panchayat. Warwat Khanderao village panchayat was served by the Kalamkhed primary health sub-centre of the Paturda primary health centre. The geographical boundaries of the Block and the area served by the primary health centre were not coincident in this case.

Paturda primary health centre served a total population of around 30,000. There were four sub-centres under the primary health centre, and three villages served directly by it. Kalamkhed sub-centre catered to a population of approximately 3,730.

The Auxiliary Nurse and Midwife and Accredited Social Health Activists (ASHA) visited the village periodically. The ASHAs had to file a monthly report to the primary health centre, where they had to record the number of cases of various illnesses (such as tuberculosis, leprosy, sickle cell anaemia, dengue, HIV-affected pregnant mothers, diarrhoea) and cases of vaccinations in that area. A meeting was held at the primary health centre on the twenty-seventh day of every month, attended by all health officials and the ASHAs. Health data on all villages were consolidated at the primary health-centre level in a specified format in this meeting. The consolidated form was sent to the Block office on the thirtieth of every month. The Block consolidated the records of every primary health centre under its jurisdiction and sent it to the district on the second day of the month.[28]

In West Bengal, the panchayati raj institutions were given the responsibility for managing all the physical assets of the Block Primary Health Centres, primary health centres and sub-centres by the Health and Family Welfare Department in 2005.[29] The function to assist in supervision and maintenance of sub-centres was devolved on the village panchayats according to Activity Mapping.

The administrative jurisdictions of the Block primary health centres and the sub-centres were different from those of the panchayats. There were 26 primary health sub-centres in the Raina I Block, and two in the Raina village panchayat. Each sub-centre served a population of 5,000 to 10,000. There was one Auxiliary Nurse Midwife per sub-centre and one health supervisor per village panchayat.

Every month each sub-centre had to send to the Block primary health centre details of all its activities, details of births and deaths, cases treated of different diseases, vaccinations, birth control and the like, according to a prescribed format.[30]

[28] Interview with the Health Supervisor of the Paturda primary health centre, February 17–23, 2014.
[29] Panchayats and Rural Development Department, Government of West Bengal (2006, pp. 14–5).
[30] Interview with the Medical Officer of Raina I Block Primary Health Centre on August 28–9, 2008.

As described above, the Block primary health centre, the ICDS centre and the village panchayat came together at the Fourth Saturday meeting. The Auxiliary Nurse Midwife and the health supervisor attended the meeting as representatives of the Health and Family Welfare Department. On the basis of this interlinked health-and-childcare system, data sharing with the panchayat and the ICDS centre becomes possible, which can also improve the quality of data from the primary health centres. The monthly data sheet was on public display at the panchayat's office. On the first Saturday of the month the data sheet was submitted to the Health and Family Welfare Department.

4.3.3.4 Land Records at the Revenue Official Office or Block Land and Land Reform Office

Maharashtra and West Bengal are located in historically different regions in terms of village land records. As mentioned before, Maharashtra lies in the erstwhile temporarily settled or *raiyatwari* areas that are cadastrally surveyed and where the land revenue agency annually compiles and updates village-level land records. Records on land use, tenure and agriculture were an integral part of the revenue system in Maharashtra. West Bengal lies in the erstwhile permanently settled or *zamindari* areas that are cadastrally surveyed but where there is no official agency of the Revenue Department at the village level for collection and annual revision of land records.

The area of the *patwari*'s revenue village was identical to the panchayat area in Warwat Khanderao. The jurisdiction of the Block Development Officer was the Block. Block (or Community Development Block) is the geographical unit for development administration. The jurisdiction of the *tehsildar* is the tehsil, which is the geographical unit for revenue administration. The two units are not the same, though they overlap considerably. Warwat Khanderao village was under the Sangrampur *tehsil* and Paturda Block.

The *patwari* (*talathi*) and *tehsildar* belonged to a separate decision-making system, independent of the panchayati raj system. Authority at the village level to collect land revenue was given to the *patwari* or *talathi* by the State's Revenue Department. The line of reporting below the State was from the village-level officer (*patwari/talathi*) to the Circle Officer, *tehsildar* and the District Collector.

The Land Measurement Department was established in 1989. The *tehsildar*'s office conducted the land measurement. The *patwari*'s work was to maintain land records and collect land revenue on the basis of this measurement.

Table 4.7 *Land Records in Maharashtra*

Village Form 7/12 (Record of Rights)
[Rules 3, 5, 6 and 7 of the Maharashtra Land Revenue Record of Rights (Preparation and Maintenance) Rules, 1971]

Village _____   Taluka _____

Survey No./Gat No.	Division of Survey No./ Gat Number.	Tenure		Name of the occupant	Account Number			
					Name of the Tenant		Rent	
Local land Name							Rs	p.
Cultivable Area		Ha.	R					
_____					Other rights			
_____								
_____								
Total								
Uncultivable Land								
ClassA Class B								
Total					Boundary and land survey symbol			
Assessment		Rs	p.					
Judi. or special assessment								

Village Form 7/12 (Crop Record)

Year	Seasons	Details of area under crop						Details of area under unmixed crop			Non-cultivating available land	Irrigated equipment		Name of occupant	Remark
		Details of area under mixed crop													
		Mixed Code No.	Irrigated	Non- irrigated	Areas under decline crop			Crop name	Irrigated	Non- irrigated	Nature	Area			
					Crop name	Irrigated	Non- irrigated								
1	2	3	4	5	6	7	8	9	10	11	12	13	14	15	16
			H. R	H. R		H. R	H. R		H. R	H. R		H. R			

The *patwari*'s main land records were maintained in Form no. 7 (*Naavn namuna saat*) and Form no. 12 (*Naavn namuna barah*) as shown in Table 4.7.[31] The record of sales and purchase of land were kept in Form no. 6 (*ferfaranchi nond wahi*) (*ferfar patra*). These land records were documented in terms of the plot and, unlike in West Bengal, they were not documented in terms of the holder. Plot numbers in the cadastral map were given in 1978. The plot-wide land record was a list of plots maintained with the plot number ("survey number"). As shown in Table 4.7, a wide range of items for each plot number, including its land uses, was recorded in this record.

According to the *patwari* of Warwat Khanderao, the land records had no information on tenants. Regardless of whether the land is leased or cultivated by the landowner himself, the landowner's name is written in the column for tenancy. Landowners do not report tenancy because they fear that the tenants may claim ownership of land. Therefore, land records in Warwat Khanderao were, in principle, land records for ownership holdings and not for operational holdings. It was almost impossible to generate operational holdings records from them.

There was no official record re-tabulated in terms of landholder. That is to say, there was no official list of landowners ("occupants") with information on their plots which were scattered everywhere. In other words, there was no official record classified according to the survey numbers held by a landowner. The *patwari* kept such a list for his operational convenience, apart from his official plot-wise land records. Even though he had such a non-official holder-wise list for his operational use, he had no record of lands located outside this revenue village and owned by the residents of this village. The information was to be updated seasonally by the *patwari* in *girdawari* (a complete enumeration of all survey numbers, which is made in every village during each crop season to compile land use, irrigation, and crop area statistics). However, this did not mean that the records are completely up to date and accurate. Under the scheme for Improvement of Crop Statistics, the National Sample Survey Organisation revealed a considerable negligence in carrying out the record on land cultivation.[32]

---

[31] Basic data of the Agricultural Census for erstwhile temporarily-settled States is compiled through re-tabulation of information available in the village land records (Ministry of Agriculture 2006a, pp. 7–8, 17).

[32] National Statistical Commission (2001), para. 4.2.6–4.2.12. Under the Improvement of Crop Statistics (ICS) scheme, an independent agency of supervisors carries out a physical verification of the *patwari*'s record on land cultivation in a sub-sample of the Timely Reporting Scheme

The *tehsil*-level land records were computerised, but the village records in Sangrampur *tehsil* were not. The computerisation started in August 2011.

Land revenue was collected at very old rates. The rates for levying were the same as those before Independence in 1947. The revenue collected was divided between the district panchayat, the Revenue Department and the village panchayat. If the total land revenue collected was Rs 9, out of it Rs 2 was given to the Revenue Department, another Rs 2 to the village panchayat, and Rs 5 to the district panchayat. The *patwari* deposited the collected tax in the Revenue Department which then divided the amount and sent it to the District Collector, who gave it to the village panchayat, Revenue Department and the district panchayat.

According to the *patwari*, the land record was still used for land reforms. No land has been acquired in the village under the Land Ceiling Acts. The ceiling for irrigated land is 24 acres and for non-irrigated land it is 52 acres. Thirteen households of the Warwat Khanderao village have been allotted some land, as the Government owns 75 acres of land in this village.

In addition to the revenue administrative duties, the *patwari* reported to the *tehsildar* and District Collector about all political happenings, outbreaks of epidemics, suicides, floods, and other natural calamities in the village. The *patwari* also supervised the village elections. A hierarchy of revenue officials – the *patwari*, *tehsildar* and District Collector under the Revenue Department – had extensive administrative powers in Maharashtra. Unlike West Bengal, where the administrative duties of the Block Land and Land Reform officer are restricted to land reforms and revenues, *tehsildars* in Maharashtra wield more administrative powers. The hierarchy of *patwaris* generally helped officers of other departments in the execution of their duties.

Originally, in the Village List of the Bombay Village Panchayats Act, 1958, "Maintenance of village records relating to land revenue in such manner and in such form as may be prescribed from time to time by or under any law relating to land revenue" has been provided within the subjects of activities

---

(TRS) sample villages and makes an assessment of discrepancies between the supervisor's and *patwari*'s crop-area entries in the sample clusters. The ICS results for the four years ending 1998–9 shows that the percentage survey numbers in which crop entries by the supervisor and the Revenue official tally with each other is around 60–70 per cent in all of India and around 40 per cent in Maharashtra, despite the *patwari* being aware that his work is subject to technical supervision.

to be devolved on village panchayats. Therefore, it was statutorily possible for village panchayats in Maharashtra to intervene in the maintenance of land records to correct and update data not only regarding seasonal land use, but also landowner–tenant relations. Besides, under the Bombay Village Panchayats Act, 1958, as amended in 2003, the village council in Maharashtra was given disciplinary control over Government and semi-Government employees working in the village. The *patwari* is one of the Government employees working in the village. Therefore, in terms of Constitutional devolution of powers, the village panchayats should be able to share information with the *patwari* and coordinate various matters using land records.

Land records were also maintained in West Bengal. Although the State had no primary reporting agency like the *patwari* at the village level in Maharashtra, the Block Land and Land Reform Office and the village-level Revenue Inspector maintained land records for villages within the Block. The Land and Land Reforms Department of the State Government was responsible for the Block Land and Land Reform officers and their land records. The panchayati raj institutions in West Bengal did not have authority over land records. They simply facilitated the selection of land-reform beneficiaries.

The Block Land and Land Reform office had a dual land-recording system; it had the land register recorded both in terms of holders and in terms of plot. As shown in Table 4.8, a page in the register was allotted for each landowner where all of the landowner's holdings within the Block's jurisdiction were listed. Besides this holder-wise land register, there was a list of plots with each plot number on the cadastral map. Unlike land records in Maharashtra, the core part of land records of the Block Land and Land Reform office was the holder-wise record. Descriptions of land were the plot number, classification (land-use classification), total area and each plot's area, and the share of the plot owned by its holder. There was no column for information on seasonal land use. Records were updated only at the landowner's request. Ordinarily, the records are not regularly updated.[33] The Land and Land Reform Department was computerising all land records. The records at Raina were being digitised, though manual records were also retained.

---

[33] Basic data (i.e. the sample frame) of the Agricultural Census for the erstwhile permanently-settled States are collected through a complete listing based on a house-to-house enquiry about operational holders in at least 20 per cent of the villages selected by simple random sampling from each stratum. Thus, the Agricultural Census in West Bengal does not rely on land records of the Block Land and Land Reform office at all; see Ministry of Agriculture (2006b, p. 2).

Table 4.8 *Land Records in West Bengal*

District:				Mouza:			Register no:	
Police Station:				J. L. No:				

Name and address of ryot	Description of title deed	Land Revenue	Road	Local body	Cess Education	Rural employment	Rural employment surcharge	
1	2	3	4a	4b	4c	4d	4e	

Description of land

Plot no.	Classi-fication	Com-ments	Total Plot Area		Share of plot owned by the holder	Area of the share owned by the holder			
			Acres	Decimal		Acres	Decimal	Hectare	Acre
5	6	7	8a	8b	9	10a	10b	10c	10d
Total no. of plots:			Total area:						

A holder-wise land register was more appropriate than a plot-wise land register in order to find the excess over the ceiling limit for individual holders. According to the Block Land and Land Reform officer at the Raina I Block, these records were used for land reform. All land in excess of the ceiling limit for individual holders is declared vested to the Government by the Land and Land Reform office. In determining surplus land, the Block Land and Land Reform Office often collaborated with adjoining Block offices to assess an individual's total holdings. This was because holders may have owned land in more than one Block, while each Block office maintained registers on landholdings just within the Block. The allocation of vested land to land reform beneficiaries was decided by a five-member committee consisting of the Block Development Officer, the Block Land and Land Reform officer, the Chairman of the Block-level committee, the Member of the Legislative Assembly, and the Secretary for agriculture and related matters (*Krishi Karmadhakshya*) of the Block-level committee.

4.3.3.5 Others

The village panchayats could gain access to data on livestock and fisheries from the respective departments. It was found that though panchayati raj institutions had authority over Khadi and cottage industries, the village panchayats did not have any authority over such industries other than collection of certain taxes and fees. Licences were granted by the Block-level committee or the district panchayat. Data from the Industrial Development office were not available with the village panchayat.

4.3.4 Census-Type Survey Organised by Central or State Government

4.3.4.1 Below Poverty Line Census

The Ministry of Rural Development conducted the Below Poverty Line Census in 2002 (also referred to as the Rural Household Survey in West Bengal) through the various State governments. This is a nationwide census-type survey conducted in rural India. Its objective is to identify households existing below the poverty line in villages at the beginning of the plan period for the selection of beneficiaries for poverty-alleviation schemes. The Below Poverty Line Census of 2002 sought to grade the relative deprivation of households on 13 indicators on a scale of 1 to 5. In West Bengal, 12 indicators were used for the Rural Household Survey.[34] Households obtaining the lowest scores in the 12 indicators were identified as being below the poverty line, with the proviso that the total number of selected households corresponded to the number of poor estimated by the Planning Commission.

The identification and selection of beneficiaries for distribution of Below Poverty Line cards under the public distribution system are based on the Below Poverty Line survey list. Beneficiaries of centrally-sponsored schemes such as the *Indira Awaas Yojana*, Indira Gandhi National Old Age Pension Scheme, and the National Family Benefit Scheme are also selected from the Below Poverty Line survey list.

The household questionnaire had two parts: Section A for basic household information and Section B for 13 (or 12) "scoring parameters" for grading the relative deprivation of each household. Section A contained: (a) a profile of each household member (name, age, sex, relation to the head of the household, and educational status); (b) average monthly income of the household in rupees; (c) the type of operational holding of land (owner/tenant/both owner

---

[34] The West Bengal Government did not use the parameter on sanitation in its Below Poverty Line survey. Hence, the Central Government schedule has thirteen parameters while the West Bengal list has twelve.

and tenant/none); (d) drinking water facility (no source of drinking water within a distance of 1.6 kilometres/source of drinking water at a distance of 1.00–1.59 kilometres/0.50–0.99 kilometres/less than 0.5 kilometre/source available within the house); and (e) social group of the household (Scheduled Caste/Scheduled Tribe/Other Backward Class/Others). Section B contained items for 13 parameters: (i) size group of operational holding of land; (ii) type of house; (iii) average availability of normal clothing (per person in pieces); (iv) food security; (v) sanitation; (vi) ownership of consumer durables; (vii) literacy status of the most literate adult; (viii) status of the household labour force; (ix) means of livelihood; (x) status of children (5–14 years); (xi) type of indebtedness; (xii) reason for migration from household; and (xiii) preference of assistance.[35]

The Below Poverty Line Census of 2002 has been widely criticised by the rural poor and their organisations, as well as by scholars. Sundaram (2003), Jain (2004), Himanshu (2008), and Usami (2010) evaluated the methodology of the Below Poverty Line Census's household identification. Even the expert group set up by the Ministry of Rural Development admitted that there were errors of exclusion and inclusion in the Census's household identification but that these remained above acceptable limits.[36]

Notwithstanding widespread discontent with using "scoring parameters" to identify Below Poverty Line households, the coverage of household members from Above Poverty Line and Below Poverty Line households in this Census was not very bad, as will be noted in section 6.6, chapter 6. Besides, the household database captured through the survey was digitised so that it could be used for other purposes. This database could assist not only in producing statistics, but also in identifying each and every rural household by name of the head of the household or by a uniquely generated household

---

[35] Out of the thirteen parameters in the Below Poverty Line Census, 2002, parameter (5) *sanitation* was not used and instead of no. (13) *preference of assistances*, another parameter, 'special kind of disability' was used in the Rural Household Survey of West Bengal. Some other parameters are also modified a little. Twelve parameters used in the Rural Household Survey of West Bengal were independently defined as follows: (i) Effective landholding of the family (together with land cultivated as registered *Barga* holder), (ii) Nature of the dwelling house, (iii) Number of garments per member, (iv) Food security, (v) Ownership of consumer items: cycle, radio, television, electric fan, pressure cooker, (vi) Educational status (of the most educated member of the family), (vii) Earning capability status, (viii) Means of livelihood, (ix) Educational status of children of nine to fourteen years (the highest to be considered for more than one child), (x) Type of loan, (xi) Reason for going out of the village for employment of the family's principal earner, and (xii) Special kind of disability.

[36] Ministry of Rural Development (2009, p. 20).

Figure 4.1 *Rural Household Survey's Household Information: Query by Design View*

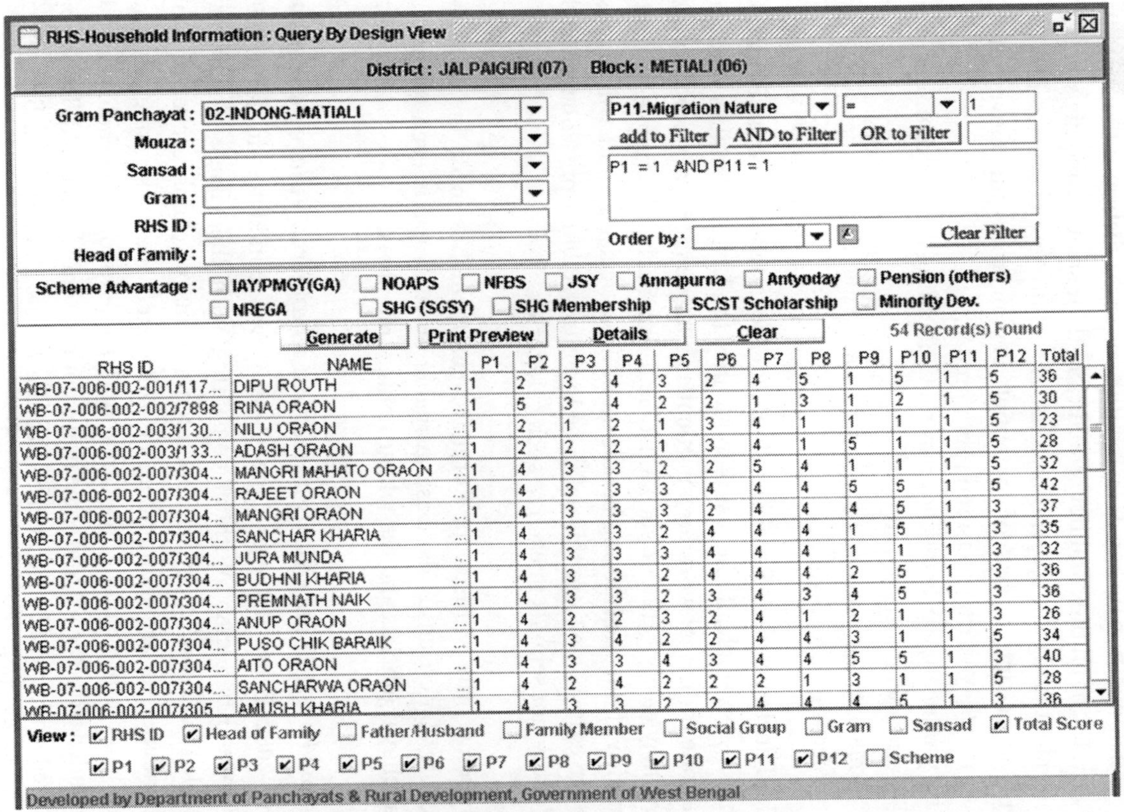

Source: Panchayats and Rural Development Department, Government of West Bengal (2008a, p. 124).

code. It could help in generating a list of households which match a set of combination of parameters. In fact, the Panchayats and Rural Development Department of West Bengal noted that the household database had been helpful by:

 i) helping the panchayati raj institutions or the district authority to prepare a list of all the rural households and their socio-economic status;
 ii) identifying and generating a list of socially vulnerable families;
 iii) generating a list of potential beneficiaries for Government and panchayati raj sponsored programmes;
 iv) producing GIS maps for grass roots planning for economic development and social justice; and
 v) making socio-economic scenarios available to civil society for a more accurate social audit.

The Panchayats and Rural Development Department of West Bengal noted that "for example, if one wants to identify the landless families who have to migrate for casual work for a particular village panchayat (*gram panchayat*), one may easily generate such a list," and, "similarly, [if] anyone wants to get an idea about the housing condition of a particular area, it will be possible to have the same from this database in figures, tabular presentation and also identify households in each of such categories." [37]

Therefore, the Ministry of Rural Development has made the 2002 Below Poverty Line Census database available on its website, even to the village panchayat officials and the village council members. [38]

Below Poverty Line Census in Warwat Khanderao Village Panchayat

The 2002 Below Poverty Line Census was conducted in June 2003 in Warwat Khanderao. Without consulting with the village panchayat, the Block Development Officer appointed a primary school teacher in Warwat Khanderao as an enumerator; he completed the task alone. Eventually suspicion arose among residents that some poor households had been excluded from the list and some non-poor households included. The suspicion caused widespread discontent with the Below Poverty Line list generated from this survey.

---

[37] Panchayats and Rural Development Department, Government of West Bengal (2008a, pp. 123–5).
[38] See BPL Census 2002.

In 2006, the village development officer of Warwat Khanderao village panchayat repeated the house-to-house survey to revise the Below Poverty Line list. However, as was the case in Raina, only some of the discrepancies were corrected.

The filled-up schedules collected from all Above Poverty Line and Below Poverty Line households and the amended Below Poverty Line list were available at the Warwat Khanderao panchayat office and on the website of the Ministry of Rural Development. This database included not only a list of households, but also a list of members of each household.

Usami, Sarkar, and Ramachandran (2010) have made an assessment of the quality of the Below Poverty Line list generated from the Below Poverty Line Census in Warwat Khanderao. The assessment was made by matching some of the parameters in that Census with comparable data collected through the census-type household surveys conducted by the Foundation for Agrarian Studies. As a result of the assessment, they found that the Below Poverty Line list generated from the Below Poverty Line Census was not accurate. The village panchayat officials' dissatisfaction with this survey was therefore justified.[39]

Below Poverty Line Census in Raina
The Below Poverty Line Census was conducted in Raina in 2005 as the Rural Household Survey. There was a similar discontent with the Below Poverty Line list generated from this survey. Therefore, as mentioned in section 4.3.2, officials of the Raina village panchayat had to conduct an independent alternative census-type survey for all households in the panchayat area and collect information on the same parameters as the Rural Household Survey.

The filled-up schedules collected from all Above Poverty Line and Below Poverty Line households and the amended Below Poverty Line list were available at the Raina village panchayat office. However, the database for Bidyanidhi village did not have the full list of members of each household. Of the 151 households listed in the Rural Household Survey database, information on household members was available only for 17.

We also obtained the database from the Ministry of Rural Development's website and made an assessment of the quality of the Below Poverty Line

[39] Usami, Sarkar, and Ramachandran (2010).

list generated from the Rural Household Survey in Bidyanidhi village. The assessment was made by matching the Rural Household Survey's data on some of the parameters with data collected through the census-type household surveys conducted by the Foundation for Agrarian Studies. As a result, we again found that the Below Poverty Line list generated from the survey was inaccurate and that the dissatisfaction with this survey among the panchayat officials was justified.[40]

Thus, the identification of households living below the poverty line using the 2002 Below Poverty Line Census caused widespread discontent among residents in both the village panchayats. Nevertheless, the database generated from the Below Poverty Line Census (or Rural Household Survey) can be used not only for the identification of households below the poverty line, but also for multiple purposes. Therefore, we will evaluate the Below Poverty Line Census (or Rural Household Survey) for such purposes in section 6.6, chapter 6.

[40] Bakshi and Okabe (2008, pp. 21–2). The two data sets, that is, the Rural Household Survey data and the Foundation for Agrarian Studies data are roughly comparable since both surveys were conducted in the same year. There were 36 households in the Below Poverty Line list, of which 32 households could be found in the Foundation for Agrarian Studies' survey list. Our analysis is restricted to these 32 households. The result of our analysis is as follows:

Female-headed households: A household headed by a woman was considered as a "special kind of disability" (P12) in the Rural Household Survey. Of the 32 households, 12 were female-headed according to the Survey. We found that seven of these households were not actually female-headed households. In two households the wives were reported as the head of the household even when the husband was present and economically active. In five cases, a widowed mother was reported as the head of the household when the actual head of the household was the working adult son.

Landholding: Of the 32 households only one was reported to own land in the Rural Household Survey. According to our survey, 12 households owned land, though the size of landholdings was very small and in all cases less than an acre.

Literacy status of the highest literate adult: In 13 cases the education status of the most educated member of the family in the two data sets did not match.

Status of the household labour force: There were some discrepancies in the two data sets. In many households adult women members were not reported to be working, thus gaining higher scores for households.

Means of livelihood: In 6 cases, the means of livelihood was reported as daily/agricultural/ other physical labour in the Rural Household Survey, whereas according to the Foundation for Agrarian Studies survey the household was self-employed in agriculture or in some other occupation or held a labour-oriented regular job in the unorganised sector. In two cases, the agricultural-labour households were classified as 'organised sector worker' and 'regular worker in unorganised sector', respectively.

Educational status of children from 9 to 14 years: Only in 6 of the 32 households the score assigned in the Rural Household Survey matched with the Foundation for Agrarian Studies' survey data.

Results of the fourth Below Poverty Line Census (the Socio-Economic and Caste Census, 2011) are forthcoming.[41] The Socio-economic and Caste Census uses a revised methodology for the identification of households below the poverty line. The Socio-Economic and Caste Census uses a two-stage method to identify poor households. In the first stage, a household is automatically excluded or included in the list if it satisfies any one criterion from a list of fourteen criteria for exclusion and five criteria for inclusion. The remaining households are ranked using seven new indicators (instead of thirteen). The indicators are binary (yes/no) indicators, thus minimising problems of scoring.

4.3.4.2 Population Census

The Population Census is conducted every ten years. The Census of India is a Union subject under the Ministry of Home Affairs. The conduct of the Population Census is the joint work of the Central and State Governments. The entire field operation, which includes house listing and population enumeration, is organised through the administrative machinery of the States. For example, the enumerator of Bidyanidhi for the Census of India 2001 was a single primary-school teacher. When we visited Bidyanidhi in February 2011, the Integrated Child Development Services (*anganwadi*) worker was the enumerator of another village.

The Population Census data (population enumeration, house listing, and housing data) is indisputably one of the most important data sources of demographic information. It consists of details of the Census house, amenities, information on households and on each household member, such as sex, age, marital status, religion, mother tongue, and language, Scheduled-Caste/Scheduled-Tribe eligibility, literacy, level of education, worker/non-worker status, economic activity, characteristics of migration, and fertility particulars. The National Statistical Commission observed that[42]

> after the 73rd and 74th constitutional amendments passed by the Parliament in 1992, the Population Census data has immense potential to serve the planning and development data needs of the *panchayati raj* institutions at the grass-roots level. The process of democratic decentralisation set in motion by the above Acts of Parliament have transferred responsibility for 29 items including primary health care, primary education, family planning, and minor developmental works to the elected local bodies. State Governments have begun the process of transferring funds to the *panchayati raj* Institutions

[41] At the time of going to press, preliminary results have been published.
[42] National Statistical Commission (2001, para. 9.2.16).

Table 4.9 *House listing and Housing Census Schedule, Census of India, 2011*

Location Particulars

State/Union Territory

District

Tahsil/taluk/panchayat samiti/Dev. Block/circle/mandal

Town/village

Ward code no. (only for towns)

House listing Block no.

1. Line number
2. Building number (Municipal or local authority or Census number)
3. Census house number
   Predominant material of floor, wall and roof of the Census house
4. Floor
5. Wall
6. Roof
7. Ascertain use of Census house
8. Condition of this Census house
9. Household number
   Total number of persons normally residing in this household:
10. Persons
11. Males
12. Females
13. Name of the head of the household
14. Sex
15. If Scheduled caste or Scheduled tribe or Other
16. Ownership status of this house
17. Number of dwelling rooms exclusively in possession of this household
18. Number of married couple(s) living in this household
19. Main source of drinking water
20. Availability of drinking water source
21. Main source of lighting
22. Latrine within the premises
23. Type of latrine facility
24. Waste water outlet connected to
25. Bathing facility available within the premises
26. Availability of kitchen
27. Fuel used for cooking
28. Radio/transistor
29. Television
30. Computer/laptop
31. Telephone/mobile phone
32. Bicycle
33. Scooter/motorcycle/moped
34. Car/jeep/van
35. Availing banking services

Table 4.10 *Household Schedule, Census of India, 2011*

---

1. Name of the person
2. Relationship to head of household
3. Sex
4. Date of birth and age
5. Current marital status
6. Age at marriage
7. Religion
8. Scheduled Caste/Scheduled Tribe
9. Disability
10. Mother tongue
11. Other languages known
12. Literacy status
13. Status of attendance in educational institution
14. Highest educational level attained
15. Worked any time during last year
16. Category of economic activity
17. Occupation
18. Nature of industry, trade or service
19. Class of worker

For marginal worker or non worker
20. Non-economic activity
21. Seeking or available for work

For other worker
22. Travel to place of work (a) One-way distance (b) Mode of travel to place of work
23. Birth place
24. Place of last residence
25. Reason for migration
26. Duration of stay in this village/town since migration

For currently married, widowed, divorced or separated woman:
27. Children surviving
28. Children ever born

For currently married woman
29. Number of children born alive during last one year

---

and *nagar palikas* to enable them implement these activities. In this changed context, the census must respond with urgency to the data needs at the district, Block, *panchayat* and village levels starting with the recently collected Census 2001 data.

The data items in the Census of India, 2011, are described in Tables 4.9 and 4.10.

Population Census data at and above the village level are published in the District Census Handbooks. As shown in Tables 4.1 and 4.2, accurate data on migration and employment statuses are not available from the village-level data source, other than the Census of India. In their absence, we have to depend on, say, brief notes in the comments column for each member of the household in the Integrated Child Development Services (*anganwadi*) village survey register.

Population Census data are obviously the core statistics for panchayati raj institutions. Census data are utilised for determining the seats and electoral boundaries for the panchayat elections, for formulating programmes and policies, and for providing a formula to calculate inter-panchayati raj shares in fund allocation.[43]

However, one of the problems in the Census of India is the frequency of data collection. It is a decennial event. It cannot be updated more frequently. Furthermore, undue delay in processing Census data is a serious problem, as pointed out by the National Statistical Commission. The final data are available with the panchayati raj institutions only after a long time lag.

Moreover, panchayati raj institutions do not have access to unit-level household data from the Population Census as it is taken as per the provisions of the Census Act, 1948, which places a legal obligation upon the public to cooperate and give truthful answers and guarantees confidentiality of their information. Information on each household from the Population Census must not be used for administrative purposes.

Village-level Census data were not available at the panchayat office in Warwat Khanderao. The village development officer said it was not useful because of the undue delay in the release of final results. The village-level Census data were available at the Block Development Office. The village-level Census data reach the Raina village panchayat late. The panchayat officials said that the Census data are fairly reliable, though the data is out-of-date by the time it reaches the panchayat.[44]

4.3.4.3 Livestock Census

The Livestock Census is conducted every five years by the Ministry of Agriculture through the State Animal Husbandry Departments with the help of their field staff. Enumerators visit houses, enterprises, and institutions to

---

[43] We discuss the potential uses of Census data at the village level in chapters 5 and 6.
[44] Interview at the Raina village panchayat office in September 2008.

collect information about the type of livestock and poultry, and the pieces of equipment used in the animal husbandry sector. However, the census data are not aggregated according to the households and their composition. The National Statistical Commission noted the excessive delay in completing the census operation and the long time lag in the availability of census results.[45] Both the village panchayats in Warwat Khanderao and Raina had access to the household-level data of the Livestock Census from the Block-level offices. However, the data were not available at the panchayat office itself.

4.3.4.4 Agricultural Census

No information about the Agricultural Census could be found at either of the two villages in Maharashtra and West Bengal. The Agricultural Census of India has been conducted by the Ministry of Agriculture since 1970–1 at five-yearly intervals as a part of the World Census of Agriculture. The Agricultural Census is expected to provide detailed statistics on the structure of operational holdings and their main characteristics such as number and area, land use, irrigation, tenancy, and cropping pattern. Reportedly, the Agricultural Census of 2005–6 covered 13,716,000 operational holdings in Maharashtra and 6,992,000 in West Bengal.[46] However, the National Statistical Commission noted serious deficiencies in the Agricultural Census. One of the principal shortcomings is attributable to its method of re-tabulation of data. The Commission stated that "its reliability rests on how accurate and up-to-date the records are. It is well known that the village records are deficient in several respects."[47] Another issue noted by the Commission is the delay in the availability of final results. According to the Commission, the time lag from the reference period can be between four and six years.

In the erstwhile temporarily-settled States, the Agricultural Census follows

---

[45] National Statistical Commission (2001, para. 4.13.3).

[46] Ministry of Agriculture (2006a, p. 57).

[47] National Statistical Commission (2001, paras 4.9.5–4.9.7). Apart from the fact that the village records are deficient in several respects, the National Statistical Commission (*ibid.*, para. 4.9.8) points out other issues in the system of the Agricultural Census as follows: "Initially, there was a fairly high-level hierarchy of officials responsible for planning and organising census operations. At the Central level there was an Agricultural Census Commissioner of India with adequate supporting staff and also a Monitoring Group under the Chairmanship of a Special Secretary. There used to be a corresponding mechanism at the State level to plan and supervise the census operations. However, over time, there has been depletion in the numbers and status of personnel in charge of the census. Apparently, the census ceased to have the same importance and priority, with the result that there has been significant erosion in the quality and timeliness of census data."

the method of re-tabulation of data from village land records.[48] The Revenue (patwari) system could have played a pivotal role in the re-tabulation of village land records. Nevertheless, the *patwari* of Warwat Khanderao had no idea of the Agricultural Census.[49] Land recording in Maharashtra is primarily by means of an ownership-holding register, not an operational-holding register. As the *patwari* of Warwat Khanderao noted, the record on tenants is unreliable. Thus, it would not be possible to produce statistics of operational holdings without village-level land records on tenants in Maharashtra.

In the erstwhile permanently-settled States, the Agricultural Census is to be taken through a complete listing by house-to-house enquiry of operational holders in a twenty per cent sample of villages. The sample villages are to include all the villages selected under the scheme for Establishment of an Agency for Reporting Agricultural Statistics.[50] The panchayat officers in Raina, however, had no idea of the Agricultural Census. According to the Block-level Agricultural Officer of Raina I Block, the final published data of the Agricultural Census and even data generated from the Establishment of an Agency for Reporting Agricultural Statistics scheme were not available at the Block-level at the time.

[48] As pointed earlier, basic data of the Agricultural Census for the erstwhile temporarily-settled States is compiled through re-tabulation of information available in the village land records. "In States where comprehensive land records exist, the data on the number and area of operational holdings according to different size-classes, social groups and gender of operational holder, would be collected and compiled on complete enumeration basis through re-tabulation of information available in the Village Land Records. This would imply covering all the survey numbers within each village and preparing a list of 'Operational Holdings' therefrom" (Ministry of Agriculture 2006a, p. 2); "Some holdings may not be located completely within the village and they may be spread over to other villages. For preparation of a list of operational holdings, necessary matching of the part-holders scattered over more than one village has to be done" (*ibid.*, p. 3); "The most important part of the Census is the preparation of the list of operational holdings. In preparing the list of operational holdings in the village, one has to go through all the survey numbers in the basic village record, viz., '*khasra* register' and/or any other equivalent local variant, and has to see whether they form part of any operational holding. One could take the *khasra* register as the base and classify all the survey numbers/sub-survey numbers held by an operational holder" (*ibid.*, pp. 7-8); "For this purpose, the primary worker can make use of the basic village land records such as land deed (*Khatauni, patta*) Register, B1 Form, Village Form 8(A) and Crop Register, which are also known as *Khasra* Register/ *Khasra Girdwar*/ *Adangal*/ Village Form VII–XII/*Pahani Patrak*, etc. *Khatauni* is a register, which gives the list of persons who own land along with the area owned. The concept followed in Agricultural Census is of Operational Holding and not the ownership holding" (*Ibid.*, p. 17).
[49] Interview at the *patwari* office in Warwat Khanderao on August 18–22, 2011.
[50] "These sample villages have to include all the villages selected under the scheme for Establishment of an Agency for Reporting Agricultural Statistics (EARAS)" Ministry of Agriculture (2006b, p. 3).

4.3.4.5 Economic Census

Neither Warwat Khanderao nor Raina village panchayat had access to data from the Economic Census. Block-level officers of both village panchayats recognised that the field operations were certainly carried out in their jurisdictions.

The Economic Census has been conducted throughout India since 1977. The Fifth Economic Census was conducted in 2005 by the Central Statistical Organisation, Ministry of Statistics and Programme Implementation of the Central Government.[51] This Census covers all the village-level units (establishments) engaged in economic activities (agricultural and non-agricultural), with the exception of those involved in crop production and plantation.[52] It covers production and/or distribution of goods and/or services other than those for the sole purpose of the producer's own consumption. Although economic units engaged in the growing of tea, coffee, rubber, tobacco, etc. are not covered by this Census, establishments engaged in the processing of tea, coffee, tobacco etc. are covered by it. Establishments with fixed premises were covered at the place of their operation. On the other hand, economic activities that are carried out without any fixed premises or location were identified at the first step through households. This "mixed household-enterprise survey" is an appropriate method of measuring the informal sector.[53]

The Fifth Economic Census in 2005 was reported to have covered 2,110,191 establishments in rural Maharashtra and 2,772,415 in rural West Bengal.[54] The census collected information on the location of each establishment, description of economic activity carried out, the nature of operations, type of ownership, the social group of the owner, use of power/fuel, the total number of workers usually engaged, its hired component, and numbers of male and female workers.

---

[51] When we visited Raina village in February 2011, the Sixth Economic Census (2012–3) was being prepared along with the house-listing operations of the 2011 Population Census. The Second (1980) and the Third (1990) Economic Censuses were integrated with the house-listing operations of the 1981 and 1991 Population Censuses, respectively.

[52] "It may be noted that while the growing of tea, coffee, rubber, tobacco, etc. are not classified as agricultural establishment for the purpose of this census, however establishments engaged in processing of tea, coffee, tobacco etc. are covered" (Ministry of Statistics and Programme Implementation 2012, p. 6).

[53] European Commission, International Monetary Fund, Organisation for Economic Co-operation and Development, United Nations, and World Bank (2009, p. 481).

[54] Central Statistical Organisation (2008).

Table 4.11 *Number of enterprises in rural areas engaged in unregistered manufacturing activities according to the Economic Census, 1990, and the Follow-up Enterprise Survey, 1989–90* in thousands

	Maharashtra	West Bengal
Economic Census, 1990	236	479
Follow-up Enterprise Survey, 1989–90	591	2418

Source: National Statistical Commission (2001), Annexe 5.15.

The National Statistical Commission noted that the number of manufacturing enterprises reported by Economic Census was generally much lower than the estimate given by the Follow-up Enterprise Survey. Table 4.11 illustrates the number of enterprises in rural areas engaged in unregistered manufacturing activities according to the Follow-up Enterprise Survey. It raises concern about the quality of data on village-level unregistered units (establishments) engaged in economic activities. If all the Economic Census data were disclosed at the village level, this discrepancy could be scrutinised.[55] Although village panchayats in both Maharashtra and West Bengal had authority over Schedule XI's subject 9 ("Khadi, village and cottage industries"), they did not have access to village-level Economic Census data.

4.3.4.6 All-India School Education Survey

Data from the All-India School Education Survey (AISES) conducted by the National Council of Educational Research and Training is disclosed on its website.[56] The village panchayats can access this website to access the AISES data. A village-wide school directory is also disclosed on the website. AISES is conducted at intervals of five-to-seven years to collect detailed data on enrolment, teachers and physical facilities in schools. Information on each village is also collected using the Village Information Form. A Block-level officer organises the survey with the help of the District Survey Officer.[57]

---

[55] "Recently, an Expert Committee to examine wide variations in data sets on the same subjects (Report released in February 2000) also studied the said divergence in the alternative data sets. According to the Report, the total number of manufacturing enterprises in the country as estimated by the FuS 1989–90 and the EC 1990 are about 144 lakhs and 54 lakhs, respectively. Thus the FuS estimate is about 2.7 times the EC count despite the fact that the FuS considered only unregistered enterprises as against the EC taking into account all types of enterprises irrespective of their status of registration or type of ownership" (National Statistical Commission 2001, para. 5.2.19).

[56] See the All India School Education Survey.

[57] A School Inspector whom we met during our follow-up research at the Marathi-medium upper-primary school, Warwat Khanderao, in October 2013 recognised this survey activity.

Although village-level data on the school regularly moves upward, the school headmaster at Warwat Khanderao was not aware of any such survey conducted by the Block-level officers.

During our fieldwork we came to know that there were three private primary (i.e. from class nursery to four) schools in the Raina panchayat area. However, the AISES village-level school directory did not have information on these three schools. It is possible that AISES underestimates privately run unrecognised schools in India.

4.3.5 Administrative Reports of the Village Panchayat

4.3.5.1 Village Schedule on Basic Statistics

As described in chapter 1, the *Basic Statistics for Local Level Development* report suggested a minimum list of variables in the form of the Village Schedule on whose basis data was to be collected. At present, the database on the Village Schedule is merely in its pilot stage. A full-fledged scheme for Basic Statistics for Local Level Development has not come into being. The Expert Committee on Basic Statistics for Local Development conducted a pilot study in nine states – Bihar, Haryana, Gujarat, Karnataka, Kerala, Meghalaya, Tamil Nadu, Tripura, and West Bengal – from 2003 to 2005. Subsequently the Ministry of Statistics and Programme Implementation started a pilot scheme on Basic Statistics in 2009–10 in 32 States and Union Territories, excluding Delhi, Goa, and Chandigarh. Based on the findings of the first phase of the pilot study, in 2011, a report called *Cross-Sectional Synthesis Report on Pilot Scheme of Basic Statistics for Local (Village) Level Development* (hereafter the *Cross-Sectional Synthesis Report 2011*) was released. The *Report on Basic Statistics for Local Level Development (BSLLD): Pilot Study in Rural Areas* (hereafter the *CSO Report 2014*) was published in 2014. Many State-level reports have also been released.[58]

So far in these country-wide pilot studies, the Village Schedule and its Field Instructions have been repeatedly tested and modified. In the pilot studies, feedback from different States and Union Territories was sought on data sources, availability of data for different items of information, and problems in data compilation.

---

[58] Synthesis reports, available at http://mospi.nic.in/Mospi_New/upload/lld_data_13jan12/state_report_2012.htm

The revised Village Schedule at present consists of the following blocks of data items:

Block 0: Descriptive identification of the village
Block 1: Particulars of data recording
Block 2: Availability of some basic facilities
Block 3: Village infrastructure
Block 4: Distance from the nearest facility
Block 5: Demographic information
Block 6: Morbidity, disability and family planning
Block 7: Health manpower
Block 8: Education
Block 9: Land utilisation
Block 10: Livestock and poultry
Block 11: Number of storage and marketing outlets
Block 12: Employment status of the villagers
Block 13: Migration
Block 14: Other social indicators
Block 15: Industries and businesses
Block 16: Information on fatality due to disasters

In principle, the data in the Schedule should be compiled once a year. If the information is not available for the year of reporting, the Ministry of Statistics and Programme Implementation directs that "latest data available may be recorded along with reference period."[59]

In the initial phase of the pilot studies conducted by the Ministry of Statistics, two Village Schedules – viz. Schedule A for periodic datasets to be compiled once in a year; and Schedule B for dynamic datasets to be compiled for each month of the reference period – were used for data compilation. However, based on experience gained in the first few years, the two Schedules were integrated into one for which data were compiled just once in a year.[60] Month

[59] "Information on age-group-wise population, employment, migration, etc. may not be available for the year of reporting at village level. In such cases, latest data available may be recorded along with reference period" (Central Statistics Office 2014, p. 126).
[60] Since the pilot scheme in 2012–3, "the concept of monthly collection of data for some items of information was dispensed with" (Central Statistics Office 2014, p. 26). The *Cross-Sectional Synthesis Report* (2011) provided by the Ministry of Statistics has already recommended that "the Schedules (both Schedule A for periodic data and Schedule B for dynamic data) need to be rationalised with a view to reduce incidence of missing data, particularly in respect of Schedule B items and to improve timeliness in completion of field work for filling out the schedules." "The two schedules may be integrated into one schedule to make it amenable to

by month dynamic data in Schedule B were converted to data "as per the last month of the reference period" (Block 13, Block 14, Block 15) or data "during the reference year" (Item 5.6 to 5.13 of Block 5).[61] A month by month dynamic dataset is certainly required for Data Needs I (i.e. data requirements for self-governance) to monitor changes of matters in the jurisdiction of the village panchayat. However, as far as the annual or five-year planning is concerned, month by month dynamic data are not a high priority requirement for Data Needs III (i.e. data requirements for micro-level planning).[62] As mentioned before, the Village Schedule on Basic Statistics was developed just for Data Needs III.[63] Thus, Schedule on Basic Statistics is compiled from secondary data and, if these are not available, the assessment of knowledgeable persons (or common knowledge among village residents) may be used. But most of the items in the Schedule have to be compiled from secondary data. The majority of data items must have documentary support. Most such data sources have already been described in sections 4.3.1 to 4.3.4. Therefore, the Schedule is merely a framework for compiling records and registers that have already been recorded by local functionaries. The *Instructions for Data Recordist* of the Schedule are as follows:

> The information in the Village Schedule is not to be collected by conducting house-to-house surveys. The information is to be recorded in the schedule from the records available at the village level and being maintained by different village-level functionaries, such as *anganwadi* workers, ANM, Panchayat Secretaries, schoolteachers, *patwaris*, village headman, and knowledgeable persons, etc. The village Directory of Census 2011, i.e., Primary Census Abstract may also be utilised as required. If required, data may be elicited from knowledgeable persons in case the particular data cannot be obtained from the records/registers.[64]

Although the *Basic Statistics for Local Level Development* report did not mention it, the Central Statistics Office suggested the use of alternative datasets from the Socio-Economic and Caste Census, 2011. The village-level data from the fourth Below Poverty Line Census (the Socio-Economic and

---

capture the required data on annual basis through one time operation once in every year" (Central Statistics Office 2011, p. vii).

[61] Central Statistics Office (2014, p. 163, 168).

[62] "The dynamic month-to-month changes are found to be very insignificant at the village level for almost all dynamic variables covered in Schedule B" (Central Statistics Office 2011, p. vii).

[63] Central Statistical Organisation (2006, p. A-1).

[64] Central Statistics Office (2014, p. 131).

Caste Census, 2011) can be used to fill in the Village Schedule. According to the Central Statistics Office,

> Most of the Directorate of Economics and Statistics (DES) informed that compilation of demographic data (Block 5) and employment data (Block 12) is difficult. However, after completion of Socio-Economic and Caste Census, data on population – sex-wise, age-wise, caste-wise and religion-wise – are available at the village level and also at each individual/ household level. These data may be aggregated as per the requirement of the BSLLD schedule.[65]

Thus, various village-level data sources are supposed to be in existence before the Village Schedule is filled-up. That is, a set of village-level data sources should be found that correspond to data items of the Village Schedule.

The Village Schedule on Basic Statistics is intended not merely to compile existing secondary data, but also to elaborate upon them. The *Instructions for Data Recordist* of the Schedule notes:

> The village-level registers should be developed and maintained through compilation of village-level statistics in order to have a continuous flow of data. The village panchayat will take the basic responsibility of maintaining proper registers at the village level.[66]

The completed Village Schedule on Basic Statistics travels upward from the village in the hierarchy. It is assumed that the "District Statistical Office (DSO) will coordinate with village panchayats and village-level functionaries from different departments for getting the information compiled in the village schedule." Completed schedules are to be received and carefully examined

---

[65] *Ibid.*, p. 126.

[66] *Ibid.*, p. 131. The CSO of the Ministry of Statistics and Programme Implementation states that "owing to the fact that village panchayat is the lowest level of three tier panchayati raj Institutions and many village level records are maintained at village panchayat level, the village panchayats may be kept as the focal point for data compilation. The data, however, may be compiled village-wise." The Ministry notes that "The panchayat secretary may be involved as a compiler or as a facilitator for compilation of the village level data . . . . In case, panchayat secretary is not in a position to compile village-level data, any village-level functionary may be engaged. If that also is not feasible, local educated persons may be engaged" (*ibid.*, p. 123). "They have also engaged a person on contract and paid him/her an honorarium for filling up the Village Schedule as per guidelines/ instructions. The person engaged was named as 'data recordist,' and preferably was the panchayat secretary himself/herself, who had successfully completed schooling up to 10+2 standard. However, if that was not feasible, then the data recordist appointed could be a school teacher or a social service volunteer who fulfils the aforesaid educational qualification. The data recordist had to compile data from the registers as far as possible" (*ibid.*, pp. 16–7).

at the District Statistical Office, the Block Statistical Office or the Block Development Office. Data entry and tabulation of data is to be conducted at the same place. The State's Directorates of Economics and Statistics (DES) should ensure consolidation and tabulation of data, and publication of the report at the village-panchayat, Block, district and State levels. Therefore, Village Schedule data can be used not only at the village level, but also at the district and State levels. There should exist three copies of the filled in Village Schedules. One copy is to be retained in the village, one at the panchayat office, and one is to be sent to the appropriate District Statistical Office, Block Statistical Office or Block Development Office.

The *Cross-Sectional Synthesis Report 2011* stated that "almost all items of information are available with village-level field functionaries like *anganwadi* workers, ANM, panchayat secretary, *patwari*, schools etc."[67] It further noted that, "there exists a considerable degree of difference in the reporting coverage of data items from State to State and also between districts within a State;" but "except for Assam, the data coverage has been found to be quite high in all the States/UTs under analysis."[68]

However, the large-scale pilot scheme launched by the Central Statistics Office in 2009 revealed that some data items of Village Schedule on Basic Statistics are missing and are not likely to be available from village records (see section 8.1–8.2 in chapter 8). The *Cross-Sectional Synthesis Report 2011* stated that a "rationalisation exercise is required to take care *inter alia* of deletion of items, which are generally missing and are not likely to be available from available village records."[69] According to the *Report*, the information content with 128 sets of data in respect of the eight States and Union Territories covered by it had "35 sets (27 per cent) of data collected from not so desirable sources. Alternative sources have been tapped in the absence of information from desired sources due to the non-availability of source records or the custodian of the records at desired places."[70] The Central Statistics Office described this problem in its *CSO Report 2014* as follows:[71]

---

[67] Central Statistics Office (2011, D-11).

[68] *Ibid.*, p. iv-v. The *Cross-Sectional Synthesis Report* covers eight States and Union Territories for its analysis: remotely located States and Union Territories (e.g. Mizoram, Andaman and Nicobar Islands), a hill State (e.g. Sikkim), the North-East States (e.g. Assam, Mizoram, Sikkim), a large backward State (e.g. Rajasthan), a small-advanced State (e.g. Haryana), and a large-advanced State (e.g. Andhra Pradesh, Tamil Nadu).

[69] *Ibid.*, p. vii.

[70] *Ibid.*, pp. v-vi.

[71] Central Statistics Office (2014, p. 125).

The Scheme has established the feasibility of collection of data at local level (village) if the following limitations are addressed:

    The pilot survey has revealed that data for some items

    a) are available only from oral enquiry,

    b) no information is available and, therefore, the data for these items are to be estimated.

The data recordist is requested to compile data from the village records as far as possible. However, if the registers are not available, the "oral enquiry method" is acceptable. According to the Central Statistics Office:

> It is suggested that estimation should not be done at the stage of compilation of data. The data which is available should only be reported. Estimation may be done by the Directorates of Economics and Statistics.[72]

The large-scale pilot scheme on Basic Statistics conducted in 32 States and Union Territories since 2009 did not cover Buldhana district, and so the Warwat Khanderao village panchayat was also not covered. Maharashtra's Akola district, which adjoins Buldhana district, was selected for the pilot scheme. The Directorate of Economics and Statistics, Government of Maharashtra, has published a State report of that pilot scheme, which gives item-wise comments on the availability of the data sources.[73]

After 2009, the large-scale pilot scheme on Basic Statistics covered Bardhaman district, and so the Raina village panchayat was covered by the survey. The Raina village panchayat office kept copies of the Village Schedule filled up for the pilot survey. The Executive Assistant of the panchayat showed us the one for Bidyanidhi village. As mentioned in section 4.2 above, the Executive Assistant understood that all the information to be filled in the Schedule had been collected by the Integrated Child Development Services (ICDS) workers, though the source code Panchayat-01 was put in for most of the items. Our discussion with the ICDS worker at Bidyanidhi on February 23, 2011 revealed that the Basic Statistics pilot survey in Bidyanidhi was conducted by a teacher from Birampur Junior High School and a resident of Bidyanidhi village. The Bidyanidhi ICDS (*anganwadi*) worker had conducted the survey for Bogra village on the basis of information obtained from the ICDS (*anganwadi*) worker at Bogra. She also obtained information on the proportion of households with electricity and some other parameters from the village panchayat office. For some information she had to conduct a house-to-house survey.

---

[72] *Ibid.*, p. 125.

[73] Directorate of Economics and Statistics (2012).

The Block Development Office trained the investigators of the Basic Statistics pilot survey and oversaw the operations. [74] An enumerator was allotted for each hamlet (*mouza*), and the Village Schedules were filled out for each hamlet in the panchayat area. According to the Block Development Officer of Raina I Block, most of the enumerators were ICDS workers. The data were consolidated by the village panchayat. The enumerators collected information from ICDS registers, Health Department records, panchayat records and interviews with villagers. The filled out Schedules were sent to the Assistant Director of Statistics of Bardhaman District. The Block office did not have the data. The 2001 Census's Village Directory was not used for filling out the Village Schedule.

Although we have identified many village-level data sources available in Raina, we found some additional data items that were not likely to be available from these sources. Some data items in the Village Schedule were not likely to have documentary evidence in Raina. We will discuss the documentary evidence of each data item in chapter 8 (sections 8.1 and 8.2).

4.3.5.2 Village-level Amenities Data (VD Data) in the District Census Handbook
The Census of India provides village-level amenities data in the village directory along with the Population Census data (the population enumeration data, and the house-listing and housing data). However, the mechanism of data collection for the former is completely different from that for the latter. While the Population Census data are collected by conducting household-to-household surveys, the village-level amenities data in the village directory are compiled primarily from secondary data (existing records and registers), and otherwise from personal assessment made by knowledgeable persons. It provides panchayats with data on amenities and infrastructure, such as location of educational institutions, medical centres, drinking water, post and telegraph, commercial and cooperative banks, agricultural, non-agricultural and other credit societies, recreational and cultural facilities, communication, approach to village, distance from the nearest town, power supply, availability of newspapers and magazines, etc. The village-level amenities data also provides data on land utilisation and irrigation. The village directory of the 2011 Census of India is supposed to include the following sections:

Section 1: Educational facilities
Section 2: Medical facilities

---

[74] Interview with Shyamsundar, Block Development Officer, Raina I Block on February 22, 2011.

Section 3: Water and sanitation

Section 4: Communication and transport facilities

Section 5: Banks, credit, and other miscellaneous facilities

Section 6: Electricity and other power/fuel availability

Section 7: Land utilisation and irrigation

Section 8: Main commodities manufactured

Section 9: Comments and observations

Amenities and land-use data are primarily collected by Census officers from the village records already maintained, for example, by the health workers, Auxiliary Nurse Midwife, ICDS worker, *chowkidar*, elected village head, and *patwari*. The reference date for data collection in the village directory of the 2011 Census of India was December 31, 2009.

The Expert Committee on Basic Statistics stated that the village directory data contains most of the critical indicators required for local-level planning, but it is available only after a time lag.[75] The Expert Committee pointed that:

> the State governments have to update the Census information on an annual basis so that year-wise information on all the basic parameters of the village is available for local-level planning. However, data from Census on Amenities and Land Use is not available for many years after the Census.[76]

For this reason, the Expert Committee proposed "a village schedule for collection of Basic Statistics for Local Level Development." In this respect, the Village Schedule is considered to be a schedule evolved from the village directory.

The village-level amenities data (VD data) was compiled for Warwat Khanderao village by the Census officers and the District Statistical Officer. The Block Development Officer was not involved.[77] This was compiled for each village in the Raina panchayat area by Block-level offices. For the 2011 Census of India, the Block Development Officer received a village questionnaire from the Census Office, which he had to consolidate and return to Census Office.[78] Although Raina panchayat officials said that the Census data were fairly reliable, they complained that the data were outdated because of late release.[79]

[75] Central Statistical Organisation (2006), p. 19.

[76] *Ibid.*

[77] Interview at the Block Development Office, Sangrampur on April 25, 2014.

[78] Interview with Shyamsundar, Block Development Officer, Raina I Block on February 22, 2011.

[79] Interview at the Raina panchayat office, Rayna in September 2008.

4.3.5.3 Self Evaluation Schedule (Raina only)
As described in section 1 of chapter 2, the Self-Evaluation Schedule for Panchayats provided by the Panchayats and Rural Development Department of West Bengal was also an important administrative report on village panchayats or their village assembly. This Schedule has been submitted to the Block Development Officer every year since 2006–7. Every village panchayat kept one copy. In this format the panchayat had to evaluate and assign scores for different indicators specified in the given format. The village panchayat received financial incentives from the State Government based on its self-evaluation.

Some institutional aspects of the panchayat, i.e. "(a) institutional functioning and good governance"; and "(b) mobilisation of revenue and utilisation of resources" were common knowledge among the panchayat officials, even though they were not documented. Information on panchayat facilities and its activities is typical of such kind of data. Besides data on institutional aspects of the panchayat, the introductory part (*Village Panchayat at a Glance*) of the Self-Evaluation Schedule contained basic data about the village panchayat, which were compiled from panchayat registers, other village-level functionaries' registers, census-type surveys, and popular knowledge.

4.3.5.4 Annual Report of the Warwat Khanderao Village Panchayat
We found at the Sangrampur Block Development Office a report containing village-level information on the Warwat Khanderao village panchayat. According to the Block Development Officer, this report was updated annually and maintained for all panchayats in the State in a uniform format. This report was a format for compiling secondary data that had already been collected by local-level functionaries. The report that we obtained consisted of five parts: Part 1: Basic information of local development; Part 2: Details of facilities available in the village; Part 3: Education facilities; Part 4: Industries and business; Part 5: Village-level work under different schemes from the last five years. The report did not contain health-related information corresponding to Blocks 6 and 7 of the Village Schedule. But it had a part like Part 5, which the Village Schedule did not contain.[80] The Block Development

---

[80] The *Basic Statistics for Local Level Development* report (Central Statistical Organisation 2006, p. 25) mentions that the Directorate of Economics and Statistics of the Maharashtra Government collected village-wise detailed information on education, health, water facilities, village amenities, and the like for the development of a GIS by the Maharashtra Remote Sensing Application Centre. However, according to the Committee, "the data were collected and validated over a period of about two years and no attempt could be made to update the data."

Officer at Sangrampur said that the District office was responsible for this Schedule.[81] The village development officer of Warwat Khanderao village panchayat maintained this Schedule for his own reference.[82]

4.3.5.5 The Raina Village Panchayat's Booklet

Protibedon is a booklet published annually by the Raina village panchayat. It is not mandatory for panchayats in West Bengal to produce such booklets/reports, but most village panchayats published such information periodically.[83] These booklets were made available free of cost to the public as a measure of transparency and accountability of the village panchayat. We obtained the 2007–8 issue of the Annual Report by Raina village panchayat (Protibedon) for our analysis. It was a 48-page document. The contents of this document were as follows:

Description of the village panchayat: The first page of the report contained general information on the panchayat, its population, land area and land use, number of schools, ICDS centres, health centres, banks, post offices, cooperatives, road length and number of beneficiaries in important schemes (pensions, number of Below Poverty Line and Antyodaya Anna Yojana cardholders, constructions under the Sajal Dhara drinking water scheme). This page also listed the names of every panchayat member and the panchayat's administrative staff.

Financial statement of accounts (Form 27): The report disclosed the financial accounts (receipts and expenditures) as specified in Form 27 of the West Bengal Gram Panchayat Accounts, Audit, Budget Rules, 2007, for the year 2007–8. In addition to the summary information in the specified format, the booklet also provided details of payments made from the receipt of Central Finance Commission funds, untied funds, the local Member of Legislative Assembly's area development fund (Bidhayak Elaka Unnayan Prakalpa), and the Sampoorna Grameen Rozgar Yojana.

---

[81] Interview at the Block Development Office, Sangrampur on August 18–22, 2011.

[82] Interview at the Block Development Office, Sangrampur on April 25, 2014.

[83] A work of research on the MGNREGS by one of the co-authors of this book (Bakshi 2011) found a similar report from Bonkati village panchayat in the Kanksa Block in the Bardhaman district. The document was titled Annual Report of Bonkati Gram Panchayat and it provided information on finances and all activities undertaken by the panchayat. In most cases, the panchayats try to publish such booklets every year, but sometimes the frequency is less. For example, the Raina village panchayat could not publish a new booklet in 2009. There is no uniform or stipulated format for such publications.

MGNREGS: Detailed information on expenditure, and person-days of employment for each project (with project code) undertaken under the MGNREGS was published.

Beneficiaries of other schemes: The report contained detailed information (number, names, amount received) on the beneficiaries of different schemes and programmes implemented by the village panchayat, such as the *Bhavisyanidhi Yojana, Indira Awaas Yojana,* pension schemes, schemes involving self-help groups, *Mahila Samriddhi Yojana,* and *Sampoorna Grameen Rozgar Yojana.* Detailed expenditures under the *Sampoorna Grameen Rozgar Yojana* and Central Finance Commission funds were reported. Since panchayats are responsible for nurturing self-help groups, the booklet also contained information on each self-help group working in the panchayat area and its bank account number.

Revised budget: The document contained the revised budget estimates for 2007–8. The revised budget estimate presented the actual receipts for the previous year and the estimated receipts for 2007–8. It also contained the budgeted, detailed expenditure of funds under the five panchayat subcommittees (*upa-samitis*).

Other information: The document provided information on different schemes (such as the MGNREGS and self-help groups) in order to spread awareness about Government schemes and programmes.

4.3.5.6 Others
The Panchayats and Rural Development Department of West Bengal provided a Block-level booklet on the village-level development profile (*Gram Unnayan Byabosthar Chitro*). The booklet mapped the position of each village panchayat in the Blocks with respect to 17 socio-economic indicators such as heath, education, food security, nutritional status, household sanitation, performance in rural development schemes, resource mobilisation and utilisation. The village panchayat-level data on the 17 indicators were compiled from the panchayat's administrative reports and secondary data sources.

Warwat Khanderao village panchayat submitted an Annual Report to the concerned Block Development Officer. The majority of the Annual Reports were annual accounts, which were consolidated at the Block level after the end of the financial year and audited annually by the Local Fund Audit Department and by the Comptroller and Auditor General once every three years. This Annual Report contained some information from the Population Census, the results of panchayat elections, information on the administrative staff, dates of the village council and monthly meetings.

4.4 CONCLUSION: IDENTIFYING POTENTIAL DATABASES FOR LOCAL SELF-GOVERNANCE

In the post-Seventy-Third Amendment regime, a new statistical domain has emerged to serve the needs of local self-governance. In chapter 2, we gave an outline of the village panchayat's data requirements to help it fulfil the roles envisaged in the Amendment. In this chapter, we have listed the data available at the two village panchayats under study, in Maharashtra and West Bengal. In the remaining chapters, we assess the potential of village-level databases to serve the data needs identified in chapter 2. In this endeavour we try to converge data needs that we have identified with the data already available at the two village panchayats under focus. Our broader objective is to understand how a new statistical system can be evolved at the village panchayat-level that can also serve the bottom-up approach to local self-governance, planning, and implementation of development programmes.

The data requirements of village panchayats for the sake of self-governance can be classified into four broad categories (Figure 4.2). The classes are not necessarily mutually exclusive. Chapters 5 to 8 discuss in detail each specific element of these data requirements and identify existing data sources that have the potential to serve such requirements.

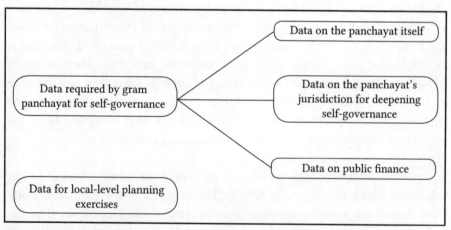

Figure 4.2 *Data requirements of village panchayats for self-governance and their planning exercises*

Chapter 5

A POTENTIAL VILLAGE-LEVEL DATABASE
ON THE PANCHAYAT

There are two kinds of data pertaining to a panchayat's self-governance – data on the panchayat itself and data on its object domain. For democratic procedures of self-governance, the village panchayat itself needs to be transparent in its functioning, even though some information on the panchayat may be common knowledge to panchayat officials. The core data on the panchayat itself pertains to the village council and the village panchayat's functions.

5.1 Records for the Village Council (Gram Sabha)

The Seventy-Third Amendment Act, 1992, envisages that citizens participate in democratic self-governance. A panchayat is a democratically elected government. The State Election Commission follows the procedure for supervising panchayat elections and prepares the electoral rolls independently of the panchayat.

The electoral roll is an essential record for the panchayat's regular activities because the village council is a body consisting of voters registered in the electoral roll. Furthermore, in Raina, electoral rolls were essential for the sub-panchayat body (i.e., the village ward or village assembly) too, which consisted of voters registered in the electoral roll within a constituency of the village panchayat. In Raina, therefore, the electoral rolls were compiled in terms of both the village wards and the village panchayat. The electoral roll contained each voter's identification number, full name, father's name, house number, age, and sex. However, it also included a record of people who were temporarily or permanently living outside the village. Therefore, it was not easy to identify valid voter records in the electoral roll. For example, according to the 2007 Foundation for Agrarian Studies survey, the total population aged 18 years and above was 809 while the number of voters in the electoral roll of Warwat Khanderao was 889. Thus, electoral rolls were not usable without a validation check with knowledgeable persons or other independent data.

Both village panchayats maintained attendance registers and minutes books for their council meetings. The "Monthly meeting attendance register" and "Proceedings book" were available in Warwat Khanderao, *Form 2* specified in the West Bengal Panchayat (Village Panchayat Administration) Rules, 2004, was also available in Raina. In Warwat Khanderao, the dates of the panchayat's monthly meetings and the village council meetings were reported to the Block Development Office in the Annual Report, while in Raina most of this information was submitted through the Self-Evaluation Schedule for Panchayats. The West Bengal Self-Evaluation Schedule requested data on the number of voters (according to the electoral roll), frequency of the village council meetings, and attendance rate at the meetings. Similar information was also requested for the subcommittees and the village development committees for self-evaluation.[1]

5.2 DATA FOR USE IN THE VILLAGE PANCHAYAT'S FUNCTIONAL DOMAIN

Data on how the panchayat functions are indispensable for self-governance. Under decentralisation, a panchayat is to perform the functions devolved to it. Many registers and records are generated and used as part of functions performed by the panchayat and its satellite agencies. A set of panchayat-level data sources found in parallel to data items of the Village Schedule is nothing other than the data generated by these village-level functionaries for operational use. Under democratic decentralisation, the panchayat has to disclose data, partly in order to fulfil democratic procedures of self-governance. The functions of the panchayat – i.e., what the panchayat has performed and is going to perform – are expected to be transparent. In order to participate in the panchayat's activities, a person needs access to the database on the village panchayat's functions.

The Panchayat Acts in both States (Section 8 of the Bombay Village Panchayats Act, 1958, and Section 18 of the West Bengal Panchayati Raj Act, 1973) envisage that the village panchayat prepares for the village council a report showing work and activities under each project, programme or scheme. Thus, the village panchayat is accountable to the village council for its activities and functions. The panchayat cannot be ignorant of matters for which it itself is responsible.

The village panchayats' functional domain is focused on "economic

---

[1] Department of Panchayats and Rural Development, Government of West Bengal (2008b).

development and social justice as may be entrusted to them, including those in relation to the matters listed in the Eleventh Schedule" (Article 243G). The village council delegates powers to subcommittees with respect to certain subjects or schemes in the functional domain of village panchayat (Section 49 of the Bombay Village Panchayats Act, 1958, and Section 66 of the West Bengal Panchayati Raj Act, 1973). In West Bengal, the village assembly may also delegate powers to the village development committee with respect to such subjects or schemes (Section 70 of the West Bengal Panchayati Raj Act, 1973).

As already discussed in chapter 2 (section 2.2.1.2), data for the panchayat's functional domain can be delineated by Activity Mapping. Without information on Activity Mapping, we cannot examine data for any level of the panchayat's functional domain.

The Second Administrative Reforms Commission observed that progress in Activity Mapping exercises was very slow in most States.[2] In fact, the actual status of Activity Mapping for the Warwat Khanderao village panchayat was different from what was envisaged in the Village List of the Bombay Village Panchayats Act, 1958. Activity Mapping in West Bengal is defined not by statute, but by executive order. As described in chapter 3 (section 3.3.7), we interviewed panchayat officials to assess "de facto Activity Mapping" for the panchayat. The panchayat officials usually knew the responsibilities assigned to them. We validated this information by follow-up interviews with the Block Development Officer and other Block-level officials. Data usage in the village panchayat's functional domain can be examined in relation to the de facto Activity Mapping, ascertained this way.

Next, we examine the possible use of the village-level databases identified in chapter 4 for this functional domain. Financial management and planning exercises are treated as special functions and are discussed in separate sections in chapter 7 and chapter 8 respectively.[3]

---

[2] Second Administrative Reforms Commission (2007, p. 45).
[3] As observed in section 3.8 in chapter 3, when a village panchayat functions within a framework of the "permissive functional domain," it may have limited responsibilities such as the basic formalities only to fill out forms. In such a case, the village panchayat has neither the responsibility of financial management, nor the authority to perform the planning exercise for a scheme. Even in such a case, from the viewpoint of self-governance, the village panchayat cannot be ignorant of matters for which it is responsible.

5.2.1 *Warwat Khanderao: Sector-wise Data Requirements*

As mentioned in chapter 3 (section 3.3.7), Activity Mapping was once legislated in Maharashtra through the Schedules of the Bombay Village Panchayat Act, 1958, and the Maharashtra Zilla Parishad and Panchayat Samiti Act, 1961. The village development officer of Warwat Khanderao panchayat pointed to Schedule I (Village List) of the Bombay Village Panchayats Act of 1958, when we asked him about Activity Mapping. However, as described in chapter 3 (section 3.3.7), the "de facto Activity Mapping" was quite different from the statutory Activity Mapping provided in Schedule I (Village List).

Primary Sector

As mentioned in relation to subject 1 ("Agriculture, including agricultural extension") of Schedule XI of the Constitution, identification of beneficiaries of schemes such as for the distribution of subsidised inputs is assigned to the Block-level committees. With regard to subject 4 ("Animal husbandry, dairying and poultry") the identification of beneficiaries of schemes such as for the distribution of subsidised inputs is assigned to the *tehsildar*. Announcement of such schemes was made by a drum-beater in Warwat Khanderao. Therefore, the Warwat Khanderao village panchayat does not require data for these functions.

However, as shown in chapter 3 (section 3.3.7), the coverage of the village panchayat's functional domain provided in Schedule I (Village List) of Bombay Village Panchayats Act, 1958, is much broader. For example, Schedule I (Village List) includes the function of "Drawing up of programmes for increasing the output of agricultural and non-agricultural produce in the village" as the sixtieth subject of activities to be devolved to the panchayats, and another function of "Improvement of agriculture (including provision of implements and stores) and establishment of model agricultural farms" as the second subject of activities. It also includes the function of making arrangements for "co-operative management of lands and other resources in village, and organisation of collective co-operative farming" as the first in the list of activities to be devolved to the village panchayats. If village panchayats in Maharashtra actually intended to perform these functions on the Village List, much more detailed data would be required by them.

With regard to subject 1 ("Agriculture") in Schedule XI, crop estimation in Warwat Khanderao was done by the *patwari*, village development officer, panchayat head and the Police *Patel.* The Agricultural Assistant or *krishi sahayak* from the State Agriculture Department signed the documents and the panchayat forwards the document to the *tehsildar.*

With regard to subject 2 ("Land improvement, soil conservation and land reform"), the distribution of vested or other land was done by the *tehsildar,* although the village panchayat sometimes had the power to make suggestions. Although the village panchayat's functioning with respect to land reforms was very limited, it could, in principle, access the *patwari's* land records if required. As "maintenance of village records relating to land revenue" has been provided as the fifty-eighth item in the list of activities to be devolved to panchayats in the Village List of the Bombay Village Panchayats Act 1958, panchayats in Maharashtra are empowered to intervene in the maintenance of land records in order to correct and update data on the seasonal use of land and the landowner–tenant relationship. As mentioned before, village functionaries, including the *patwari,* are statutorily under the control of the village panchayat as provided by the 2003 Amendment to the Bombay Village Panchayats Act.

With regard to subject 3 ("minor irrigation") in Schedule XI, the village panchayat was responsible only for basic formalities such as filling out forms and attaching documents. These were then sent to the Block-level committee which forwarded them to the District Collector. Warwat Khanderao village panchayat had access to plot-wise information on irrigation in the *patwari's* land records (Form 7/12).

Education

As mentioned in subject 17 ("education, including primary and secondary schools"), almost no function was assigned to Warwat Khanderao village panchayat. The function for improving school infrastructure was the responsibility of panchayats until 2010, but was assigned to the school management committee after 2010. One panchayat member, the school headmaster and parents were members of the committee for primary and upper-primary schools. However, "spread of education" and "other educational and cultural objects" are statutorily subjects that are to be devolved to village panchayats. But the Warwat Khanderao village panchayat did not perform these functions at all. With regard to subject 20 ("libraries"), a charitable trust owned the village library and a committee supervised the library.

Health and Child Development

As mentioned in relation to subject 23 ("health and sanitation, including hospitals, primary health centres and dispensaries") in Schedule XI, the State Sanitation Scheme is implemented by the village panchayat. The Warwat Khanderao village panchayat prepared a priority list for the State Sanitation Scheme. Certainly, subjects 24 "preservation and improvement of public health" and 23 ("maternity and child welfare") are statutorily provided as the panchayat's functional domain in Schedule I (Village List) of the Act of 1958.

Warwat Khanderao village panchayat had access to the village Integrated Child Development Services' registers. Although the primary health centre and sub-centres were located outside the panchayat area, an Auxiliary Nurse Midwife regularly visited Warwat Khanderao. The Integrated Child Development Services' workers sometimes collaborated with the Auxiliary Nurse Midwife for immunisation and other tasks.

The village panchayat was also an implementing agency for the Rural Sanitation Wing (*Grameen Swachchhata Vibhag*) of the Central Government. In the 2002 Below Poverty Line Census, households which reported not having a toilet were given a grant of Rs 2200 each. The money was allotted under a scheme called the Rural Sanitation Programme (*Nirmal Gaon Seva*).[4] Therefore, data on latrines in "scoring parameters" in the village-wise lists generated from the 2002 Census was essential for this function.

With regard to subject 24 ("family welfare") in Schedule XI, the village panchayat had no specific role in respect of implementation of schemes. The National Maternity Benefit Scheme was implemented by the primary health centres under the Public Health Department.

With regard to subject 25 ("women and child development"), the committee for women and children (*Mahila Bal Samiti*) mobilised social support against social evils and discrimination against women. It discussed and resolved matters related to women's and child welfare. Construction of Integrated Child Development Services' (*anganwadi*) centres and coordination of their activities were functions assigned to the panchayat. The Integrated Child

---

[4] Institutional Strengthening of Gram Panchayats (ISGP): the panchayat receives grants to construct community infrastructure and buildings that cannot be otherwise constructed under the NREGS. The Scheme has been functional since 2010–1. (Interview with the panchayat head at Warwat Khanderao in August 2011.)

Development Services' registers maintained at the village were an essential data set for the functional domain of "women and child development."

Income-generating activities were undertaken by self-help groups but these were organised by non-governmental organisations in Warwat Khanderao.

Poverty Alleviation and Social Welfare
According to the panchayat head of Warwat Khanderao, the panchayat's functional domain regarding subject 16 ("poverty alleviation programme") and subject 27 ("welfare of the weaker sections, and in particular, of the Scheduled Castes and the Scheduled Tribes") was restricted. The panchayat head complained, "the panchayat only fills out the forms; all rights are with the Block-level committee" for the poverty alleviation programme, and that "the panchayat had no specific role in respect of implementation of schemes for SCs and STs."[5] Thus the data needs of the village panchayat in this regard were also reduced. However, his remark revealed that the Block-level committee did have a certain role in the poverty alleviation programme at the village level.

As discussed, the Mahatma Gandhi National Rural Employment Guarantee Scheme (MGNREGS) was not functional in Warwat Khanderao, the panchayat's authority over the scheme notwithstanding. The Warwat Khanderao village panchayat issued 270 job cards in 2012-3.

The Warwat Khanderao village panchayat did not directly receive *Indira Awaas Yojana* funds from the Government agencies. The village panchayat sent a list of houseless people to the Block-level committee. The Committee selects beneficiaries under the *Indira Awaas Yojana* from this list. There were 171 buildings in the village. The *Indira Awaas Yojana* houses were allotted to those who reported not having a house in Below Poverty Line Census. Therefore, the village panchayat needed the village-wise Below Poverty Line households list to suggest a list of beneficiaries to the Block-level committee.

The Indira Gandhi National Old Age Pension Scheme was implemented by the *patwari* under the *tehsildar*'s supervision. The *Sanjay Gandhi Niradhar Yojna* and the National Family Benefit Scheme were also implemented by the *tehsildar*. According to the panchayat head, the village panchayat was responsible only for formalities such as filling out forms and attaching

[5] Interview with the panchayat head at Warwat Khanderao on August 18–22, 2011.

documents, the Block-level committee did everything else. However, the panchayat did compile a list of prospective names for the *Sanjay Gandhi Niradhar Yojna*. The *patwari*, panchayat head and Police *patel* signed and sent it to the *tehsildar*, who forwarded it to the Sub-Divisional Officer. The village-wise Below Poverty Line households list was used to prepare the beneficiaries list because these schemes primarily cover households below the poverty line.

With regard to subject 28 ("public distribution system") in Schedule XI, the village panchayat was responsible for identifying beneficiaries of the *Antyodaya* and *Annapurna* schemes. The *Dakshata* panchayat subcommittee distributed ration cards. Along with the Food Supply Officer, it heard complaints about supply through the Public Distribution System. The Below Poverty Line households list was required to discharge this function.

As far as the functions pertaining to "poverty alleviation and social welfare" are concerned, the Block-level committees were given more rights than the village panchayats.[6] More importantly, the *tehsildar* was still the most powerful official in the Warwat Khanderao village panchayat.

Historically, the village panchayat's functions with respect to poverty alleviation were limited and remains unclear even in Schedule I (Village List) of the Bombay Village Panchayats Act, 1958. The only provision made for poverty alleviation in the Village List was the fifteenth subject of activities:

> "Promotion of social and moral welfare of the village including promotion
> of prohibition, the removal of untouchability, amelioration of the condition
> of backward classes, eradication of corruption, and the discouragement of
> gambling and useless litigation."

There is no further provision for the "amelioration of the condition of the backward classes." By contrast, details are provided for Block-level committees and district panchayats to fulfil the subject of "programmes for welfare of backward classes" in Schedule I and Schedule II of the Maharashtra Zilla Parishad and Panchayat Samiti Act, 1961. The demarcation of duties between Block-level committees and village panchayats is also unclear in the Acts.

Infrastructure
As mentioned in chapter 3 (section 3.3.7), all responsibilities for subject 11

[6] Interview with the panchayat head at Warwat Khanderao in August 2011.

("drinking water") are assigned to the village panchayat. Besides Schedule I (Village List), the water supply scheme was added to the duties of the panchayat in 1981 by Section 45 of the Bombay Village Panchayats Act, 1958. As mentioned in section 3.3.8, the water supply scheme was a very important development activity in the Warwat Khanderao village panchayat.

Water supply facilities such as tanks and tubewells were recorded in *Item no. 25 Permanent Asset Register* of the panchayat's register. Water tax from these facilities was also recorded in *Item no. 10 Tax collection receipt book* of the panchayat's register.

With regard to subject 13 ("Roads, culverts, etc.") in Schedule XI, connectivity within the panchayat area was a function assigned to village panchayats. The village panchayats had to raise money and then make a list of works to be completed. All roads within the jurisdiction of the village panchayat, with information like length, width, and other descriptions, were recorded in *Item no. 26 Details of road under village panchayat jurisdiction* of the panchayat's register.

All responsibilities with regard to subject 14 ("rural electrification"), rest with the Maharashtra State Electricity Board. No function was assigned to the Warwat Khanderao village panchayat for this subject.

Responsibilities pertaining to subject 29 ("Maintenance of community asset"), rested with the village panchayat as far as they are its own assets.

All buildings, gutters, public toilets, water supply, wells, tanks etc. were to be recorded in *Item no. 25 Permanent asset register* of the village panchayat. Land acquired from the State government and district panchayat and open spaces acquired by the panchayat were also to be recorded in *Item no. 27 Land and barren space register.*

The Annual Report contained data items concerning some of the community assets to be maintained by the village panchayat (whether or not facilities are available, and if not available, then distance in kilometres to those facilities).

Industry and Commerce
Although Schedule I (Village List) of the Bombay Village Panchayats Act, 1958, included "promotion, improvement and encouragement of cottage and village industries" as the forty-seventh item in the list of activities to be

devolved to village panchayats, the Warwat Khanderao village panchayat had no specific role regarding subject 8 ("small scale industries") and subject 9 ("khadi, village and cottage industries") in Schedule XI of the Constitution.

The Annual Report contained data items of "industries and business." Block 15 of the Village Schedule on Basic Statistics contains data on the number of small-scale enterprises and workers therein. However, the large-scale pilot scheme on Basic Statistics since 2009, which covered Akola, a district adjoining the Buldhana district, could not find documentary evidence for these data items. "Data is totally missing. There is no such arrangement to collect such data at the village level."[7] They had to depend on locally knowledgeable persons.

The Warwat Khanderao village panchayat had some authority over subject 22 ("markets and fairs"). In fact, the village panchayat collected a fee from shop owners as professional tax. Normally stalls for the weekly market (*haat, bazaar*) were auctioned every year and the village panchayat kept the auction money. The person who paid the highest amount in the auction rented out the site to different stall-holders. According to the panchayat head, the highest bid for the right to collect tax from the weekly market was Rs 5000 in 2012, which was part of the panchayat's own-source revenue. Schedule I (Village List) of the Bombay Village Panchayats Act, 1958, included functions such as the "establishment and maintenance of markets, provided no market shall be established without prior permission of the *Zilla Parishad*" and "control of fairs, bazars, tonga stands and car stands" as the seventieth and seventy-first items in the list of activities to be devolved to the village panchayats. However, the Warwat Khanderao village panchayat did not have any exhaustive tax lists on trade equivalent to *Form 9 Assessment List* in the Raina village panchayat.

5.2.2 Raina: Sector-wise Data Requirements and Availability

The Activity Mapping exercise in West Bengal was carried out by delegated legislation in the form of executive orders.[8] The Executive Assistant of Raina village panchayat spoke of Activity Mapping in West Bengal. The Block Development Officer of Raina I Block was also aware of Activity Mapping and the demarcation of duties between the Block office and the village panchayats.

---

[7] Directorate of Economics and Statistics, Government of Maharashtra (2012).
[8] Executive order No. 6102/PN/O/dated 7.11.2005, No. 3969/PN/O/dated 25.07.2006, and No. 4769/PN/O/ dated 29.10.2007.

Primary Sector

As mentioned above in relation to subject 1 ("agriculture, including agricultural extension"), subject 4 ("animal husbandry, dairying and poultry"), and subject 5 ("fisheries") of Schedule XI of the Constitution, identification of beneficiaries of schemes such as for distribution of subsidised inputs were functions assigned to the village panchayats in West Bengal. For these functions village panchayats and the village development committees in West Bengal needed a list of eligible persons or households engaged in these primary sector activities. In order to perform these functions, unit-level data were preferable to aggregate numbers. They can constitute a checklist for village panchayats and the village development committees to identify beneficiaries. For example, in Raina, whenever the Agricultural Department distributed mini-kits, fertilizers, seeds, and other benefits, the department specified the number of beneficiaries to select from each panchayat or village assembly. The Agricultural Department required only estimates of the number of beneficiaries and the quantity of subsidised inputs. The village panchayat then informed the village electoral wards, and the village development committee selected the beneficiaries. In this process, unit-level data was more useful for selecting beneficiaries. In this absence of unit-level data, the village panchayats and the village development committees had to depend on the villagers' knowledge for selection of beneficiaries.

The Raina village panchayat had access to departmental data on livestock and fisheries. The Livestock Census data may be used for "vaccination of animals against epidemic," with regard to subject 4 ("animal husbandry, dairying, and poultry") of Schedule XI of the Constitution. However, at present, the Livestock Census data is not aggregated in relation to households, although data is collected from houses, enterprises, and institutions.

With regard to subject 2 ("land improvement, soil conservation, and land reform"), identification of beneficiaries for distribution of vested lands to the landless was a function assigned to village panchayats. Land records available at the Block Land and Land Reform office were essential for land reforms. For this purpose, the Block Land and Land Reform office declared vested lands and the village development committees selected beneficiaries for granting title deed.

According to the Executive Assistant, the Raina village panchayat sometimes worked on land improvement projects though it was not listed in the panchayat's Activity Mapping. The village development committees identified projects in the Action Plans for land improvement. Based on these Action Plans, the village panchayat prepared estimates and sent the project proposal to the Block Development Office. On its approval of the budget and disbursement of funds, the village panchayat then implemented the project. In order to support such projects, the village panchayats and village development committees had to depend on villagers' knowledge about the status of their land. In Raina, there was no reliable plot-wise record even for land utilisation. Land records at the Block Land and Land Reform office were updated only when a landholder seeks and applies for a mutation of records.[9]

With regard to subject 3 ("minor irrigation, water management, and watershed development"), the village panchayat may use data on area irrigated by source in Block 9 of the Village Schedule on Basic Statistics and in the village directory's data in the District Census Handbook. However, unlike Warwat Khanderao village panchayat in Maharashtra where the panchayat had access to plot-wise information on irrigation in the *patwari's* land records, Raina village panchayat did not have access to the updated plot-wise information on irrigation. Accordingly, aggregate data on area irrigated should not be presumed to be reliable. The village panchayat had to depend on people's knowledge on this matter.

With regard to subject 6 ("social forestry and farm forestry") and subject 7 ("minor forest produce"), the village panchayat may use records for the Mahatma Gandhi National Rural Employment Guarantee Scheme and the *Swarna Jayanti Gram Swarozgar Yojana* only when the concerned social forestry projects are related to these schemes.

Education
As mentioned in Schedule XI's subject 17 ("education, including primary and secondary schools"), the School Education Department is the nodal department for administering primary education. Parallel to this system, the Panchayats and Rural Development Department of West Bengal introduced an alternative para-teacher scheme, *Sishu Siksha Karmasuchi* in 1997–8 with the objective of providing primary schools for students in areas without access

---

[9] In order to support such projects, the village panchayat would also seek different types of information about land. For example, the Task Force on Devolution of Powers and Functions to panchayati raj institutions constituted by the Ministry of Rural Development suggested in its Activity Mapping that the village panchayat may assist technical experts in conducting soil tests and help in ensuring that feedback from soil testing reached farmers (Ministry of Rural Development 2001, p. 56).

to the formal education system. The Department started *Madhyamik Siksha Karmasuchis* under the alternative system of primary education in 2003–4 in order to extend the coverage of para-teachers upto class eight. Identification of villages and supervision of these alternative school education schemes were functions assigned to panchayats in Activity Mapping in West Bengal.

The village panchayat may have access to the school registers and the village-level register of all children (see chapter 4, section 4.3.3.2). In addition, the village panchayat had access to the village survey register and the child register maintained at the Integrated Child Development Services' centre in the village.

With a view to assessing the quality of functioning of both *Sishu Siksha Karmasuchi* and *Madhyamik Siksha Karmasuchi*, different aspects of their functioning were captured by the Panchayats and Rural Development Department of West Bengal in working out a composite index known as the School Efficiency Index.[10] Several parameters, such as net enrolment, drop-out rates, school infrastructure (including the number of schools, availability of electricity, drinking-water facility, separate toilets for girls and availability of school buildings with a sufficient number of classrooms), number of teachers, attendance of teachers and students were used to assess the quality of functioning of the *Sishu Siksha Karmasuchi* and *Madhyamik Siksha Karmasuchi*.[11]

As mentioned in Schedule XI's subject 19 ("adult and non-formal education"), the functions of (i) publicity and supervision of Adult High Schools to impart education up to *Madhyamik* level to interested adult learners who are not enrolled in any formal school and (ii) regular contact with literates/neo-literates for attendance in Continuing Education Centre were assigned to the village panchayat. With regard to subject 20 ("libraries"), the establishment and maintenance of libraries and reading rooms, and supervision of the activities of Rural Libraries/Community Library-cum-Information Centre were functions assigned to the village panchayat. Accordingly, information on Adult High Schools, the Continuing Education Centre and libraries was also necessary. This information was considered common knowledge among the village residents. However, in order to discharge these functions, the village panchayat required unit-level information on the quality and

---

[10] Panchayats and Rural Development Department, Government of West Bengal (2009a, p. 64).
[11] Jalan and Panda (2010).

maintenance of each facility rather than data on existence (non-existence) or total number of these as recorded in data items in the Village Schedule on Basic Statistics (Block 2 "availability of some basic facilities," and Block 3 "village infrastructure"). Data focused solely on the existence or total number of such facilities do not suffice on the ground for executing the functions assigned to the village panchayats.

Health and Child Development
In the context of subject 23 ("health and sanitation, including hospitals, primary health centres and dispensaries") of Schedule XI of the Constitution, village panchayats in West Bengal were assigned wide ranging functions, such as the maintenance of sub-centres, monitoring of community health and disease surveillance to pre-empt outbreaks through self-help groups, and preventive measures against spread of communicable diseases.[12] With regard to subject 24 ("family welfare") mobilisation of people for immunisation, and assisting people in adopting family planning measures through efficient functioning of sub-centres were functions assigned to the village panchayat. With regard to subject 25 ("women and child development") alerting parents to the value of pre-school education and immunisation of their children, organising self-help groups for women, construction of Integrated Child Development Services' centres (*anganwadi*), and the convergence meeting at the panchayat level were also functions assigned to the village panchayat.

As described in chapter 4, section 4.3.3.1, for convergence of health-related activities, the village panchayat's subcommittee (*upa-samiti*) member on education and public health, functionaries of the Health and Family Welfare Department, field-level functionaries of Integrated Child Development Services programme under the Women and Child Development and Social Welfare Department, and representatives of self-help groups formed an interlinked health and child-care system in West Bengal. The convergence of these activities was assigned to the village panchayat. A regular meeting of panchayat functionaries, the "Fourth Saturday meeting," was held at the panchayat office every month. On the basis of this strong coordination mechanism, data sharing about births and deaths, morbidity, and the status of sanitation and drinking water supply in the panchayat area became possible. The records of the primary health centre and its sub-centres, Integrated Child Development Services' registers maintained at the village, and other data

---

[12] Institutional Strengthening of Gram Panchayat (ISGP): see fn. 3 above.

related to public health and child-care were combined and compiled at the panchayat's office for preparing the monthly chart.

The village panchayat also required data on self-help groups in its jurisdiction to mobilise them. The booklet published by the Raina village panchayat – *Protibedon* – contained information on self-help groups functioning in the village panchayat's jurisdiction.

The census-type household survey conducted in Raina in 2008 on instructions from the district panchayat to evaluate the rural sanitation scheme (see chapter 4, section 4.2.2) contained data on access to toilets and some socio-economic features of the households, such as social category (Scheduled Caste, Scheduled Tribe and Others). Even its unit-level household data were available at the panchayat office. Data on latrines in the household list generated from the Below Poverty Line Census was also available for the panchayat's use.

Poverty Alleviation and Social Welfare
As mentioned in section 3.3.8 in chapter 3, in relation to subject 16 ("poverty alleviation programme"), subject 26 ("social welfare"), and subject 27[13] ("welfare of the weaker sections") in Schedule XI of the Constitution, village panchayats in West Bengal act as a direct implementing agency for Government schemes such as the *Sampoorna Grameen Rozgar Yojana*, Mahatma Gandhi National Rural Employment Guarantee Scheme, *Indira Awaas Yojana*, Indira Gandhi National Old Age Pension Scheme, Provident Fund for Landless Agricultural Labourers, National Family Benefit Scheme, *Kishori Shakti Yojana* and *Balika Samriddhi Yojana*. In each of these schemes, the village panchayats received funds directly from Government agencies for its implementation. The village panchayats were responsible for maintaining financial accounts for each scheme.

As mentioned in chapter 3 (section 3.3.8), the village panchayat was the most important unit of local government in respect of the Mahatma Gandhi National Rural Employment Guarantee Scheme (MGNREGS). The village panchayat had a responsibility to issue job cards after registering the households, prepare a development plan and maintain a shelf of possible

---

[13] These activities are mapped separately to the subject of "Women and Child Development" and the subject of "Welfare of women and children" in Activity Mapping in West Bengal. See Third State Finance Commission of West Bengal (2008), Annexure XII.

works to be taken up under the scheme as and when the demand for work arose.[14] The MGNREGS was a flagship scheme for the village panchayat itself.

Although the MGNREGS was a centrally-sponsored scheme, the Raina village panchayat maintained its own National Rural Employment Guarantee Act (NREGA) register. According to the NREGA, 2005, "the village council shall conduct regular social audits of all the projects under the Scheme taken up within the village panchayat." Therefore, "the village panchayat shall make available all relevant documents including the muster rolls, bills, vouchers, measurement books, copies of sanction orders and other connected books of account and papers to the village council for the purpose of conducting the social audit" (Section 17).

The village panchayat also required data on basic infrastructure to maintain a roster of possible works to be taken up under the MGNREGS. According to Section 4(3) of the NREGA, 2005, the focus of this scheme was on the following works in the concerned panchayat's order of priority:[15]

(i) water conservation and water harvesting;

(ii) drought proofing (including afforestation and tree plantation);

(iii) irrigation canals including micro and minor irrigation works;

(iv) provision of irrigation facility to land owned by households belonging to the Scheduled Castes and Scheduled Tribes or to land of beneficiaries of land reforms or that of the beneficiaries under the Indira Awas Yojana of the Government of India;

(v) renovation of traditional water bodies, including desilting of tanks;

(vi) land development;

(vii) flood control and protection works including drainage in water logged areas;

(viii) rural connectivity to provide all-weather access; and

(ix) any other work which may be notified by the Central Government in consultation with the State Government.

Creating durable assets and strengthening the livelihood resource base of the rural poor were important objectives of this scheme. The principles of community ownership and maintenance were applied to community-

[14] "With the launching of the National Rural Employment Guarantee Act w.e.f. 2/2/2006 in ten districts in the first phase, and in seven more districts w.e.f. 1/4/2007 in the second phase, the SGRY was subsumed with NREGA in those districts" (Panchayats and Rural Development Department, Government of West Bengal 2008a , p. 53).

[15] Schedule I of the National Rural Employment Guarantee Act, 2005.

based assets.[16] With a view to implementing the MGNREGS, therefore, a database on community-based assets and other infrastructure in each village assembly area was required with respect to the above works (i) to (ix). As will be mentioned later, some of the records on the village panchayat's assets were available from the panchayat registers. However, in order to obtain information on all infrastructure, such as water tanks, watershed protection, irrigation facilities, water bodies, status of land, drainage, rural roads, village panchayats and village development committees had to depend in part on the villagers' knowledge. For the implementation of this scheme, the village panchayat required unit-level information on quality and maintenance of each infrastructure rather than data on presence (or absence) of each kind of infrastructure as recorded in some data items in the Village Schedule (such as those in Block 2 "Availability of some basic facilities") and the village directory data in the District Census Handbook.

The village panchayat would also require data for estimating the demand for works to be provided by this scheme. The Department of Panchayats and Rural Development states in Section 12 of the notification of the West Bengal Rural Employment Guarantee Scheme, 2006:

> For the purpose of identification of sufficient quantity of works the likely estimation of the demand is essential. This shall be done on the basis of the Below Poverty Line population, number of Marginal Agricultural Labourers, Migration figures and other parameters as may be decided by the district for each village panchayat.[17]

Thus, data or variables such as the population living below the poverty line and number of marginal agricultural labourers are required.

Raina village panchayat also oversaw the implementation of the *Swarna Jayanti Gram Swarozgar Yojana* (*SGSY*), though it was not directly involved in the funding and administration of the scheme. As mentioned in relation to subject 25 "Women and child development", the village panchayat assists in the formation and functioning of self-help groups under the *SGSY*. In West Bengal, the convergence of *SGSY* with MGNREGS was also pursued. The Department of Panchayats and Rural Development states:

---

[16] Notification of the Government of West Bengal, Department of Panchayats and Rural Development, No. 684-RD/NREGA/18S-1/06 dated 02/02/2006. However, "appropriate arrangements for having an agreement with the owner of the land would have to be made by the Panchayati Raj Institutions or other bodies."

[17] Panchayats and Rural Development, Government of West Bengal.

More development has taken place in getting assistance of the SHGs for development of awareness about the programme and augmenting participation of the women and improving the delivery system. The latter includes the capable SHG members being utilised as Supervisors of scheme and growing nurseries under NREGS for social forestry as well as development of horticulture.[18]

Here again the village panchayat required unit-level data on self-help groups in its jurisdiction.

As mentioned in chapter 3 (section 3.3.7), beneficiary selection for the *IAY* through village wards and distribution of funds to individuals were functions assigned to the village panchayat in West Bengal.[19] In Raina too, *IAY* beneficiaries were selected from the Below Poverty Line list. Beneficiary selection for the National Family Benefit Scheme (NFBS) and for the Indira Gandhi National Old Age Pension Scheme (IGNOAPS) through village wards was also a function assigned to the village panchayat. The Below Poverty Line household list can be used to discharge functions for the NFBS and the IGNOAPS because these schemes primarily cover households below the poverty line.

Identification of PROFLAL beneficiaries and collection of its subscriptions were also functions assigned to the panchayat. The Raina village panchayat had its own records for the Provident Fund for the PROFLAL. There were about 1500 Provident Fund account holders in the Raina village panchayat area. For this scheme, the land records at the Block Land and Land Reform Office (BLLRO) were required because eligible persons needed to apply to the village panchayat with documents on landholdings obtained from the BLLRO in order to participate in this scheme. People who owned less than 0.5 acres of land were eligible for the scheme.

As mentioned in chapter 3 (section 3.3.8) in Schedule XI's subject 28 "public distribution system," the beneficiary selection for the *Antyodaya* and *Annapurna* schemes was one of the village panchayat's functions. The Below Poverty Line household list was used to implement these schemes.

Infrastructure
As noted in chapter 3 (section 3.3.8), the identification of schemes and

[18] Panchayats and Rural Development, Government of West Bengal (2009a, p. 95).
[19] Activity Mapping in West Bengal relates this scheme to subject 10 (Schedule XI) "Rural housing" as well.

locations for wells, tanks, tubewells (ordinary handpumps), their construction and maintenance, and open wells were functions assigned to the village panchayat with regard to subject 11 ("drinking water") in Schedule XI of the Constitution. The village panchayat maintained registers of the facilities under construction. Raina village panchayat also maintained a tubewell register.

With regard to subject 13 ("roads, culverts, etc."), connectivity between villages within the panchayat area was also a function assigned to the village panchayat. Responsibilities for construction and upgrading roads/culverts not exceeding Rs 2 lakhs rest with it. Raina village panchayat did not have a panchayat register comparable to the data under *Item no. 26 Details of road under village panchayat jurisdiction* in panchayat registers in Maharashtra. However, a Core Network Plan (CNP) was ported on GIS-based maps for each Block, which was uploaded on the website.[20] The CNP, consisting of existing roads as well as roads to be constructed for eligible unconnected habitations under the *Pradhan Mantri Gram Sadak Yojana* (*PMGSY*), was prepared and approved by the district panchayat for each district. The *PMGSY* was launched by the Government of India to provide connectivity to unconnected rural habitations as part of a poverty reduction strategy.[21]

Under subject 14 ("rural electrification") in Schedule XI, the elected village head issued certificates for the electrification of hamlets (*mouzas*). The village panchayat also mobilised consumers through self-help groups for generating awareness. The Village Schedule on Basic Statistics (Block 2 "Availability of some basic facilities") contained a data item on "Household electricity connection *at least for one household in the village* (Yes-1, No-2)." The village directory data in the District Census Handbook contained similar data items. However, according to the Integrated Child Development Services worker in Bidyanidhi, unit-level information on households with electricity connections was not available with the panchayat.[22]

Under subject 29 ("Maintenance of community assets"), the village panchayat had the following functions: (i) maintenance of community assets such as public tanks, *ghats*, public channels, reservoirs, wells, streets, drains, culverts, lamp posts etc., (ii) construction and maintenance of resting place for travellers and pilgrims, rest houses, cattle sheds, cart stands, and protection and repair

---

[20] Pradhan Mantri Gram Sadak Yojana.
[21] Panchayats and Rural Development, Government of West Bengal (2009a, pp. 103–4).
[22] Interview with an ICDS worker at Bidyanidhi on February 23, 2011.

of buildings or other property vested in it, and (iii) power to acquire, hold and dispose of immovable property with the State government's approval.

Raina village panchayat did not have a comprehensive list of the community assets under its jurisdiction. In our interview, the panchayat officials said that such facilities were within common knowledge. The information was available but not always recorded. The village panchayat maintained registers of facilities that were currently under construction. Such community assets were not always recorded, notwithstanding section 23 in the West Bengal Panchayat (Gram Panchayat Accounts, Audit and Budget) Rules, 2007, which stipulated that

> a village panchayat shall maintain in Form 20 a register for all immovable properties possessed by it and also of all public roads, paths and water courses within the concept and meaning of section 25 and records of all lands, buildings, tanks, ferries, fisheries, markets, huts and any other property vested in and controlled or created by the village panchayat.

Here, Form 20 is the *Register of immovable properties* described in chapter 4 (section 4.3.1).

Facilities under Raina village panchayat's control were partly recorded in *Form 9 Assessment list* specified in the 2006 Amendments of the West Bengal Panchayat (Gram Panchayat Administration) Rules, 2004. The *Form 9 Assessment list* included in Part VIII ("roads/ferry/bridges or other assets or resources from where tolls/fees may be collected") and in Part-IX a "list of remunerative assets under the control of the village panchayat." However, these records were prepared exclusively for the purpose of tax assessment. Indeed, data on the *Form 9 Assessment list* is useful for another function: "fixing and collection of toll, fee, rate as user charges for these community assets," which was also assigned to the village panchayat in West Bengal with regard to subject 29 "Maintenance of community assets."

However, unless the community assets were revenue sources or were under construction, they were not recorded in the panchayat registers in Raina. [23] As mentioned in chapter 2 (section 2.2.1.3), data on all panchayat facilities

---

[23] The Third State Finance Commission of West Bengal points to a similar issue on asset registers at the district panchayat level. "Some of the panchayat bodies, particularly the district panchayats (ZPs), have under their management and ownership various types of assets – land, buildings, water bodies, hats and bazaars, ferries, etc., but most of the ZPs do not maintain proper asset registers" (Third State Finance Commission of West Bengal 2008, p. 36).

was required not only for managing them as revenue resources, but also for maintaining those facilities. The tax system on the panchayat's assets may be simple for operational convenience, but maintenance of such assets has to be exhaustive. For the maintenance of assets, therefore, the list of assets needs to be comprehensive and needs to examine the details of each asset's quality and maintenance.

The Village Schedule on Basic Statistics (Block 2 "Availability of some basic facilities" and Block 4 "Distance from the nearest facility") included data items regarding community assets. These pertained only to the existence of each type of asset and the distance from the asset. This information was far from comprehensive and did not mention the quality and maintenance of the assets. As information on basic facilities is common knowledge in the panchayat area, the village panchayat may compile a list of its own assets if required.

Industry and Commerce

As mentioned in chapter 3 (section 3.3.8) in the context of subject 8 ("small scale industries, including food processing industries") in Schedule XI, the identification of micro-enterprise/entrepreneurs for Block-level committees and district panchayats for organising entrepreneur development programmes was a function assigned to the village panchayat. With regard to subject 9 ("khadi, village and cottage industries"), the panchayat had the function of group formation for these industries and identifying needs for skill development training. However, we found that the Raina village panchayat did not have any authority over such industries other than collection of certain taxes and fees. The licences were granted by higher bodies in the panchayati raj hierarchy.

Block 15 of Village Schedule on Basic Statistics contains data on the number of small-scale enterprises and workers therein. Although identification of micro-enterprise/entrepreneurs was as such a function assigned to the village panchayat, no record on each unit of such industries was available with it. Data from the Industrial Development Office (IDO) were also not available with the panchayat. A brief note on the occupation of each member of households in the Integrated Child Development Services' village survey register was a possible source of such unit-level data in Bidyanidhi village. The Socio-Economic and Caste Census 2011 has also collected data on non-agricultural own account enterprises as a "main source of household income." If village-level Economic Census data were made available, it could be used as information about these data items.

As mentioned in chapter 3 (section 3.3.8) in the context of subject 22 ("markets and fairs"), the panchayat's functions included management of village markets (*haat/bazaar*) transferred to the village panchayat, and construction and regulation of markets, holding and regulation of fairs, village markets, and exhibition of local produce and products of local handicrafts/home industries.

As mentioned in chapter 4 (section 4.3.1), the *Form 9 Assessment list* included a list of persons liable to pay registration/renewal fee for running a trade (wholesale or retail) within the panchayat area.

However, the main sources for the data items of Block 11 "Number of storage and marketing outlets" and Block 15 "Industries and business (the number of small-scale enterprises and workers therein)" in the Village Schedule were the villagers' common knowledge.

5.3 OTHER DATA FOR PANCHAYAT ADMINISTRATION

5.3.1 Coordination of Activities between the Village Panchayat and Outside Agencies

As stated in section 2.3 in chapter 2, in the transition to Constitutional devolution, line departments or parallel bodies are working in the village panchayat's functional domain, independently of the panchayati raj system. Therefore, the latter has to coordinate activities of these outside agencies in order to work in its functional domain. The village panchayats have to coordinate matters in their functional domain not only with the higher tiers of the panchayati raj, but also with outside agencies which are under the control of the line departments. The panchayati raj institutions (even the village panchayat) needed a comprehensive sector-wise list of current Central and State schemes and programmes, i.e., a "scheme census."

Village-level functionaries, such as revenue officials, health workers, health supervisors, technical assistants of the MGNREGS and schoolteachers also work in the panchayat's functional domain, using funds provided by the State or Central Government, independently of the panchayati raj system. They generate and maintain their own databases independently of the panchayats. When the panchayat has control over these agencies, they are considered the panchayat's satellite agencies. They can be designated as agents to keep track of matters of self-governance on behalf of the panchayat.

Panchayats can also coordinate these outside agencies to establish a data-sharing mechanism. In practice, such a data-sharing mechanism is crucial for the panchayat to develop its village-level statistical database. An important recommendation of the *Basic Statistics for Local Level Development* report is the formulation of formal data-sharing mechanisms between the village panchayat and different agencies working in the panchayat area.[24] The report directed that, "Efforts should be made to ensure coordination of activities among all these potential sources of regular information at the panchayat level ensuring that quality of data so gathered is maintained."

In Warwat Khanderao village panchayat, the panchayat head was familiar with the sector-wise information on current Central and State schemes and programmes. Therefore, it is possible for the Warwat Khanderao village panchayat to compile, if required, a comprehensive list of on-going Government schemes within the panchayat area. In fact, "Village-level work under different schemes from the last 5 years" was to be listed in the Annual Report described in chapter 4 (section 4.3.5.4). The list contained information on "year," "work name," "sanctioned amount," "present status of work (completed/uncompleted)," and "evaluation" of each scheme of the

---

[24] Central Statistical Organisation (2006, pp. 17, 23–6, 28–9). "A great amount of information is available from the records of *anganwadi* workers, health/ANM workers and land record registers. Efforts should be made to ensure coordination of activities among all these potential sources of regular information at panchayat level ensuring that quality of data so gathered is maintained." (*ibid.*, p. 17). In Karnataka: "[c]onsolidation and sharing of data between various development agencies take place at the district level. On eleventh of every month, there is a Karnataka Development Programme (KDP) meeting at the district level and representatives of all the developmental agencies participate in the meeting. Once in a quarter, the Minister in-charge of the district chairs the KDP meeting. The data sets available with different agencies are shared in these meetings. The Chief Planning Officer of the *zilla panchayat* is vested with the responsibility of compiling and maintaining local-level statistics on various aspects. The items of information thus being collected include population, infrastructure, education and literacy, area and land utilisation, crop production, livestock, industrial units, cooperatives, credit and loans, health and family welfare, etc. The compilation and consolidation of local-level statistics is, however, being undertaken as a one-time operation rather than as a continuous regular operation. There is also no direct involvement of DES in the compilation and consolidation of these statistics though the officers and staff involved in the exercise in *zilla* and taluk panchayats are taken from the DES" (*ibid.*, pp. 23–4). In Maharashtra: "There is no formal data sharing mechanisms between different agencies working at village panchayat, *tehsil* or district levels." (*ibid.*, p. 25). In Haryana: "There is no data sharing between various agencies functioning at the village panchayat, *panchayat samiti* and *zilla parishad*s. The functionaries of different departments do have a vertical system of reporting and at no stage do the data get integrated to have a holistic view of any geographical region in all the dimensions of development. The panchayati raj institutions do not have any access to such data sets and recently an exercise has been initiated to collect comprehensive data on village characteristics

Twelfth Planning Commission, *Dalit Basti Sudhar Yojana*, *Thakkar Bappa*, *Rajiv Gandhi Gramin Niwara Yojana* and the *Indira Awaas Yojana*.

As described in chapter 3 (section 3.3.5), under the Bombay Village Panchayats Act, 1958, as amended in 2003, in Maharashtra the village council has been given disciplinary control over the Government and semi-Government employees working in the village. In Warwat Khanderao village panchayat, therefore, all such village-level functionaries are statutorily under the control of the panchayat. However, a strong coordination mechanism did not exist in Warwat Khanderao. Village-level functionaries with whom the panchayat has the potential to establish a coordination mechanism are the Integrated Child Development Services workers. Warwat Khanderao village panchayat had subcommittees (e.g. Woman and Child Committee and Child Development Committee) to coordinate activities of the Integrated Child Development Services programme, although, as mentioned in the last chapter, they were not presently functional. The Warwat Khanderao village panchayat also had the potential to establish a data-sharing mechanism with the revenue official.

Before 2008, the Village Education Committee was formed at Warwat Khanderao with the panchayat head as its president. However, under the Right to Education Act, 2009, the concept and formation of the Committee was scrapped. Authority over this matter has been taken away from the panchayat.

In Maharashtra, there was no strong formal data-sharing mechanism among the outside agencies working at the village, Block (*tehsil*) and district levels. There were multiple lines of control and various reporting mechanisms. The *Basic Statistics for Local Level Development* report notes,

---

and infrastructure in respect of each village through a pre-designed schedule. The effort is still continuing with some success" (*ibid.*, p. 26). The report further notes, "The functionaries at the village level particularly the *anganwadi* workers, ANMs, panchayat secretaries and revenue officials maintain a large number of registers, records and reports containing up-to-date data on every aspect of each village. There is, however, no mechanism to check the reliability of such statistics and to consolidate them at the village panchayat level" (*ibid.*, p. 28). "The concerned Line Department presently maintains the collected data only and panchayats are generally not consolidating and maintaining such data. The situation needs to be changed and the village panchayats should consolidate, maintain, and own village-level data. All the functionaries at the village level including the *anganwadi* worker, ANM, and revenue officials should share the data possessed by them with the respective village panchayats. Such data should be verified, consolidated, and maintained by the panchayats in pre-designed formats. The panchayats should also own such data" (*ibid.*, p. 29).

In the case of revenue officials, the line of reporting is from the village officer (*talati*) to the Circle Officer, *tehsildar* and District Collector. The channels of reporting in the case of different functionaries at village panchayat, Block Development Office and District panchayat office are through the respective line of control of the respective departments. The reports being received by different departments are generally not being integrated at any stage.[25]

The Block Development Officer is expected to coordinate the activities of these line departments, because the officer receives all information about planning and implementation of schemes by other departments. However, according to our interview with the Block Development Officer of Sangrampur, Buldhana District, Maharashtra,[26] the *tehsildar* in Maharashtra wielded greater administrative powers as he was the Programme Officer for all programmes under the Ministry of Rural Development. Thus, the power of the Block Development Officer was restricted.

Thus, the institutional coordination mechanism in panchayati raj institutions was not strong in Maharashtra. As far as the Warwat Khanderao village panchayat was concerned, a data-sharing mechanism could be instituted under the Bombay Village Panchayats Act, 1958, as amended in 2003. At the time of the survey, however, such a mechanism was not in place.

In contrast, in Raina village panchayat, there were registers on current Central and State schemes and programmes. The West Bengal Panchayat (Gram Panchayat Accounts, Audit and Budget) Rules, 2007, specify *Form 16: Programme register* and *Form 17: Scheme register* for this purpose. The date of meeting of village panchayat or *upa-samiti* sanctioning the Scheme, the serial no. and its description, the proposed expenditure, date of commencement of the scheme, and details of expenditure are recorded in *Form 17 Scheme register*. However, the schemes and programmes recorded in *Form 16* and *Form 17* were only those sanctioned by the village panchayat/subcommittee meetings. The schemes and programmes carried out within the panchayat area by line departments which deal with matters not devolved to the village panchayat, for example some activities of the Agriculture Department, were not always recorded in *Form 16* and *Form 17*. Contact details of line departments and parallel bodies for each Central and State scheme and programme were

---

[25] Central Statistical Organisation (2006, p. 25). For example, "Though the jurisdiction of the Block Development Office is the same as *tehsil*, both the Block Development Officer and the *tehsildar* have two different offices."
[26] Interview at the Block Development Office, Sangrampur on April 25, 2014.

provided on the last page of the Raina village panchayat's booklet *Protibedon*.

The Executive Assistant of Raina village panchayat was aware of each Central or State scheme and programme. Therefore, it was possible for Raina village panchayat to compile, if required, a comprehensive list of on-going Government schemes within its area.

In Raina, the *Krishi Prani Sahayak* (under the Department of Animal Resources Development), the *Krishi Prajukti Sahayak* (under the Department of Agriculture), the fisheries officer (under the Department of Fisheries), health supervisor (under the Department of Health and Family Welfare), the female health assistant (under the Department of Health and Family Welfare), the Auxiliary Nurse Midwife (under the Department of Health and Family Welfare), the Integrated Child Development Services' supervisor (under the Department of Woman and Social Welfare), and the Revenue Inspector (under the Department of Land and Land Reforms) were the departmental liaison officers responsible for assisting the village panchayat. Furthermore, as mentioned in chapter 3 (section 3.6), five subcommittees (*upa-samitis*) – (i) Finance and Planning, (ii) Agriculture and Animal Resources Development, (iii) Education and Public Health, (iv) Women and Child Development and Social Welfare, and (v) Industries and Infrastructure – were given wide powers to call for information and inspect any work in progress in Raina. Thus, there was considerable data-sharing and administrative synergy between village-level functionaries and panchayat officials.

We found that the Raina village panchayat had a strong coordination mechanism with the Integrated Child Development Services' supervisor, auxiliary nurse midwife, health supervisor and representatives of self-help groups in the "Fourth Saturday meeting." On the basis of such institutional coordination, data sharing about births and deaths, cases of morbidity, and the status of sanitation and drinking water supply in the panchayat area become possible for these agencies. The records of the primary health centre and its sub-centres, the Integrated Child Development Services' registers maintained at the village, and other data related to public health and child care were matched or compiled at the panchayat office.

This data-sharing mechanism made it possible to check the reliability of each item of data from different sources, which ensured the quality of that item of data. There was no such formal data-sharing mechanism in Warwat Khanderao village panchayat.

5.3.2 Data on Panchayat's Personnel

As mentioned in chapter 2 (section 2.2.1.3), data on the panchayat's personnel, including elected panchayat representatives and their administrative staff, reflect the basic human resource of the panchayat's general administration. It is required for transparent self-governance in the post-Seventy-Third-Amendment regime.

As panchayat officials know the panchayat's personnel, this information can be easily documented and disclosed. Data on elected representatives may be validated by the records of the State Election Commission. Data on panchayat-level administrative staff may be validated through the panchayat registers.

5.3.3 Data on Panchayat's Assets

Data on the panchayat's assets show the foundations of the panchayat's general administration. It is also required for transparent self-governance. The shortcomings of data on the panchayat's assets have been mentioned in sections 5.2.1 and 5.2.2 above, under subject 29 "Maintenance of community assets" of Schedule XI of the Constitution.

The Village Schedule on Basic Statistics contains data items on some basic facilities of the village in Block-2, Block-3, and Block-4. However, except for the distance from "panchayat HQS" in Block-4, its focus is not necessarily on the village panchayat's general administration infrastructure. It has also not addressed the quality and maintenance of the panchayat's office building.

The Self-Evaluation Schedule in West Bengal asked whether the village panchayat had its own building, whether there was a big hall (with seats for at least sixty people) for meeting/training, drinking water, clean toilets, electricity, a telephone, fax line, and computer with internet access in the panchayat building. These queries were addressed to ensure the quality and maintenance of some of panchayat's own infrastructure for the sake of general administration. The panchayat officials had the necessary knowledge to respond to these queries.

In this respect, the Village Schedule on Basic Statistics is not focused on the panchayat itself. As information on basic facilities is common knowledge in both the village panchayats, they can compile, if required, data on their own assets to make their working more transparent.

Chapter 6

POTENTIAL DATABASES ON
VILLAGE PANCHAYAT'S JURISDICTION

In addition to data on the panchayat, governance requires data on the object domain (i.e. the "target") of its functions. Since the local region is the object of the panchayat's governance, its object domain is primarily its geographically-defined jurisdiction. In addition, its jurisdiction delineates a local society of people living within the boundary of the region. Therefore, the village panchayat's object domain is the particular local society of that region. Accordingly, data on panchayat's jurisdiction include data on panchayat's territory in spatial terms, along with data on the local society of that region.

A village panchayat is not responsible for everything in its geographical area; it is responsible only for matters concerning its functional domain. The object domain of the panchayat's governance is exclusively with respect to its functional domain (described as the panchayat itself in the previous chapter). This does not mean that data on the panchayat's functioning can double up as data on its object domain. The latter should be distinguished from the panchayat's functioning as such. As described in chapter 2 (section 2.2.2), the panchayat's functioning is not self-contained. While it is true that data on its functioning precisely reflects the shape of the panchayat itself, that object domain of its function may be external to the panchayat. In fact, we often find unrecorded elements of the object domain in relation to the panchayat's functioning. These elements, as can be expected, are external to the panchayat. A part of local society may be left out of the administrative record system. Or, the panchayat may discover unknown administrative needs in this unrecorded aspect of the object domain. The panchayat and its satellite agencies require more objective data and knowledge independently of their usual administrative records.

Many registers and records are generated and used as part of the functions performed by the panchayat and its satellite agencies. However, since there may be unrecorded aspects of the object domain of its function, these administrative records must be cross-checked by other data or through the villagers' common knowledge. The village panchayat may liaise with other agencies for cross-checking these records with different data sources. A data-sharing mechanism with outside agencies is required to cross-check village-level registers and records. The recommendation of the *Basic Statistics for Local Level Development* report to establish formal data-sharing mechanisms between village panchayat and different agencies working in the panchayat area not only serves the purpose of saving costs of additional data collection, but also allows cross-checking the reliability of the different data sources. The report noted that the functionaries at the village level, particularly the ICDS workers (*anganwadi*), ANMs, panchayat secretaries, and revenue officials maintain a large number of registers, records and reports containing up-to-date data on every aspect of each village. There is, however, no mechanism to check the reliability of such statistics and to consolidate them at the village panchayat level.[1]

As noted in chapter 4 (section 4.2), some types of information on the village community were common knowledge to most villagers.[2] Therefore, as will be illustrated in the context of the village-level discussion on the Below-Poverty-Line list (see section 6.4.4),[3] the village council members' common knowledge can be one of the reference points for cross-checking data. In this way a panchayat can strengthen its self-governance, re-examining unrecorded elements in the object domain external to the panchayat itself.

6.1 *Village Panchayat's Spatial Data*

Self-governance by panchayat requires data on its territory (i.e., its jurisdiction in spatial terms). This data presupposes spatial information including information from maps and the geographical information systems (GIS). Both Warwat Khanderao and Raina village panchayats have access to traditional cadastral maps (available at the *patwari's* office in Warwat Khanderao and at the Block Land and Land Reform Office in Raina). Their respective State governments have already established GIS to draw outlines of the area. Data on area and location of the panchayat area can be mapped on the basis of such spatial information.

Data items on the distance from the nearest basic facilities in the Village Schedule on Basic Statistics (Block 4 "Distance from the nearest facility"), Annual Report of the Warwat Khanderao Village Panchayat (Part 2 "Details of facilities available in the village"), and village directory data in the District

---

[1] Central Statistical Organisation (2006, p. 28).

[2] Bakshi and Okabe (2008, pp. 24–5, 27).

[3] For details see section 4.2.4.1 as well.

Census Handbook describe the location of the panchayat area. Distance from the nearest facilities is not documented in the village-level records, but is common knowledge among villagers in both village panchayats (see section 4.2, chapter 4).

As already mentioned in chapter 4 (section 4.3.3.4), land records in both Warwat Khanderao and Raina contained data on the area of each plot. From these the total cultivated area (in hectares or acres) in the region can be computed. For example, the *patwari* of Warwat Khanderao was able to estimate the area of the village, that is, the total area of Warwat Khanderao village to be 1300 acres and out of which 1236.122 acres of land is cultivated. The rest of the land is used for drainage and housing.

Land-use information for Raina was not available in the land records at the Block Land and Land Reform Office. As already pointed out, records are updated only when a landholder seeks and applies for a change in the records. In contrast, the Warwat Khanderao village panchayat had access to land-use information in the *patwari's* land record.

For precise unit-level information on village infrastructure, both village panchayats could depend on the exhaustive list of houses in the property tax (or house tax) register. If the property tax (or house tax) register is validated in village council or village ward meetings, it is considered accurate.

The numbers of each type of livestock in an area can be obtained only from the quinquennial Livestock Census, data from which are available at the respective Block-level offices of the two village panchayats.

6.2 DATA ON RESIDENTS IN PANCHAYAT'S JURISDICTION

People residing in the panchayat's jurisdiction are not only its object domain, but also the main actors in the panchayat's activities. Therefore, a database on people resident in the region is an integral part of panchayat-level databases.

The Population Census is the core source of statistics for the panchayati raj institutions. As the National Statistical Commission stated, it is a multi-purpose data set to serve a wide range of data needs at the grass roots of the panchayati raj.[4] It has already been utilised for determining seats and the

---

[4] National Statistical Commission (2001), para. 9.2.16.

electoral boundaries for the panchayat election. As shown in Tables 4.1 and 4.2 (chapter 4), for example, data on migration and on employment status of villagers were not available in the panchayat offices (the panchayat has access only to brief notes on migration and occupation of each member of the household in the comments column of the Integrated Child Development Services village survey register). The Population Census data contain these details. However, the National Statistical Commission has noted the unnecessary delay in processing Census data. The panchayat officials in both villages also mentioned this problem. More importantly, the limitation of the Population Census is that unit-level private information collected by it must not be used for local administrative purposes as it is collected under the provisions of the Census Act, 1948.

The village panchayat and sub-panchayat bodies touch the everyday life of each and every village resident. These bodies are sometimes responsible for helping a certain group or individuals to improve their capabilities. At present, however, there is no official list of all residents in the panchayat's jurisdiction. The village panchayat and sub-panchayat bodies need a comprehensive people's list ready for disaggregation. We will examine in section 6.6 the Integrated Child Development Services village survey register and the Below Poverty Line Census (or the Socio-Economic and Caste Census, 2011) as sources for a core list of residents.

6.3 DATA ON DEMOGRAPHIC MOVEMENT

Some of the data on the panchayat's jurisdiction is dynamic (chapter 2, section 2.2.2.2). Incidents and events in the area reflect changes in the status of its jurisdiction. Some of these changes are recorded by the panchayat itself and others by outside agencies. Among these records, data on vital events and migration of people resident in a panchayat's jurisdiction are indispensable for maintaining accurate information on its residents.

The National Statistical Commission noted that the birth and death registers in the Civil Registration System have the potential to provide records of vital events at the local level.[5] However, as will be observed in section 6.7, the place of registration in the system was not the place of usual residence, so that vital events recorded in it were not always related to people actually living in the panchayat's area of jurisdiction. Vital records in the Integrated

---

[5] Ibid., para. 2.7.8.

Child Development Services registers, which keep track of births at the place of usual residence, are more appropriate for data on self-governance for the panchayat's jurisdiction. In Warwat Khanderao and Raina, these two vital records can be cross-checked with each other. In Raina, as mentioned in chapter 4 (section 4.3.3.1), on the basis of the interlinked health-and-childcare system, data sharing among the interlinked agencies is possible. At the Fourth Saturday meeting, data on institutional births are collected from health department officials and the number of home births is collected from the Integrated Child Development Services worker (*anganwadi*) and both are combined and compiled at the panchayat office for preparing their monthly chart. The data-sharing mechanism makes it possible to check the reliability of data from each source.[6] The child register for all children in the village, compiled from an annual house-to-house survey conducted by the school teachers can also be used to validate the vital records.

Data on in- and out-migration are also crucial for self-governance by the panchayat. However, many States reported that data items on migration in the Village Schedule on Basic Statistics (Block 13 "Migration") have no documentary evidence in the village. As there is no official system of recording migration, no accurate data on this item is available in the village.[7] As a result, village panchayats are ignorant of this important aspect of their jurisdiction. While the decennial Population Census collects data on migration, the data are not available until ten years later. Therefore, the data potential of the Integrated Child Development Services village survey register is immense. This register is updated every five years. When a new survey is conducted, households that have migrated temporarily are deleted from the register.[8]

Moreover, as mentioned in chapter 4 (section 4.3.3.1), the village survey register in Bidyanidhi has a comments column, that notes, for a given point in time, information on deaths, marriages or migrations within a household. However, as it is a comments column, the exact date of an event is not always available and thus limits its operational use. Based on the pilot study of Basic Statistics in the Akola district, the Maharashtra Government reported that information on in- and out-migrations is only available from the Integrated

---

[6] Bakshi and Okabe (2008, p. 26).

[7] Central Statistics Office (2014, pp. 69-70).

[8] However, as mentioned in chapter 4 (section 4.3.3.1), in cases where some of the household members have migrated (for example, a son and his family while the parents stayed behind), details of all members of the undivided household are recorded even when the migration is permanent.

Child Development Services (*anganwadi*) records, and age-wise classification for this information is not available.[9]

6.4 DATA ON EACH MAJOR FUNCTION IN THE PANCHAYAT'S OBJECT DOMAIN

6.4.1 Primary Sector

The Agricultural Census is expected to provide detailed statistics on the structure of operational holdings and their main characteristics (such as number and area, land use, irrigation, tenancy, and cropping patterns). The Agricultural Census addresses a major part of the panchayat's object domain in the primary sector. It can help identify administrative needs in the primary sector. Nevertheless, the potential of sub-district-level data of the Agricultural Census is not discussed in either State.

The population enumeration data in the Census of India includes data on the "category of economic activity" (cultivator/agricultural labourer/worker in household industry/other worker) on a decennial basis. Below Poverty Line Census 2002 collected data on "type of operational holding of land" (owner/tenant/both owner and tenant/none) and the Socio-Economic and Caste Census 2011, collected data on the "main source of household income" (cultivation/manual casual labour/parttime or fulltime domestic service/ foraging, rag picking/ nonagricultural own-account enterprise/begging, charity, alms collection/others) and data on "land owned" (ownership/total unirrigated land in acres/total irrigated land in acres). The Integrated Child Development Services village survey register has brief notes in the comments column on the occupation of each household member.

In Maharashtra, where the *patwari's* land records are maintained, all villages, including Warwat Khanderao, are purportedly covered by the Agricultural Census through re-tabulation of the revenue records. A list of operational holdings is compiled, matching part-holders scattered over more than one village. [10] Nevertheless, the *patwari* at Warwat Khanderao has no idea of the

---

[9] *Ibid.*, p. 70.

[10] "For preparation of a list of operational holdings, necessary matching of the part-holders scattered over more than one village has to be done. A holding may cut across the boundary of a village/*patwari* circle/Revenue Inspector Circle/*tehsil*/District/State. As in the previous Censuses, the *tehsil* will be the outer limit for pooling of all the parcels of an operational holding. If a holding is spread over more than one *tehsil*, that part of the holding which is lying outside the *tehsil* of residence of operational holder will be treated as a separate operational holding" (Ministry of Agriculture 2006a, p. 3).

Agricultural Census operation.[11] Actually, the re-tabulation of the village land records should be an insignificant matter, since land records in Maharashtra are primarily of ownership holding, not operational holdings. As pointed out by the *patwari*, information on tenants is inaccurate. Regardless of whether land is leased or cultivated by the landowner, the landowner's name is put in the column for tenancy. Landowners do not report tenancy because of the fear that the tenants may claim ownership. Therefore, even though the *patwari's* land records are re-tabulated, the accuracy of the results is questionable. In other words, it will be possible to produce statistics of operational holdings only with village-level land records on tenants.

Since the Bombay Village Panchayats Act, 1958, has the function of "maintenance of village records relating to land revenue," the fifty-eighth subject in the list of activities to be devolved to the village panchayats, the village panchayats in Maharashtra have the potential to revise information on tenants. Statutorily, the village land records can be a matter of concern to the panchayat or village council members.

If the Agriculture Census data are made available to panchayats, detailed statistics on operational holdings can be cross-checked by the information from the Population Census, the Below Poverty Census (or the SECC 2011), as well as villagers' local knowledge.

In West Bengal, where there are no comprehensive land records, the Agricultural Census is conducted through a house-to-house enquiry on operational holders in a 20 per cent sample of villages, including all the sample villages selected under the scheme for Establishment of an Agency for Reporting Agricultural Statistics (EARAS).[12] However, as mentioned in chapter 4, the panchayat officials in Raina did not have access to the Agricultural Census data. According to an Agricultural Officer of Raina I Block, no data from the Agricultural Census, and not even data generated from the EARAS scheme, were available at the Block level.

If the Agriculture Census data were available to the panchayats, the statistics on operational holdings could be cross-checked with information from other sources. The statistics of the Agricultural Census and unit-level data in the

[11] Interview at the *patwari's* office in Warwat Khanderao on August 18–22, 2011.
[12] "These sample villages have to include all the villages selected under the scheme for Establishment of an Agency for Reporting Agricultural Statistics (EARAS)" (Ministry of Agriculture 2006b, p. 3).

Below Poverty Line Census or the Integrated Child Development Services village survey register can be useful for the village panchayat and the village development committees for assessing the exhaustiveness of the list of eligible persons or households engaged in agriculture under the schemes for distributing subsidised inputs. The selection of beneficiaries can then be carried out objectively so that administrative services reach each beneficiary.

6.4.2 Education

Data on the major part of the panchayat's object domain of education comes from the village school register and the village-level register of all children based on an annual house-to-house enquiry conducted by the school teachers. This annual enquiry can validate the record of students in the village school register. In fact, as mentioned in chapter 4 (section 4.3.3.2), some children in Bidyanidhi are sent to private schools outside the village and are, therefore, not counted in the village school register. In Raina panchayat area, there are three private primary schools (for classes nursery to four), but they are not found in the village-level school directory generated from the All India School Education Survey. The annual house-to-house enquiry counts children enrolled at schools outside the village. The Integrated Child Development Services child register and their village survey register also cover these children.

Data on literate and illiterate people is useful to explore the panchayat's object domain (possible beneficiaries) with respect to adult education. The decennial Population Census provides the size of the illiterate population. The village-wise unit-level database on households generated from the Below Poverty Line Census 2002, contained data on adult literacy in each household.[13] The Socio-Economic and Caste Census 2011, collected data on "highest educational level completed" (including "Illiterate") for each person in the household. The census-type surveys independently conducted by the panchayati raj institutions – particularly household surveys conducted in 2008 on the district panchayats' instructions to evaluate the rural sanitation scheme (chapter 4, section 4.3.2) – also collected data on literacy and the educational attainment of the most educated member of the household with some other socio-economic features of the households, such as eligibility for

---

[13] The Below Poverty Line Census database in Warwat Khanderao also contains data on each household member with respect to education status (including literacy status), but this person-wise information was not available at Bidyanidhi.

a special social category (Scheduled Caste, Scheduled Tribe, Others). Unit-level household data are also available at the panchayat office. The village survey register also contains unit-level data on the educational attainment of each household member. These data on literacy can be cross-checked with each other.

6.4.3 Health and Child Development

Most of the data on the panchayat's object domain of functions pertaining to health and child development are from the records at the primary health centre and the village Integrated Child Development Services registers. As already mentioned, the data-sharing mechanism in Raina on the basis of such interlinked health and child care system among the village panchayat, the ICDS centre, and the Primary Health Centre, make it possible to cross-check the reliability of each item of data from different sources. Since the Integrated Child Development Services workers (*anganwadi*) in Warwat Khanderao sometimes work jointly with the Auxiliary Nurse Midwife for tasks such as immunisation, there is a possibility of data-sharing between them.

6.4.4 Poverty Alleviation and Social Welfare

The Below Poverty Line Census 2002 (and the Socio-Economic and Caste Census 2011) are the major data sources on the panchayat's object domain of functions pertaining to poverty alleviation and social welfare. However, there was widespread discontent in both Warwat Khanderao and Raina village panchayats about the Below Poverty Line lists generated from this Census. Both panchayats have conducted a house-to-house re-survey to revise the list generated from the BPL Census 2002 (also referred to in West Bengal as the Rural Household Survey). It was a significant achievement of the decentralisation process after the Seventy-third Amendment that village panchayats have independently conducted house-to-house re-surveys to revise the Below Poverty Line lists.

This fact suggests that both panchayats can organise and conduct a house-to-house re-survey in their respective jurisdictions. This experience shows that they have the ability and expertise to identify discrepancies in data from surveys conducted by higher organisations. Such arguments between the village panchayat and other organisations about the accuracy of village data suggest that the quality of village data is a matter of concern to the panchayat.

Data from Below Poverty Line Census 2002 (and the Socio-Economic and Caste Census 2011) can be cross-checked with information from the Population Census and the village survey register. In section 6.6, we will compare lists of persons and households generated from the Below Poverty Line Census 2002, and the Integrated Child Development Services village survey register, and match each person and household in these lists. We will analyse micro-level discrepancies in these lists.

These village-level discussions on the Below Poverty Line list reveal that the villagers' popular knowledge, and ultimately, the direct democracy of the villagers, can also be one of the sources of information for cross-checking village-level records. Initial doubts about the Below Poverty Line list arose from the common knowledge of villagers.

6.4.5 Infrastructure

All community assets owned by village panchayats are recorded in panchayat registers such as the *Item no. 25 Permanent asset register* in Warwat Khanderao and *Form 20 Register of immovable properties* in Raina. However, unless the community assets are revenue sources and/or are under construction, they are actually not thoroughly documented in the panchayat registers.

In the two selected village panchayats, basic facilities present in the panchayat area are of common knowledge. The information is available but not always recorded. As the panchayat is a meeting place for village people, even if data are undocumented, most information on the panchayat can be derived from their "common knowledge."[14] Therefore, the two village panchayats may compile a list of their own assets, if required.

6.4.6 Industry and Commerce

The main village-level data source for industrial and commercial establishments is the Economic Census. It covers all the village-level units (establishments) engaged in economic activities, except those involved in crop production. Industrial information on, for example, the establishment's location, the description of the economic activity carried out, the nature of

---

[14] "As it [panchayati raj institutions] is a meeting place for the village people, if some data are collected without records, probability of getting correct information is very high" (Central Statistics Office 2011, D-21).

the operation, the type of ownership, the social category of the owner, the use of power/fuel, the total number of workers employed, its hired component and the composition of male and female workers is collected in the Economic Census.

In chapter 4, we ascertained how the field operations of the Economic Census were carried out at the village. The Economic Census directly addresses "small scale industries, including food processing industries," "khadi, village, and cottage industries," and commercial establishments in the panchayat's area of jurisdiction. Nevertheless, no data from the Economic Census were available at panchayati raj institutions.

It is the villagers' common knowledge which is the main source for data items of the Village Schedule's Block 15 on "industries and business (the number of small scale enterprises and workers therein" and Block 11 on "number of storage and marketing outlets." However, information on non-agricultural unorganised establishments is a matter of dispute. For example, as the National Statistical Commission observed, the number of enterprises in rural areas engaged in unregistered manufacturing activities, according to the Economic Census, is contentious. If the Economic Census data are disclosed at the village level, these discrepancies could be examined in detail.

The Integrated Child Development Services village survey register has brief notes on occupation for each household member in the comments column. This is one source of unit-level information on such economic activities. The Socio-Economic and Caste Census 2011, also collected data on non-agricultural own-account enterprises as the "main source of household income." The population enumeration data in the Census of India includes data on the "category of economic activity" ("worker in household industry"/ "other worker," apart from "cultivator" and "agricultural labourer"). These data on non-agricultural establishments can be used to cross-check the validity of village-level data in the Economic Census.

6.5 REQUIREMENTS FOR KEEPING VILLAGE-LEVEL RECORDS ON THE PANCHAYAT'S JURISDICTION

The village-level records in India evolved to meet the requirements of a highly centralised system of administration. In the post-Seventy-Third Amendment regime, however, the way of recording matters in the village must benefit the panchayat's self-governance. For the most effective use of data for self-governance, village-level records have to be documented accurately in relation to people resident in the panchayat's jurisdictional area. Even when a record seems to be available at the village, its recording structure may not be oriented to people resident in that area and cause difficulty in the use of data.

There are two such issues. The first issue is that the administrative jurisdiction of outside agencies may be different from that of village panchayat so that village-level data cannot be taken from the records maintained by these agencies. For example, the geographical boundaries of the Block and the area served by the primary health centre are not coincident in rural Maharashtra. The administrative jurisdiction of the Block primary health centres and sub-centres in rural West Bengal may also be different from the jurisdiction of the panchayats. As for Raina village panchayat, jurisdictional boundaries of the two sub-centres were identical to the boundaries of the panchayat area. The boundaries of the two sub-centres did not cut across the panchayats' boundaries. But the jurisdiction of a sub-centre covers more than one village so that the data maintained by it need to be separated for each village. Similar problems arise elsewhere in India. The Ministry of Statistics and Programme Implementation indicates that:

> In view of the fact that jurisdictions of local institutions are overlapping over villages, village-level data cannot be culled out from the records maintained by these institutions. In such cases, a mechanism may be evolved to get the village-level data from the institutional data with the help of other available records/the other village-level functionaries. [15]

Even if no such problem arises, a second issue emerges: village-level records may not be related to people actually residing in the panchayat area. The place of registration in the Civil Registration System is the place of occurrence of the vital event and not the place of usual residence of the person in question. Therefore, it does not register children born outside the panchayat's jurisdiction because their mothers return temporarily to their native villages for delivery or go to a nearby town for institutional delivery. Thus, the recording structure of the Civil Registration System is not oriented to children resident in the panchayat's jurisdiction. If all children born outside the jurisdiction of the relevant panchayat or municipality are born inside the boundary of the State, the number of children born outside each panchayat or municipality will balance out each other in the State. Therefore, this issue

---

[15] Central Statistics Office (2014, p. 142).

does not interfere with the use of macro-level data for large States. It is not a matter of serious concern for highly centralised systems of administration. However, following the Seventy-Third Amendment regime, the favoured data source with respect to village-level births has shifted from records such as the Civil Registration System to records such as the Integrated Child Development Services (*anganwadi*) child registers which record the child's place of usual residence. Therefore, panchayat officials in Raina claimed that the birth registers maintained by Integrated Child Development Services workers (*anganwadi*) are the most reliable source on child births.

A similar issue arises with the *patwari's* land records. While the land record includes information on landowners who live outside the village in question but who own plots in the village, the same land record does not include information on landowners who live in the village but who do own plots outside that village. This can hinder data use.

The *patwari* in Warwat Khanderao, besides his plot-wise land records, has a list of landowners ("occupants") living in the village to link with information on all their plots within the village. But he has no information on their plots lying outside his jurisdiction. Therefore, the Agricultural Census has tried to solve this problem (although the purpose of this Census is to compile a list of "operational holdings" and not ownership holdings). The *Manual of Schedules and Instructions for Data Collection* (Land Record States) for the Agricultural Census describes the re-tabulation of village-level land records as follows:

> Some holdings may not be located completely within the village and they may be spread over to other villages. For preparation of a list of operational holdings, necessary matching of the part-holdings scattered over more than one village has to be done. A holding may cut across the boundary of a village/*patwari* Circle/Revenue Inspector Circle/Tehsil/District/State. As in the previous Censuses, the *tehsil* will be the outer limit for pooling of all the parcels of an operational holding.[16]

Village panchayats in Maharashtra can solve this problem by citing the Bombay Village Panchayats Act, 1958, which makes "maintenance of village records relating to land revenue" a subject of activities to be devolved to panchayats. The panchayati raj institutions in Maharashtra also have the potential to pool "the part-holdings scattered over more than one village" using the same method as the Agricultural Census.

[16] Ministry of Agriculture (2006a, p. 3).

The Block Land and Land Reform Office in West Bengal has a dual land recording system. It has in addition to the plot-wise ownership holdings registers, holder-wise land registers that bring together information on all their ownership holdings within the Block area. This dual land recording system is useful for land reforms to find land in excess of the ceiling limit for individual holders.

A similar issue also arises in the data of All India School Education Survey (AISES). In AISES data, students are recorded at the place of their schools. While the data includes information on students who live outside the village in question but are enrolled at schools located there, it does not include information on students who live in the village but are enrolled at schools outside it. However, the village-level register of all children based on an annual house-to-house survey conducted by the school teachers includes children enrolled at schools outside that village.

Thus, under the post-Seventy-Third-Amendment regime, the requirement for village-level records has shifted to a new type of documentation that is focused on the place of usual residence of the people concerned. The new type of records has to be organised entirely in relation to people resident in the panchayat area and meet the demands of democratic self-governance.

6.6 PEOPLE'S LIST AND A PEOPLE-ORIENTED RECORDING PRINCIPLE

People living under the jurisdiction of a panchayat are its main actors. The panchayat – especially the village panchayat and its sub-panchayat bodies – is the nearest available administrative institution for people living in villages. Therefore, it is expected to be a democratic and people-oriented local government.

In order to be a people-oriented local government, the panchayat requires a comprehensive People's List: a comprehensive list of all persons and households living in its jurisdiction. The panchayat needs this list even though the Population Census covers every village, because unit-level records produced by the Population Census are not available to it. Without a complete list of residents in its jurisdiction, the panchayat's public policies would be inefficient or discretionary, and less objective. It would be difficult for the panchayat to formulate its public policies in relation to its residents. At present, however, no such comprehensive list of people is available with the panchayat office.

The panchayat secretary of Warwat Khanderao argued that he could use the electoral roll with the property tax register (house tax register), if necessary, to identify households and individuals in the panchayat area. These lists can be used to identify target beneficiaries for Government schemes. However, the electoral roll is a list of adult persons and therefore does not cover all residents; it covers only the adult (18 years and above) population. In adition, the electoral roll may include persons temporarily or permanently living outside the village. The number of voters in the electoral roll of Warwat Khanderao was 889 out of a total population of 809, aged 18 and above. Out of 809 persons in the Foundation for Agrarian Studies (FAS) survey data, 662 persons were identified in the voters' list.

The property tax register contains information on each house in the panchayat's jurisdiction, with its corresponding owner and house number,[17] but does not contain any information on members of the owner's household. Furthermore, if more than one "household" (a group of persons normally living together and getting food from a common kitchen) lives in the house, no household other than the owner's would be covered by the property tax register. Therefore, it does not necessarily cover all the households.

In the electoral rolls, house numbers are given to voters to indicate voters living in the same house. In Warwat Khanderao we tried to match the households and house numbers in electoral rolls with the FAS households. We could locate 209 house numbers given to voters in the electoral roll in the FAS database. But the actual number of households in the FAS database in these 209 house numbers matching with the electoral roll was 239. The reason is that some house numbers were given to more than one FAS household. The number of house numbers given to more than one FAS household was

Table 6.1 *Comparison of Electoral Roll of Warwat Khanderao with Foundation for Agrarian Studies (FAS) Data*

No. of FAS households with House Numbers in the electoral roll	239
No. of House Numbers of FAS households matched with the electoral roll	209
No. of FAS households with more than one House Number	16
No. of House Numbers given to more than one FAS household	37

[17] As far as Warwat Khanderao is concerned, house numbers in the property tax register (house tax register) and house numbers according to the voters' list are different. The two sets of house numbers are not necessarily linked with each other.

37, whereas the number of FAS households to which more than one house numbers were given was 16.

The village panchayat requires not only aggregate data, but also unit-level records for data retrieval. In fact, in an interview, a panchayat leader at Raina stated that a kind of People's List would be most desirable for the panchayat's activities. Thus, we examine some records that have the potential to function as comprehensive lists of residents in the jurisdiction of a panchayat, that is, the Integrated Child Development Services village survey register and the village-wise households list of the Below Poverty Line Census.

There was widespread discontent among village residents regarding the Below Poverty Line list generated from the Survey data. On the basis of a micro-level discrepancy analysis, comparing each head of household in the Below Poverty Line list with the corresponding person in the FAS survey list, we found that some parameters estimated by the Below Poverty Line Census were very inaccurate. However, as will be seen below, the coverage of persons in the Census was in itself not unsatisfactory.

On the one hand, the more frequently updated a People's List is, the more usable it becomes. In this respect the village survey register is preferable as the core for a People's List as it is updated regularly. On the other hand, although the Below Poverty Line Census database is not updated regularly, it is available in a digitised format. This helps not only in producing statistics but also in identifying each and every rural household by a uniquely generated household code.

The panchayat leader at Raina who told us in an interview that a type of People's List is desirable for his panchayat's activities also said that the village-wise list of all households from the Rural Household Survey is not too bad for this purpose. He said this notwithstanding his dissatisfaction with the accuracy of the list of the Below Poverty Line households and with the scores obtained by households on each of the parameters.

Table 6.2 *Total number of persons in Warwat Khanderao*

FAS Survey database	1308
BPL Census database	1322
ICDS village survey register	1319

Table 6.3 *Total number of persons in Bidyanidhi*

FAS Survey database	643
BPL Census database	***
ICDS village survey register	896

Using the FAS database as the point of reference, we made an assessment of the village survey register and the Below Poverty Line Census 2002 (or the Rural Household Survey) databases. We evaluated whether these databases could be used as a People's List in the villages. The assessment was done at two levels, for individuals and for households. As far as the individual People's List is concerned, the number of persons in these two lists is shown in Tables 6.2 and 6.3.

The BPL Census database for Bidyanidhi contained a complete list of all households, and the scores obtained by each household on each of the parameters used for identification of the poor. However, the database did not list the members of each household. Of the 151 households listed in the Below Poverty Line Census database, information on household members was available for only 17. For this reason, the data could not be used for our micro-discrepancy analysis and the number of persons in the Below Poverty Line Census database is left blank in Table 6.3.[18]

In our micro-level discrepancy analysis,[19] we compared each person and household in these lists with the corresponding person and household in the database collected from census-type household surveys conducted by the FAS. We tried to match each and every person and household in these candidate lists with the corresponding person and household in the database. First, we tried to match them using their names, ages, etc. We then conducted a follow-up interview for unmatched cases with persons in the village, including village-level functionaries. On the basis of the interviews, we corrected the spelling of names and tried to match them again as far as possible. There was no standard romanisation of the Devanagari or Bengali scripts. There were also entry errors and spelling mistakes. Nicknames were sometimes used for children. Therefore, it was not easy to undertake data-matching. From the follow-up interview we found several reasons for the discrepancies. Finally, we examined the overall matching status of person-wise and household-wise lists.

[18] See below for an explanation of the discrepancies found in Bidyanidhi between the different lists.
[19] OECD (2002, p. 53).

Table 6.4 *Micro-level data matching: A sample from Warwat Khanderao*

Matching status								FAS Database					ICDS village survey register			BPL Census				
Person's Serial No in FAS Database	Household's Serial No in FAS Database	Person's Serial No in BPL census	Household's Serial No in BPL Census	Person's Serial No in ICDS Register	Household's Serial No in ICDS Register	Serial No in Voter's List	House No in Voter's List	Family Name #	Name #	Sex	Age	Relationship	Cleaned Name #	Age	Sex	Name of Head of Household #	Member Name #	Gender	Age	Relation With Head
310	60	1092	261	322	75	678	182	K.	B.	M	22	Son	K.B.P.	Not Available	M	K.P.R.	K.B.P.	M	18	Son
311	61	1090	261	323	76	679	182	K.	G.P.	M	35	Self	K.G.P.	28	M	K.P.R.	K.G.P.	M	30	Son
312	61	1093	261	324	76	680	182	K.	M.	F	31	Wife	K.M.G.	26	F	K.P.R.	K.M.G.	F	26	Others
313	61		261	325	76			K.	S.	F	9	Daughter	K.S.G.	8	F					
314	61		261	326	76			K.	S.	M	6	Son	K.S.G.	5	M					
315	61		261	325.1	76			K.	S.	F	24 m	Daughter	K.S.G.	1	F					
316	62	869	214	311	73	484	127A	K.	G.S.	M	30	Self	K.G.S.	25	M	K.G.S.	K.G.S.	M	26	Self
317	62	870	214	312	73	485	127A	K.	U.	F	22	Wife	K.U.G.	21	F	K.G.S.	K.U.G.	F	20	Wife
318	62	871	214	313	73	482	127A	K.	M.	F	65	Mother				K.G.S.	K.M.S.	F	70	Mother
319	62		214		73			K.	K.	F	12m	Daughter								
320	63	438	116		/	478	127	P.	W.S.	M	38	Self				P.W.S.	P.W.S.	M	45	Self
321	63	439	116		/			P.	U.B.	F	28	Wife				P.W.S.	P.U.W.	F	25	Wife
322	63		116		/			P.	D.	F	24 m	Daughter								

Note: # Only initials, not names, are shown in this table. However, data-matching was more difficult than the sample shown in this table. We had to correct the spelling of names. There was no standard romanisation of the Hindi or Marathi scripts. There were also entry errors and spelling mistakes. Nicknames were sometimes used for children.

The "matching status" of each of the lists with the persons list in the FAS database is shown in Tables 6.5 and 6.6. In the tables, row entries show the matching status of each list in the left column with each list in the first row. As the list shown in the left column is the reference point, the matching status of, say, list x with list y is not identical to the matching status of list y with list x.

Table 6.5 *Final results of person-to-person matching, Warwat Khanderao*

	FAS survey		BPL Census		ICDS village survey register	
	Matched	Not matched	Matched	Not matched	Matched	Not matched
FAS survey database	***	***	973	335	956	352
BPL Census database	973	349	***	***	908	414
ICDS village survey register	956	363	908	411	***	***

Table 6.6 *Final results of person-to-person matching, Bidyanidhi*

	FAS survey		ICDS village survey register	
	Matched	Not matched	Matched	Not matched
FAS survey database	***	***	632	11
ICDS village survey register	632	264	***	***

Table 6.7 *Percentage of matched cases, Warwat Khanderao in per cent*

Age code	Female	Male	Total
5 and below	26.1	24.3	25.2
5–10	63.9	71.9	68.0
10–15	81.5	80.0	80.8
15–20	75.6	92.5	83.7
20–25	40.0	84.2	61.5
25–30	84.0	69.6	76.4
30–50	86.1	92.4	89.2
50–55	84.2	85.0	84.6
55–60	82.1	95.7	88.2
60–65	73.7	96.3	87.0
65–70	80.0	100.0	89.5
70 and above	27.3	87.5	63.0
Total	69.6	79.1	74.4

The lists of individuals in Below Poverty Line Census database and the village survey register in Warwat Khanderao were not of good data quality. They did not properly document 20 to 30 per cent of the village population.

As shown in Table 6.7, non-matched persons in Below Poverty Line Census database were concentrated in the category of children under 10 years, women around 20 years old and women older than 70. There was a four-year time lag between the Below Poverty Line Census (June 2003) and the FAS survey (May 2007). But the matching status of children aged four through ten years was also not satisfactory. Some children's names were not recorded in the list and some names were misspelt. Some young women had married men who were resident in other villages during those four years. It was sometimes difficult to identify families to which elderly widows belonged; they were sometimes recorded as family members of one of their children, and sometimes under one-person households. Except for children and elderly widows, about 80 to 90 per cent of residents in the Below Poverty Line Census database were matched with the persons' list of the FAS database. The matching status of Muslims in the Below Poverty Line Census database was also not as good as expected.

As shown in Table 6.8, the matching status of Scheduled Caste and Nomadic Tribe (NT) persons in the village survey register was not particularly dissatisfying, but the status of Muslims stood out. The Integrated Child Development Services worker and the teacher of the Zilla Parishad Urdu Primary School said that all village children in Warwat Khanderao were included in the Integrated Child Development Services registers. However, there were inaccuracies in the records for Muslim families. Some of the errors arose because of entry errors and spelling mistakes. There was no standard romanisation of the Devanagari script, nicknames instead of given names are sometimes used for children, thus compounding the problem. In addition, the Integrated Child Development Services worker, a Buddhist woman,

Table 6.8 *Percentage of matched cases in both lists, Warwat Khanderao in per cent*

Caste group	ICDS village survey register	BPL Census
Muslim	52.6	68.5
Nomadic tribe	72.9	79.2
OBC	80.6	75.0
Scheduled caste	86.8	77.2
Total	72.9	74.4

was not clear about discrepancies in the child register records for Muslim children. The teacher from the Zilla Parishad Urdu Primary School said that they had applied for separate Integrated Child Development Services centres (*anganwadi*), but that this was not sanctioned since there were very few Muslim children in the village. We interviewed five Muslim households that did not send their children to the Integrated Child Development Services centre for pre-schooling. The families reported that they do not send their children because the centre was far away and the concerned worker did not come to collect the children. The family members did not have time to drop the children there. They also reported that the children often went to the closer Urdu school where they could eat with their older siblings. All the students of the Zilla Parishad Urdu Primary School also went to the *madrasa*, namely the Ziya-ul-Quran, in the morning and the evening to learn Arabic. This situation may also have affected the coverage and accuracy of records collected by the Integrated Child Development Services workers.

The person-wise list in the village survey register in Bidyanidhi was of high quality. As shown in Table 6.6, it covered most persons in the village, that is, 98.3 per cent of persons in the FAS survey database on Bidyanidhi. Information was updated regularly. Non-matched cases in the village survey register were as many as 264. However, that is not necessarily a sign of the weakness of this register. The current status of most of the unmatched cases was specified in the register, as shown in Table 6.9. In Bidyanidhi, even with the village survey register being updated every five years, a lot of information on births, deaths, marriages, and migrations was added later and modified. The register included records on children born after the FAS survey and persons marrying and coming to the village after the survey,

Table 6.9 *Reasons for discrepancies between FAS survey data and ICDS survey data, Bidyanidhi*

Born after FAS survey	49
Died before FAS survey	29
Married and left the village	29
Married into the village after the survey	28
Non-resident	95
Other	6
Unspecified	26
(Blank)	2
Total	264

which suggests that this information is updated regularly. However, details of all members of undivided households were still recorded even when a member of the household had migrated permanently. Therefore, the register included records of non-residents, such as persons who have married outside and left the village. It also included records of persons who died before the FAS survey. Their details remained with explanatory notes. Thus panchayat officials in Raina valued the registers maintained by the Integrated Child Development Services workers.

Household-to-household matching was an even more difficult exercise than person-to-person matching. As far as a household-wise people's list is concerned, the numbers of all families in these candidate lists are shown in Tables 6.10 and 6.11. Unlike the total number of persons, the total number of households varied considerably depending on the lists. The definition of "household" looks identical across these lists, that is, "a group of persons normally living together and taking food from a common kitchen." However, in some situations, it may be difficult for enumerators to strictly apply this definition of a household. In fact the *Instruction Manual for Enumerators: Socio-Economic and Caste Census 2011 – Rural* (Ministry of Rural Development) indicated this issue as follows:

> In a few situations, it may be difficult to apply the definition of household strictly as given above. For example, a person living alone in a Census house, whether cooking meals or not, will have to be treated as a single member household. [20]

Table 6.10 *Total number of households, Warwat Khanderao*

FAS survey	250
BPL Census	306
ICDS village survey register	295
Census 2001	286
Census 2011	316

Table 6.11 *Total number of households, Bidyanidhi*

FAS survey	142
BPL Census	151
ICDS village survey register	109
Census 2001	131
Census 2011	162

[20] Ministry of Rural Development (2011, p. 13).

The *Manual* further indicated:

> If any female member of a household decides to declare herself as a
> separate household, she should be recorded as a separate household. Widowed,
> separated, second wives, single women are some examples of women who
> could declare themselves as a separate household.

A group of persons living together could be considered a joint family, or
sub-divided into several nuclear families. Where a married son lived with his
parents and others, he and his family could be either regarded as members of
the larger joint family or as forming a separate household. A similar problem
arose with elderly persons living with their adult children.

The sub-division of a household leads to a lower Below Poverty Line score,
which causes respondent bias among persons who want Below Poverty Line
cards. Consequently, the definition of "household" in the Socio-Economic and
Caste Census 2011 was modified a little, allowing for the actual respondent
bias.[21] The Expert Group chaired by N. C. Saxena (to advise the Ministry of
Rural Development on the methodology for conducting the BPL Census for
the Eleventh Five Year Plan) provided the following definition of household:

> Household will mean:
>   A joint family comprising all adults and children who eat from a common
> hearth and reside under a common roof.
>   However, for the purpose of inclusion and survey (but not exclusion), within
> households which may even share a kitchen and a roof, the following will be
> treated as separate households:
> - a single woman
> - old individuals or couples in which one or both are beyond the age of 60
>   years.
> - every adult with TB, leprosy, disability, mental illness or HIV AIDS with
>   spouse and children; and
> - bonded labourers with spouse and children.

Thus, any couple or even a single woman/widow may declare herself as
a separate household. Therefore, the definition of household in the Below
Poverty Line Census 2002 (and Socio-Economic and Caste Census 2011) is
slightly different from other censuses or surveys.[22] As a result, the household

---

[21] Ministry of Rural Development (2009, p.33).
[22] Himanshu (2010) is of the view that "while the National Sample Survey Organisation and
the Census recognise a common kitchen as the basis of identifying a household, the Below
Poverty Line (BPL) census and the Mahatma Gandhi National Rural Employment Guarantee
Scheme (MGNREGS) use the definition of a nuclear household."

size ascertained in the Below Poverty Line Census tends to be smaller than in other surveys. The number of households in the Below Poverty Line Census list tends to be larger than in other lists.

The matching status between two household-wise lists and the list of households of the FAS database is shown in Tables 6.12 and 6.13. In these

Table 6.12 *Household-to-household matching, Warwat Khanderao*

	FAS survey		BPL Census		ICDS village survey register	
	Matched	Not matched	Matched	Not matched	Matched	Not matched
FAS survey	***	***	231	19	200	50
BPL Census	241 (230)*	65 (76)*	***	***	230	76
ICDS village survey register	221	74	244	51	***	***

Notes: (i) Matched household does not mean that all household members match with each other. It is the case where more than one household member of both households match with each other.
(ii) * Matched head of household in BPL Census list found in the persons' list of the other databases — FAS database and the ICDS village survey register.

Table 6.13 *Household-to-household matching, Bidyanidhi*

	FAS survey		BPL Census		ICDS village survey register	
	Matched	Not matched	Matched	Not matched	Matched	Not matched
FAS survey	***	***	134*	8*	138	4
BPL Census	139*	12*	***	***	140*	11*
ICDS village survey register	99	10	91*	18*	***	***

Notes: (i) Matched household does not mean that all household members match with each other. It is the case where more than one household member of both households match with each other.
(ii) * This marks matching between heads of household in the BPL Census list and the list of all household members in the other two databases —FAS survey database and the ICDS village survey register. If the head of household in the BPL Census list is found among household members in the compared database, then the household is considered as a matched household. More than one head of household in the BPL Census list can be found in a single household in the compared database. In such a situation, all BPL households are considered as "matched." The BPL Census database for Bidyanidhi does not contain all the members of each household, hence individual members could not be compared across databases.

tables, row entries show the matching status of each household list in the left column with each household list given in the first row. (A matched household is one in which at least one household member of both households matches, and it does not necessarily mean that all household members match in both lists.)

As shown in Tables 6.5, 6.12, and 6.13, the matching can be done directly between the Integrated Child Development Services village survey register and the village-wise list of the Below Poverty Line Census. It can be done without using the list in the FAS database. The Integrated Child Development Services village survey register or the list of the Below Poverty Line Census can also be used as a point of reference.

If the village panchayat were to designate a core list of people and check its reliability on the basis of data-sharing mechanisms among different data sources, the quality of data in the people's lists could be improved in Warwat Khanderao as well. The village survey register or the database from census-type surveys can serve as a core population list. Besides the Below Poverty Line Census, other census-type surveys such as those organised by panchayati raj institutions or the Central/State Governments can also help build a population list.

The following person-wise lists, in part, are available in the village as checklists to validate and update the core people's lists: 1. the electoral roll together with the property tax register (house tax register); 2. records at the primary health centre; 3. birth and death register of the Civil Registration System; 4. records at the village school (especially where an annual survey is conducted by school teachers of all households in the village); and 5. the Mahatma Gandhi National Rural Employment Guarantee Scheme register.

There are possible ways of generating population lists through data sharing. Our suggestions are:

Alternative 1: The village panchayat can designate and coordinate the village survey register as the core list of the people in the village. The Integrated Child Development Services workers (*anganwadi*) or a group of officials in an interlinked health-and-childcare system can then update it regularly. Databases from census-type surveys can be used to further check its reliability. Further, the various checklists mentioned above can be used to validate in part and update the ICDS village survey registers.

Alternative 2: The village panchayat can initially designate a database from a census-type survey such as the BPL Census (or the Socio-Economic and Caste Census 2011) as being the core list of the population. The Integrated Child Development Services workers (*anganwadi*) or a group of officials in an interlinked health-and-childcare system can then update the list regularly. Subsequently, the various checklists mentioned above can be used to validate in part and update the initial core list.

Alternative 3: As the project to create the National Population Register (NPR) is ongoing, the village panchayat can designate the NPR as the core list of the people. The NPR is a process of mandatory registration of all usual residents of a locality under the Citizenship Act, 1955, and the Citizenship (Registration of Citizens and Issue of National Identity Cards) Rules, 2003. The first phase of the project, which required the registration of usual residents through a door-to-door survey, was completed with the first phase of Census 2011 in April–September 2010. However, collection of biometric information and issuing citizenship identity cards under the project remain controversial due to the fact that the collection of biometrics does not have statutory backing in the Citizenship Rules 2003, and the obvious overlap between the NPR and the Unique Identification Authority of India project of the Central Government, which also entails collecting biometric data and issuing a unique identification number to all citizens.

The ICDS village survey register is not recorded digitally, whereas the Below Poverty Line Census database and some of the checklists mentioned above are maintained in a digitised form. It would be useful for the village panchayat if the database from the ICDS village survey register was digitised at the Block or district level.[23] It would be useful even as a paper document if there were columns for comments in which to record additional information on each record. In fact panchayat officials in Raina considered the registers maintained by the Integrated Child Development Services workers (*anganwadi*) reliable, even though they were not digitised.

6.7 SHIFT IN REQUIREMENT FOR THE PRINCIPLE OF BIRTH RECORDING

The National Statistical Commission stated that the Civil Registration System (CRS) has the potential to provide estimates of vital events at the

---

[23] The digitisation of the work of the *anganwadis* has been implemented in November 2015.

local level.[24] However, our analysis of the CRS in the two villages showed that vital village-level records are not necessarily related to people residing in that area. The existing CRS is often not reliable for supplying databases for the purpose of self-governance.

There are two ways of recording vital events: at the place of occurrence or at the place of usual residence.[25] The CRS determines the place of registration according to the place of occurrence of vital events. Such events in the life of a resident occurring outside the jurisdiction of the panchayat are not registered in the CRS of that panchayat, even if that resident usually lives in the panchayat area. For example, the CRS of a village panchayat does not register children born outside its jurisdiction because their mothers may return temporarily to their native villages for delivery or go to nearby towns for institutional delivery. In this respect, the recording principle of birth records in the CRS does not suit the vision of self-governance.

Using the FAS survey database as a point of reference, we conducted a micro-level discrepancy analysis, comparing each and every birth event recorded in the CRS of the Warwat Khanderao village panchayat from 2002 to 2007 with the corresponding person in the FAS database – that is, all children in the age group of five years and below. Furthermore, we conducted interviews with all households in which children were born between 2002 and 2007, and whose names were not in the CRS but present in the FAS database.[26]

The major finding that emerges out of our assessment is that, even if we assume a 100 per cent registration, the CRS gives information only for births occurring within the village, whereas in most cases mothers go to their parental villages for delivery or go to the nearest town for institutional delivery. As shown in Table 6.14, out of 130 children in the 0–5 age group in 2007 in the FAS database, only 22 per cent were registered under the CRS at the Warwat Khanderao village panchayat. About 63 per cent of the children were not registered there but were registered at other village panchayats or local bodies. Thus, the birth of most children in the age group 0–5 years in the FAS database was registered outside the Warwat Khanderao village panchayat. Almost all institutional births were recorded as demanded by law. However, since there was no medical facility in Warwat Khanderao village, mothers had

[24] National Statistical Commission (2001), para. 2.7.8.
[25] United Nations (2001, p. 59).
[26] Okabe and Surjit (2012).

Table 6.14 *Details of registration of children of ages less than or equal to five,* Warwat Khanderao *village, May 2007* in per cent

Category	Number (in per cent)
All children less than or equal to age five appeared in FAS database in 2007	130 (100.0%)
Registered births in the CRS at Warwat Khanderao or elsewhere	111 (85.4%)
Registered births in the CRS at Warwat Khanderao	29 (22.3%)
Registered births in the CRS elsewhere outside Warwat Khanderao	82 (63.1%)
Unregistered births in the CRS neither at Warwat Khanderao nor elsewhere	18 (13.8%)
Other	1 (0.8%)
Registered births in the CRS at Warwat Khanderao but not in the FAS database in 2007	40
Mother came to Warwat Khanderao for delivery	23
Other	17

Source: PARI survey data 2007.

to approach facilities located in neighbouring towns. Moreover, it is a general custom that mothers return to their parents' home for the first delivery.

Conversely, the registers under CRS at the village panchayat in Warwat Khanderao included 23 children whose births were registered in the village because their mothers, who were married to men resident in other villages, came temporarily to Warwat Khanderao for delivery. Thus the information from CRS of a particular village cannot be used for the purpose of obtaining data on children which is needed for local administration as it does not cover all children resident in that village.[27]

The micro-level picture on birth records is somewhat different from the macro-level view based on the Sample Registration System (SRS) or the National Family Health Survey.[28] If all children born outside the jurisdiction of the relevant panchayat or municipality are born inside the boundary of the State, the number of children born outside each panchayat or municipality would balance out each other in the State. Therefore, this issue does not seriously impair the use of birth records as macro-level data in large States. Although both the CRS and the SRS provide us with State-level macro data, we envisaged difficulties in using the CRS data for the purpose of local-level

[27] A similar exercise could not be carried out for Bidyanidhi. On our visit to the Raina panchayat office on September 10, 2009, we found that birth registers were only available from August 2005 onwards. The FAS survey in Bidyanidhi was conducted in May–June 2005. All children recorded in the FAS survey were thus born before the present registers began.

[28] International Institute for Population Sciences (2007).

administration. Certain systematic changes are required to establish birth registration at the place of usual residence if the CRS data are to meet the increasing requirement and demand for decentralised databases in the post-Seventy-Third Amendment regime.

At the same time, we examined the potential of the ICDS (*anganwadi*) child registers in Warwat Khanderao. These registers do not have the problem of undercounting children since all children, whether born in the village of their residence (here Warwat Khanderao) or in the native village of their mothers or at medical facilities located in a neighbouring town, are to be registered in the child register. In principle, the place of registration of the ICDS child register is the place of usual residence, whereas the place of registration in the CRS is the place of the event's occurrence.

We also tried to match each child in the ICDS child register for the period 2005–7 with children mentioned in the FAS database for Warwat Khanderao (see Table 6.15). Out of 51 children in the FAS database born between 2005 and May 2007, 33 children (or 65 per cent) were recorded in the ICDS child register during and after 2005 to May 2007. Out of 50 children recorded in the ICDS child register for 2005 to May 2007, 29 children (or 58 per cent) were mentioned in the FAS database. Therefore, although the ICDS child register may cover more children in the village than the CRS's birth register, the quality of its data is debatable and merits further investigation.

Further, we tried to match each child in the ICDS child register for the period

Table 6.15 *Results of matching for the period of 2005–7, Warwat Khanderao*

	FAS survey		ICDS child register	
	Matched	Not matched	Matched	Not matched
FAS survey database	***	***	33 (64.7 %)	18 (35.3 %)
ICDS child register	29 (58.0 %)	21 (42.0 %)	***	***

Table 6.16 *Results of matching for the period January 2000 to June 2007, Bidyanidhi*

	FAS survey		ICDS child register	
	Matched	Not matched	Matched	Not matched
FAS survey database	***	***	54 (88.5 %)	7 (11.5 %)
ICDS child register	54 (91.5 %)	5 (8.5 %)	***	***

January 2000 to June 2005 with children present in the FAS database in Bidyanidhi (see Table 6.16).[29] We compared this list with the list of children aged 5 years and below from the FAS survey data. According to the ICDS child register, 59 children were born in the village between January 2000 and June 2005. According to the FAS survey data, 61 children were in the age group 0–5 years in June 2005. The names of 54 children were found in both the lists. We examined this discrepancy closely, allowing for some divergence on account of temporary or permanent migration and misreported age during the FAS survey.[30] From this analysis we were able to conclude that the coverage of the ICDS child register in Bidyanidhi was excellent.

The ICDS child registers, recorded in the place of usual residence, were intended to include the births of all children resident in the village, and so they were useful as a basis for village-level administration and planning. After the Seventy-third Amendment, therefore, the favoured data source with respect to village-level births had been shifting from records such as the CRS to those such as the ICDS child registers which were related directly to people resident in the panchayat area.

6.8 CONCLUSION

In this chapter we described some potential data sources on the panchayat's jurisdiction. In our analysis we found that a People's List or list of households and individuals residing within the panchayat's jurisdiction is essential for self-governance. However, the village panchayats do not have such a list ready at their disposal. We thus assessed two potential lists that can serve

[29] We were able to obtain the child register for 2006 from the ICDS centre. The 2005 child register was not available because the then ICDS worker at the centre had joined in 2006.

[30] Five names in the ICDS list were not found in the survey list. In three of the five cases, the households to which the children belonged (identified by the name of the child's father) were not found in the survey database. It could be that the households were not present in the village at the time of the survey. There is also a possibility that the particular household had settled in the village after June 2005 (but before January 2006). In the remaining two cases, the children's names were not recorded during the survey. Both the children belonged to the same household and the error was corrected during a later survey conducted in the same household in 2006. Seven children in the survey list were not found in the ICDS list. These children were reported to be 5 years old. Hence, there is a high possibility that their age was under-reported during the survey and hence their names were not registered at the ICDS centre. There are reasons to believe that ICDS data on age are more accurate than the survey data. First, data on children's date of birth were not collected in the household survey, but the ICDS register records the date of birth of each child. Secondly, in four of the eight cases, other children from the same household were recorded in the ICDS register.

as a people's list, i.e., the Below Poverty Line Census list and the Integrated Child Development Services household registers. We also evaluated the data quality of these two sources in the two villages.

The ICDS household register can suit the purpose as the same format is used across ICDS centres in India and data are updated regularly. The quality of ICDS data in Bidyanidhi was very good, though the ICDS register data at Warwat Khanderao was not satisfactory. The quality of ICDS records needs to be improved at the village level.

The Below Poverty Line surveys also used uniform templates across the country and were digitised. However, the surveys were not held at regular intervals and the data were not necessarily accurate. Besides, since the Below Poverty Line surveys were done in a centralised manner, it was not easy for village agencies to make changes in the data.

In order to make data from village agencies other than panchayats suitable for use by panchayats there needs to be a reorientation of the recording principle that allows for aggregation and disaggregation of data according to the geographical jurisdiction of the panchayati raj institutions. The recording principle of the present statistical system in India caters to the needs of centralised planning, and is, thus, not suitable for decentralised decision making.

Chapter 7

POTENTIAL VILLAGE-LEVEL DATA FOR PUBLIC FINANCE

This chapter discusses the financial data available at the two village panchayats under study. Five types of financial data necessary for local self-governance are described and discussed here. These are:

(i) Village panchayat accounts
(ii) Own-source revenues
(iii) Intergovernmental fund transfers between the Centre, States and panchayati raj institutions
(iv) Fiscal relationship between State Governments and village panchayats
(v) Funding streams for all schemes and programmes within the village panchayat's jurisdiction.

7.1 DATA ON PANCHAYAT ACCOUNTS

7.1.1 Panchayat Accounts Data in Maharashtra

The Warwat Khanderao village panchayat maintains account data in its registers as shown in Table 4.5 (chapter 4). Under provisions of Section 62(4) of the Bombay Village Panchayats Act, 1958, village development officers are required to prepare annual accounts. The village panchayat is to submit annual accounts to the village council for approval.

We authenticated the accounting data in the *Annual Budget Report on Village Panchayats in Maharashtra*. As shown in Table 7.1, the total revenue and expenditure of the Warwat Khanderao village panchayat in 2007–8 amounted to Rs 166,117.32 and Rs 157,354.00, according to the Report. Own-source revenues were Rs 86,456.89. Grants from Government agencies were not recorded except for the grant for the *Sampoorna Grameen Rozgar Yojana* (Rs 25,117), Twelfth Finance Commission grant (Rs 35,281.43) and Government subsidy for remuneration/salary, meeting allowance (Rs 9900), etc. The Twelfth Finance Commission grant recorded in the Report can be considered as an untied fund. Untied funds are not tied to specific schemes or activities, but there are specific rules regarding the expenditure of such funds.

As mentioned in chapter 3, according to the Comptroller and Auditor General, 63 out of the test-checked 80 village panchayats in Maharashtra had submitted their annual accounts every year to the village council for approval for the period 2003–8. None of the test-checked 80 village panchayats had submitted their annual accounts to the district panchayats during that period. The Comptroller and Auditor General's scrutiny of records revealed that 70 out of the test-checked 80 village panchayats did not maintain Form 3 through Form 27 required in the Bombay Village Panchayats (Budget and Accounts) Rule, 1959. The Comptroller and Auditor General argued that "this also shows lack of proper control and supervision of GPs by higher officials like BDO of PS and CEO of ZP."[1] As far as the Warwat Khanderao village panchayat was concerned, we ascertained the existence of such forms as shown by the panchayat secretary. The village panchayat submitted annual accounts to the village council for approval. In addition, the Warwat Khanderao village panchayat submitted the Annual Budget Report to the Block Development Officer.

According to the Comptroller and Auditor General, test-checking of cash books of six village panchayats selected from three district panchayats revealed that cash books were not consistently maintained from 2003 to 2008. It was also observed that village panchayats were making huge cash payments in violation of all codal instructions.[2] We ascertained the existence of a cash book in the Warwat Khanderao village panchayat, shown to us by the panchayat secretary. However, the village panchayat was severely understaffed. The panchayat secretary, who visited Warwat Khanderao village only twice a week, was responsible for maintaining accounts along with many other responsibilities for panchayat administration.

The annual accounts of the Warwat Khanderao village panchayat were consolidated at the Block level and audited by the Local Fund Audit Department annually and by the Comptroller and Auditor General once in three years.[3] Accounting data of the Warwat Khanderao village panchayat were produced primarily in relation to its own source of revenues. Therefore,

[1] Comptroller and Auditor General (2008, pp. 38–40).
[2] *Ibid.*, p. 37. "According to Rule 5(A) of the Bombay Village Panchayats (BVP) (Budget & Accounts) Rules, 1959 payment of any sum in excess of Rs 500 out of the village fund shall be made by cheque, signed by the Sarpanch and Secretary of the GP . . . Scrutiny of the records revealed that in 72 selected GPs, money was drawn in cash from the village/scheme funds and payments in excess of Rs 500 in 1511 cases involving an amount of Rs 88.47 lakh were made in cash to the parties concerned during the period 2003–4 to 2007–8."
[3] Interview at the Block Development Office, Sangrampur on April 25, 2014.

accounting data on the Central and State schemes implemented within the village panchayat's jurisdiction constituted a large information vacuum for the financial management of the panchayat. Since the Warwat Khanderao village panchayat is not responsible for maintaining annual accounts for schemes in which it is not directly involved, it was not able to include information in its Annual Budget Report on grants from the State and Central Governments. Since the progress of financial devolution to panchayats is slow, the village panchayat-level accounts cannot cover all grants from the State and Central Governments.

Even though the accounting data is focused mainly on funds from its own source of revenues, it does not provide details of revenues collected through the *patwari* system to be allocated to the village panchayat. Revenues under *patwari* system are collected outside the panchayat raj system. Data on expenditure in the Annual Budget Report was reported as shown in Table 7.1.

However, the revenue and expenditure data were not classified by functions in respect of 29 subjects mentioned in Schedule XI of the Constitution. Although the Government of Maharashtra adopted in 2003 the new accounting system for panchayati raj institutions as prescribed by the Comptroller and Auditor General, the new system was being introduced only at the district panchayat level.[4] Yet the district panchayats and Block-level committees did not compile the accounts in this format.[5] The Comptroller and Auditor General's scrutiny of their records showed that none of the selected Block-level committees and village panchayats had prepared and submitted their accounts in the formats prescribed in 2003–8. The Block Development Officer who exercises jurisdiction over Warwat Khanderao certainly knew of the new format, but, he said, it was introduced only at the district panchayat level.[6] In fact it was introduced neither at the Block Development Office at Sangrampur, nor at the Warwat Khanderao village panchayat. The village council in Warwat Khanderao could cross-check the accounting data maintained at the village panchayat with data from the Block Development Office or data audited by the Local Fund Audit Department and the Comptroller and Auditor General.

[4] "It was also envisaged that the formats for preparation of budget and keeping accounts by PRIs shall be prescribed by C&AG. Accordingly, C&AG had prescribed the Budget and Accounts formats for PRIs in 2002. These formats were approved by Government of Maharashtra (GOM) and circulated to all ZPs (November 2003) for implementation with effect from 2001-02" Comptroller and Auditor General of India (2008, pp. 9–10).

[5] *Ibid.*, p. 22, 42.

[6] Interview at the Block Development Office that exercises jurisdiction over Warwat Khanderao on August 18–22, 2011.

Table 7.1 *Annual budget report on village pachayats in Maharashtra, village panchayat office, Warwat Khanderao 2007–8*

Serial no.	Particulars	Total income in current year		Particulars	Total expenditure in current year
1	**Village fund**		**1**	**Village fund**	
	1. Property tax	80197		1. Panchayat head remuneration	3600
	2. Street-light tax			2. Panchayat member meeting allowance	690
	3. Sanitation and water tax			3. Travelling allowance	156
	4. Shops and small enterprises			4. Employee salary and Provident Fund	18920
	5. Fair			5. Employee uniform	390
	6. Entertainment tax			6. Official expenditure (stationery and Xerox)	8095
	7. Cycle and other vehicle tax			7. Maintenance	2429
	8. Toll tax			8. Sanitation	
	9. *Jakhat* tax			9. Electricity bill	25200
	10. Octroi			10. Water supply (pending)	
	11. Forest development tax			10a. Bleaching powder	2400
	12. Service tax			10b. Pump repairing	2032
	13. Other deposit tax			10c. Maintenance of tap	
2	**Non-tax income**			10d. Maintenance of dam	
	1. Market fee (Auction)	1500		10e. Maintenance of well	
	2. Rickshaw stand fee			10f. Other (furniture)	3800
	3. Car stand fee			10g. Maintenance of street light	1966
	4. Allocation received from 12 Finance Commission (5 per cent) and SGRY	3832		11. Equipments and others	
	5. General			12. Education and health	
	6. Private			13. Subsidy for toilet construction	1200
	7. Sanitation fee			14. Roads and gutter cleaning	6250
	8. Cattle grazing fee			15. Other construction	
	9. D.V.F. interest (2.5 per cent)			16. Library	
	10. Land lease fee			17. To maintain roads	7450
	11. Interest deposit (Bank)	3959.89		18. Social Welfare for Dalit and Tribal hamlets (10 per cent)	4050
	12. Land rent			19. DVD F contribution	801
	13. Cattle shed			20. Women and child welfare	
	14. Donations			21. Social and cultural work	
	15. Other fees (Grant-in-aid)	800		22. Cattle shed	
3	**Transferred fund**			22a. Fine	
	1. Stamp duty	3700		22b. Fodder	
	2. Sub-tax	1770		22c. Donation	
	3. Land revenue			Miscellaneous	7797
	4. Levelling of land			Total	

Table 7.1 (*continued*)

Serial no.	Particulars	Total income in current year		Particulars	Total expenditure in current year
5.	Minor minerals		2	**Government subsidy expenditure**	
6.	Aid for street light			Toilets in Dalit *basti*	
7.	Tap water supply (50 per cent subsidy)			Water supply	
8.	Assistance for backward and tribal areas			Construction	
9.	Subsidy other than fair and festival tax			Schools	
10.	Compensation for toll			Health	
11.	Other subsidy			Agriculture	
	Total transfer fund			Other (Public welfare works)	4510
4	**Government subsidy deposits**		**3**	**Government subsidy expenditure (Schemes)**	
1.	Toilet			SJSY	
2.	Development of Dalit *basti*			JGSY	
3.	Water supply/TCL subsidy	60		SGRY	25150
4.	Construction			Twelfth Finance Commission	30115
5.	School			Small expenditure	
6.	Remuneration/salary, meeting allowance	9900		Deposits	
	Total government subsidies			Instalment, Interest and bank commission	353
5	**Funds from MP, MLA and backward area development**			Advances	
1.	DRDA			Total	157354
2.	Central government subsidies			General, water supply, Twelfth Finance Commission*	136220.16
2a.	SGSY			Total	293574.16
2b.	JGSY				
2c.	SGRY	25117			
2d.	Twelfth Finance Commission	35281.43			
2e.	Hamlet development scheme				
	Total				
6	**Opening balance**	127456.84			
	Total (1+2+3+4+5)	166117.32			
	Grand total	293574.16			

Notes: (i) The original accounts were in Marathi. The table is the researchers' translation of the accounts.
(ii) * "General, water supply, Twelfth Finance Commission" is unspecified, which may include closing balance.

Since the progress of financial devolution to village panchayats is either slow or stalled in Maharashtra, the panchayat has to consult the accounting data at the Block or district level to find information about grants from the State and Central Governments.

7.1.2 Panchayat Accounts Data in West Bengal

The Raina village panchayat maintains accounts data as a part of the panchayat registers. The West Bengal Panchayat (Gram Panchayat Accounts, Audit and Budget) Rules, 2007, specify the format for accounting. We saw some of the filled-up forms. Unlike Maharashtra, even sub-panchayat bodies and subcommittees of the village panchayat prepare outline budgets. The Executive Assistant under the elected village head's direction draws up an outline budget. The Executive Assistant of the village panchayat, with the assistance of the secretary and other employees, prepares monthly, half-yearly and annual statements of receipts and payments. The village panchayat is expected to submit its annual account to the village council for approval. The elected village head cannot sanction any funds for a scheme, programme or project without considering the views of the members of subcommittees to whom powers have been delegated by the village panchayat. Accounting data of village panchayats are brought under the internal audit of the Panchayat Audit and Accounts Officer posted at the Block office.[7]

The booklet named *Protibedon*, prepared by the Raina village panchayat contained the accounting data maintained by the Raina village panchayat. Thus, as far as the Raina village panchayat is concerned, the accounting data was transparent and open for discussion among villagers. This information was disclosed precisely for the purpose of accountability to the villagers. It was not intended to be sent upward to the district or the State level. It was also not submitted to higher officials like the Block Development Officer.

According to *Protibedon*, the total revenue and expenditure for 2007–8 was Rs 16,666,309.53 and 16,725,805.20, respectively. Of the total revenues, the

[7] The Third State Finance Commission of West Bengal (2008, pp. 110–1) attaches importance to the Panchayat Audit and Accounts Officer. It notes, "The main problem has, however, remained at the GP level where substantial amounts are being spent for implementation of various assigned schemes. The services of the Panchayat Audit and Accounts Officer posted at the Block office are often used for various other purposes by the Block Development Officer (BDO). Authority responsible for internal auditing the panchayat offices should be independent of any tier of panchayat bodies. Offices of the Panchayat Audit and Accounts Officer should desirably be made independent of *panchayat samitis*."

largest component was amount received and spent on the Mahatma Gandhi National Rural Employment Guarantee Scheme (Rs 12,948,347 or 77.7 per cent). Of the remaining amount (Rs 3,717,962.53), own-source revenue was Rs 253,218 (1.5 per cent), untied funds from the Central and the State Finance Commissions were Rs 563,172 (3.4 per cent), MP/MLA Local Area Development Fund was Rs 215,000 (1.3 per cent). The remaining amounts were receipts from various Government schemes and grants. Hence the major source of revenue and expenditure for the Raina village panchayat was from Government schemes, the most important being MGNREGS.

Both the State Finance Commission and the Examiner of Local Accounts are concerned with the weakness of financial management of panchayati raj institutions in West Bengal. As noted in chapter 3, in the process of auditing 18 district panchayats, 151 Block-level committees and 3,214 village panchayats during 2008–9, the Examiner of Local Accounts found that the internal audit of Bankura and Bardhaman district panchayats, 67 Block-level committees and 1,252 village panchayats was not conducted for a period ranging from one to five years.[8] According to the Examiner of Local Accounts, this is indicative of inefficient internal controls in the panchayati raj institutions in West Bengal. The West Bengal Panchayat (Gram Panchayat Miscellaneous Accounts and Audit) Rules, 1990, prescribe that the internal audit of village panchayats shall be conducted by the Panchayat Accounts and Audit Officers at least once a month.

All village panchayats in West Bengal are to maintain accounts specified by the West Bengal Panchayat (Gram Panchayat Accounts, Audit, and Budget) Rules, 2007. In its 2008–9 audit, the Examiner of Local Accounts found that 29 Block-level committees (out of 151) and 28 village panchayats (out of 3214) did not prepare the account in the prescribed format. The Examiner of Local Accounts found that 735 panchayati raj institutions did not maintain the Demand and collection register (Form 7), 1039 of them did not maintain the Appropriation register (Form 15) and 1589 did not maintain the Advance register (Form 14).[9]

In the Raina village panchayat, however, we ascertained that these forms were maintained by the Executive Assistant. The village panchayat submitted annual accounts to the village council for approval. The Raina village

[8] Examiner of Local Accounts, West Bengal (2009, pp. 17, 19, 20).
[9] *Ibid.*, pp. 19, 85–6.

panchayat also distributed to the public the brochure *Protibedon*, which contained detailed accounting data.

The Examiner of Local Accounts found in its audit that the Jalpaiguri district panchayat, 17 Block-level committees and 85 village panchayats did not reconcile differences between the cash book and pass book balances of banks and treasuries as of March 31, 2008. The Third State Finance Commission of West Bengal suggested that "the accounts [kept] by all the three tiers are not in order" as different sources mention different figures.[10] We verified the existence of a cash book at the Raina village panchayat. It was maintained by the full-time Executive Assistant. In West Bengal, the double entry system of accounts was introduced with computerisation, which has been initiated and completed in the district panchayats. However, the same was in progress in Block-level committees and village panchayats. We met the Panchayat Accounts and Audit Officer of Raina Block in charge of the Raina village panchayat.[11] He was able to show us a filled-up annual statement of receipts and payments (Form 27) of the Raina village panchayat dated October 23, 2009.

In West Bengal, the village panchayat is the main implementing agency for all the major Central and State Governments' schemes and programmes. Under these schemes, the village panchayats receive funds directly from Government agencies for their implementation. Scheme-related funds constituted the bulk of panchayat receipts in Raina. As a result, "receipts of grant-in-aid from Central/State Government" and "payments out of grant-in-aid from Central/State Government" were recorded in the accounting data (see Table 7.2).

The Raina village panchayat also provided information on untied funds from the Central and State Finance Commissions. In fact, "Receipts of grant-in-aid from Central/State Government for programme implementation as untied fund under the recommendation of (i) Central Finance Commission, (ii) State Finance Commission, and (iii) others" was recorded in the accounting data (see Table 7.2).

---

[10] Third State Finance Commission of West Bengal (2008, p. 33). The Commission stated "The analysis indicates the evidence adduced by the Auditors and Examiner of Local Accounts before the Commission."

[11] Interviews at the Raina panchayat office and Raina I Block Development Office in February 2011.

Table 7.2

Form – 27
[see rules 27(2) and 27(3)]
Part – I
Half-yearly/Annual Statement of Receipts and Payments of .... Gram Panchayat for the
period from...........to ....

Receipts				Payments		
Particulars	Opening balance (Rs)	Receipts during the period (Rs)	Total amount (Rs)	Particulars the period (Rs)	Payments during	Closing balance
A. Receipts of grant-in-aid from Central/ State Government: 1. For programme implementation: (a) As sponsored programmes- (i) WBREGS (ii) IGNOAPS (iii) IAY (iv) .... (b) As assigned functions- (i) .... (ii) .... (c) As untied fund under the recom-mendation of- (i) Central Finance Commission (ii) State Finance Commission (iii) others .... 2. For establishment: (a) Honorarium for elected village head, deputy *pradhan* and director (b) Fixed Travelling allowances of members of				A. Payments out of grant-in-aid from Central/State Government: 1. For development works: (a) As sponsored programmes- (i) WBREGS (ii) NOAPS (iii) IAY (iv) .... (b) As assigned functions- (i) .... (ii) .... (c) As untied fund under the reco-mmendation of- (i) Central Finance Commission (ii) State Finance Commission (iii) others .... 2. For establishment: (a) Honorarium for elected village head, deputy *pradhan* and director (b) Fixed Travelling allowances of members of vill-		

Table 7.2 (*continued*)

Receipts				Payments		
Particulars	Opening balance (Rs)	Receipts during the period (Rs)	Total amount (Rs)	Particulars the period (Rs)(Rs)	Payments during	Closing balance
village panchayat including elected village head (c) Salary of employees (d) Allowance for tax collector				age panchayat including elected village head (c) Salary of employees (d) Allowance for tax collector		
B. Contribution from ZP/PS/ other agency: (i) MP LAD (ii) BEUP (iii) SHG training and so on				B. Payment out of contribution from ZP/PS/ other: Agency... (i) MP LAD (ii) BEUP (iii) SHG training and so on		
C. Own source revenue: (i) Tax (ii) Non-tax (iii) Others				C. Payment out of own source revenue (Specify): (i) (ii) (iii)		
D. (a) Loans/ advances/deposits: (b) Interest on savings bank accounts: From- (i) WBREGS (ii) IAY (iii) SGRY (iv) NOAPS (v) MP LAD (vi) Own Source Revenue and so on				D. (a) Repayment of loans/advances/ deposits, etc.: (b) Bank charges, commissions, etc. for- (i) WBREGS (ii) IAY (iii) SGRY (iv) IGNOAPS (v) MP LAD (vi) Own Source Revenue and so on		
E. Miscellaneous receipts: Total:				E. Miscellaneous payments: Total:		

Source: West Bengal Panchayat (Gram Panchayat Accounts, Audit and Budget) Rules, 2007.

There is as yet no standardised format in West Bengal that gives a detailed breakdown of expenditures in the panchayat accounting system. The format of annual statement of receipts and payments of the village panchayat (Form 27) specified in the West Bengal Panchayat (Gram Panchayat Accounts, Audit, and Budget) Rules, 2007, does not give detailed information on expenditures. For example, as shown in Table 7.2, an untied fund under the recommendation of the Central or State Finance Commission is present on both the receipts and payments sides of the annual statement. The latter does not clarify payment details of the untied fund, let alone provide a detailed breakdown classified by functions, programmes and activities capturing the expenditure under all 29 subjects mentioned in Schedule XI of the Constitution. As a result, sector-wise allotment and expenditure therefrom cannot be identified in panchayat accounts. Therefore, the Third State Finance Commission of West Bengal stated,

> analysis of expenditure by the panchayats at three tier level is more difficult as the state of affairs with respect to data availability and reliability is more precarious in this field. Panchayat and Rural Development Department (P&RD) Annual Reports give the year-wise expenditure of the Central Government flagship schemes only. Funds for State Government schemes including those for salary and pensionary benefits are released and credited to the local fund accounts and bank accounts of the panchayat bodies, expenditure from which are hardly monitored.[12]

The Simplified Accounting System prescribed by the Comptroller and Auditor General had not been introduced in West Bengal at the time of our study, even though the System provides the object heads which represent each object item of expenditure in relation to Schedule XI. The system of accounting in West Bengal has no similarity to the codes list for functions, programmes and activities as prescribed by the Comptroller and Auditor General.[13] The Panchayat Accounts and Audit Officer at the Raina I Block certainly knew of the new format but said that it had not been introduced in West Bengal.[14]

---

[12] Third State Finance Commission of West Bengal (2008, pp. 32–3).

[13] "The Secretary, MOPR requested (October 2009) the Chief Secretaries of all States and Union Territories to operationalise the format with effect from April 2010. The State Government had intimated (May 2010) that they had already adopted cash based Double Entry System of Accounting in all tier of PRIs . . . The P&RDD [Panchayats and Rural Development Department] developed and introduced (April and June 2003) two software packages, namely Integrated Fund Monitoring and Accounting System (IFMAS) and Gram Panchayat Management System (GPMS) for maintenance of accounts and database for ZP/PS and GP respectively" Examiner of Local Accounts West Bengal (2009, p. 6).

[14] Interview at the Raina I Block Development Office in February 2011.

Thus, without details of expenditures in the accounting data, the panchayat's financial needs cannot be accurately assessed. In particular, its expenditures cannot be assessed in relation to its functional domain, the database for which we discussed in chapter 5 (section 5.2.2).

However, *Protibedon* gave a detailed breakdown of the Raina village panchayat's expenditure, particularly of the Central Finance Commission and untied funds.[15] For example, in 2007–8, the panchayat obtained Rs 219,498 from the Central Finance Commission. It spent Rs 78,209 on the expansion and construction of the panchayat's office, Rs 32,578 to purchase a computer, Rs 16,600 for construction of culverts at two locations, Rs 18,640 for road repair, Rs 36,562 for distributing chickens to self-help groups, and the remaining for the maintenance of wells. Similar detailed information was presented for expenditure from the untied funds. This information was disclosed only for displaying accountability to the villagers. It is detailed but specific to the village panchayat. The information is not relayed upward to the district or the State authorities. Nevertheless, the fact that a detailed breakdown of the Raina village panchayat's expenditure was independently disclosed to the public, suggests that it could produce such data if required. The information cannot move upward to the district panchayat or the State without a uniform format across village panchayats.

Since accounting data in the Raina village panchayat is internally audited by the Panchayat Accounts and Audit Officer and statutorily audited by the Examiner of Local Accounts every year, the village council should be able to cross-check the accounting data with data checked by these auditors. Since *Protibedon* has not been published since 2008, one cannot discuss at present the expenditures of the village panchayat in relation to its functional domain.

7.2 DATA FOR ASSESSING OWN-SOURCE REVENUE

Own-source revenue is important for the fiscal autonomy of the panchayati raj institutions since they have control over its use. Further, data on own-source revenue is required for inter-governmental financial adjustment that aims at financing any resource gap between administrative needs and financial capability (including tax collection capability).

---

[15] Raina village panchayat (2008).

7.2.1 Own-Source Revenue in Maharashtra

Maharashtra lies in the temporarily settled or *raiyatwari* areas. The *patwari's* work is to keep land records and collect land revenue on their basis. However, accounting data at the Warwat Khanderao village panchayat did not properly reflect the revenues allocated under the *patwari* system. We could not identify in its accounting data the amount of funds coming from the *patwari* system. According to the Block Development Officer, Sangrampur Block, the amount of land revenue collected by the *patwari* is negligible. The land registration fee on land purchases and transfers is much higher than land revenue.

At present, the major own-tax revenue source for panchayats in many States is property tax. The Warwat Khanderao village panchayat also collected property tax under the name of house tax. As described in chapter 4 (section 4.3.1), all taxable buildings under the panchayat's jurisdiction are recorded in *Item no. 7 General Receipt Book* and *Item no. 8 House tax*. Thus, the Warwat Khanderao village panchayat has a list of houses in its jurisdiction. It updates this register every four years. We authenticated the one updated in 2005–6. Unpaid taxes are recorded in *Item no. 9 Tax demand-collection and Balance register*. According to the panchayat secretary, about 71 per cent of house tax was collected every year.

There are 255 houses in the village that are required to pay house tax. In 2010–1, a total of 173 houses paid this tax. The total tax assessment for the entire village was Rs 43,337. In 2010–1, the actual collection of house tax was Rs 30,828. In order to assess and evaluate the base of house tax, aggregate

Table 7.3 *Own-Source revenue, Warwat Khanderao village panchayat*

Own-Source Revenue				
2007–8	Rupees	2011–2	Rupees	Per cent
		Property tax	59,891	23.1
Property tax,		Street light	7,340	2.8
Street-light tax,	80,197	Sanitation	5,835	2.2
Sanitation and water tax		Water tax	78,313	30.2
		General water tax	21,626	8.3
		Private water tax	86,400	33.3
		Total	259,405	100.0
Non-tax income				
Market fee (Auction)	1,500			
Interest deposit (Bank)	3959.89	Interest deposit (Bank)	1380	

Note: Since 2009, new water taxes have been imposed in Warwat Khanderao village.
Source: Annual Budget Report on Gram Panchayats in Maharashtra 2007–8 and 2011–2.

data collected by census type-household surveys (such as the Census of India, especially the house-listing and housing data, and the Below Poverty Line Census) may be usable, though the house tax register is a list of "houses" (or house owners) alone, and not a list of "households."

The Warwat Khanderao village panchayat also keeps registers for other revenue sources. According to the panchayat head, water tax is a major source of income for the village panchayat. Tax receipts from water supply (from underground pipes) are recorded in *Item no. 10 Tax Collection Receipt Book*. Under the Maharasthra Rural Water Supply Scheme, two 18,000-litre water tanks were constructed in the village. The village panchayat also owned a tubewell and 110 households were connected to it. A 5,000-litre tank was also filled with this tubewell. Eight general taps have been constructed. Water tax of Rs 75 per household was imposed for drawing tubewell water, Rs 250 on all households for tank water, and Rs 720 on those households that have taps in their houses. Although the amount of water tax was combined with that of property tax (house tax) etc. in 2007–8, the share from the water tax was more than 70 per cent of the total amount in 2011–2.

7.2.2 Own-Source Revenue in West Bengal

West Bengal lies in the erstwhile permanently settled or *zamindari* areas. The land records that give the total extent of land held by individual holders were used for levying land revenue in the Raina village panchayat. The revenue inspector's office is responsible for obtaining the records of total land ownership among individual holders, and assessing and collecting land revenue at prevailing rates. According to the Block Land and Land Reforms Officer of the Raina I Block, there was no land revenue expected from holdings smaller than four acres.

As described in chapter 4 (section 4.3.1), the Raina village panchayat collects property tax (tax on land and buildings) using *Form 6 Register for market value of land and building located within the village panchayat* specified in West Bengal Panchayat (Gram Panchayat Administration) Rules, 2004, and its Amendments, 2006. According to the Panchayats and Rural Development Department of West Bengal, property tax contributes around 40 per cent of the village panchayats' total own source revenue. As far as Raina village panchayat was concerned, property tax contributed 56.7 per cent of total own-source revenue. Based on *Form 6* and other forms, an assessment list of persons liable to pay tax on land and buildings within the panchayat area is

Table 7.4 *Own-Source revenue, Raina village panchayat*

Own-source revenue	Rupees	Per cent
Property tax	144,125	56.7
Professional tax	32,970	13.0
Toll tax	35,735	14.0
Vehicle registration fees	410	0.2
House construction fees	11,180	4.4
Sale of trees	2564	1.0
Contingency	447	0.2
Miscellaneous	1771	0.7
Leasing of pond	12,500	4.9
Cattle shed	600	0.2
Receipt from principal etc.	1360	0.5
Scrap fund	350	0.1
Sale of old newspapers etc.	60	0.0
Transport charges	9088	3.6
Birth and death registration fees	58	0.0
Sale of old sacks	1133	0.4
Total	254,351	100.0

Source: Protibedon (2008, pp. 3–5).

to be prepared using Part-I of *Form 9 Assessment List (List of persons liable to pay tax on land and building within the village panchayat)* to be approved by the meetings of the village panchayat and the village electoral wards. Therefore, the list of persons liable to pay tax on land and buildings was open for discussion in the village council. Unpaid taxes are to be recorded in *Form 7 Register for Arrears and Current Demand and Collection of Taxes* in the Gram Panchayat Rules, 2007. When we visited the Raina panchayat office in February 2011, we were shown a "Panchayat Property Tax Assessment Sheet." In Raina, all households in the village were taxed. Even a landless household had to pay a minimum annual tax of Rs 3. In Raina, the village panchayat collected property tax for agricultural land as well as on homestead land and houses.[16] There were 3581 property tax assessed in the Raina village panchayat. According to the Executive Assistant, the total tax assessed in the financial year 2009–10 was Rs 137,395 and actual collection was Rs 106,000

---

[16] Land is valued at Rs 25,000 per acre. A house is valued at Rs 10,000 for a *pucca* construction, Rs 2000 for a *kutcha* construction, and Rs 4000 for a semi-*kutcha* construction. Tax is assessed at 6 per cent of the total value of property. The tax rate is 1 per cent if the assessed value is up to Rs 1000 and 2 per cent if the assessed value is higher than Rs 1000 (interview with Executive Assistant at the Raina panchayat office on 14 September 2009).

on the current assessment. He estimated that approximately 80 per cent of the tax assessees paid each year.

In general, the collection rate for tax, fees, and rates in West Bengal is not considered high. The Examiner of Local Accounts found that "3,068 gram panchayats could collect only 23.93 crore in the shape of tax, fees, rates etc. against total demand of 95.01 crore during 2007–8. Thus, the collection was only 25 per cent of the total demand."[17] The Third State Finance Commission suggested that "it is . . . true that there are no firm figures of own revenue of the PRI bodies – different sources have mentioned different figures. The Commission also failed to get firm figures as the PRI bodies did not furnish the information asked for."[18] According to the Commission, figures on own-source revenue may be much less than what has been shown in the *Annual Administrative Report* of the Panchayats and Rural Development Department. It concludes, "The results of the study reflect that the per capita collection of own revenue is much less than what has been shown in the Annual Reports of the Department."[19]

As in the Warwat Khanderao village panchayat, in order to assess and evaluate the base of property tax, aggregate data collected by census-type household surveys such as the Census of India (especially the house-listing and housing data) may be usable.

Village panchayats in West Bengal, in principle, can impose a conservancy rate, drainage rate and a general sanitary rate, fees for grazing cattle on vested land, for the use of burning *ghats*, registration of shallow or deep tubewells, licensing of dogs, birds and domestic animals, toll for use of roads, bridges, ferries vested in them or under their management, and rates such as water rate, lighting rate and fees for arranging sanitary arrangements at places of worship, pilgrimage, fairs and *melas*, and fees for registration of trades and income from assets generated by them.[20] However, the Third State Finance Commission observed, "Although in terms of numbers, there are as many as 66 different types of taxes, fees and charges which can be imposed by them, most of the levies are only in the statute books and are just not levied as none of these revenue handles is significant from the view point of

[17] Examiner of Local Accounts West Bengal (2009, p. 19).
[18] Third State Finance Commission of West Bengal (2008, p. 28).
[19] *Ibid.*, p. 30.
[20] *Ibid.*, p. 27. Also see West Bengal Panchayat (Gram Panchayat Administration) Rules 2004, Part II, Chapter X (Imposition of Taxes, Fees and Rates by Panchayats).

generating revenues except the Property Tax."[21] Own-source revenue for the Raina village panchayat is shown in Table 7.4.

The Third State Finance Commission of West Bengal pointed out that "some of the panchayat bodies, particularly the ZPs (district panchayats), have under their management and ownership various types of assets – land, buildings, water bodies, *hats* and *bazaars*, ferries, etc., but most of the ZPs do not maintain proper Asset Registers."[22]

7.3 DATA FOR INTER-GOVERNMENTAL FUND ALLOCATION

As mentioned in chapter 2 (section 2.4.4), the asymmetry between taxation power and the responsibility to meet their functional requirements necessitates transfer of funds from higher tiers of government to the local governments either through untied grants or through a share in other State taxes or as part of various development schemes. This requires the Centre–State and the State–local inter-governmental funds transfer, and further inter-panchayati raj funds allocation. In section 2.4.4, chapter 2, we defined such fiscal transfers as inter-governmental financial adjustment. Generally, fiscal transfers among local bodies require principles for fund allocation. India has created a necessary condition towards rationalising State–local inter-governmental financial adjustment by creating the State Finance Commissions through the Seventy-Third and Seventy-Fourth Amendments.[23]

7.3.1 Inter-Governmental Fund Transfer in Maharashtra

Details of recommendations and reports of the State Finance Commission (SFC) of Maharashtra are not available in the public domain and we were not able to access the SFC reports. A report on budget transparency in India prepared by the Centre for Budget and Governance Accountability in 2011 identified the following (among others) as major gaps and shortcomings in budget transparency in Maharashtra:

1. The report of the latest finance commission has not yet been published.

---

[21] *Ibid.*, p. 34.

[22] Third State Finance Commission of West Bengal (2008, p. 36). It further states, "The Commission feels that there is considerable scope of augmentation of resources through proper management of the assets owned by them and/or transferred to the PRI bodies."

[23] The Twelfth Central Finance Commission (2004, pp. 149–51, 159–60) argues that State Finance Commissions have not worked properly in most of the States. Oommen (2008, p. 9) argues that "the State Finance Commissions have not performed their onerous tasks satisfactorily."

2. The executive does not hold consultations with the legislature on the memoranda/demands to be submitted by the State to Finance Commission and Planning Commission.

3. It does not make public the memoranda submitted to the Finance Commission and Planning Commission.

4. The State Government either does not present the Action Taken Report on the recommendations of the SFC to the legislature, or when it does, it is delayed by more than a year after the submission of the SFC report.[24]

According to the Comptroller and Auditor General's report of local bodies in Maharashtra for 2010–1, the second State Finance Commission had recommended the allocation of 40 per cent of the State revenues to local bodies. However, the State Government did not accept the recommendation. In 2010–1, 15.9 per cent of the State revenues were allocated to local bodies. We could not verify if the State follows a uniform principle in allocating funds to local bodies and determining the amount of allocation across local bodies.

7.3.2 Inter-Governmental Fund Transfer in West Bengal

The State Finance Commissions of West Bengal have provided a principle and methodology for allocating "untied funds."[25] The four units of self-governance, namely, the urban local bodies, district panchayats, Block-level committees, and village panchayats have been assessed on a State-wide basis with some common and specific indicators, the choice of which has been greatly influenced by the availability, reliability, and transparency of the database. Each of these indicators has been assigned a definite weight, indicative of its role and importance in the combined index.

The principle and methodology of fund allocation provided by the Third State Finance Commission are as follows. At the outset, the State has been divided into a Municipal and a panchayati raj population and all allocable funds available at the State level have been apportioned accordingly: 76 per cent for panchayati raj institutions and 24 per cent for urban local bodies. The Commission recommends a larger share of the panchayati raj fund for village panchayats since "there is a growing shift in the focus of development activities towards the GP [Gram Panchayat] level under the evolving decentralised planning environment." Sub-allocations of the panchayati raj fund are as follows:

---

[24] Centre for Budget and Governance Accountability (2011).
[25] Third State Finance Commission of West Bengal (2008, p. 133ff.).

District panchayats (*zilla parishads*)	12 per cent
Block-level committees (*panchayat samitis*)	18 per cent
Village panchayats (*gram panchayats*)	70 per cent

Further, the proportionate share for each panchayat among all the village panchayats is calculated using a combined index that comprises indicators and their relevant weights. The combined index for a village panchayat (GP_i) will work out as:

$$GP_i = 0.598 \, GP_{1i} + 0.1 \, GP_{2i} + 0.1 \, GP_{3i} + 0.1 \, GP_{4i} + 0.051 \, GP_{5i} + 0.051 \, GP_{6i}$$
where i=1, 2, ... to n (number of village panchayats).

These indicators and the relevant weights accorded to each are provided under:

1 (a). Undifferentiated population	0.500
1(b). Backward population segments	0.098
1. Weighted population (GP_{1i})	0.598
2. Female non-literates (GP_{2i})	0.100
3. Food insecurity (GP_{3i})	0.100
4. Marginal workers (GP_{4i})	0.100
5. Total population without drinking water or paved approach or power supply (GP_{5i})	0.051
6. Sparseness of population [inverse of population density] (GP_{6i})	0.051

The Third State Finance Commission stated the following:

As a complete set of more recent data was unavailable we have had to rely on the detailed data set that was made available by the 2001 Census right down to the Gram Panchayat level. For Food Insecurity parameters we have used the data provided by the Rural Household Survey.[26]

The premise of the combined index is that the administrative need for resources for development is strongly and positively correlated with the population size (1[a]) and backwardness (1[b], 2 through 6) of the region. However, the combined index does not include a parameter for financial capability. The combined index only for urban local bodies includes the parameter of "ratio of own revenue to total revenue," but there is no such parameter in the index for the panchayati raj institutions. As the inter-governmental financial adjustment, in principle, aims at financing a shortfall between administrative needs and financial capability, information included in the combined index for village panchayats is insufficient in this respect.

[26] *Ibid.*, p. 133.

Not only data from the Population Census and Rural Household Survey (2005), but also some of the village-level data such as the Village Schedule Data on Basic Statistics may be used to construct indexes for fund allocation among village panchayats. These may compensate for data constraints at the panchayat level.

7.4 SEPARATE BUDGET WINDOW FOR THE STATE GOVERNMENT–PANCHAYAT FISCAL RELATIONSHIP

It has become absolutely essential for the State Government to arrange for a separate budget head in which devolution of funds, pertaining to all matters devolved to panchayats, are separately indicated. If the State government produces a list of State departments whose funds are channelised through the local government sector window and decides upon the formula for distribution of local government components, the panchayati raj institutions can prepare the plan for their areas based on specific ideas about the financial resources available to meet their responsibilities.[27] In this regard, Kerala is the only State whose budget is disaggregated to the level of each local government.[28] Appendix IV of the State budget gives details of funds allocated to each local self-government institution, under different heads of accounts. Each village panchayat can easily find out about its budget directly from the State budget.

Parallel to this separate budget window, the Thirteenth Central Finance Commission recommends that all States adopt an accounting framework and codification pattern consistent with the Model Panchayat Accounting System prescribed by the Comptroller and Auditor General.

7.4.1 State Government–Panchayat Fiscal Relationship in Maharashtra

The village development officer of Warwat Khanderao said that the village panchayat estimates a fund flow for the current year to be approximately 10 per cent higher than the previous year's fund flow. It does not know in advance the precise amount of funds to the panchayat.

7.4.2 State Government–Panchayat Fiscal Relationship in West Bengal

According to the Executive Assistant of the Raina village panchayat and the

---

[27] Planning Commission (2008b, p. 37).
[28] *Ibid.*, p. 36.

Panchayat Accounts and Audit Officer at the Raina I Block Development Office, the village panchayat does not know the exact fund flow for the next year. Therefore, the panchayat estimates a fund flow that is 10 per cent higher than the previous year's. The budget outline is then sent for approval to the Block-level committee. Based on the fund flow till December each year, the village panchayat prepares a revised or supplementary budget which is sent for approval in February.[29] As described before, the village panchayats in West Bengal are still overwhelmingly dependent on grants from the Central and State Governments. This fact suggests that, unlike panchayats in Kerala, the ones in West Bengal cannot estimate their budget in relation to fund allocation from budgets of the Central and State Governments.

Arrangement for separate budget windows in the State budget is said to be underway in West Bengal.[30] The Third State Finance Commission of West Bengal recommended that West Bengal Government should review Kerala's experience.[31] Arrangement for separate budget windows in the State departments presupposes that the State Government has taken the obligatory steps for devolving functions to the panchayati raj institutions with appropriate Activity Mapping. However, the Third State Finance Commission was critical of the current status of functional devolution in West Bengal, because devolution through Activity Mapping has been done only by executive order. Such orders are not published in the official gazette as required under the West Bengal Panchayats (Amendment) Act, 1994. Separate budget windows are not put in place, unless formal notifications for such devolution of functions are published in the official gazette as required by law.

---

[29] Interviews at the Raina panchayat office and Raina I Block Development Office in February 2011. Their working formula is as follows. The total fund for panchayat consists of
Administrative Fund: 25 per cent
Women and Child Development Fund: 10 per cent
Backward Class Development Fund: 15 per cent
Atithi Bhata: 2 per cent
Handicapped: 2 per cent
Other Development Funds: Rest
[30] Panchayats and Rural Development Department, Government of West Bengal (2009a, p. 129).
[31] Third State Finance Commission of West Bengal (2008, pp. 131–2). It notes, "The efforts reportedly made by the States of Kerala and Karnataka may not be irrelevant in this connection. In Kerala, the Government has devolved the functions and announced local government-wise share of funds under three tier PRIs for five years starting from 2006–7. A separate document has been annexed as part of the State budget indicating local government-wise allotments. The funds are automatically credited to the local governments and the local governments are allowed to carry over 20 per cent of their funds to the next financial year."

7.5 DATA ON FUNDING FOR ALL SCHEMES AND PROGRAMMES WITHIN THE PANCHAYAT'S JURISDICTION

As mentioned in chapter 5 (section 5.3.1), it is potentially possible for the Warwat Khanderao village panchayat to compile a comprehensive list of ongoing Central and State schemes and programmes carried out in the panchayat area, since its officials, such as the panchayat head, are knowledgeable about sector-wise information on current Central and State schemes and programmes. However, at present it is difficult to obtain financial data on all schemes and programmes including those carried out by outside agencies within the village panchayat's jurisdiction.

The Raina village panchayat has *Form 16 Programme register* and *Form 17: Scheme register* to keep track of ongoing Central and State schemes and programmes. Both forms contain detailed information on expenditure. However, as mentioned in chapter 5 (section 5.3.1), the schemes and programmes recorded in *Form 16* and *Form 17* are only those sanctioned by the panchayat/subcommittee meetings. *Form 16* and *Form 17* do not contain information on schemes and programmes carried out within the panchayat's jurisdiction by departments dealing with matters not devolved to the panchayat, for example a wide variety of activities of the Agriculture Department, as illustrated in Table 3.7 (chapter 3). The Raina village panchayat does not necessarily know about the funding streams of outside agencies working within the jurisdictional area of the panchayat. Therefore, the "scheme census" is again required in this regard. It needs to cover information on funding streams for each scheme entrusted to outside agencies working within the jurisdiction of the panchayat. Various documents such as the State budget and Central Government documents provide detailed information for the "scheme census." This resource mapping exercise often becomes a reconstruction of the financial picture from available bits and pieces of data.[32] Therefore, the Planning Commission suggests that the mapping of budgets and conveying them to every panchayat should be the responsibility of the States and the District Planning Committees.[33]

---

[32] Planning Commission (2008b, p. 78). It observes, "Below the Block level, the resource mapping exercise often becomes a process of reconstruction of the financial picture from available bits and pieces of data."

[33] *Ibid.*, p. 77.

Chapter 8

A POTENTIAL DATABASE FOR LOCAL-LEVEL PLANNING, WITH SPECIAL REFERENCE TO THE VILLAGE SCHEDULE ON BASIC STATISTICS

A vision for any planning exercise must have a strong empirical basis in "rigorous compilation and analysis of baseline data, which needs to be as institutionalised and strong as the planning system itself."[1] The process of building a vision is referred to as an "envisioning" exercise in planning documents.[2] The planning exercise would be impossible in a situation where the panchayat cannot have its own vision or initiative. The planning exercise is a special function that is possible only in a functional domain that is characterised by a high degree of autonomy.

Several core statistical databases can be used for the panchayat-level planning exercise. The Census of India (including the population enumeration data, house-listing and housing data, and the village-level amenities data from Census village directories) is indisputably one of the core statistical databases for micro-level planning in rural India.[3] The Below Poverty Line Censuses (and the Socio-Economic and Caste Census 2011) can also be a core database, one that provides panchayats with unit-level data on households and persons. The Census of India and the Below Poverty Line Censuses aim at essential aspects of local development and poverty alleviation programmes. Nevertheless, they do not cover all aspects of the data requirements for micro-level planning. Even the wide-ranging dataset of the Census of India is not entirely in tune with the functional domain of the panchayats. Besides, these census results are not updated regularly and thus do not furnish panchayats with the most recent information with which to prepare annual or five-year plans.

As mentioned in chapter 2 (section 2.5.6), the latest effort to meet the data requirements for micro-level planning and its implementation in rural India

---

[1] Planning Commission (2008b, p. 13). This exercise is referred to as the "stock-taking report" (*ibid.*, pp. 57–8).

[2] Planning Commission (2008b, p. 65).

[3] The National Statistical Commission (2001, para. 9.2.16) states that "after the 73rd and 74th Constitutional Amendments passed by the Parliament in 1992, the Population Census data has immense potential to serve the planning and development data needs of the panchayati raj institutions at the grass roots level."

(Data Needs III) is reflected in the *Basic Statistics for Local Level Development* report. The terms of reference of the report were to identify the data "for use in micro-level planning of various developmental programmes."

The framework for the Village Schedule provided by the *Basic Statistics* report is based on a review of the efforts of various groups and committees in India. In addition, the Village Schedule and its Field Instructions have been repeatedly tested and modified through pilot studies, including the large-scale pilot scheme launched by the Ministry of Statistics and Programme Implementation in 2009. In the course of the pilot studies, feedback from different States was sought on data sources, the availability of data for different items of information, problems in compilation of data, etc. The Village Schedule has been upgraded on the basis of these reports.

The baseline data with which to create a planning vision can be freely defined by the panchayats, and is a matter open for discussion. A minimum requirement for the baseline data for use in planning exercises is thus difficult to define. This chapter discusses this issue with special reference to the baseline data in the Village Schedule on Basic Statistics.

8.1 BLOCK-BY-BLOCK ASSESSMENT OF THE VILLAGE SCHEDULE ON BASIC STATISTICS

The Village Schedule on Basic Statistics is a framework to summarise village-level secondary data along with the personal assessment of knowledgeable persons (or common knowledge among village people). A set of panchayat-level data sources is assumed to exist in parallel to most data items of the Village Schedule. We have discussed these sources in chapter 4. We can now examine the availability of data sources for each data item of the Village Schedule.

As we have already discussed Activity Mapping in both village panchayats in Maharashtra and West Bengal in sections 3.7 (chapter 3) and 5.1.1–5.1.2 (chapter 5), we can also evaluate the utility of the Village Schedule on Basic Statistics for the subject functions listed in Schedule XI of the Constitution. For an analytical study of the relationship between each data item and the subjects listed in Schedule XI, information on Activity Mapping in the concerned State is indispensable. A clear idea of the concrete activities or schemes related to each subject of Schedule XI is required to assess the usefulness of each data item. Without such a clear idea of specific operational and activity-related responsibilities, it is difficult to discuss the utility of each item of data. We can now examine a particular relationship between each data item in the Village Schedule and each function listed in Schedule XI, although the *Basic Statistics for Local Level Development* report has not explicitly indicated that relationship. Data items in the Village Schedule should be consistent with the minimum requirement for use in micro-level planning for the subject functions listed in Schedule XI.

We shall discuss on a Block-by-Block basis (i) the kinds of data sources available at the village level in relation to each data item of the Schedule, and (ii) the reason for the usefulness of such data in performing the functions listed in Schedule XI. Using information from feedback reports from some States and Union Territories[4] in the pilot scheme conducted by the Ministry of Statistics since 2009, we can also compare our findings in the two survey villages with the feedback reports.[5]

Most of the data items in Block 2 were not documented in village-level records and were common knowledge among village residents. Some data items, such as sources of drinking water and self-help groups, have documentary evidence but the rest do not. Officials of both village panchayats whom we interviewed said that this information is common knowledge. According to the *Cross-sectional Synthesis Report* on the large-scale pilot scheme on Basic Statistics in 2009, village panchayats were able to fill up most of the data items in Block 2.[6] The report stated that as the panchayat office is "a meeting place for the village people, if some data are collected without records, the probability of getting correct information is very high."

---

[4] The *Cross-sectional Synthesis (CSO) Report* covers eight States and Union Territories, viz., Andaman & Nicobar, Andhra Pradesh, Assam, Haryana, Mizoram, Rajasthan, Sikkim, and Tamil Nadu. Feedback reports covered in the *CSO Report 2014* are 23 States and Union Territories, viz. Andaman & Nicobar, Andhra Pradesh, Arunachal Pradesh, Assam, Chhattisgarh, Goa, Gujarat, Haryana, Himachal Pradesh, Jharkhand, Kerala, Maharashtra, Manipur, Meghalaya, Mizoram, Odisha, Puducherry, Punjab, Rajasthan, Sikkim, Tamil Nadu, Uttar Pradesh, and Uttarakhand. Thus, Bihar, Chandigarh, Dadra & Nagar Haveli, Daman & Diu, the NCT of Delhi, Jammu & Kashmir, Karnataka, Lakshadweep, Madhya Pradesh, Nagaland, Tripura, and West Bengal are not covered by either report. Apart from the above two reports, Jammu & Kashmir, Karnataka, Lakshadweep, and Nagaland have provided their State or Union Territory reports on the Ministry of Statistics and Planning Implementation's website.
[5] The pilot scheme of the Ministry of Statistics and Planning Implementation was conducted in Maharashtra and West Bengal: in its Phase I in both Maharashtra (Akola district) and West Bengal (Bardhaman district), and in Phase II in Maharashtra (Akola district). However, the *CSO Report 2014* does not cover any feedback from West Bengal.
[6] Central Statistics Office (2011).

Village schedule

Block 0: *Descriptive identification of the village*

Sl. no.	Item	Name	Code as per Census 2011			
0.1	State/UT					
0.2	District					
0.3	*Tehsil*/ Sub-Division					
0.4	Block					
0.5	Panchayat					
0.6	Village					
0.7	Reference Year			2	0		

Block 1: *Particulars of data recording*

Sl. no.	Item	Panchayat Secretary/ Other designated Primary Worker	Block Statistical Officer	District Statistical Officer
(1)	(2)	(3)	(4)	(5)
1.1	Name (block letters)			
1.2	Sex (M/F)			
1.3	Date(s) of (i) Recording/ Inspection (ii) Receipt (iii) Scrutiny (iv) Despatch	DD MM YY	DD MM YY	DD MM
1.4	Signature			

Most of the data items in Block 2 are relevant to subject 29 (maintenance of community assets) of Schedule XI. Besides, some data items are relevant to the planning exercises for the functional domain with regard to subject 14 (rural electrification: data item 2.1), subject 15 (non-conventional energy sources: data item 2.2), subject 11 (drinking water: data item 2.4), subject 3 (minor irrigation: data items 2.5 and 2.6), and subject 13 (roads, culverts, bridges, ferries, waterways and other means of communication: data items 2.12, 2.13, and 2.15) in Schedule XI. Data items 2.7, 2.10 and 2.11 are useful to coordinate credit linkage with regard to subject 1 (agriculture), subject 8 (small scale industries), and subject 9 (khadi, village and cottage industries),

Block 2: *Availability of some basic facilities*

Sl. no.	Item	Item code	Source code
(1)	(2)	(3)	(4)
2.1	Household electricity connection at least for one household in the village (Yes - 1, No - 2)		
2.2	Use of renewable source of energy by at least for one household in the village (Yes - 1, No - 2)		
2.3	At least one cable connection within the village (Yes - 1, No - 2)		
2.4	Major source of drinking water for the village (tap - 1, tubewell/hand pump - 2, well - 3, reserved tank for drinking water - 4, any other source - 9)		
2.5	Drainage system passes through the village (Yes - 1, No - 2)		
2.6	Benefit is being received from Government controlled irrigation system by at least one villager (Yes - 1, No - 2)		
2.7	Whether any type of cooperative society including cooperative credit society is functioning within the village (Yes - 1, No - 2)		
2.8	Whether any self-help group is functioning within the village (Yes - 1, No - 2)		
2.9	Whether any adult education course is in operation within the village (Yes - 1, No - 2)		
2.10	If there is any credit society other than cooperative credit society (Yes - 1, No - 2)		
2.11	Whether there is any commercial bank or agricultural bank (Yes - 1, No - 2)		
2.12	Whether there is *pucca* street (Yes - 1, No - 2)		
2.13	Frequency (per day) of State Transport/ Private buses to nearest city (No facility - 1, Less than 5 - 2, At least 5 - 3)		
2.14	Whether there is any crèche (Yes - 1, No - 2)		
2.15	Whether there are street lights (Yes - 1, No - 2)		

etc. Data item 2.7 can also be used to deal with the first item in the list of activities, i.e., "making arrangements for co-operative management of lands and other resources in village, and the organisation of collective co-operative farming," which is to be devolved to panchayats in the Village List of the Bombay Village Panchayats Act, 1958. Data item 2.8 is relevant in implementing the *Swarnjayanti Gram Swarozgar Yojana.* Other data items

Block 3: *Village Infrastructure*

Sl. no.	Facilities	Last year	Source code
(1)	(2)	(3)	(4)
3.1	No. of factories set up within the vicinity (5 km radius) of the village		
3.2	No. of new bridges constructed within the vicinity (5 km radius) of the village		
3.3	No. of business establishments with large turnover (more than one crore annually) set up within the vicinity (5 km radius) of the village		
3.4	Orchards with area 1.0 hectare and more planted within the vicinity (5 km radius) of the village (Yes - 1, No - 2)		
3.5	Forest area declared within the vicinity (5 km radius) of the village (Yes - 1, No - 2)		
3.6	Percentage of households having access to safe drinking water		
3.7	Percentage of houses according to structure (a) *Kuṭcha* (b) *Semi-pucca* (c) *Pucca*		
3.8	Percentage of houses with latrines Sanitary Others (a) Individual (b) Shared		

are relevant to planning for subject 19 (adult and non-formal education: data item 2.9) and subject 25 (women and child development: data item 2.14).

Issues pertaining to data items 3.1 to 3.5 in Block 3 were common knowledge or could be obtained from knowledgeable persons among village residents. Data on items 3.1 and 3.3 that were in the Industrial Development Office were not available with the village panchayat. The sub-State-level data of the Economic Census were also not available with the panchayati raj institutions. A validation check for data items 3.4 and 3.5 is possible only when land records and cadastral maps are available.

Data items 3.6 to 3.8 require the aggregation of a large amount of data on households or houses, and therefore, subjective assessment by knowledgeable persons is not adequate for obtaining such aggregates. All subjective assessments require validation checks. In Warwat Khanderao, data item 3.6

had documentary evidence in *Item no. 9 Tax demand-collection and balance register* and *Item no. 10 Tax collection receipt book* in the panchayat register. For example, the Warwat Khanderao village panchayat imposes a water tax of Rs 75 per household on 110 households with a tubewell connection. The Raina village panchayat had a format for the *List of enterprises/persons liable to pay registration fees for providing supply of water from deep-tubewell/ shallow-tubewell fitted with motor-driven pumpsets in GP* (Part-V of the Form 9 Assessment List) specified in the 2006 Amendments of the West Bengal Panchayat (Gram Panchayat Administration) Rules, 2004, but, as shown in Table 7.4 in chapter 7, the village panchayat did not receive any water tax.

Both village panchayats had documentary evidence for data item 3.7 in their property tax registers, i.e. in *Item no. 8 House tax* in Warwat Khanderao, and in *Form 6 Register for market value of land and building located within GP* specified in the West Bengal Panchayat (Gram Panchayat Administration) Rules, 2004, in Raina. The Below Poverty Line Census data was available with both village panchayats for data item 3.8, which contains data on households without a toilet. Besides, in Raina, unit-level household data of the census-type household survey conducted in 2008 to evaluate the rural sanitation scheme were available. This database contained data on access to toilets and some socio-economic features of households, such as whether or not they belonged to special social groups (Scheduled Caste, Scheduled Tribe, others).

According to the *Basic Statistics for Local Level Development* report (2014), out of the 23 feedback reports received from different States and Union Territories,

> almost all the States/UTs are of the view that information for items in this block is neither available nor reliable and adequate. A few States viz. Haryana, Jharkhand, Maharashtra, Tamil Nadu and Uttarakhand have highlighted that information on i) number of business establishment with large turnover (more than one crore annually) set up within vicinity (5 km radius) of the village, ii) percentage of houses according to structure i.e., *katcha*, Semi-*pucca* and *pucca*, iii) percentage of houses with latrine (Individual and Shared) is not readily available, and since this information is collected from knowledgeable persons ... may not be reliable.[7]

A feedback report from Maharashtra in the 2014 *Basic Statistics* report noted,

---

[7] Central Statistics Office (2014, p. 53).

The proper record books are available but not properly maintained. It is observed that village development officer is too busy with other works hence he doesn't find time for updation [*sic*] of these records . . . Since the *gram sevak* is a busy person, the DSO took the help of other village level workers like *anganwadi sevika* or ASHA worker to solve all of the above difficulties.[8]

Data item 3.5 is relevant to planning exercises for the functional domain with regard to subject 6 (social forestry and farm forestry) and subject 7 (minor forest produce) in Schedule XI. Data items 3.6, 3.7, and 3.8 are respectively relevant to subject 11 (drinking water), subject 10 (rural housing), and subject 23 (health and sanitation) in Schedule XI of the Constitution.

As mentioned in chapter 4 (section 4.2), most data items in Block 4 were not documented in the village-level records but can be derived from the common knowledge among villagers. Officials of both village panchayats told us in interviews that such information is common knowledge. Therefore, no significant problem in compiling the information for this Block was reported in the 2014 *Basic Statistics* report.[9]

Data items in Block 4 are relevant to planning exercises for the functional domain with regard to subject 13 (roads, culverts, bridges, ferries, waterways, and other means of communication: data items 4.3 to 4.5 and 4.34 to 4.35), subject 17 (education), subject 18 (technical training and vocational education: data items 4.6 to 4.19 and 4.36 to 4.39), subject 4 (animal husbandry, dairying, and poultry: data item 4.20), subject 23 (health and sanitation, including hospitals, primary health centres, and dispensaries: data items 4.21 to 4.28), subject 28 (public distribution system: data item 4.31), subject 22 (markets and fairs: data item 4.32), subject 26 (social welfare, including welfare of the handicapped, and mentally retarded: data items 4.36 to 4.39), subject 25 (women and child development: data item 4.45), subject 21 (cultural activities, etc.: data items 4.47 to 4.48), and subject 20 (libraries: data item 4.49). Data item 4.46 can be used to deal with the first subject in the list of activities, i.e., "making arrangements for co-operative management of lands and other resources in village, (and)organisation of collective co-operative farming," to be devolved to the village panchayats in the Village List of the Bombay Village Panchayats Act, 1958.

Data items 5.1 and 5.2 in Block 5 can be obtained from the Population

[8] *Ibid.*
[9] *Ibid.*, p. 54.

Census, albeit after a considerable time lag. As described in chapter 6 (section 6.6), both village panchayats can also obtain updated information for data items 5.1 to 5.4 from the Integrated Child Development Services workers (*anganwadi*). According to the 2014 *Basic Statistics* report, "In the pilot study, a large number of States/UTs have observed that information for items 5.1 to 5.5 is not readily available. These States have reported that wherever this

Block 4: *Distance from the nearest facility*

Sl. no.	Item	Distance in km (in two digits)	If distance is '00' then number	Source code
(1)	(2)	(3)	(4)	(5)
4.1	Panchayat HQs		X	
4.2	Tehsil HQs		X	
4.3	Bus stop			
4.4	Metalled road			
4.5	All weather road			
4.6*	Pre-primary school (without separate toilet for girls)			
4.7*	Primary school (without separate toilet for girls)			
4.8*	Middle school (without separate toilet for girls)			
4.9*	Secondary school (without separate toilet for girls)			
4.10*	Higher secondary school (without separate toilet for girls)			
4.11*	Pre-primary school (with separate toilet for girls)			
4.12*	Primary school (with separate toilet for girls)			
4.13*	Middle school (with separate toilet for girls)			
4.14*	Secondary school (with separate toilet for girls)			
4.15*	Higher secondary school (with separate toilet for girls)			
4.16	College with degree course			
4.17	College with masters degree course/ university			
4.18	Industrial training Institute (ITI)			
4.19	Non-formal education centre (NFEC)			
4.20	Veterinary sub-centre/dispensary			

Block 4 *(continued)*

Sl. no.	Item	Distance in km (in two digits)	If dist- ance is '00' then number	Source code
(1)	(2)	(3)	(4)	(5)
4.21	Sub-centre (Health)			
4.22	Public health centre (PHC)			
4.23	Community health centre			
4.24	Government hospital			
4.25	Allopathic medicine shop			
4.26	Homeopathic medicine shop			
4.27	Ayurvedic medicine shop			
4.28	Other medicine shop			
4.29	Post office			
4.30	Bank			
4.31	Fair price shop			
4.32	Weekly market			
4.33	Fertilizer/pesticide shop			
4.34	Internet (physical) facility			
4.35	PCO			
4.36	Special school for the blind			
4.37	Special school for the mentally retarded			
4.38	Vocational training school/centre			
4.39	Institution/organisation for rehabilitation of disabled persons			
4.40	Railway station	X		
4.41	Airport	X		
4.42	District HQs	X		
4.43	State capital	X		
4.44	Police station/Beat Office/Outpost	X		
4.45	Anganwadi–noon meal centre			
4.46	Cooperative society			
4.47	Community centre			
4.48	Recreational area (Club, Park, Garden)			
4.49	Public library			

Notes: Distance in km to the nearest integer may be given. If the facility is available within the village, '00' may be given. Distance more than 99 km may also be given as 99.
* Only Government and semi-Government should be reported

Block 5: *Demographic information on Items 5.1 to 5.5, as on 1st April of the reference year* in numbers

Sl. no.	Data item	Population in different age groups						Source code	
(1)	(2)	(3)	(4)	(5)	(6)	(7)	(8)	(9)	(10)
5.1	Population	0–4 years	5–14 years	15–17 years	18–49 years	50–59 years	60 years & above	Total	
5.2									
	Female								
	Male								
	Households								

(1)	(2)	(3)	(4)	(5)	(6)	(7)	(8)
		SC	ST	OBC	General	Total	
5.3	Total no. of households						
5.4	Total no. of households headed by women						
5.5	No. of households living below poverty line						

Items 5.6 to 5.13 during the reference year

Sl. no.	Births	Girls	Boys	Source code
(1)	(2)	(3)	(4)	(5)
5.6	Live birth			
5.7	Still birth			
5.8	Deaths (below age 1 year)			

Other deaths (after completion of first birthday)	1–4 years	5–14 years	15–49 years	50–59 years	60 years & above	Total	
(1) (2)	(3)	(4)	(5)	(6)	(7)	(8)	
5.9 Female							
5.10 Male							

5.11	No. of deaths of women (age groups: 15–49 years) at the time of childbirth
5.12	No. of pregnant women
5.13	Number of Medical Termination of Pregnancy (MTP) cases

information is available, it is not up to date." In practice, however, "a major chunk of information has been collected from the *anganwadi* worker or the health worker."[10] As observed in Warwat Khanderao and Raina, the Integrated Child Development Services workers maintained a record of each household (in the village survey register) within their jurisdiction. In fact, according to the feedback report from Assam, Haryana, Kerala, and Maharashtra in the 2014 *Basic Statistics* report, they consulted the Integrated Child Development Services registers. However, they pointed out that "the age-wise information is available with the *anganwadi sevika* and the ANM worker but tabulation of this information as per given age group is very difficult."[11] At the same time, feedback reports in the 2014 *Basic Statistics* report from Rajasthan, Tamil Nadu, and Uttarakhand suggested that they did not use the Integrated Child Development Services registers and used estimated data by asking knowledgeable persons.[12]

Data item 5.5 can be obtained from the Below Poverty Line list available at both village panchayats, although it is not updated regularly. However, a feedback report in the 2014 *Basic Statistics* report from Assam noted that "no specific data of households (HHs) below the poverty line is available. Issue of BPL Cards cannot justify that HH is below the poverty line."[13]

Data items 5.6 to 5.11 can be obtained at Warwat Khanderao and Raina from the Integrated Child Development Services registers, the records at the primary health centres (and their sub-centres), or the birth and death registers of the Civil Registration System. As mentioned in chapter 6 (section 6.7), however, births and deaths outside the village were often not recorded in the Civil Registration System because the place of occurrence is taken to be the place of registration. Data items 5.12 and 5.13 can be obtained from the records of the primary health centres or the Integrated Child Development Services registers. The Integrated Child Development Services worker often works with the health worker (Auxiliary Nurse Midwife or Accredited Social Health Activist) on these matters.

The demographic information in Block 5 can be used for multiple purposes,

---

[10] *Ibid.*, p. 55.
[11] *Ibid.*, p. 56. "Therefore, special compilation is required for generating data as per BSLLD village schedules (A & B) like age group wise/social group wise etc" (Directorate of Economic and Statistics of Karnataka 2012).
[12] Central Statistics Office (2014, pp. 56–7).
[13] *Ibid.*, p. 55.

such as subject 23 (health and sanitation, including hospitals, primary health centres, and dispensaries), subject 24 (family welfare), subject 25 (women and child development), subject 26 (social welfare), subject 27 (welfare of the weaker sections, and in particular, of the Scheduled Castes and the Scheduled Tribes), subject 16 (poverty alleviation programme), and subject 28 (public distribution system).

Data items 6.1 and 6.2 were documented in the records of the primary health centres and their sub-centres. Data on disability in the Population Census 2011, and the Socio-Economic and Caste Census 2011, can cater to data items 6.3 to 6.7, although it is not updated regularly. Otherwise, these data items have to rely on the oral enquiry method with the help of the

Block 6: *Morbidity, disability and family planning*

Sl. no.		Name three common diseases in the village in descending order of prevalence			Source code
(1)	(2)	(3)	(4)	(5)	(6)
6.1	Chronic				
6.2	Seasonal				

Number of disabled persons by type of disability

		Female			Male			
(1)	(2)	(3)	(4)	(5)	(6)	(7)	(8)	(9)
Type of disability		0–59 Years	60 years and above	Total	0–59 Years	60 years and above	Total	Source code
6.3	Visual							
6.4	Hearing							
6.5	Speech							
6.6	Locomotor							
6.7	Mental illness							

Number of married persons

		Less than 15 years	15–17 years	18–20 years	21 years and above	Source code
(1)	(2)	(3)	(4)	(5)	(6)	(7)
6.8	Female					
6.9	Male					
6.10	Percentage of couples using any type of family planning method					

health worker.[14] Data items 6.8 and 6.9 can be obtained from the Integrated Child Development Services village survey registers. Data item 6.10 can be obtained from the records of the primary health centres and their sub-centres. As Integrated Child Development Services workers work with the Auxiliary Nurse Midwife or the Accredited Social Health Activist, they partly shared data with the primary health centres.

A special compilation is required for generating age-group-wise data for data items 6.3 to 6.9. A feedback report in the 2014 *Basic Statistics* report from Maharashtra noted that "age group and sex-wise compilation of disabilities is very difficult because this information is not updated."[15]

Data items 6.1 and 6.2 are relevant to subject 23 (health and sanitation, including hospitals, primary health centres, and dispensaries) in Schedule XI of the Constitution. Data items 6.3 to 6.10 are relevant to the planning exercises for subject 26 (social welfare, including welfare of the handicapped, and mentally retarded: data items 6.3 to 6.7), and subject 26 (family welfare: data items 6.8 to 6.10).

Data items in Block 7 can be obtained from the records of the primary health centres and their sub-centres. Feedback reports in the 2014 *Basic Statistics* from Kerala, Maharashtra, and Uttarakhand noted that information on non-Government facilities was not always available in secondary sources so that data had to be collected from knowledgeable persons.[16] Block 7 is obviously relevant to the planning exercises for subject 23 (health and sanitation, including hospitals, primary health centres, and dispensaries) in Schedule XI.

Data items 8.1 to 8.4 can be obtained from the Population Census. The unit-level household data on the literacy status of the most literate adult in each household and unit-level person data on each household member with respect to education status (including literacy status) were generated by the Below Poverty Line Census 2002.[17] The Socio-Economic and Caste

---

[14] *Ibid.*, p. 59. A feedback report in the *CSO Report 2014* from Haryana points out that "Data are not available for all disabled persons. Data available at social welfare office are related to beneficiaries (physically handicapped) only. However, the available data are not age wise" (*ibid.*, p. 58).

[15] *Ibid.*, p. 58.

[16] *Ibid.*, pp. 59–60.

[17] However, a major part of the unit-level person data of the Below Poverty Line Census was not available for Bidyanidhi village.

Block 7: *Health manpower*

	Number of health officials									
	Government facilities				Non-government facilities					
Type of system	Female		Male		Female		Male			Source code
	Doc-tor	Trained Nurse/ Comp-ounder etc	Doc-tor	Trained Nurse/ Comp-ounder etc	Doc-tor	Trained Nurse/ Comp-ounder etc	Doc-tor	Trained Nurse/ Comp-ounder etc		
(1) (2)	(3)	(4)	(5)	(6)	(7)	(8)	(9)	(10)		(11)
7.1 Allopathic										
7.2 Ayurvedic										
7.3 Unani										
7.4 Siddha (Tradi-tional medicine system)										
7.5 Homoeopathic										
7.6 Other/ naturopathy										

Census 2011 also collected data on the "highest educational level completed" (including "illiterate") for each person in the household. In Raina, other unit-level household data on the number of literate members and the educational attainment of the most educated member of the household within special social groups (Scheduled Caste, Scheduled Tribe, others) was produced from the census-type survey independently conducted by the panchayati raj institutions in 2008 to evaluate the rural sanitation scheme (see section 4.3.2, chapter 4). However, these data were not updated regularly. The Integrated Child Development Services village survey register is expected to contain data on the educational attainment of each household member and should be updated regularly. The feedback report in the 2014 *Basic Statistics* report from Maharashtra pointed out that the *anganwadi sevikas* were requested to help compile this data.[18]

Data items 8.5 to 8.24 can be obtained from the village school register and the village-level register of all children on an annual house-to-house enquiry conducted by the schoolteachers. Village-wise data of the All India School Education Survey are also usable to some extent.

[18] Central Statistics Office (2014, p. 62).

Block 8: *Education*

(1) (2)	SC (3)	ST (4)	OBC (5)	General (6)	Total (7)	Source code (8)
Literate population (aged 7 years and above) in	SC	ST	OBC	General	Total	Source code
8.1 Female						
8.2 Male						
Literate population (aged 15–24 years) in numbers	SC	ST	OBC	General	Total	
8.3 Female						
8.4 Male						

(1) (2)	Female (3)	Male (4)	Source code (5)
A: Primary classes (I–V)	Female	Male	Source code
8.5 Number of students enrolled			
8.6 Number of students attending schools			
8.7 Number of new entrants/fresh entry			
8.8 Number of students discontinued the studies			
8.9 Reasons for discontinuation of studies			
B. Middle classes (VI–VIII)			
8.10 Number of students enrolled			
8.11 Number of students attending schools			
8.12 Number of new entrants/fresh entry			
8.13 Number of students discontinued the studies			
8.14 Reasons for discontinuation of studies			
C. High school (IX–X)			
8.15 Number of students attending schools			
8.16 Number of new entrants/fresh entry			
8.17 Number of students discontinued the studies			
8.18 Reasons for discontinuation of studies			
D. Senior secondary school (XI–XII)			
8.19 Number of students enrolled			
8.20 Number of students attending schools			
8.21 Number of new entrants/fresh entry			
8.22 Number of students discontinued the studies			
8.23 Reasons for discontinuation of studies			
8.24 Number of children aged 6–14 years, never enrolled in school			

Notes: Reasons for discontinuation of studies (i) Economic - 1 (ii) Non-economic - 2
(For items 8.5 to 8.21, the reference date may be taken as September 30 of the year)

Block 9: *Land utilisation*

Sl. no.	Items	Area in hectares (up to two decimal places)	Source code
(1)	(2)	(3)	(4)
9.1	Geographical area of the revenue village		
9.2	Reporting area for land utilisation		
9.3	Area under forest		
9.4	Barren and unculturable land		
9.5	Area under non-agricultural uses		
9.6	Area not available for cultivation (9.4+9.5)		
9.7	Land under miscellaneous trees		
9.8	Permanent pasture and other grazing land		
9.9	Cultivable wasteland		
9.10	Current fallow		
9.11	Fallow lands other than current fallows		
9.12	Net area sown		
9.13	Area sown more than once		
9.14	Total cropped area (gross area)		
9.15	Land under still water		
9.16	Social forestry		
9.17	Marshy land		

Area irrigated by source (in hectares)

9.18	Government canals		
9.19	Wells /tubewells		
9.20	Tanks		
9.21	Micro-irrigation		
9.22	Other source		
9.23	Total irrigated land (9.18 to 9.22)		

Number of operational holdings by size-classes

9.24	Marginal......... (below 1 hectare)		
9.25	Small .... (1–4 hectares)		
9.26	Medium..........(4–10 hectares)		
9.27	Large............. (10 hectares and above)		

Natural resources

9.28	River length (km)		
9.29	Area of water bodies (other than river) (ha)		
9.30	Mines (number)		

Data items in Block 8 are directly relevant to subject 17 (education, including primary and secondary schools) of Schedule XI.[19] Data items 8.1 to 8.4 are useful for multiple purposes, including subject 19 (adult and non-formal education).

Data items 9.1 to 9.23 can be estimated from land records and cadastral maps at the *patwari's* office in Warwat Khanderao and at the Block Land and Land Reform Office in Raina. The *patwari's* land record is updated regularly unless there is negligence in carrying out the record on land cultivation. The Block Land and Land Reform Officer's land record is not updated regularly. Data from the scheme for Establishment of an Agency for Reporting Agricultural Statistics might be usable in Raina, but it is not available yet.

There is no documentary existence with respect to data items 9.24 to 9.27 have in either Warwat Khanderao or Raina. The Below Poverty Line Census 2002 collected data on the "type of operational holding of land" (owner/tenant/both owner and tenant/none). However, these were not classified by size of operational holdings. As mentioned in chapter 4 (section 4.3.3.4), the *patwari's* land record in Maharashtra (*Form no. 7*) is primarily an ownership holding register and its information on the landowner–tenant relationship is quite inaccurate. Since the Agricultural Census for the erstwhile temporarily-settled State is conducted through the re-tabulation of information available in the village land records, the Agricultural Census data in Maharashtra, accordingly, does not reflect actual operational holdings. Therefore, the operational holding data from the Agricultural Census is presently not useful for Maharashtra even if its sub-State-level data were disclosed. As for West Bengal, the operational holding data from the Agricultural Census and the scheme for Establishment of an Agency for Reporting Agricultural Statistics can be potentially useful, but are not yet available.

"Maintenance of village records relating to land revenue" has been listed as the fifty-eighth subject of activities to be devolved to village panchayats in the Village List of the Bombay Village Panchayats Act, 1958. Therefore, village panchayats in Maharashtra are able to intervene in the maintenance of land records in order to correct or update data not only on season-wise land use, but also on the landowner–tenant relation. Data items 9.28 to 9.30 in Block 9 have to rely on the assessment of knowledgeable persons or the *patwari*.

---

[19] "Among the other Blocks, Block 8 appeared to be tough for the recordists" (Central Statistics Office 2011, D-27).

In the 2014 *Basic Statistics* report, Assam, Goa, Kerala, Meghalaya, and Sikkim reported non-availability of data for Block 9.[20] Feedback reports from Kerala reported that ward-wise data for this Block were not available though panchayat-wise data were collected from the District Statistical offices.[21] A feedback report from Haryana (an erstwhile temporarily settled area) noted that "data related to items 9.24 to 9.27 are not available accurate(ly)."[22]

Data items 9.1 to 9.27 in Block 9 are relevant to planning exercises for subject 1 (agriculture), subject 2 (land improvement, implementation of land reforms, land consolidation, and soil conservation), and subject 6 (social forestry and farm forestry) of Schedule XI of the Constitution. Data items 9.18 to 9.23 and 9.28 to 9.29 are also relevant to subject 3 (minor irrigation, water management, and watershed development).

Data items in Block 10 can be obtained from the Livestock Census. However, it is difficult to gain annual data as the Livestock Census is conducted once every five years and is not updated regularly. A feedback report from Haryana noted, "that data as per latest livestock census are available, otherwise no data related to livestock are compiled at any level." Block 10 is relevant to subject 4 (animal husbandry, dairying, and poultry) of Schedule XI of the Constitution.

As noted before, most data items in Block 11 were not documented in the village-level records but were common knowledge among village people.

Block 10: *Livestock and poultry*

Sl. no.	Livestock/poultry	Number	Source code
(1)	(2)	(3)	(4)
10.1	Cattle (including ox, bullock, yak, mithun, etc.)		
10.2	Buffaloes		
10.3	Sheep		
10.4	Goats		
10.5	Horses, ponies, mules, donkeys, camels etc		
10.6	Pigs		
10.7	Hens and ducks		
10.8	Any other livestock and poultry		

---

[20] Central Statistics Office (2014, p. 62).
[21] *Ibid.*, p. 63.
[22] *Ibid.*

Block 11: *Number of storage and marketing outlets*

Sl. no.	Marketing outlets	Number	Source code
(1)	(2)	(3)	(4)
11.1	Fair price shops		
11.2	Regular market/Mandis		
11.3	Cold storages		
11.4	Godown/warehousing facility		
11.5	Others shops		

Panchayat officials in both Warwat Khanderao and Raina revealed that this information was indeed common knowledge. The Raina village panchayat collected some professional tax from shop owners. Block 11 is related to subject 22 (markets and fairs) and subject 28 (public distribution system).

Data items in Block 12 were not regularly documented in the village-level records, nor were they common knowledge among villagers. These data items have no documentary evidence except for the Population Census which is not updated regularly. Although the Integrated Child Development Services village survey register contains a brief note on occupations in the comment column for each member of the household, it is far from adequate for data on the employment status of villagers.

Block 12: *Employment status (employment/unemployment) of the villagers, only for persons six years and above* in numbers

Sl. no.	Sectors	Male	Female	Total	Source code
(1)	(2)	(3)	(4)	(5)	(6)
12.1	Self-employed in agriculture sector				
12.2	Self-employed in non-agriculture sector				
	Employed as regular wage/salaried employee				
12.3	(i) In agriculture sector				
12.4	(ii) Non-agriculture sector				
12.5	Rural labourer				
12.6	Unemployed				
12.7	Unemployed between age 15–24				
12.8	Not in the labour force				

According to feedback reports in the 2014 *Basic Statistics* report, the situation for different States was as follows: "category-wise village level data on employment/unemployment are not available" (Assam); "perfect figures of employment and unemployment sector wise data are not available" (Gujarat); "no data are available for employment, only estimated data are available" (Haryana); "no register is available in any office to supplement this Block. Census figures 2001 are utilised" (Kerala); "there is no proper record available at village level for compilation of employment status data" (Maharashtra); "data not available" (Rajasthan); "collection of data available is insufficient" (Tamil Nadu); and "records are not maintained at panchayat level" (Uttarakhand).[23]

Data items in Block 12 are useful for several purposes. For example, village panchayats can use them to estimate the demand for work to be provided by the Mahatma Gandhi National Rural Employment Guarantee Scheme with regard to subject 16 (poverty alleviation programme) of Schedule XI. As far as Maharashtra is concerned, "preparation of statistics of unemployment" has been provided as the Seventy-Fourth subject of activities to be devolved to village panchayats in the Village List of the Bombay Village Panchayats Act, 1958. Data items in Block 12 are also relevant to subject 1 (Agriculture: data items 12.1 and 12.3), subject 8 (Small-scale industries) and subject 9 (khadi, village and cottage industries: data items 12.2 and 12.4).

As there were no official systems of recording migration, no accurate migration data were available at the village level. Some data can be obtained from the comments column for each member of the household in the village survey register. Information on deaths, marriages or migration for each member of the household was noted in this column. However, the exact date of the event was not always available. When a new survey was conducted, households that had migrated temporarily were deleted from the register. Nevertheless, as mentioned in chapter 4 (section 4.3.3.1), in cases where some of the household members had migrated, details of all members of the undivided household were recorded even when the migration was permanent. In addition, a special compilation would be required to generate data for each age group. The Population Census also collects migration data every ten years, but these have not been updated recently.

Many feedback comments in the 2014 *Basic Statistics* report stated that "there is no system of recording migration data. So it is difficult to get exact

[23] *Ibid.*, pp. 66–7.

Block 13: *Migration (as per the last month of the reference period)*

		Out-migration			
		0–14 years	15 years & above	Total	Source code
(1)	(2)	(3)	(4)	(5)	(6)
13.1	Female				
13.2	Male				
		In-migration			
13.3	Female				
13.4	Male				

figures."[24] According to Kerala's feedback report, "registers are not available in any office." The difficulty was solved "by collecting data from oral reports of knowledgeable person."[25] Maharashtra's feedback report pointed out that "information regarding in and out migration can only be available from records of *anganwadi* register but age-wise classification of this information is not available. No other official record is maintained at the village level." [26] Demographic information in Block 13 is a core statistic for rural development, and useful for multiple purposes.

Data items in Block 14 have no documentary evidence for them and require subjective assessments by knowledgeable persons. Maharashtra's feedback report in the 2014 *Basic Statistics* report noted that "these data are collected from knowledgeable person(s) which are not reliable."[27] A feedback report from Odisha noted that "some items of this Block are not available in the recorded form. Because of social reasons people are reluctant to share information."[28]

Data items 14.1, 14.2, and 14.5 are related to subject 16 (poverty alleviation programme), etc. Data item 14.6 is relevant to subject 25 (women and child development) of Schedule XI.

Data items in Block 15 were not documented in the village-level records. Neither data from the Industrial Development office nor village-level data of the Economic Census were available with the village panchayats. Some

---

[24] *Ibid.*, p. 68.
[25] *Ibid.*
[26] *Ibid.*, p. 68.
[27] *Ibid.*, p. 72.
[28] *Ibid.*, p. 70.

Block 14: *Other social indicators, as per the last month of the reference period*

Sl. no.	Other selected social indicators	Number		Source
	Item	Female	Male	code
(1)	(2)	(3)	(4)	(5)
14.1	Street children			
14.2	Beggars			
14.3	Juvenile delinquents			
14.4	Drug addicts			
14.5	Child workers (Aged 14 years or less)			
14.6	Incidence of violence against women (only cognisable reported cases)			

enterprises and workers therein may be known to the people of the village. However, information on small, informal-sector enterprises may not always be common knowledge. The Raina village panchayat collects professional tax from shopowners. Otherwise, data on the number of enterprises have no corresponding documentary evidence at the village level. Data on the number of workers by type of enterprise have no documentary evidence except for the Population Census data, which is updated once in ten years.

According to Kerala's feedback report in the 2014 *Basic Statistics* report, the "number of enterprise, available from the panchayat register is partial. Updation is only done as and when new enterprises are registered . . . Data are collected from knowledgeable persons."[29] According to Haryana's feedback report, "In small villages where establishments are less, accurate data can be collected but in big villages it is based only on the knowledge of informants."[30] According to Maharashtra's feedback report, "Up-to-date record is not maintained, especially of commercial units which are outside the village but inside the village boundary are found unrecorded."[31] A feedback report from Andhra Pradesh suggested that the "6th Economic Census data can be used for this Block."[32]

Block 15 is obviously relevant to subject 8 (small-scale industries, including food processing industries), and subject 9 (khadi, village, and cottage

---

[29] *Ibid.*, p. 74.
[30] *Ibid.*, p. 73.
[31] *Ibid.*, p. 74.
[32] *Ibid.*, p. 71.

Block 15: *Industries and business as on March 31 of the reference year* in numbers

Sl. no.	Enterprises	Only self-employed enterprises (own-account enterprises)			Other enterprises (with at least one paid worker)					Source code
		No. of units	No. of self-employed workers		No. of units	No. of self-employed workers		No. of paid workers		
			Female	Male		Female	Male	Female	Male	
(1)	(2)	(3)	(4)	(5)	(6)	(7)	(8)	(9)	(10)	(11)
15.1	Blacksmith's shop									
15.2	Shops selling agricultural equipment									
15.3	Agricultural seed shops									
15.4	Manufacturing of fishing nets									
15.5	Processing of fish									
15.6	Mining and quarrying									
15.7	Well/tubewell making									
15.8	Flour mills									
15.9	Saw mills									
15.10	Sugar cane crushing									
15.11	Weaving mills									
15.12	Grocery shop									
15.13	Tailoring									
15.14	Car/scooter/cycle repair shop									
15.15	Tea stall									
15.16	Sweet shop									
15.17	*Pan/bidi*/cigarette shop									
15.18	Meat Shop									
15.19	Slaughterhouse									
15.20	Tyre repair shop									
15.21	Goldsmith/jewellery shop									
15.22	Shoe repair shop									
15.23	Brick/kiln making									
15.24	Food processing (other than fishing)									
Dispensary and medicine shops										
15.25	(a) Allopathic									
15.26	(b) Homoeopathic									

Block 15 (*continued*)

Sl. no.	Enterprises	Only self-employed enterprises (own-account enterprises)			Other enterprises (with at least one paid worker)					Source code
		No. of units	No. of self-employed workers		No. of units	No. of self-employed workers		No. of paid workers		
			Female	Male		Female	Male	Female	Male	
(1)	(2)	(3)	(4)	(5)	(6)	(7)	(8)	(9)	(10)	(11)
15.27	(c) Ayurvedic									
15.28	Carpentry									
15.29	Restaurants (other than tea stalls)									
15.30	Masonry/helpers									
15.31	Rickshaw pullers									
15.32	Auto/taxi drivers									
15.33	Tutorial Home/centre									
15.34	Telephone booth (STD)									
15.35	Fish shop									
15.36	Poultry farming and selling									
15.37	Fruits and/or vegetables shops/vendors									
15.38	Stationery shops									
15.39	Beauty parlours									
15.40	Massage parlours									
15.41	Milk processing									
15.42	Electronic and electric equipment shop									
15.43	Hardware shop									
15.44	Cell phone shop									
15.45	Internet café									
15.46	Any other enterprise not listed above									

Block 16: *Information on fatality due to disasters*

				Number of deaths					
(1)	(2)	(3)	(4)	(5)	(6)	(7)	(8)	(9)	(10)
Sl. no.	Name of the disaster	Female			Male			Total	Source code
		0–14 years	15 years & above	Sub-total 1	0–14 Years	15 years & above	Sub-total 2		
1									
2									
3									
4									
5									

Source codes:

1. Panchayat - 01
2. *Anganwadi* worker - 02
3. Health worker (ANM/ FHW/ MHW/etc.) - 03
4. *Patwari* (Land Records) - 04
5. Village headman - 05
6. Local school - 06
7. Local doctor - 07
8. PHC/sub-Centre/hospital - 08
9. Knowledgeable Persons/others (female- 09, male- 10)

industries) of Schedule XI. Data items 15.25 to 15.27 are related to subject 23 (health and sanitation), which includes matters on dispensaries.

There is no panchayat register for data items in Block 16.[33] However, according to feedback from States and Union Territories in the 2014 *Basic Statistics* report, "as such no significant problem was faced by them for compilation/collection of information for this block."[34] In Maharashtra, the *patwari* reported to the *tehsildar* and District Collector about information on deaths caused by natural disasters.

[33] This Block has been inserted in the Village Schedule on Basic Statistics since Phase III of the Ministry of Statistics and Planning Implementation's pilot study commissioned in 2012–3. Before that, no such Block was present in the Schedule. Therefore, we have not conducted interviews on this Block in the field.
[34] Central Statistics Office (2014, p. 75).

8.2 DOCUMENTARY EVIDENCE OF VILLAGE SCHEDULE DATA ON BASIC STATISTICS

The Village Schedule on Basic Statistics gives a framework for the compilation not only of secondary data (existing records and registers), but also information from knowledgeable persons. However, as described in chapter 4 (section 4.3.5.1), most of the data items in the Schedule are assumed to have documentary evidence. A set of village-level data sources that has already been documented by local-level functionaries is expected to exist in parallel to most of the data items in the Village Schedule.

For villages under the Raina village panchayat that were actually covered by the Ministry of Statistics' pilot scheme on Basic Statistics in its first phase since 2009, we ascertained that all the data items in the Village Schedule were filled up. However, as observed earlier, some data items were not obtained from the village-level records or registers. Some data items such as in Block 2, Block 3, Block 4, and Block 11 were not documented but were obviously common knowledge among villagers. For example, as the panchayat is a meeting place for villagers, the probability of getting correct information on data items in Block 4 (distance from the nearest facility) was very high. However, some data items were not documented in any village-level record, nor were they common knowledge among villagers. Some data items required aggregation of a large number of items of information so that subjective assessment by knowledgeable persons is not adequate as a data source. These include data items in the following Blocks: Block 9 "land utilization," Block 12 "employment status," Block 13 "migration," and Block 15 "industries and business."

As already mentioned, there was no reliable record of operational holdings even in the erstwhile temporarily settled areas such as Warwat Khanderao. There was no updated land use record in the erstwhile permanently settled areas like Raina. Although the village survey register contained a brief note on occupations and migration in/ the comments column for each member of the household, the note was neither accurate nor exhaustive. Although village-level data in the Economic Census should include data on small-scale enterprises and workers, they are not disclosed at present. Therefore, data items in these Blocks need substantial refinement and should be rationalised to improve their quality.[35] However, these data items are not unimportant for

---

[35] Central Statistical Organisation (2006, p. 17). The report adds, "The Village Schedule in its present form needs substantial refinement and clarity on the basis of the experience gained through pilot studies regarding data availability."

rural development. Thus, a fundamental reform needs to be introduced in these data sources. The recording systems used by village-level functionaries need to be fundamentally reorganised.

Kerala's feedback report in the 2014 *Basic Statistics* report suggested, for example, that by paying a yearly honorarium to the Integrated Child Development Services workers, their services can be utilised for maintaining and updating registers in accordance with the Village Schedule with the permission of the State Government.[36] The *Basic Statistics* report also recommended that staff, particularly the panchayat secretary in coordination with the Integrated Child Development Services workers, Auxiliary Nurse Midwives, and *patwaris*, work on obtaining financial support for the compilation of village-level statistics at the village panchayat level.

As already mentioned, an important recommendation made by the *Basic Statistics* report is to establish formal data-sharing mechanisms between the panchayat and different agencies working in the panchayat area. In chapter 6 (section 6.6), we discussed a possible data-sharing mechanism to prepare a village-level population list (People's List). In addition, data on occupation or migration may be included in the list if it is urgently required. Such a reform in the village-level recording system may meet the data requirements of Block 12 and Block 13. As mentioned in chapter 4 (section 4.3.3.4), village panchayats in Maharashtra have the potential to establish a data-sharing mechanism with *patwari* agencies to intervene in maintenance of land records and correct and update data regarding season-wise land use or data regarding the landowner–tenant relation. It is statutorily possible for village councils in Maharashtra to have disciplinary control over the *patwari* system under the Bombay Village Panchayats Act, 1958, as amended in 2003. Such intervention will develop the land records to meet the data requirement in Block 9.[37] As for village panchayats in West Bengal, data from the Agricultural Census or the scheme for the Establishment of an Agency for Reporting Agricultural Statistics can be useful when obtained through a complete house-to-house enquiry about operational holders. Otherwise, land-use information might be added to the land records maintained by the Block Land and Land Reform office and village-level Revenue Inspector. Sub-

---

[36] Central Statistics Office (2014, p. 56, 58).

[37] The State Government may disclose to panchayats the village-level spatial data on the geographical information system (GIS), as has already been made public on Google Maps. This can help the panchayats to check the reliability of cadastral maps and land-use information maintained by the *patwari*.

State-level data of the Economic Census may be disclosed to examine its discrepancies and be used for data items in Block 11 and Block 15.

8.3 PLANNING EXERCISE AT THE VILLAGE LEVEL AND POSSIBLE USE OF THE VILLAGE SCHEDULE ON BASIC STATISTICS

The village-level planning exercise is feasible only for a functional domain over which the panchayat has a high degree of autonomy. The panchayat cannot make any plan concerning functions that lie outside its functional domain. Therefore, we should evaluate the utility of the Village Schedule on Basic Statistics in relation to the functional domain of a particular panchayat.

The utility of the Village Schedule depends on the tier of the panchayati raj – village panchayat, Block-level committee or district panchayat – because Activity Mapping differs from tier to tier. The Village Schedule assumes its utilisation at the panchayat and district levels. In fact, one copy of the Village Schedule is to be retained with the village panchayat as a "permanent document for every village,"[38] and another copy is to be sent to the District Statistical Office.[39] Its utility at the village panchayat level will be different from its utility at the district level.

8.3.1 Utility of the Village Schedule on Basic Statistics for Warwat Khanderao Village Panchayat

"Preparation of plans for the development of the village" is a function listed in Schedule I (Village list) of the Bombay Village Panchayats Act, 1958. The village panchayat is to place, before the first meeting of the village council in every financial year, "the development and other programmes of work proposed for the current financial year" (Section 8). Nevertheless, as observed in chapter 3 (section 3.12), all of the Village Schedule data is not so important for Warwat Khanderao village panchayat for the purpose of "preparation of plans for the development of the village," as the panchayat's authority to carry out planning exercises is substantially limited in reality. Information in the Village Schedule proves to be, as it were, "excessive" for Warwat Khanderao village panchayat, considering the narrow autonomy in its functional domain. The village panchayat will fill up most data items not for

[38] Central Statistics Office (2014, p. 148).
[39] Central Statistical Organisation (2013, p. 4). The *Instructions for Data Recordist* specify that "Three copies of both the village schedules are to be filled-in. One copy is to be retained at the village, second copy at the panchayat, and the third copy is to be sent to the concerned DSO."

use in its own planning exercises, but in order to report to the district office.

As already noted in chapter 3, most schemes in Warwat Khanderao, except for schemes for drinking water, roads, sanitation, Integrated Child Development Services, Mahatma Gandhi National Rural Employment Guarantee Scheme, and public distribution, were implemented by agencies such as the line departments, *tehsildar*, Block-level committee, and the district panchayat. As described in detail in chapter 5 (section 5.2.1), most subject functions regarding the primary sector, such as subject 1 (agriculture, including agricultural extension), subject 2 (land improvement, soil conservation, and land reform), subject 3 (minor irrigation), and subject 4 (animal husbandry, dairying, and poultry) of Schedule XI were, in practice, assigned to the Block-level committee or *tehsildar*. Under the Right to Education Act, 2009, almost no function was assigned to the Warwat Khanderao village panchayat with regard to subject 17 (education, including primary and secondary schools). The panchayat head insisted that functions assigned to the village panchayat with regard to social welfare and the poverty alleviation programme covered only basic formalities such as completing paperwork, while the rest was implemented by the Block-level committee or *tehsildar*. The village panchayat had no specific role regarding subject 8 (small-scale industries) and subject 9 (khadi, village, and cottage industries). Besides there was no strong coordination mechanism between the Warwat Khanderao village panchayat and village-level functionaries working in the panchayati raj institutions independently of the panchayati raj system. The only village-level functionaries with whom the village panchayat had a coordination mechanism were the Integrated Child Development Services workers.

Thus, in most functional domains provided in Schedule XI of the Constitution, the Warwat Khanderao village panchayat cannot act even as an implementing agency of the State or Central Government. The institutional mechanisms of the Central and State schemes bypass and ignore the panchayat or, at best, seek only a "cursory and token linkage."[40]

The only area of functions for which the Warwat Khanderao village panchayat can carry out envisioning a feasible plan was the functional domain related to schemes for drinking water, roads and sanitation, Integrated Child

---

[40] Planning Commission (2008b, p. 6). The *Manual* notes, "the institutional mechanisms envisaged continue to bypass panchayats or at best, seek only a cursory and token linkage. Most such schemes envisage a line department sponsored hierarchy of missions and parallel bodies for actual planning and implementation."

Development Services, and public distribution. The water supply scheme was an important development activity in the Warwat Khanderao panchayat area. The Integrated Child Development Services centre has become fully functional in Warwat Khanderao. Its workers sometimes jointly worked with the Auxiliary Nurse Midwife and the Accredited Social Health Activist. Accordingly, the data items in the Village Schedule on Basic Statistics pertaining to carrying out micro-level planning by the Warwat Khanderao village panchayat must focus on this, limited, functional domain.

In contrast, the Village Schedule data on Basic Statistics was relevant to a broader range of functions of the concerned Block-level committee. In Maharashtra, the scope of autonomy in the functional domain is broader for the Block-level committee than the village panchayats under its jurisdiction. As mentioned in chapter 5 (section 5.2.1), responsibility for some schemes implemented in Warwat Khanderao was assigned not to the village panchayat but to the Block-level committee. For example, identifying beneficiaries of schemes, such as the distribution of subsidised agricultural inputs, was assigned to the latter with regard to subject 1 "agriculture." The *Swarnajayanti Gram Swarozgar Yojana* was implemented by the Block-level committee for Warwat Khanderao. As witnessed by the panchayat head, although the village panchayat only fills up forms for the poverty alleviation programme, the rest of the work is done by the Block-level committee.

The power of the Block Development Officer to carry out planning exercises in Maharashtra was also somewhat limited. Although "sector planning officers" in the Block Development Office (a sector refers to a geographical area comprising ten to fifteen villages) were responsible for all planning activities for each scheme/programme of the Ministry of Rural Development with the help of the village development officer, its power was limited as compared to the *tehsildar*. While the Block Development Officer is the executive officer for all matters related to the panchayat, the *tehsildar* is the Programme Officer for all programmes under the Ministry of Rural Development.

8.3.2 Utility of the Village Schedule on Basic Statistics for Raina Village Panchayat

The Village Schedule data on Basic Statistics is usable in Raina for compiling a minimum number of statistics for planning. Information in the Village Schedule is not excessive for the needs of the Raina village panchayat, considering its comparative autonomy in the functional domain.

The West Bengal Panchayati Raj Act, 1973, authorises all tiers of panchayati raj institutions to prepare annual and five-year plans. Furthermore, the West Bengal State Government pursued a bottom-up approach to planning with a special focus on village panchayats and their village assemblies. The onus of development activities was placed on the panchayat and ward levels in West Bengal. At the ward level, the village development committees were entrusted the task of preparing village-level plans ("Action Plan"), which was the basis of the panchayat's own plan. The Raina village panchayat and its wards also acted as implementing agencies of the State or Central Government schemes, as in Maharashtra. The projects that could be taken up under the different schemes and funding were specified by the funding authority of the State or the Central Government, and so the village panchayat had limited authority in planning for such schemes. Nevertheless, the power of the West Bengal village panchayats even over sponsored schemes was greater than in Maharashtra for the following reasons. First, the devolution of finance and functionaries to the village panchayats had advanced more in West Bengal than in Maharashtra. In numerous schemes, the panchayats received funds directly from the Government agencies. Second, the West Bengal village panchayats and their wards had some policy handles to mobilise people using Government schemes. Although schemes such as the Mahatma Gandhi National Rural Employment Guarantee Scheme and the *Swarnjayanti Gram Swarozgar Yojana* are tied to predetermined objectives given by the Central Government, they leave considerable scope for the panchayat's own work priorities.

The village development committees of each village assembly were able to select beneficiaries for distribution of subsidised inputs for the primary sector on the basis of the number of panchayat-wise or ward-wise beneficiaries specified by line departments such as the Agriculture Department and the Animal Resources Development Department (chapter 5, section 5.2.2). The committees were able to identify projects in the Action Plans for land improvement. Based on these Action Plans, the village panchayat prepared estimates and sent project proposals to the Block Development Office that approved the budget and sent the funds back to the village panchayat. The panchayat was able to identify locations for minor irrigation projects and their beneficiaries. Vaccination of animals against epidemics was also a function assigned to the village panchayat. In order to execute social forestry projects in wastelands and on the roadsides, the village panchayat was able to select sites for planting and execution of work through self-help groups or the village development committees.

In the functional domain pertaining to the primary sector, the scope of panchayat autonomy in carrying out planning exercises was limited. However, the village panchayat or the village assembly can select beneficiaries or locations for schemes according to their own priorities. All data items in Block 9 (land utilization) and Block 10 (livestock and poultry) are relevant for planning exercises for this functional domain. Data items 2.5 and 2.6 (on irrigation) in Block 2, data items 3.4 and 3.5 (on orchards and forest areas) in Block 3, and data item 4.20 (on veterinary sub-centre/dispensary) in Block 4 are also relevant for this functional domain.

The Raina village panchayat was also able to identify school-less hamlets (*mouzas*) for opening schools under alternative education schemes (*Sishu Siksha Karmasuchi* and *Madhyamik Siksha Karmasuchi*) and to send proposals to the Block-level committee (chapter 5, section 5.2.2). Panchayati raj institutions in West Bengal took the initiative under these alternative school education schemes. Providing adult and non-formal education through adult high schools and the Continuing Education Centres as well as the establishment of libraries were duties assigned to the village panchayats. For the purpose of planning in the functional domain of education, all data items in Block 8 (education), data item 2.9 (on adult education) in Block 2, and data items 4.6 to 4.19, 4.36 to 4.38 and 4.49 (on distance from the nearest education facilities) in Block 4 are relevant.

As noted in chapter 5 (section 5.2.2), the village panchayat was assigned a wide variety of functions with regard to subject 23 (health and sanitation, including hospitals, primary health centres and dispensaries), and subject 25 (women and child development). The village panchayat maintained and supervised sub-centres of the primary health centre. It organised self-help groups of women and involved these in monitoring community health. Disease surveillance to pre-empt outbreak of epidemics and preventive measures against the spread of communicable diseases were also functions assigned to it. The village panchayat worked with the Health Department to implement programmes under the National Rural Health Mission. The coordination of the Integrated Child Development Services activities and construction of its centres were additional functions. It can assist couples in family planning with regard to subject 24 (family welfare). Village panchayats in West Bengal had taken initiatives for the convergence of public health activities through the monthly "Fourth Saturday meeting" at the panchayat office with the Integrated Child Development Services supervisor, the Auxiliary Nurse Midwife, and health supervisor, representatives of self-help groups, and panchayat officials (chapter 3, section 3.5). The meeting reviewed the performance of different departments in the delivery of public health services (immunisation, ante- and post-natal services, registration of births and deaths, nutritional status of children, and water supply and sanitation). The meeting "encourages the panchayati raj institutions (PRIs) to chalk out their action plan for improvement with local interventions."[41] Therefore, all data items in Block 5 (demographic information), Block 6 (morbidity, disability, and family planning), and Block 7 (health manpower) are relevant to planning exercises for the functional domain pertaining to health and child development. Data item 2.14 in Block 2, data item 3.8 in Block 3, data items 4.21 to 4.28 (on distance from the nearest medical facilities), and 4.45 in Block 4, data item 14.6 in Block 14, and data items 15.25 to 15.27 in Block 15 are also relevant to this functional domain.

As stated in chapter 5, village panchayats in West Bengal were the direct implementing agency for Government schemes, such as *Sampoorna Grameen Rozgar Yojana (SGRY)*, Mahatma Gandhi National Rural Employment Guarantee Scheme (MGNREGS), *Indira Awaas Yojana* (IAY), Indira Gandhi National Old Age Pension Scheme (IGNOAPS), Provident Fund for Landless Agricultural Labourers (PROFLAL), National Family Benefit Scheme (NFBS), *Kishori Shakti Yojana,* and the *Balika Samriddhi Yojana.* Under each of these schemes, the village panchayats received funds directly from Government agencies. A village panchayat can identify projects in its area to be taken up under the MGNREGS and can prepare a development plan, considering the recommendations of the village council, and the village assembly meetings. In this respect, the MGNREGS leaves some scope for the priorities of each village panchayat. In addition the village panchayat bodies in West Bengal were able to mobilise people utilising self-help groups under the *Swarnjayanti Gram Swarozgar Yojana* (SGSY). The convergence of SGSY with MGNREGS was also pursued in West Bengal by seeking assistance of self-help groups for the MGNREGS.[42] The village panchayat also selected beneficiaries for the *Antyodaya* and *Annapurna* schemes with regard to subject 28 "public distribution system" of Schedule XI. Thus, all data items in Block 5 "demographic information," especially data items 5.3 to 5.5, Block 12 "employment status," and Block 14 "other social indicators," especially data items 14.1 to 14.2 and 14.5 are relevant to planning exercises for the functional domain pertaining to poverty alleviation and social welfare. Data item 3.7 (on

[41] Panchayats and Rural Development Department, Government of West Bengal (2007, p. 49).
[42] Panchayats and Rural Development Department, Government of West Bengal (2009a, pp. 95–7).

house structures) in Block 3 and data item 2.8 (on self-help groups) in Block 2 are also relevant to this functional domain. Data items 4.36 to 4.39 and data items 6.3 to 6.7 may also be related to social welfare. Data items 4.31 and 11.1 are relevant to the public distribution system. Block 13 "migration" is usable for multiple purposes.

The Raina village panchayat helped construct wells, tanks, tubewells (ordinary handpumps) with regard to subject 11 (drinking water) of Schedule XI. It also issued a certificate on the electrification of hamlets with regard to subject 14 (rural electrification). Maintenance of community assets such as public tanks, *ghats*, public channels, reservoirs, wells, streets, drains, culverts, lamp posts, etc. was also assigned to it in view of subject 29 (maintenance of community assets). Creation of durable assets and strengthening the livelihood resource base of the rural poor were important objectives of the MGNREGS. The principle of community ownership and maintenance is applied for such assets. Therefore, the village panchayat was expected to identify such projects in its area and prepare a development plan. In this way, the village panchayat had autonomy in creation of community assets under the MGNREGS. Data items 2.1, 2.2, 2.4 to 2.6, 2.12, 2.13, and 2.15 in Block 2 (availability of some basic facilities), data item 3.6 in Block 3 (village infrastructure), and data items 4.3 to 4.5 in Block 4 are relevant to planning exercises in the functional domain of infrastructure.

With regard to subject 8 (small-scale industries), the village panchayat can facilitate group formation for khadi, village, and cottage industries and identify needs for skill development training. However, we could not find any specific role of the Raina village panchayat in respect to this functional domain. It can also manage local markets (*haats/bazaars*) transferred to the panchayat's jurisdiction. It can set up and regulate local markets, and it can hold and regulate fairs (*melas*). Block 15 (industries and business), Block 11 (number of storage and marketing outlets), and data item 12.2 (on self employed in non-agriculture sector) in Block 12 can be used for planning for the functional domain of industry and commerce.

8.4 VILLAGE-LEVEL DATA SOURCES TO SUPPLEMENT THE VILLAGE SCHEDULE ON BASIC STATISTICS IN PLANNING EXERCISES

As shown in Figure 1.1 (chapter 1), there is a set of data sources in the village parallel to most data items in the Village Schedule. Therefore, the data recordist is requested to compile as much data as possible from the village-level records.[43] However, the village dataset is used as more than documentary evidence for the Village Schedule. For local-level planning, the village panchayats (and village councils) have to depend on village-level data sources for supplementary data not reflected in the Village Schedule. Some of these supplementary data are discussed below.

8.4.1 Supplementary Data on Current and Past Performance of a Panchayat and its Satellite Agencies

The village panchayat (including the village council) requires data on its current and past performance in its functional domain. For the planning exercises, the village panchayat (including the village council) needs to supplement the Village Schedule data with data on the current status and history of performance of a particular village panchayat and its satellite agencies. The Village Schedule does not contain data on performance of the village panchayat and satellite agencies, which we have discussed in section 5.2 of chapter 5. Without data on the current and past performance of the village panchayat and satellite agencies working in its functional domain, the village panchayat (including the village council) cannot assess progress, shortfalls, and gaps in output in implementing previous plans. Without this performance data, the village panchayat (including the village council) will not only be unable to prepare plans for the future, but also not be able to monitor the execution ("output") of the previous plan.

In chapter 5, we have discussed data on the current status of performance of a particular village panchayat and its satellite agencies working in the panchayat's functional domain. In fact, many records and registers are documented as a part of functions performed by village-level functionaries and these describe their functional domain. These data sources have been described in section 4.1 of chapter 4 as "registers and records collected and maintained by the village panchayat" and "registers and records collected and maintained by other village-level agencies." Work done by the village panchayat and its satellite agencies and assets created through that work are documented in these records and registers. For example, the Raina village panchayat had a "works register" to keep track of public works done by the panchayat under various schemes. The Panchayat Acts in both States (Section 8 of the Bombay Village Panchayats Act, 1958, and Section 18 of the West Bengal Panchayati Raj Act, 1973) require the village panchayat to

---

[43] Central Statistics Office (2014, p. 125, 131).

prepare for the village council a report showing any work and activities done under different projects, programmes, or schemes.

In addition to the registers on their work and assets, many lists of beneficiaries – IAY, *Annapurna Anna Yojana, Paani Parota Yojana*, MGNREGS register and records at the primary health centre (and its sub-centres) – are generated in the panchayats' functional domain and their satellite agencies. Village-wide aggregate data (statistics) can be produced from these lists of beneficiaries to work out key indicators for the planning exercise.[44] A retrospective review of their functional domain is also required of the village panchayat (and village wards) in order to have a long-term vision for planning exercises. For the retrospective review, a data archive on the panchayat's functional domain is necessary. Activity Mapping in West Bengal, recognising the need for such a data archive, asks for the following functions to be assigned to the village panchayat with regard to subject 20 (libraries) of Schedule XI:

> Sending copies of guidelines and booklets for all development programs, Annual Report, Budget, Annual Plan of GP, and information on social issues to Rural Library or Community Library cum Information Centre (CLIC) for general information of public.

Needless to say a copy of the Village Schedules retained with the village panchayat may also be stored as a "permanent document for every village" every year in order to highlight the significant features of development in chronological order.[45]

8.4.2 Supplementary Data to Re-Examine the Village Panchayat's Unrecorded Object Domain

We often find unrecorded elements in the object domain of the panchayat and its satellite agencies outside the coverage of their administrative registers and records. In chapter 2 (section 2.2.2) we discussed, for example, unrecorded eligible households excluded from the Below Poverty Line list and unregistered children outside the coverage of the Civil Registration System. The data recordist of the Village Schedule on Basic Statistics is requested to compile as much data from these records and registers as possible. However, there may also be an unrecorded domain outside the coverage of the Village Schedule data. The accuracy of the Village Schedule's documentary evidence

[44] Planning Commission (2008, p. 129) mentions the "summary of processes followed for getting the village/ward-level wish-lists prepared."
[45] Central Statistics Office (2014, p. 148).

was compromised in this regard. The village panchayats (including village wards) may need data or information on the unrecorded object domain of the panchayat's functioning and its satellite agencies so as to ascertain unknown administrative needs for planning exercises.

In order to identify unrecorded areas in the functions of the panchayat and its satellite agencies, a cross-check is sometimes possible between data from the Village Schedule and other data or information (chapter 6). For example, both Warwat Khanderao and Raina village panchayats cross-checked their respective Below Poverty Line lists by conducting an independent house-to-house re-survey. In order to explore the possible object domain outside the coverage of birth registration in the Civil Registration System, the panchayat can cross-check the Civil Registration System data with other administrative records such as the Integrated Child Development Services child registers and records at the primary health centre.

The *Basic Statistics* report's recommendation to establish formal data-sharing mechanisms between the panchayat and different agencies working in the panchayat area saves not only on the cost of additional data collection, but also helps in cross-checking the quality of different data sources. Some types of information on the village community are common knowledge to most villagers.[46] In those cases, such common knowledge among villagers can be a reference point for the purpose of cross-checking. In both Warwat Khanderao and Raina village panchayats, initial doubts about the Below Poverty Line list were raised on the basis of the peoples' common knowledge. Thus, common knowledge is a significant source of information, even though assessments based on it may not be necessarily conclusive.

8.4.3 Supplementary Data on Public Finances of Village Panchayat

As mentioned in chapter 2, the Village Schedule on Basic Statistics focuses on Data Needs III (data required for micro-level planning and its implementation). However, the planning exercise is constrained by budgetary considerations. Therefore, it is debatable whether data items on the financial status of the village panchayat are to be included in the Village Schedule or not. At present the Village Schedule does not include data items on the panchayat's finances so that it has to be supplemented with financial data about the village panchayat. For the planning exercise of a village panchayat financial

---

[46] *Ibid.*, pp. 24–5, 27.

data on all schemes and programmes, including those carried out by outside agencies within the panchayat's functional domain, are also required.[47]

8.4.4 Unit-level Information for the Village Panchayat's Planning Exercise

The village panchayat (including village wards) requires unit-level information for its planning exercise since it is the closest administrative institution to people living in villages. While aggregate data with a macroscopic view is more often required for administrative units at the district than at the village level, unit-level data is more often required for the village level than for the district level. The Village Schedule on Basic Statistics is used to compile aggregate data, and cannot include full details of unit-level information or lists of households, persons, events, facilities or establishments, or of plots or areas.

A list of every concerned unit is the direct base of aggregate data (statistics). However, a list has more uses. A list of every unit is more flexible for multiple uses in planning exercises than the already aggregated data (statistics) produced from such a list. The village panchayat can retrieve a particular group of units from the list for its planning exercise. Disaggregated numbers on the group can also be derived from the list. Among other things, a priority list can also be made from the list.

Preparing a priority list of beneficiaries, a priority list of facilities to be created, a priority list of schemes to be implemented is, in practice, an integral part of the micro-level planning exercise. We have seen that in West Bengal most of the beneficiaries of Government schemes were selected by the village development committees. In this process, unit-level information is indispensable for the village panchayat and the village development committees to select beneficiaries; the State departments require only approximate figures to estimate the number of beneficiaries and the aggregate allocation of benefits. Without an exhaustive check list of eligible persons or households, the selection of beneficiaries cannot be done objectively and the subsidised inputs cannot properly reach each beneficiary. The possibility for establishing a People's List has already been discussed in chapter 6 (section 6.6). The People's List is a list of every unit (resident) which can also be used in people-oriented micro-level planning exercises.

---

[47] Planning Commission (2008b, p. 78). Therefore, the Planning Commission (*ibid.* p. 77) suggests that the overall responsibility of mapping budgets and conveying them to every panchayat belongs to the District Planning Committees and the State Government.

Table 8.1 *Percentage of all villages in India served by various amenities*

	Percentage of total inhabited villages	
Amenity provided	1981	1991
Education	90.44	93.27
Medical	17.4	31.01
Drinking water	100	100
Post and telegraph	28.57	29.63
Market (*haat*)	10.92	10.55
Communication	47.32	64.44
Pucca road	37.44	42.23
Power supply	67.08	95.76

Note: These figures are compiled from Census 1981 and 1991.
Source: Planning Commission (2007, p. 239).

Further, the village panchayat often requires unit-level information on the location, quality and maintenance of village facilities. It cannot be content with information on the existence (or non-existence) or total number of village facilities as recorded in data items in the Village Schedule, Block 2 (availability of some basic facilities), Block 3 (village infrastructure), and Block 4 (distance from the nearest facility). Obviously, the information on the existence (or non-existence) of facilities is for use in upper-level administrative units such as the Block, district, or the State. This data is certainly very useful, for instance, to figure out district-wise indicators such as the percentage of villages served by each facility in their jurisdiction, as illustrated in Table 8.1. These indicators show performance across different types of amenities provided by upper-level administrative units. These indicators assess progress, shortfalls, and gaps in the performance of the upper-level administrative units. However, the utility of the information on the existence (or non-existence) of these facilities is obviously not much for village panchayats. Information on its facilities needs to be more detailed. For example, information on "major source of drinking water for the village (tap- 1, tubewell/handpump- 2, well- 3, reserved tank for drinking water- 4, any other source- 9)" in data item 2.4 in Block 2 may not be very useful for the Warwat Khanderao village panchayat which keeps a panchayat register for *Item no. 10 Tax collection receipt book* with a precise description of two 18,000-litre water tanks, a tubewell and a 5000-litre tank filled using this tubewell.

The development plan and the list of possible works to be taken up under the

MGNREGS require information on existing village infrastructure, such as water tanks, watershed protection, irrigation facilities, water bodies, status of land, drainage, and rural roads. However, the required type of information has to be unit-level data on the location, quality, and maintenance of each facility.

In West Bengal the Core Network Plan consisting of every road and road to be constructed to eligible unconnected habitations under the *Pradhan Mantri Gram Sadak Yojana* has been ported on GIS-based maps for each Block.[48]

Some unit-level information may be common knowledge among the village council members, in which case the recording of such units will be unnecessary paperwork. However, unit-level information regarding a large number of units such as population, households, houses, etc. is often beyond the common knowledge of villagers even in the Warwat Khanderao village panchayat and the Bidyanidhi village ward with a population of 1479 and 719 respectively (Census of India 2011). Even though unit-level information is required for the village panchayat and ward levels' planning exercise, this does not mean that aggregate data are of no use. Among other things, the Village Schedule data is useful for making comparisons with other villages.

8.5 Possible Use of Village Schedule on Basic Statistics in the District-Level Planning Exercise

The Maharashtra Government has traditionally focused on the district as a basic unit of planning and development. In fact, many functions are assigned to the district panchayats in Schedule I of the Maharashtra Zilla Parishad and Panchayat Samiti Act, 1961 (Section 101). In West Bengal, although the main focus of development activities is on the village panchayat level, many functions are assigned to the district panchayats in Activity Mapping. Accordingly, the Village Schedule on Basic Statistics may have a broad utility at the district level in both States.

However, in order to carry out the planning exercises, the District Planning Committees and the district panchayats also need information from the village-level data sources to supplement the Village Schedule data. This can be accomplished in the following three ways:

[48] For GIS based thematic mapping for Rural Roads, see www.trendswestbengal.org/pmgsy.

Table 8.2 *Population size of administrative units*

District level	
Buldhana	2,586,258
Bardhaman	7,717,563
Block level	
Sangrampur	137,092
Raina - I	180,952
Village panchayat level	
Warwat Khanderao	1479
Raina	15569
Sub-panchayat level	
Bidyanidhi	719

Source: Census of India 2011.

1. Both bodies can supplement the Village Schedule data with data on the past and current status of performance of the village panchayats and their satellite agencies.[49] For the purpose of preparing plans, the District Planning Committees and the district panchayats can create key indicators out of registers and records maintained by the village panchayats and their satellite agencies. Indeed, the *Manual for Integrated District Planning* states that "key indicators should be identified for nodal reporting institutions (*anganwadis*, public health centres, and primary schools) from their data registers, for highlighting and upward transmission."[50]

There are two alternative channels for the District Planning Committees and district panchayats to gain access to data sources in all the villages in their jurisdiction: direct access to village-level data sources, and indirect access to them through district- or Block-level agencies. The District Planning Committees and district panchayats can approach district-level agencies that have lines of reporting mechanisms from the village-level, instead of using direct access to village-level data sources. Many district-level agencies such as the District Collector, the District

---

[49] As mentioned in chapter 1, this enquiry is methodologically limited to village-level data sources. Some data used for medium- and large-scale projects of the panchayati raj institutions are beyond its scope because such data can be collected or recorded directly by an upper-tier institution, independently of the villages. Therefore, data on the overall performance of district panchayat are beyond the scope of this book.

[50] Planning Commission (2008b, p. 128).

Programme Officer (in charge of the Integrated Child Development Services), the District Health Officer, the District Project Office (along with the District Information System for Education), and the District Registrar have lines of reporting mechanisms.[51] However, any delay in upward data transmission can be due to a problem with the official reporting system in rural India.[52] Thus, the choice of the channel for the District Planning Committees and the district panchayats for accessing the village-level data sources will depend on the prevailing situation with regard to data reporting.[53]

2. In order to reveal the unrecorded areas among the village panchayat's functions, the District Planning Committees and district panchayats can cross-check the Village Schedule data with other data or information. They can aggregate the Village Schedule data in their jurisdiction and compare it with other aggregates or estimates obtained from different agencies working in the functional domain of the village panchayats. The District Planning Committees and district panchayats can also use the sampling method to cross-check the Village Schedule data. For such a cross-check, both bodies need data-sharing with other agencies.

3. The District Planning Committees and district panchayats can supplement the Village Schedule data with data on public finance of all the village panchayats in the jurisdiction of the district panchayat. For the purpose of planning exercises, the District Planning Committees and district panchayats can work out the district-level aggregate data of every village panchayat's finances. The preference for direct or indirect access to village-level data on finances again depends on the prevailing situation of data reporting. The Thirteenth Central Finance Commission argues that "accurate data on the financial performance of local bodies are best obtained from accounts of the local bodies themselves, apart from the budget documents of the State Governments."[54]

[51] In a sense, the Village Schedule on Basic Statistics is an effort to establish another information channel to transmit village-level data directly to the District Statistical Office.

[52] National Statistical Commission (2001, para. 9.3.30). The Commission's report observes, "Even in States that have achieved high levels of registration, there is a considerable delay in reporting of statistics from the local registrars, eventually delaying the compilation of vital statistics at the State and National levels. A lot of paperwork required and pending at the level of the Registrar is one of the major reasons for the delay in submission of returns."

[53] Isaac and Franke (2000, p. 110) note: "in many places the secondary data collected from the field offices did not tally with the published statistics of the Block and district levels."

[54] Thirteenth Finance Commission (2009, p. 168).

For the planning exercise, financial data on all schemes and programmes including those carried out by outside agencies in the villages within the panchayati raj institutions functional domain will be also be required by the District Planning Committees and district panchayats.[55] As mentioned in chapter 7 (section 7.5), various documents such as the State budget documents and Central Government documents are again required for detailed information.

Unit-level information is sometimes important for the planning exercise even at the district level. However, the District Planning Committees and district panchayats are not the institutions closest to people living in villages. Their jurisdiction covers a large area and large populations compared to the village panchayats' jurisdiction. Thus, unlike the village panchayats (and village wards), the District Planning Committees and district panchayats need aggregated data (statistics) with a macroscopic view for the "envisioning" exercise.

[55] Planning Commission (2008b, p. 78).

Chapter 9

CONCLUSION

This study describes a new statistical domain in rural India that has emerged in the wake of the decentralization process initiated by the Seventy-third Amendment to the Indian Constitution. Most of the data generated and used by village panchayats was the by-product of their administrative requirements or of other satellite agencies of the State Government. However, there has been no intensive discussion on the quality and usefulness of these data sources available in the village. This study has examined these data sources at the village panchayat level in the light of the needs generated by the Seventy-third Amendment. We identified three categories of data needs:

   I data required for self-governance, of which data required for managing the transition to full-scope Constitutional devolution are a special component;

  II data required for matters of public finance; and

  III data required for micro-level planning for economic development and social justice, and its implementation.

Out of these three categories of data, Data Needs I and II are the core data requirements of the panchayats. The emerging statistical domain, among other things, is related to this core data requirement. It is emerging precisely in order to serve the functional domain that is now devolved to the village panchayats. Democratic self-governance within the functional domain drives the data requirements of village panchayats since the Seventy-third Amendment. Micro-level planning by village panchayats—a pre-requisite of advanced democratic decentralisation—is only possible if they have robust democratic self-governance over their functional domain. In this regard, the *Basic Statistics on Local Level Development* report identified Data Needs III on the basis of its terms of reference "for use in micro-level planning of various developmental programmes."

In most States and Union Territories the progress in Activity Mapping exercises (the delineation of functions of the different tiers of local governments under a given subject matter) has been very slow.[1] At present it is a major bottleneck in the decentralisation process in rural India.[2] Without a clearly delineated functional domain of the panchayat, one cannot discuss its corresponding statistical domain. This book has had to devote many pages to this complicated issue.

The *Basic Statistics on Local Level Development* report recommends that the Village Schedule compile village-level data precisely because the report found that in almost all States and Union Territories various kinds of data are regularly collected by village-level functionaries and maintained in their records or registers. In fact, many village-level functionaries, such as panchayat officials, revenue officials, Integrated Child Development Services (*anganwadi*) workers, Auxiliary Nurse Midwives, Accredited Social Health Activists, health supervisors, technical assistants of the Mahatma Gandhi National Rural Employment Guarantee Scheme, and school teachers are working in the panchayat's functional domain. However, the dataset used in the village has more than documentary value for the Village Schedule. Most panchayat-level data sources found in parallel to data items of the Village Schedule are nothing other than administrative records and registers documented by village-level functionaries for their operational use.

Through our study of this new statistical domain, we can begin building a panchayat-level database from the bottom upwards. We found that the village panchayat has the potential to develop high-quality databases to meet the core data requirements for democratic self-governance. This study has reached, albeit through a different approach, the same conclusion as the *Basic Statistics on Local Level Development* report, i.e., that the village panchayat can "consolidate, maintain and own village-level data" in this era of democratic decentralisation. It can own a record-based system of statistical databases,[3] along with the official Census data. Administrative records and registers generated by village-level functionaries are the basic dataset for the system because this dataset is documented for direct use in the village panchayat's functional domain (as described in chapter 5). What is more, when these datasets are updated regularly, it is impossible to maintain them without the direct involvement of village-level functionaries. Therefore, the core system of statistical databases is an extension of the village-level administrative records system.

[1] Second Administrative Reforms Commission (2007), p. 45.
[2] Oommen (2008), p. 7.
[3] Sridhar (2013). See also United Nations Economic Commission for Europe (2007).

The *Basic Statistics on Local Level Development* report is a framework to summarise such village-level secondary data along with subjective assessments by knowledgeable persons on matters of common knowledge among villagers. We should distinguish summary data in the Village Schedule from the above-mentioned record-based system of statistical databases. The latter provides more than documentary evidence for the former. The record-based system of statistical databases is to be utilised for democratic self-governance over the panchayat's functional domain, regardless of whether it is summarised in the Village Schedule for planning exercises at the village panchayat and district levels. The first priority is to strengthen the village-level administrative records system. Therefore, this enquiry focused on the administrative records and registers in a village.

In order to maintain such a record-based system of statistical databases, however, a data-sharing mechanism between the village panchayat and other village-level agencies working in the former's functional domain is indispensable. The village panchayat has the potential to coordinate such a data-sharing mechanism. We reaffirm the recommendation made by the *Basic Statistics on Local Level Development* report: "Efforts should be made to ensure coordination of activities among all these potential sources of regular information at the Panchayat level ensuring that quality of data so gathered is maintained."[4] Based on such coordination, a village panchayat can own a database available at its office or can have access to databases through its satellite agencies. A good example of this was the sharing of data in West Bengal at the Fourth Saturday Meeting comprising the village panchayat, Integrated Child Development Services (*anganwadi*) centre, and the Block Health Centre. Indeed, as we saw in our case study, the Raina village panchayat had the authority to coordinate such satellite agencies to maintain the data-sharing mechanism, which enabled it to produce a booklet (*Protibedon*) of panchayat-level datasets and distribute it to village council members. However, most village panchayats (as our Maharashtra example showed) have to overcome the division of powers between the panchayat and line departments in order to create such a data-sharing mechanism.

In chapter 6 (section 6.6), we demonstrated a possible data-sharing mechanism to construct a village-level population list (People's List). We suggested a way of generating a village-level population list from the bottom upwards. Although a top-down approach by the Central Government to provide such

---

[4] Central Statistical Organisation (2006), p.17.

lists through the National Population Register or the Socio-Economic and Caste Census, 2011, is in progress, this book suggests an alternative approach that begins bottom upwards to construct the population list.

The Below Poverty Line Census was conducted for direct use in the village panchayats' functional domain, for instance, for the purpose of household identification. Therefore, the village panchayats' core system of statistical databases needs to be combined with the Below Poverty Line Census. The Census of India (including population enumeration data, house-listing and housing data, and the village level amenities data) is indisputably a benchmark for producing panchayat-level statistical data. Data sharing by the village panchayat with Central or State Governments in the form of other official censuses such as the Agricultural Census and the Economic Census remains unrealised at present. This will remain an issue of discussion in the future.

The data-sharing mechanism between the village panchayat and other agencies working in its functional domain serves not only the purpose of saving costs of additional data collection, but also helps in cross-checking the reliability of different data sources. The data-sharing and data triangulation mechanisms help improve the quality and validation of data from different sources. Cross-checking different data sources also enables the village panchayat to strengthen self-governance by examining unrecorded areas of administration under village-level functionaries.

Some types of information on a village are common knowledge to most residents of that village. Therefore, this common knowledge can be a reference point for ascertaining the quality of village-level data. In fact, village residents in both Warwat Khanderao and Raina village panchayats initially questioned the Below Poverty Line lists generated from the Below Poverty Line Census 2002 (the Rural Household Survey in West Bengal). The micro-level knowledge of villagers in both village panchayats brought to light the fact that some poor households had been excluded from the lists. It is a very significant step in the decentralisation process after the Seventy-third Amendment that village panchayats have independently conducted house-to-house re-surveys to revise the Below Poverty Line lists. This occurrence shows that village panchayats can identify discrepancies in data from surveys conducted by other organisations. The arguments between the village panchayat and other organisations about the accuracy of village-level Below Poverty Line lists suggest that the quality of village-level data is a matter of concern to the people of a village, and is indicative of the village panchayat's ability to construct its own quality databases.

The quality of village-level data sources pertaining to the panchayat's functional domain depends on how much use the village panchayat and its satellite agencies make of these data sources. So, for example, disputes arose over the accuracy of the Below Poverty Line lists because these lists are actually used in village administration. At the same time, as in Warwat Khanderao, the quality of the birth registers in the Civil Registration System can be questioned because birth certificates are not required, for example, for school admissions. The more data are functional and used, the more alert the agency accountable for their data quality is. That is why this enquiry focused on the use of data sources.

Since village panchayats (and sub-panchayat bodies such as village assemblies in West Bengal) are the administrative institutions closest to the people in villages, unit-level information on village society is crucial. Unit-level records and registers are ready for aggregation, but are primarily used for the identification and selection of beneficiaries of public policies and for delivery of services. The strengthening of the village panchayat's self-governance will enhance the utility of unit-level records and registers. As in the disputes over the accuracy of the village-level Below Poverty Line list, the villagers' micro-level knowledge is reliable. In this way, the village panchayat and sub-panchayat bodies are the institutions best suited to correct micro-level discrepancies in administrative records and registers. This is precisely an advantage of the bottom-up approach to these databases against the top-down approaches by upper levels of government. Policy decisions will have to be taken, however, with regard to the persons and functionaries to whom access is granted to unit-level data for administrative purposes.

After the Seventy-third Amendment, as discussed in chapter 6, the requirement for data-recording principles at the village-level has shifted to a new type of documentation that is focused on the place of usual residence of the people concerned. The new type of records has to be organised entirely in relation to residents of the panchayat area for the sake of democratic self-governance.

We found some serious shortcomings in the panchayats' financial data, data on community assets in the panchayat area, on land utilisation and agrarian relations, on migration, on employment, and on industry and commerce. A comprehensive systemic reform needs to be considered in order to overcome these shortcomings in the existing administrative records systems.

The National Statistical Commission has drawn attention to "the foundation on which the entire edifice of Administrative Statistical System was built," and denounced the move to "divert attention from the solution of the real systemic problem of the decentralised Indian Statistical System."[5] Indeed, securing the village panchayat-level database from the bottom up is a problem of decentralisation.

As this enquiry is methodologically limited to village-level data sources, some data used for medium- and large-scale projects at the Block and district levels are beyond the scope of this study. We could not sufficiently discuss panchayat databases above the level of the village panchayat, even though we acknowledge that such databases at tiers above the village have significant implications for local self-government. As this study primarily covers the period from April 2005 to March 2011, we also have not discussed the details of issues regarding the National Population Register and the Socio-Economic and Caste Census, 2011. This study also did not discuss village panchayat-level databases in relation to the geographical information systems, which have been making remarkable progress. However, this book aims to help understand the kinds of village panchayat-level statistical databases that address the emerging statistical domain in India.

In this book we examined the question of the data required by institutions of self-government at the village level, that is, village panchayats, to fulfil their Constitutional duties. We did so by constructing what may be called an anticipatory list of the data needs of the village panchayat derived from the list of functions specified by the Seventy-third Amendment to the Constitution. We then examined all the sources of data that existed at the village in two village panchayats, one each in West Bengal and Maharashtra, in which we conducted detailed case studies. Our study was thus based on an examination of secondary data on (and post-Independence discussion of) panchayats and their data needs, and on our examination of village-level registers and primary village-level household data. We explored the ways

---

[5] National Statistical Commission (2001, paras 14.3.10, 14.3.17). This insight was provided by the Commission (*ibid.*, para. 14.3.20) in the context of a critical review of the Modernisation Project proposed by the then Department of Statistics. The Commission stated: "the project will have to shift its focus from expansion of sample surveys to improvement of the systemic issues of the Administrative Statistical System."

in which village panchayats can build a system of village-based statistical databases, and suggested ways of generating and developing such databases from the grassroots upwards.

There is, of course, much research that remains to be done in the field: we need, for instance, detailed studies of issues that emerge from top-down approaches to building village panchayat-level databases using techniques of small area estimation along with data from sources such as the National Population Register and the Socio-Economic and Caste Census of 2011. Nevertheless, we hope that this book contributes in a small way to the effort to build the administrative infrastructure for local self-government that was set in motion after the statutory establishment of panchayati raj in rural India.

FUNCTIONS OF VILLAGE PANCHAYAT

SUBJECTS OF ACTIVITIES OF VILLAGE PANCHAYAT,
BOMBAY VILLAGE PANCHAYAT ACT, 1958

Agriculture

1. Making arrangement for cooperative management of lands and other resources in village; organisation of collective cooperative farming
2. Improvement of agriculture (including provision of implements and stores) and establishment of model agricultural farms
3. Bringing under cultivation waste and fallow lands vested by Government in the panchayats
4. Reclamation of wasteland and bringing wastelands under cultivation with the prior permission of the State Government
5. Establishment and maintenance of nurseries for production of improved seeds and encouraging their use
6. Crop experiments
7. Crop protection
8. Ensuring conservation of manurial resources; preparing compost and sale of manure
9. Securing minimum standards of cultivation in the village with a view to increasing agricultural production
10. Assistance in the implementation of land reform schemes
11. Establishment of granaries

Animal Husbandry

12. Improvement of cattle and cattle breeding and general care of livestock

Forests

13. Raising, preservation, improvement and regulation of the use of village forests and grazing lands, including lands assigned under section 28 of the Indian Forests Act, 1927

Social Welfare

14. Relief of the crippled, destitute and the sick
15. Promotion of social and moral welfare of the village, including promotion of prohibition, the removal of untouchability, amelioration of the condition of backward classes, eradication of corruption, and the discouragement of gambling and useless litigation
16. Women's and Children's organisation and welfare.

Education

17. Spread of education
18. Other educational and cultural objects
18-A. (Maintenance and Repairs of Primary School Buildings) vesting for the time being in the district committee (*zilla parishad*)
19. Provision of equipment and playgrounds for schools
20. Adult literacy centres, libraries and reading rooms
21. Rural Insurance

Medicine and Public Health

22. Providing medical relief
23. Maternity and child welfare
24. Preservation and improvement of public health
25. Taking of measures to prevent outbreak, spread or recurrence of any infectious disease
26. Encouragement of human and animal vaccination
27. Regulation by licensing or otherwise of tea, coffee and milk shops
28. Construction and maintenance or control of slaughterhouses
29. Cleansing of public roads, drains, *bunds*, tanks, and wells (other than tanks and wells used for irrigation), and other public places or works
30. Reclaiming of unhealthy localities
31. Removal of rubbish heaps, jungles, growth, prickly pears, filling in of disused wells, insanitary ponds, pools, ditches, pits or hollows, prevention of water-logging in irrigated areas and other improvements in sanitary conditions
32. Construction and maintenance of public latrines
33. Sanitation, conservation, prevention and abatement of nuisance and disposal of unclaimed corpses and animal carcasses
34. * * * *1
35. Excavation, cleansing and maintenance of ponds for supply of water to animals.
36. Management and control of bathing or washing *ghats* which are not managed by any authority.

1 Entry 34 was deleted in 1997.

37. Provision, maintenance and regulation of burning and burial grounds

Building and Communications

38. Maintenance and regulation of the use of public buildings, tanks and wells (other than tanks and wells used for irrigation) vesting in or under the control of the panchayats.
39. Removal of obstructions and projections in public streets or places and in sites, not being private property, which are open to the public, whether such sites are vested in the panchayat or belong to Government (removal of unauthorised cultivation of any crop on any grazing land or any other land not being private property)
40. Construction, maintenance and repair of public roads, drains, *bunds* and bridges: provided that, if the roads, drains, *bunds*, and bridges vest in any other public authority such works shall not be undertaken without the consent of the authority
41. Planting of trees along roads, in marketplaces and other public places and their maintenance and preservation
42. Provision and maintenance of playgrounds, public parks, and camping grounds
43. Construction and maintenance of *dharmasalas*
44. Extension of village sites and regulation of buildings in accordance with such principles as may be prescribed
45. Lighting of the village

Irrigation

46. Minor irrigation

Industries and Cottage Industries

47. Promotion, improvement and encouragement of cottage and village industries

Cooperation

48. Organisation of credit societies and multi-purpose cooperative societies
49. Promotion of cooperative farming.

Self-Defence and Village Defence

50. Watch and ward of the village: provided that the cost of watch and ward shall be levied and recovered by the panchayat from such person in the village, and in such manner, as may be prescribed
51. Village Volunteer Force and Defence Labour Bank

52. Rendering assistance in extinguishing fires and protecting life and property when fire occurs

53. Regulating, checking and abating of offensive or dangerous trades or practices

General Administration

54. Preparation, maintenance, and upkeep of panchayat records

55. Numbering of premises

56. Registration of births, deaths and marriages in such a manner and in such form as may be laid down by the Government by general or special order in this behalf

57. Collection of land revenue (when entrusted by the State Government under section 169)

58. Maintenance of village records relating to land revenue in such manner and in such form as may be prescribed from time to time by or under any law relating to land revenue

59. Preparation of plans for the development of the village

60. Drawing up of programmes for increasing the output of agriculture and non-agricultural produce in the village

61. Preparation of the statement showing requirement of supplies and finances needed for carrying out rural development schemes

62. Establishment, control and management of cattle pounds

63. Destruction of stray and ownerless dogs and pigs

64. Disposal of unclaimed cattle

65. Construction and maintenance of houses for the conservancy staff of the panchayat

66. Reporting to proper authorities village complaints which are not disposable by the panchayat

67. Making surveys

68. Acting as a channel through which assistance given by the Central or State Governments for any purpose may reach the village

69. Establishment, maintenance and regulation of fairs, pilgrimages and festivals

70. Establishment and maintenance of markets, provided no market shall be established without prior permission of the district panchayat.

71. Control of fairs, *bazaars*, tonga stands and car stands

72. Establishment and maintenance of warehouses

73. Establishment and maintenance of works or the provision of employment in time of scarcity.

73-A. Provision of employment to needy local persons seeking manual work under any scheme for employment guarantee undertaken or adopted by, or transferred to, the panchayat

74. Preparation of statistics of unemployment

75. Assistance to residents when any natural calamity occurs
76. Organising voluntary labour for community works and works for the uplift of the village
77. Opening fair price shops
78. Control of cattle stands, threshing floors, grazing grounds and community lands.
79. Securing [or continuing] postal facilities of experimental post offices in the village by providing for payment of non-refundable contribution to the Posts and Telegraphs Department, wherever necessary]

Illustrative Activity Mapping in West Bengal

The Panchayats and Rural Development Department worked out a format for Activity Mapping in West Bengal. The main features of the activities specified in the mapping format are given below:[2]

Item no.	Subject (as per Schedule XI)	Activities	Activities of district committees	Activities of Block-level committees	Activities of village panchayat
1.	Agriculture, including agricultural extension	1. Distribution of mini-kits, seeds, bio-fertilizer at subsidised price	1. Sub-allotment of mini-kits, seeds, bio-fertilizer (at subsidised price) to intermediate panchayat (*panchayat samiti* – PS) for distribution among farmers	1. Fix target for distribution of mini-kits, seeds, bio-fertilizer (at subsidised price) to village panchayats	1. Beneficiary selection for distribution of mini-kits, seeds, equipment at subsidised prices
			2. Distribution of agricultural equipment	2. Fix target for each PS for distribution of agricultural equipment	2. Monitor proper and timely distribution of agricultural equipment on the basis of technical possibilities and field situation
			3. Awareness campaign and wide publicity among farmers		3. Awareness campaign and wide publicity among farmers
			4. Management of agrifarm		4. Estimation of need-based requirement of seeds

[2] See Government of West Bengal (2005 and 2007).

(continued)

Item no.	Subject (as per Schedule XI)	Activities	Activities of district committees	Activities of Block-level committees	Activities of village panchayat
2.	Land improvement, implementation of land reforms, land consolidation and soil conservation	1. Watershed development programme/ *Hariyali* scheme covering soil conservation, irrigation afforestation, etc.			
		2. Distribution of vested lands to the landless		2. (i) Pre-distribution survey of undistributed agriland and preparation of a priority list of beneficiaries (ii) Distribution of *patta* to landless people	2. Identification of beneficiary for distribution of vested land
3.	Minor irrigation, water management and watershed development	1. Development of minor irrigation system		1. Seeking technical vetting of executive engineers through district council (ZP) for minor irrigation schemes beyond the competence of intermediate panchayat (PS) and joint supervision / monitoring of schemes	1. Identification of locations for projects and beneficiaries
		2. Construction of tanks and field channels			2. Construction of percolation tanks, field channels within the village panchayat
		3. Management of deep tubewells and cluster of shallow tubewells			3. Maintaining minor irrigation schemes, collecting water charges through user committee for new projects

(continued)

Item no.	Subject (as per Schedule XI)	Activities	Activities of district committees	Activities of Block-level committees	Activities of village panchayat
					handed over to PRIs
		4. Watershed development programme		4. Watershed development programme / *Hariyali* scheme	
4.	Animal husbandry, dairying and poultry	1. To identify beneficiaries of different animal husbandry, dairy and poultry schemes		1. Beneficiary selection for different schemes	
		2. Breed upgrading through distribution of improved variety of livestock	2. Distribution of improved variety of livestock to Blocks	2. Collection of improved variety of livestock from district farm and determining scale of distribution to panchayats	2. Distribution of improved variety of birds/small animals to farmers
			3. Rearing of birds and small animals: family scheme and individual scheme		3. Providing facility for hatching
		4. Vaccination programme	4. Drawing up action plan for vaccination programme for the district	4. Monitoring of the situation to prevent outbreak of epidemic	4. Vaccination of animals against epidemic
		5. Artificial insemination programme	5. Action plan for artificial insemination programme for the district	5. Monitoring of artificial insemination programme; identifying problem areas and covering gap	5. Execution of artificial insemination with the help of *Prani Bandhu* at fixed price
5.	Fisheries	1. Identification of beneficiaries, ponds, derelict, semi-derelict tanks		1. Approval of beneficiaries, ponds, open-cast pits, derelict / semi-derelict tanks for pisciculture	1. (i) Identification of beneficiaries and their ponds and open-cast pits (ii) Identification and selection of derelict/semi-derelict tanks

(continued)

Item no.	Subject (as per Schedule XI)	Activities	Activities of district committees	Activities of Block-level committees	Activities of village panchayat
		2. Organising training and awareness camps	2. Action plan for all sorts of training and awareness camps in consultation with the Asst. Director of Fisheries	2. Organisation of training and selection of training venue	2. Holding awareness camps
		3. Distribution of mini-kits	3. Allocation of funds and components for Blocks in kind	3. Credit access to fish farmers from financial institutions	3. Supply of lime and mini-kits
		4. Helping fish farmers to access credit from financial institutions		4. Excavation of tanks	4. Improvement of tanks for pisciculture
		5. Improvement of tanks for fish cultivation			
6.	Social forestry and farm forestry	1. To establish nurseries for supply of saplings and seedlings			1. To establish nurseries for supply of saplings and seedlings
		2. Execution of social forestry projects in wastelands and roadsides			2. Selection of sites for plantation and execution of the work through self-help groups / village development committees
		3. Establishing Progeny Nursery		3. Establishing Progeny Nursery for fruit-bearing trees	
7.	Minor forest produce	1. Maintenance of social forestry through self-help groups / village development committees for livelihood		1. Distribution of inputs for micro-enterprises like *sal*-leaf plate-making, saplings of fruit trees and providing assistance for income-generating activities	1. Maintenance of social forestry through self-help groups/village development committees

(continued)

Item no.	Subject (as per Schedule XI)	Activities	Activities of district committees	Activities of Block-level committees	Activities of village panchayat
		2. Distribution of sale proceeds to self-help groups / village development committees			2. From sale proceeds the panchayat will get a share to recoup actual expenditure. The balance amount will go to self-help groups/village development committees for livelihood
8.	Small-scale industries, including food processing	1. Development of small enterprises and entrepreneurs	1. Organisation of entrepreneur development programmes	1. Selection of trainees/venue for training programmes	1. Identification of micro-enterprise/entrepreneurs
		2. Skill development training programmes	2. Organising skill development training programme	2. Selection of entrepreneurs for training	
		3. Organising credit facility	3. Coordination between entrepreneurs and financial institutions for credit linkage	3. Developing microenterprise / self-enterprise with bank credit	
9.	Khadi, village and cottage industries	1. Identification of beneficiaries and forming groups	1. Action plan for development of microenterprise	1. Selection of trainees/venue for skill development training	1. Group formation and selection of activities programme
		2. To arrange training for skill development/ upgradation of artisans			2. Identification of training needs for skill development training and beneficiaries
		3. Motivation of artisans			3. Motivation of rural artisans
		4. To assist in accessing credit from financial institutions by artisans		4. Accessing credit from financial institutions	4. Organisation of awareness camps at the panchayat level

(continued)

Item no.	Subject (as per Schedule XI)	Activities	Activities of district committees	Activities of Block-level committees	Activities of village panchayat
10.	Rural housing	1. Beneficiary selection for housing schemes			1. Beneficiary selection in meetings of rural ward (*gram sansad*)
		2. Financial assistance to beneficiaries			2. Distribution of funds to individuals
		3. Monitoring and supervision		3. Monitoring and supervision	
11.	Drinking water	1. Identification of schemes, locations			1. Identification of schemes and locations
		2. Formulation of projects and schemes	2. Formulating major water supply schemes (piped water supply)	2. Selection of location and beneficiaries for piped water schemes in consultation with village panchayats	
		3. Technical approval of schemes	3. Technical approval of schemes beyond the competence of Block-level committees	3. Seeking technical approval from district panchayat for projects beyond the competence of Block-level committees	
		4. Execution of schemes	4. Execution of schemes beyond the competence of Block-level committees	4. Execution of schemes (e.g. DTW/Mark-II/Tara Hand Pump) beyond the competence of village panchayats	4. Construction of wells, tanks, tubewells (ordinary hand pump)
		5. Maintenance and periodical disinfection		5. Handing over schemes to panchayats/user committees for day-to-day maintenance	5. Repair of tubewells, periodical chlorination of open wells and disinfection of tubewells

(continued)

Item no.	Subject (as per Schedule XI)	Activities	Activities of district committees	Activities of Block-level committees	Activities of village panchayat
12.	Fuel and fodder	1. Promotion of biogas plant training in construction of smokeless *chulhas*		1. To provide assistance and supervision in construction of biogas plants	1. Awareness generation and wide publicity
		2. Augmentation of fodder production through distribution of mini-kits, sale of seeds, *Kishan Bon*, fodder demonstration, etc.	2. (i) Fixing scale of distribution of mini-kit, seeds, manure per Block; (ii) Policy decision on purchase of seeds and sub-allotment of funds to different Blocks	2. (i) Supply of mini-kits to different panchayats and fixing scale of distribution of mini-kits per village panchayat; (ii) Monitoring and supervising distribution of mini-kits and sale of seeds to farmers	2. (i) Distribution of mini-kits, seeds, manure to farmers; (ii) Field demonstration to farmers
13.	Roads, culverts, brid-, ges, ferries, waterways and other means of communication	Planning, construction, upgrading roads, culverts:			
		1. For connectivity between Blocks and district roads	1. Constructing and upgrading roads/culverts exceeding Rs 10 lakhs		
		2. For connectivity within Block and between village panchayats		2. Constructing and upgrading roads/culverts amounting to Rs 2 to 10 lakhs	
		3. Connectivity between villages within the panchayat (WBM and earthen roads)			3. Constructing and upgrading roads, culverts, not exceeding Rs 2 lakhs
		4. Bridges	4. Construction of bridges		
14.	Rural electrification including distribution of electricity	1. Issuing certificates regarding electrification of villages (*mouzas*)			1. Issuing certificates by village head for electrification of villages (*mouzas*)
		2. Preparation of master plan for		2. To ensure co-ordinated efforts	

(continued)

Item no.	Subject (as per Schedule XI)	Activities	Activities of district committees	Activities of Block-level committees	Activities of village panchayat
		linking different villages (*mouzas*) with the network		between panchayat and other departments in respect of development of electricity infrastructure	
		3. Mobilising consumers		3. Organising workshops/ seminars at Block level for awareness generation	3. Mobilising consumers through authorised franchisees of WBSEB (self-help groups) for connectivity to households
		4. Identification of graded self-help groups	4. Identification of suitable graded self-help groups through DRDC and Standing Committee on Women and Child Development (*Nari o Shishu Unnayan Sthayee Samiti*) and capacity building of self-help groups for working as franchisees of West Bengal State Electricity Distribution Company Limited (WBSEDCL)		
		5. Energy management	5. Demonstration of energy-saving devices in Block-level committee office	5. Awareness generation regarding efficient management of energy	
		6. Energy-saving devices and demonstration of models			6. Demonstration of energy-saving devices in village panchayat office
		7. Monitoring constitution of Licensing Board in the district for issuing licences	7. Monitoring constitution of Licensing Board in the district for issuing licences		

(continued)

Item no.	Subject (as per Sched-ule XI)	Activities	Activities of district committees	Activities of Block-level committees	Activities of village panchayat
15.	Non-con-ventional energy sources	1. Identification of potential consumers			1. Identification of potential con-sumers of alter-native sources of energy
		2. Technical and financial assistance for installation of biogas in potential households		2. Extending technical and fin-ancial assistance for installation of biogas in poten-tial households	
		3. Development of demonstration models of biogas		3. Development of demonstration models of biogas, alternative sources of energy and bio-fuel for publicity	
		4. Development of energy parks	4. Development of energy parks for demonstration of alternative sources of energy and biofuel		
		5. Awareness generation for harnessing alter-native sources of energy, inclu-ding biofuel	5. Organising workshops/semi-nars to emphasise the need of har-nessing alternative sources of energy		5. Organising awareness camps for harnessing alternative sour-ces of energy including biofuel
16.	Poverty alleviation programmes	Planning, benefi-ciary selection and implementa-tion of (a) *SGRY*, (b) REGS, (c) *SGSY*, (d) *IAY*, (e) IGNOAPS, (f) NFBS, (g) Total Sanitation Cam-paign (TSC), etc.	1. Planning and implementation of works/schemes under *SGRY* exceeding Rs 10 lakhs	1. Planning and implementation of works/ schemes under *SGRY* between Rs 2 lakhs and 10 lakhs	1. Planning and implementation of works/ schemes under *SGRY* not excee-ding Rs 2 lakhs
			2. To inform State Government for giving unemploy-ment assistance under REGS; receipt of funds from State Govern-ment and allotment	2. Approval of action plan and schemes under REGS	2. Preparing list of prospective workers, distri-bution of job cards, planning and implemen-tation for works under REGS

(continued)

Item no.	Subject (as per Schedule XI)	Activities	Activities of district committees	Activities of Block-level committees	Activities of village panchayat
			of funds to BDOs, sending utilisation certificates to State Government		
			3. To allot funds under *IAY* to panchayats to ensure expenditure of 3% of funds for handicapped persons and sending compiled report of fund utilisation to State Government	3. Monitoring and supervision of *IAY* programme, collection of report and UC from all panchayats and sending to district panchayats	3. Identification and selection of beneficiaries for *IAY* through village assembly; handing over funds to beneficiaries
				4. Approval of names of pensioners under IGNOAPS received from village panchayat	4. Identification of beneficiaries for IGNOAPS through village assembly and disbursing pension to beneficiaries
				5. Sending names of beneficiaries under NFBS to Sub-Divisional Officer for approval	5. Identification of beneficiaries under NFBS through village assembly; recommmending names to Block-level committee; releasing funds to beneficiaries through 'account payee' cheques
			6. Releasing funds to Block-level committees for capacity building, organising Sanitary Marts and awareness campaigns	6. Selection of NGOs for running Sanitary Marts and organising awareness camps through NGOs/Clubs/voluntary organisations for total sanitation	6. Awareness camps and motivating people for sanitary toilets; listing of names for toilet construction and handing it over to Sanitary Mart. Meeting with teachers and

(continued)

Item no.	Subject (as per Schedule XI)	Activities	Activities of district committees	Activities of Block-level committees	Activities of village panchayat
					members of village education committee for school sanitation
17.	Education, including primary and secondary schools	1. Identification of school-less hamlets (*mouzas*)	1. Identification of school-less hamlets (*mouzas*) in district for preparation of status report	1. Collection of proposals for new *SSK/MSK* from panchayats and sending the plan to district panchayat for approval	1. Identification of school-less hamlets (*mouzas*) for opening *SSK/MSK* and sending proposals to Block-level committee
		2. Organising alternative school education: *Shishu Shiksha Karmasuchi* (SSK) and *Madhyamik Shiksha Karmasuchi* (MSK); improvement of school infrastructure, e.g. buildings, toilet, kitchen, etc.	2. Preparation of action plan for organising *SSK/MSK* in district	2. Construction of *SSK/MSK* from SGRY/RIDF/ untied funds/ own-source revenue, etc.	2. Construction of *SSK/MSK* through own fund/*SGRY*/ untied funds/ local contributions and funds received from Block-level committee
		3. Information collection/supervision/monitoring through EMIS and District Information System for Education	3. Supervision/ monitoring and report collection through District Information System for Education	3. Collection of information through EMIS and District Information System for Education and analysis of information	3. To supervise attendance of teachers and students, quality of midday meals, distribution of books
			4. Fund release for teachers' salary	4. Release of fund for salary of teachers of *SSK/MSK*	
18.	Adult and non-formal education	1. To impart education up to *Madhyamik* level to interested adult learners not enrolled in schools	1. Consideration of proposal for opening of new Adult High School. (To be forwarded to the MEE Department with recommendation or otherwise)	1. Publicity and Supervision of Adult High Schools.	1. Publicity and Supervision of Adult High Schools

(continued)

Item no.	Subject (as per Schedule XI)	Activities	Activities of district committees	Activities of Block-level committees	Activities of village panchayat
		2. Monitoring and supervision of Continuing Education Centres	2. Planning, Monitoring and Supervision by the *Zilla Saksharata Samiti*	2. Monitoring and supervision of Continuing Education Centres	2. Regular contact with Literates/Neo-literates for attendance at Continuing Education Centres
19.	Libraries	1. Establishment and maintenance of libraries and reading rooms and supervision of activities of rural libraries	1. Supervision of activities of district libraries	1. Supervision of activities of sponsored libraries	1. Establishment and maintenance of libraries and reading rooms and supervision of activities of rural libraries/ CLIC
		2. Dissemination of information on Rural Development Programmes, social issues, locally available resources, functioning of PRIs	2. Sending information to District Library: (i) copies of guidelines/ booklets for all development programmes (ii) Annual Report/ Budget/Annual Plan of district panchayat (iii) information on social issues	2. Sending information to Sponsored Library: (i) copies of guidelines/ booklets for all development programmes (ii) copy of Annual Report/ Budget/Annual Plan of Block-level committee (iii) information on social issues	2. Sending copies of guidelines/ booklets for all development programmes, Annual Report/ Budget/Annual Plan of village panchayat and information on social issues to Rural Library/ CLIC for general information of public
		3. Disbursing salaries to organisers of CLIC		3. Disbursing salaries to organisers of CLIC	
		4. Audit of CLIC by Panchayat Audit and Accounts Officer		4. Audit of CLIC by Panchayat Audit and Accounts Officer	
20.	Cultural activities	1. Celebration of red-letter days	1. Selection of Blocks and release of funds	1. Liaison with village panchayats for organising programmes/ campaigns	1. Wide publicity campaigns and selection of venues
		2. Organising folk festivals	2. Selection of themes for folk	2. Selection of village panchayat	2. Selection of venues for

(continued)

Item no.	Subject (as per Schedule XI)	Activities	Activities of district committees	Activities of Block-level committees	Activities of village panchayat
			festivals	for organising folk festivals and providing infrastructural support	festivals and identification of participants
	3. Workshops on Tagore songs, Nazrul songs, and folk songs	3. Supply of musical instruments and selection of teachers			
	4. Selection of films for each Block	4. Contact with cinema hall owners and fixing time for film shows	4. Contact with schools for publicity among students	4. Distribution of entry tickets/cards	
21.	Markets and fairs	1. Management of village markets up to an area of 5 acres	1. Management of village markets transferred to district panchayat by State Government	1. Management of village markets transferred to Block-level committee by State Government	1. Management of village markets transferred to village panchayats by State Government
		2. To provide licences to hold fairs or	2. Issuing licences to hold fairs		
		3. To issue licence for *haat* or market		3. To issue licences for establishing markets	
		4. To hold village markets and fairs	4. Acquire and maintain village markets		4. Construction and regulation of markets, holding and regulation of fairs, village markets and exhibition of local produce and products of local handicrafts/home industries
22.	Health and sanitation, including hospitals, Primary Health	1. Maintenance of sub-centres, Bureau of Primary Health Care, Primary Health Centres,		1. Maintenance of Bureau of Primary Health Care and Primary Health Centres	1. Maintenance of sub-centres

(continued)

Item no.	Subject (as per Schedule XI)	Activities	Activities of district committees	Activities of Block-level committees	Activities of village panchayat
	Centres and dispensaries	District Hospital			
		2. Procuring materials and their distribution	2. Lifting of materials from State headquarters and supply to different Blocks	2. Local purchase of non-medical items required by Primary Health Centres and Bureaus of Primary Health Care as may be authorised by Health and Family Welfare Department	2. Local purchase of non-medical items required by sub-centres as may be authorised by Health and Family Welfare Department
		3. Monitoring and supervision of service delivery system	3. Compilation of reports and returns from Block level and analysis for monitoring crucial public health indicators	3. Compilation of monthly reports from sub-centres and village panchayats, and analysis for monitoring crucial public health indicators	3. Involving self-help groups in monitoring community health
		4. Involving community in promoting preventive health care management	4. Developing information, education and communication materials	4. Planning and organisation for information, education and communication activities	4. Disease surveillance to pre-empt outbreak, preventive measures against spread of communicable diseases
23.	Family welfare	1. Universal immunisation including Pulse Polio programme	1. Fund allotment, monitoring and supervision of immunisation programme, including Pulse Polio programme	1. Implementation of immunisation programme	1. Mobilisation of people for immunisation
		2. To assist people in adopting family planning measures through efficient functioning of sub-centres and supervision of	2. Development of infrastructure for institutional delivery	2. Promotion of institutional delivery	2. Promoting planned family norms and practices

(*continued*)

Item no.	Subject (as per Schedule XI)	Activities	Activities of district committees	Activities of Block-level committees	Activities of village panchayat
		health workers' work			
		3. Organisation of sterilisation camps	3. Organising sterilisation camps for eligible couples		3. Awareness camps for family planning and sterilisation
		4. Training of traditional birth attendants (*dais*)		4. Organising training of traditional birth attendants (*dais*)	
24.	Women and Child Development	1. Mobilising social support against social evils discriminating against women	1. Selection of beneficiaries for non-institutional care of children up to 18 years	1. Recommendation of beneficiaries for non-institutional care of children up to 18 years	1. Awareness generation in villages to motivate parents for pre-school education and immunisation of their children
		2. Formation of self-help groups	2. Monitoring formation of self-help groups, providing financial assistance and creating marketing support for self-help groups	2. Formation of self-help groups and providing training for key activities and group management	2. Formation of self-help groups
25.	Social Welfare	1. Identification of beneficiaries for social welfare schemes		1. Recommendation of names of beneficiaries for pension schemes to the District Magistrate for approval	1. Identifying beneficiaries for *Kishori Shakti Yojana* and pension schemes
		2. Issue of Below Poverty Line certificates for *Balika Sambriddhi Yojana*			2. Issuing Below Poverty Line certificates for beneficiaries of Balika *Sambriddhi Yojana*
		3. Identification of beneficiaries for PROFLAL (Provident Fund for Landless	3. Sanction and allotment of fund for payment to beneficiaries	3. Maintenance of PROFLAL accounts and payment of money on	3. Identification of PROFLAL beneficiaries and collection of subscriptions

(continued)

Item no.	Subject (as per Schedule XI)	Activities	Activities of district committees	Activities of Block-level committees	Activities of village panchayat
	Agricultural Labourers)			maturity of scheme or death of beneficiary	
26.	Welfare of women and children	1. Construction of *anganwadi* centres		1. Supervision of construction of *anganwadi* centres	1. Recommendation of sites for *anganwadi* centres and construction of *anganwadi* centres
		2. Monitoring and supervision of programmes and convergence of Integrated Child Development Services' activities	2. Monitoring and supervision of *anganwadi* centres and convergence of activities		2. Convergence of ICDS activities and reporting of functioning of *anganwadi* centres in the convergence meeting at the village panchayat level
27.	Public distribution system	1. Identification of beneficiaries of *Antyodaya* and *Annapurna* schemes	1. Approval of beneficiary list	1. Preparation of list of beneficiaries for Below Poverty Line cards	1. Identification and selection of beneficiaries for distribution of Below Poverty Line cards, *Antyodaya* cards and *Annapurna* cards
		2. Lifting of foodgrains from Food Corporation of India	2. Monitoring lifting of foodgrains from Food Corporation of India	2. Monitoring distribution of foodgrains to MR dealers	2. Monitoring distribution of foodgrains from MR shops to beneficiaries
		3. Distribution of ration cards		3. Monitoring preparation and distribution of ration cards	
		4. Selection of Farmers' Cooperative Societies		4. Selection of Farmers' Cooperative Societies for purchase of paddy	4. Providing certificates confirming procurement of paddy from farmers at Minimum Support Price

(continued)

Item no.	Subject (as per Schedule XI)	Activities	Activities of district committees	Activities of Block-level committees	Activities of village panchayat
		5. Fixing targets for each rice mill	5. Fixing targets for each rice mill		
		6. Milling of paddy and storing of rice	6. Monitoring milling of paddy and storing of rice in godowns		
28.	Maintenance of community assets	1. Development and maintenance of public assets, such as buildings, shopping centres, passenger sheds, bathing *ghats*, ferry *ghats*, tanks, community centres, auditoria, playgrounds, etc.	1. Manage or maintain any institution for promotion of livelihood, education, health, communication, tourism or public utility works, including auditoria, dispensaries, diagnostic clinics, bus-stands, guest houses, eco-parks constructed by it or vested in it for control and management	1. Management and maintenance of any institution for promotion of livelihood, education, health, communication, tourism or public utility works, including village markets, auditoria, bus-stands, eco-parks, guest houses constructed by it or vested in it for control and management	1. Maintenance of community assets such as public tanks, *ghats*, public channels, reservoirs, wells, streets, drains, culverts, lamp posts, etc.
		2. Construction and maintenance of public assets	2. Management of roadside land		2. Construction and maintenance of resting places for travellers and pilgrims, rest-houses, cattle sheds, cart stand, and protection and repair of buildings or other property vested in it
		3. Fixing and collecting rents/ user charges	3. Fixing and collecting toll, fees, rates as user charges	3. Fixing and collecting tolls, fees, rates as user charges	3. Fixing and collecting tolls, fees, rates as user charges

Source: Third State Finance Commission of West Bengal (2008, Annexure XII).

The Task Force on devolution of powers and functions upon panchayati raj institutions worked out a format for Activity Mapping of "Agriculture." The main features of the activities specified in the mapping format are given below:

Item-1	Activity	Distribution of functions		
		District panchayat (*zilla panchayat*)	Intermediate panchayat (*panchayat samiti*)	Village panchayat (*gram panchayat*)
Agriculture including agricultural extension	1. Increasing agricultural, horticultural and vegetable production	(i) To develop necessary agricultural infrastructure	(i) To help in crop yield estimation through maintaining links with various agencies and village panchayats/farmers	(i) Estimation of crop yield and maintaining a database
		(ii) To prepare a comprehensive crop plan	(ii) To advise suitable cropping system based on location-specific characteristics	(ii) To assist in preparation of a crop plan
		(iii) To develop and maintain a database for cropping pattern, land use and inputs use for planning	(iii) To assist DP in organising farmers' fairs, *kisan mela*, etc.	(iii) To assist in advising farmers about remunerative crop activities and crop diversification
		(iv) To maintain inventory of technological options	iv) To organise on-farm verification trials and demonstration of new technologies	(iv) To assist in identifying progressive farmers for adoption and diffusion of new technologies
		(v) To propagate adoption of new technologies	(v) Reporting and initiating action plan for different items	(v) To help in providing custom hiring services for plant protection equipment and farm implements
		(vi) To organise farmers' (*kisan*) *melas*, fairs and exhibitions	(vi) To coordinate activities of field-level extension workers and officials	(vi) To generate awareness in use of organic vermiculture, etc.
		(vii) To arrange awards to best progressive farmers	(vii) To act as a link between DP and village panchayats for transfer of knowledge and technologies	
		(viii) To protect bio-diversity and promote profitable crop technologies		
	2. Assessment and distribution of inputs	(i) To prepare a consolidated plan for input requirement	(i) Assessing inputs needs for village panchayats and forwarding consolidated request to DPs	(i) To assist in assessing needs of various inputs such as seeds, fertilizers, pesticides.

(continued)

Item-1	Activity	Distribution of functions		
		District panchayat (*zilla panchayat*)	Intermediate panchayat (*panchayat samiti*)	Village panchayat (*gram panchayat*)
		(ii) To acquire and arrange distribution of inputs in time	(ii) Ensuring timely availability of required inputs to village panchayats	(ii) To assist in timely distribution of adequate inputs to farmers
		(iii) To improve adequate storage facilities for inputs	(iii) Arranging storage and transport facilities for inputs	
		(iv) To monitor distribution of quality inputs	(iv) Close monitoring of the inputs delivery system	
	3. Credit support	(i) Preparing a credit plan	(i) To assist in preparing credit plans	(i) To assist in assessing credit needs of various groups of farmers and crops.
		(ii) Ensuring timely credit availability and linkage between agricultural development and credit institutions, and monitoring credit mobilisation	(ii) Ensuring timely credit from formal institutions	(ii) Exercising social control and regulating interest areas and recovery of loans from formal and informal credit institutions
		(iii) Help in strengthening cooperative credit institutions	(iii) Monitoring credit delivery system.	(iii) Help in formation of self-help groups
	4. Extension support	(i) To maintain linkage with research and training organisations and agriculture departments	(i) To monitor the visit of extension workers to village. farms	(i) Identifying suitable plots for conducting soil and demonstration
		(ii) To ensure regular visits of extension staff and to help in disseminating new technologies	(ii) To prepare plans for visiting extension workers and monitor their work	(ii) Selecting farmers for participating in farmers' (*kisan*) *melas* and training
		(iii) To ensure regular training of extension officials for updating their knowledge of advancements in technologies	(iii) To advise and identify extension officials for training	
			(iv) To assist scientists in identifying local problems for designing	

(continued)

Item-1	Activity	Distribution of functions		
		District panchayat (*zilla panchayat*)	Intermediate panchayat (*panchayat samiti*)	Village panchayat (*gram panchayat*)
			their research work relevant to local needs (v) Ensuring better linkages between farmers and extension staff	
	5. Soil testing	(i) To establish soil-testing laboratories and own them (ii) To monitor soil-testing work	(i) To monitor soil-testing work (ii) To help in identifying locations for soil-testing work (iii) To help farmers for improvement of soil fertility as per soil-testing results	(i) To assist technical experts in conducting soil tests (ii) To help in giving feedback from soil-testing to farmers (iii) Selection of beneficiaries for relief of natural calamities and undertaking distribution of assistance
	6. Post-harvest management	(i) To establish and improve storage facilities (ii) To develop marketing infrastructure at suitable locations (iii) Monitoring regulated marketing (iv) To control private traders from exploiting farmers (v) To ensure correct weights and measures (vi) Supervision of crop insurance facility	(i) Maintenance of godowns (ii) To organise market committees and maintain market yards (iii) Regular market charges and ensure correct weights and measures (iv) Ensuring quick sale of products and payment to farmers	(i) To help in organising farmers for group sale in bulk (ii) To assist in increased awareness about better storage facilities for seeds and foodgrains
	7. Risk management	(i) To assess losses due to natural calamities and formulate rehabilitation plans (ii) To monitor and supervise relief operations (iii) To arrange crop insurance schemes	(i) To estimate crop losses and report of action (ii) To monitor relief operations (iii) To help in identifying farmers for crop	(i) Reporting of losses due to natural calamities and rehabilitation requirements (ii) To supervise relief operations and distribution of materials (iii) To motivate farmers for using

(continued)

Item-1	Activity	Distribution of functions		
		District panchayat (*zilla panchayat*)	Intermediate panchayat (*panchayat samiti*)	Village panchayat (*gram panchayat*)
		and coordination among insurance agencies	insurance schemes	crop insurance schemes
		(iv) Preparation of contingency agricultural plans	(iv) To assist in providing benefits from crop insurance schemes	(iv) To assist in the implementation of contingency plan

Source: Ministry of Rural Development (2001).

BIBLIOGRAPHY

Bakshi, A. (2011), "Weakening Panchayats in West Bengal," *Review of Agrarian Studies*, vol. 1, no. 2.

Bakshi, A., and Okabe J. (2008), "Panchayat Level Databases: A West Bengal Case Study," *CITS Working Paper 2011–14*, Center for International Trade Studies, Faculty of Economics, Yokohama National University, Yokohama, available at http://www.econ.ynu.ac.jp/cits/publications/paper.html, viewed on November 30, 2014.

Barr, Julian, Basavraj, Settihalli, Girdwood, Alison, Harnmeijer, Jan Willem, Mukherjee, Anuradha, Prakash, Siddartha, and Thornton, Hilary (2007), *Evaluation of DFID Country Programmes Country Study: West Bengal State Programme, Final Report*, ITAD with KIT, and Verulam Consultants Private Ltd., available at http://www.oecd.org/derec/unitedkingdom/39770200.pdf, viewed on November 30, 2014.

Below Poverty Line Census (2002), available at http://bpl.nic.in/index.php?bpl=Y, viewed on November 30, 2014.

Central Statistical Organisation (2006), *Report of High Level Expert Committee on Basic Statistics for Local Level Development*, Ministry of Statistics and Programme Implementation, Government of India, New Delhi, available at http://mospi.nic.in/Mospi_New/upload/lld_data_13jan12/lldreport_ssd.pdf, viewed on November 30, 2014.

Central Statistical Organisation (2008), *Economic Census 2005: All India Report*, Ministry of Statistics and Programme Implementation, Government of India, New Delhi, available at http://mospi.nic.in/Mospi_New/upload/economic_census_2005/index_6june08.htm, viewed on November 30, 2014.

Central Statistical Organisation (2013), *Basic Statistics for Local Level Development: Instructions for Data Recordist*, vol. I, Ministry of Statistics and Programme Implementation, Government of India, New Delhi.

Central Statistics Office (2011), *Cross-Sectional Synthesis Report on Pilot Scheme of Basic Statistics for Local (Village) Level Development: Based on Results of the Pilot Scheme on BSLLD Executed in Selected States and UTs*, Ministry of Statistics and Programme Implementation, Government of India, New Delhi, available at http://mospi.nic.in/Mospi_New/upload/lld_data_13jan12/synthesis_report_11mar11.pdf, viewed on November 30, 2014.

Central Statistics Office (2014), *Report on Basic Statistics for Local Level Development (BSLLD) Pilot Study in Rural Areas*, Ministry of Statistics and Programme

Implementation, Government of India, New Delhi, available at http://mospi.nic.in/ Mospi_New/upload/lld_data_13jan12/Report_pilot_study_RuralAreas11sept14. pdf, viewed on November 30, 2014.

Centre for Budget and Governance Accountability (2011), *Transparency in State Budgets in India: Maharashtra*, New Delhi, available at http://www.cbgaindia. org/files/policy_briefs/Maharashtra.pdf, viewed on January 23, 2015.

Chakrabarti, Bhaskar, Chattopadhyay, Raghabendra, and Nath, Suman (2011), "Local Governments in Rural West Bengal, India and their Coordination with Line Departments," *Commonwealth Journal of Local Governance*, Issue 8/9, May–Nov, available at http://epress.lib.uts.edu.au/ojs/index.php/cjlg, viewed on November 30, 2014.

Chander, Avinash (2008), *Report on District Planning: Status and Way Forward*, Socio-Economic Research Division of Planning Commission, New Delhi, available at http://planningcommission.nic.in/reports/sereport/ser/ser_distplan.pdf, viewed on November 30, 2014.

Chaudhuri, Siladitya, and Gupta, Nivedita (2009), "Levels of Living and Poverty Patterns: A District-Wise Analysis for India," *Economic and Political Weekly*, vol. 44, no. 9.

Committee on Plan Projects (1959), *Report of the Team for the Study of Community Projects and National Extension Service* (Chairman: Balwantrai Mehta), Government of India, New Delhi.

Comptroller and Auditor General (2008), *Audit Report (Local Bodies) for the Year Ended March 2008*, Comptroller and Auditor General of India, New Delhi.

Comptroller and Auditor General (2009), *Model Accounting System for Panchayats (Formats, Guidelines and List of Codes)*, Comptroller and Auditor General and Ministry of Panchayati Raj, Government of India, New Delhi, available at http:// www.panchayat.gov.in/model-accounting-system1, viewed on November 30, 2014.

Comptroller and Auditor General (2014), *Report of the Comptroller and Auditor General of India on Local Bodies for the Year Ended 31 March 2013*, Government of Maharashtra, New Delhi.

Council of Europe (1985), "European Charter of Local Self-Government," Strasbourg.

Deshpande, Ravi, and D'Souza, Marcella (2009), *Panchayat Raj on the Ground: Issues in Village-Level Panchayat Raj Operation*, Watershed Organisation Trust, Pune.

Directorate of Economics and Statistics (2010), *Statistical Abstract of Maharashtra State, 2007–8*, Government of Maharashtra, Mumbai.

Directorate of Economics and Statistics (2012), *Basic Statistics for Local Level Development: Report on Pilot Scheme (Akola District in Maharashtra)*, Government of Maharashtra, Mumbai, available at http://mospi.nic.in/Mospi_New/upload/lld_ data_13jan12/state_report_2012.htm, viewed on November 30, 2014.

Directorate of Economics and Statistics (2012), *Basic Statistics for Local Level Development: A Pilot Study of Dharwad District*, Government of Karnataka, Bangalore.

DISNIC Programme Division (2005), *DISNIC-PLAN Project: Phase-II (Information*

Technology for Micro-Level Planning) A Project Sponsored by the Planning Commission, National Informatics Centre, Department of Information Technology, Ministry of Communications and Information Technology, Government of India, New Delhi.

Dongre, Ambrish, Chowdhury, Anirvan, and Barik, Suddhasattwa (2011), *Do Gram Panchayats Get their Money?: A Case Study of Gram Panchayat Fund Flows in Birbhum District, West Bengal*, PAISA Report, Accountability Initiative, New Delhi.

Eleventh Finance Commission (2000), *Report of the Eleventh Finance Commission*, New Delhi.

Elvers, E., and Rosén, B. (1997), "Quality Concept for Official Statistics," *Encyclopedia of Statistical Sciences*, John Wiley & Sons, New York.

European Commission, International Monetary Fund, Organisation for Economic Co-operation and Development, United Nations, and World Bank (2009), *System of National Accounts 2008*, available at http://unstats.un.org/unsd/nationalaccount/sna2008.asp, viewed on November 30, 2014.

Examiner of Local Accounts, West Bengal (2009), *The Report of the Examiner of Local Accounts on Panchayati Raj Institutions for the Year Ending 31 March 2009*, Government of West Bengal.

Gazetteers Department (n.d.), "Tahsildars and Naib Tahsildars," Government of Maharashtra, Mumbai, available at http://akola.nic.in/gazetteers/maharashtra/gen_admin_tahsildar.html, viewed on November 30, 2014.

Government of Maharashtra (2008), *Annual Budget Report on Gram Panchayats in Maharashtra 2007–8*, Comptroller and Auditor General and Ministry of Panchayati Raj, Government of India, New Delhi.

Government of Maharashtra (2012), *Annual Budget Report on Gram Panchayats in Maharashtra 2011–2*, Comptroller and Auditor General and Ministry of Panchayati Raj, Government of India, New Delhi.

Government of West Bengal (2006–7), *Gram Panchayater Abasthaner Mulyayaner Pratibedan, 2006–7* (Self-Evaluation Schedule of Gram Panchayat 2006–7), Panchayats and Rural Development Department, Kolkata.

Himanshu (2008), "What Are These New Poverty Estimates and What Do They Imply?" *Economic and Political Weekly*, vol. 43, no. 43.

Himanshu (2010), "Poverty's Definitional Woes," *Live Mint*, May 27.

International Institute for Population Sciences (2007), *National Family Health Survey (NFHS-3) 2005–6*, vol. I, Mumbai, available at http://www.rchiips.org/nfhs/nfhs3_national_report.shtml, viewed on November 30, 2014.

International Institute for Population Sciences (2010), *District Level Household and Facility Survey 2007–8*, Mumbai, available at http://www.rchiips.org/pdf/INDIA_REPORT_DLHS-3.pdf, viewed on November 30, 2014.

Isaac, Thomas T. M., and Franke, Richard W. (2000), *Local Democracy and Development: People's Campaign for Decentralised Planning in Kerala*, LeftWord Books, New Delhi.

Jain, Sachin Kumar (2004), "Identification of the Poor: Flaws in Government Surveys," *Economic and Political Weekly*, vol. 39, nos 46–47.

Jalan, Jyotsna, and Panda, Jharna (2010), *Low Mean and High Variance: Quality of Primary Education in Rural West Bengal*, Centre for Studies in Social Sciences, Calcutta.

Japan International Cooperation Agency (2008), *Draft Final Report: The Study on the Improvement of Internal Revenue Allotment (IRA) System in the Republic of the Philippines*, KRI International Corp, Tokyo.

Kashyap, Anirban (1989), *Panchayati Raj: Views of Founding Fathers and Recommendations of Different Committees*, Lancers Books, New Delhi.

Kerala Administrative Reforms Commission (1959), *Report of the Administrative Reforms Committee* (Chairman: E.M.S. Namboodiripad), Trivandrum.

Kumar, Girish (2006), *Local Democracy in India: Interpreting Decentralisation*, Sage Publications, New Delhi.

Laliberté, L., Grünewald, W., and Probst, L. (2004), *Data Quality: A Comparison of IMF's Data Quality Assessment Framework (DQAF) and Eurostat's Quality Definition*, available at http://dsbb.imf.org/Applications/web/dqrs/dqrswork/, viewed on November 30, 2014.

Marx, Karl (1843), *Kritik des Hegelschen Staatsrechts, Marx-Engels-Werke (MEW)*, vol. 1 (*Critique of Hegel's Philosophy of Right*, Part 3), Berlin, available at https://www.marxists.org/archive/marx/works/1843/critique-hpr/index.htm, viewed on November 30, 2014.

Marx, Karl (1959), *Ökonomisch-philosophische Manuskripte, Karl Marx Friedrich Engels Gesamtausgabe* (*Economic and Philosophic Manuscripts of 1844*), Progress Publishers, Moscow, available at http://www.marxists.org/archive/marx/works/1844/manuscripts/preface.htm, viewed on November 30, 2014.

Mathew, George (1995), *Status of Panchayati Raj in the States of India*, Concept Publishing Company, New Delhi.

Ministry of Agriculture (2006a), *Agricultural Census 2005–6: Manual of Schedules and Instructions for Data Collection* (*Land Record States*), Government of India, New Delhi, available at http://agcensus.nic.in/report/ac_lr_200506.pdf, viewed on November 30, 2014.

Ministry of Agriculture (2006b), *Agricultural Census 2005–6: Manual of Schedules and Instructions for Data Collection* (*Non-Land Record States*), Government of India, New Delhi, available at http://agcensus.nic.in/report/ac_nlr_200506.pdf, viewed on November 30, 2014.

Ministry of Agriculture and Irrigation (1978), *Report of the Committee on Panchayati Raj Institutions* (Chairman: Asoka Mehta), Department of Rural Development, Government of India, New Delhi.

Ministry of Human Resource Development (2009), *All India School Education Survey*, Department of Educational Surveys and Data Processing, Government of India, New Delhi, available at http://aises.nic.in/home, viewed on November 30, 2014.

Ministry of Panchayati Raj (2011), *Roadmap for the Panchayati Raj (2011–16): An All India Perspective*, Government of India, New Delhi.

Ministry of Rural Development (2001), *Report of the Task Force on Devolution of Powers and Functions upon Panchayati Raj Institutions*, Government of India, New Delhi.

Ministry of Rural Development (2009), *Report of the Expert Group to Advise the Ministry of Rural Development on the Methodology for Conducting the Below Poverty Line (BPL) Census for the 11th Five Year Plan*, Government of India, New Delhi.

Ministry of Rural Development (2011), *Instruction Manual for Enumerators: Socio-Economic and Caste Census 2011—Rural*, Government of India, New Delhi.

Ministry of Statistics and Programme Implementation (2012), *Guide for Enumerators and Supervisors*, Government of India, New Delhi, available at http://mospi.nic. in/Mospi_New/upload/census_2012/EC_main_2012.htm, viewed on November 30, 2014.

Mukherjee, Amitava (ed.) (1994), *Decentralisation: Panchayats in the Nineties*, Vikas Publishing House, New Delhi.

National Statistical Commission (2001), *Report of the National Statistical Commission*, New Delhi, available at http://mospi.gov.in/nscr/hp.htm, viewed on November 30, 2014.

OECD (2002), *Measuring the Non-Observed Economy: A Handbook*, Organisation for Economic Co-operation and Development, Paris.

Office of the Registrar General, India (1998), *Handbook of Civil Registration*, 4th edn, New Delhi.

Office of the Registrar General, India (2009), *Annual Report on Vital Statistics of India based on CRS-2009*, New Delhi, available at http://www.censusindia.gov.in/2011-Common/CRS.html, viewed on November 30, 2014.

Office of the Registrar General, India (2011), *Annual Report on Vital Statistics of India based on CRS-2011*, New Delhi, available at http://www.censusindia.gov.in/2011-Common/CRS.html, viewed on November 30, 2014.

Okabe, Jun-ichi and Surjit, V. (2012), "Village-Level Birth Records: A Case Study," *Review of Agrarian Studies*, vol. 2, no. 1, available at http://www.ras.org.in/ village_level_birth_records, viewed on November 30, 2014.

Oommen, M.A. (ed.) (2008), *Fiscal Decentralisation to Local Governments in India*, Cambridge Scholars Publishing, Newcastle.

Panchayats and Rural Development Department (2006), *Annual Administrative Report 2005–6*, Government of West Bengal, Kolkata.

Panchayats and Rural Development Department (2007), *Annual Administrative Report 2006–7*, Government of West Bengal, Kolkata, available at http://www. wbprd.gov.in/HtmlPage/Reports.aspx, viewed on November 30, 2014.

Panchayats and Rural Development Department (2008a), *Annual Administrative Report 2007–8*, Government of West Bengal, Kolkata.

Panchayats and Rural Development Department (2008b), *Self- Evaluation Schedule for Gram Panchayats 2007–8*, Government of West Bengal, Kolkata.

Panchayats and Rural Development Department (2009a), *Annual Administrative Report 2008–9*, Government of West Bengal, Kolkata.

Panchayats and Rural Development Department (2009b), *Roadmap for the Panchayats in West Bengal: A Vision Document*, Government of West Bengal, Kolkata, available at http://www.wbprd.gov.in/HtmlPage/Reports.aspx, viewed on November 30, 2014.

PARI (2007), Survey data, Project on Agrarian Relations in India, Foundation for Agrarian Studies, Bengaluru.

Planning Commission (1952), *First Five Year Plan 1951–6*, New Delhi.

Planning Commission (2007), *Maharashtra State Development Report*, Academic Foundation, New Delhi.

Planning Commission (2008a), *Eleventh Five Year Plan 2007–12*, Volume I, Government of India, New Delhi.

Planning Commission (2008b), *Manual for Integrated District Planning*, Government of India, New Delhi, available at http://planningcommission.gov.in/reports/genrep/mlp_idpe.pdf, viewed on November 30, 2014.

Pradhan Mantri Gram Sadak Yojana, available at www.trendswestbengal.org/pmgsy, viewed on November 30, 2014.

Rai, Manoj, Nambiar, Malini, Paul, Sohini, Singh, Sangeeta U., and Sahni, Satinder S. (eds) (2001), *The State of Panchayats: A Participatory Perspective*, Samskriti, New Delhi.

Raina Gram Panchayat (2008), *Protibedon*, Raina, West Bengal.

Rajaraman, Indira (2003), *A Fiscal Domain for Panchayats*, Oxford University Press, New Delhi.

Rao, Govinda M., and Rao, Vasanth U.A. (2008), "Expanding the Resource Base of Panchayats: Augmenting Own Revenues," *Economic and Political Weekly*, vol. 43, no. 4.

Rural Development Statistics (2011-2), National Institute of Rural Development, Ministry of Rural Development, Government of India, New Delhi, available at http://www.nird.org.in/Rural%20Development%20Statistics%202011-12/rds index.html, viewed on June 30, 2015.

Sasaki, Yu (2005), "Decentralisation or Retreat of the State?: Comparison of House Tax Collection in Village Panchayats in Madhya Pradesh and Tamil Nadu," *Journal of the Japanese Association for South Asian Studies*, vol. 17.

Second Administrative Reforms Commission (2007), *Sixth Report on Local Governance: An Inspiring Journey into the Future*, New Delhi, available at http://arc.gov.in/6-1.pdf, viewed on November 30, 2014.

Sen, Amartya (1992), *Inequality Re-Examined*, Oxford University Press, New York.

Sridhar, V. (2013), "The Data Challenge at the Gram Panchayat Level," *The Hindu*, November 8, available at http://www.thehindu.com/business/Economy/the-data-challenge-at-the-gram-panchayat-level/article5329852.ece, viewed on November 30, 2014.

Sundaram, K. (2003), "On Identification of Households Below Poverty Line in BPL

Census 2002: Some Comments on the Proposed Methodology," *Economic and Political Weekly*, vol. 38, no. 9.

Synthesis reports, available at http://mospi.nic.in/Mospi_New/upload/lld_data_13jan12/state_report_2012.htm, viewed on November 30, 2014.

Third State Finance Commission of West Bengal (2008), *Report of the Third State Finance Commission, West Bengal*, available at http://www.wbfin.nic.in/Page/publication.aspx?type=16, viewed on November 30, 2014.

Thirteenth Finance Commission (2009), *Report of the Thirteenth Finance Commission*, New Delhi.

Thygesen, Lars (1995), "The Register-Based System of Demographic and Social Statistics in Denmark: An Overview," *Statistical Journal*, vol. 12, no. 1, United Nations Economic Commission for Europe.

Twelfth Finance Commission (2004), *Report of the Twelfth Finance Commission*, New Delhi.

UNICEF (2005), *The "Right" to Start to Life*, United Nations Children's Fund, New York, available at http://www.unicef.org/publications/index_25248.html, viewed on November 30, 2014.

United Nations (2001), *Principles and Recommendations for a Vital Statistics System, Revision 2*, Statistics Division, United Nations.

United Nations Economic Commission for Europe (2007), *Register-Based Statistics in the Nordic Countries*, United Nations, Geneva.

Unnikrishnan, P.V. (2012), *Strategic Management of Information Communication Technologies in the Third World Context*, Ph.D. thesis submitted to University of Kerala, Department of Future Studies, Thiruvananthapuram.

Usami, Yoshifumi, Sarkar, Biplab, and Ramachandran, V.K. (2010), 'Are the Results of BPL Census 2002 Reliable?' presented at International Conference on Environment, Agriculture and Socio-Economic Change in Rural India, Kyungpook National University, Daegu, South Korea, March 29–30, available at http://www.agrarianstudies.org/UserFiles/File/Usami_Biplab_Ramachandran_Reliability_of_BPL_Census1.pdf#search='BPL+census+2002', viewed on November 30, 2014.

INDEX

Aam Admi Bima Yojana, 171

Accelerated Irrigation Benefits Programme (AIBP), 34–5

Accelerated Rural Water Supply Programme (ARWSP), 34

Activity Mapping, 22, 23, 24, 25, 40, 49, 52, 54, 55, 58, 84, 85, 90, 91, 92, 116, 118, 122, 128, 147, 182, 217, 227, 229, 293, 296, 339

Agricultural Census (2005–6), 199

Akola, 108, 224, 246

All-India School Education Survey (AISES), 202, 249, 255, 309

Andhra Pradesh, 39, 317

Anganwadi; see Integrated Child Development Services (ICDS)

Annapurna scheme, 84, 90, 95, 222, 232, 328

Antyodaya scheme, 84, 90, 95, 172, 212, 222, 232, 328

Arabic, 180

Assam, 39, 306, 312, 315

Backward Regions Grant Fund, 49

Balika Samriddhi Yojana, 90, 229, 328

Balwantrai Mehta Committee, 65, 66

Bardhaman (district), 62, 209, 212

Bardhaman (town), 62, 63

Basic Statistics for Local Level Development report, 51, 55, 57, 73, 155, 177, 203, 205, 211, 237, 238, 243, 296, 297, 301, 306, 309, 312, 315, 316, 320, 321, 332, 339, 340, 341

Below Poverty Line Census (2005); see Rural Household Survey (2005)

Below Poverty Line Census (2011); see Socio-Economic Caste Census (2011)

Below Poverty Line Census, West Bengal (2002); see Rural Household Survey, West Bengal (2002)

Bengali, 258

Bhandara, 108

Bharatiya Janata Party, 11

Bhavishyanidhi Yojana, 213

Bidhayak Elaka Unnayan Prakalpa, 212

Bidyanidhi (village), 7, 9, 59, 63–5, 68, 87, 160, 177, 181, 194, 195, 208, 235, 246, 249, 258, 260, 262, 265, 270, 271, 308, 335

Bihar, 203

Birampur (village), 177

Bogra, 208

Bombay Local Fund Audit Act (1930), 107

Bombay Village Panchayats (Budget and Accounts) Rule (1959), 110, 111, 274

Bombay Village Panchayats Act (1958), 20, 36, 79, 80, 85 107, 116, 123, 163, 164, 176, 181, 186, 216, 217, 218, 219, 222, 223, 224, 238, 239, 248, 254, 273, 302, 312, 315, 321, 323, 330

Bonkati (village panchayat), 212

Buldhana (district), 7, 59, 99, 208, 224, 239

Census Act (1948), 32, 153, 198, 245

Census of India (2011), 196–7, 209, 267, 307, 335

Central Statistical Organisation, 159

Citizenship Act (1955), 267

Citizenship (Registration of Citizens and Issue of National Identity Cards) Rules (2003), 267

Civil Registration System (CRS), 29, 34, 165, 170, 176, 179, 245, 253, 254, 266, 267, 268, 269, 270, 271, 331, 343

Communist Party of India (Marxist), 11

Comptroller & Auditor General of India's (Duties, Powers and Conditions of Services) Act (1971), 107

Congress Party, 11

Constitution (Seventy-Third Amendment) Act (1992); see Seventy-Third Amendment (1992)

Dalit Basti Sudhar Yojana, 238

Damodar (river), 62

Department for International Development

(DFID), Government of the United Kingdom, 104, 120
Devanagari, 258

Eleventh Central Finance Commission, 40, 42, 45
Establishment of an Agency for Reporting Agricultural Statistics (EARAS) scheme, 200, 248, 312, 321
Expert Committee on Basic Statistics for Local Development, 203, 210

Fifth Economic Census (2005), 201
First Finance Commission of West Bengal, 114
Follow-up Enterprise Survey, 202
Foundation for Agrarian Studies (FAS), 7, 9, 59, 63, 194, 215, 256, 258, 261, 262, 265, 268, 270, 271

Gadgil Formula, 44
Goa, 313
Gram Panchayat Rules (2004), 166
Gram Panchayat Rules (2007), 167, 170, 287
Gujarat, 203, 315
Gupta, S.P., 3

Haryana, 203, 237, 306, 308, 313, 317
Hazare, Anna, 109
Himachal Pradesh, 39

India, 155
Indira Awaas Yojana (*IAY*), 34, 82, 84, 88, 94, 96, 109, 117, 189, 213, 221, 229, 232, 238, 328, 331
Indira Gandhi National Old Age Pension Scheme (IGNOAPS), 83, 88, 94, 96, 189, 221, 229, 232, 328
Information Kerala Mission (IKM), 155
Institutional Strengthening of Gram Panchayat (ISGP) scheme, 96
Integrated Child Development Services (ICDS) / *anganwadi*, 4, 10, 25, 33, 34, 37, 65, 72, 75, 83, 90, 93, 94, 95, 96, 145, 152, 158, 159, 160, 171, 173, 174, 175, 176, 177, 179, 180, 181, 195, 198, 208, 220–1, 227, 233, 240, 244, 245–7, 249, 250, 251, 252, 254, 261, 262, 263, 266, 267, 270, 271, 272, 303, 306, 308, 309, 314, 321, 324–5, 327, 332, 337, 340, 341

Jalpaiguri, 112, 280
Japan International Cooperation Agency, 47

Kalamkhed, 181, 182
Karnataka, 39, 203, 237
Karnataka Development Programme (KDP), 237
Kerala, 6, 9, 39, 48, 53, 103, 118, 155, 203, 292, 293, 306, 308, 313, 315, 316, 317, 321
Kishori Shakti Yojana, 90, 229, 328
Kolhapur, 108

Madhya Pradesh, 39, 42
Madhyamik Shiksha Karmasuchi, 88
Maharashtra, 7, 29, 41, 59, 65–6, 67, 70, 71, 72, 74, 75, 76, 79, 80, 84, 93, 95, 98, 99, 100, 103, 106, 107, 108, 109, 113, 114, 115, 116, 120, 121, 121, 122, 123, 165, 167, 170, 176, 179, 181, 183, 186, 187, 199, 201, 202, 214, 239, 246, 247, 248, 253, 254, 275, 278, 285, 296, 306, 308, 309, 312, 315, 316, 317, 320, 321, 325, 326, 335, 344
Maharashtra Gramin Paani Parota Yojana, 94
Maharashtra Remote Sensing Application Centre, 212
Maharashtra Rural Water Supply Scheme, 286
Maharashtra State Development Report (2007), 41
Maharashtra Village Panchayat (Audit of Accounts) Rules (1961), 107
Maharashtra Zilla Parishad and Panchayat Samiti Act (1961), 80, 107, 218, 335
Mahatma Gandhi National Rural Employment Guarantee Scheme (MGNREGS), 34, 49, 54, 75, 88, 93, 94, 95, 96, 97, 98, 117, 120, 165–6, 171–2, 212, 213, 221, 226, 229, 230, 236, 266, 279, 315, 324, 326, 328, 329, 331, 335, 340
Mahatma Gandhi Tanta Mukti Gaon Mohim, 77
Mantralaya (Mumbai), 109
Manual for Integrated District Planning, 22, 35, 36, 37, 48, 50, 51, 52, 336
Marathi, 179, 180, 202
Marathwada, 77
Meghalaya, 203, 313
Mehta, Balwantrai, 1
Mid-Day Meals Programme (MDM), 34
Ministry of Agriculture, 198
Ministry of Home Affairs, 195

Ministry of Rural Development, 189, 190, 192, 193, 325
Ministry of Statistics and Programme Implementation, 203, 204, 206, 253, 296, 297
Ministry of Women and Child Development, 174

National Bank for Agricultural and Rural Development (NABARD), 52
National Council of Educational Research and Training (NCERT), 202
National Family Benefit Scheme (NFBS), 83, 94, 189, 221, 229, 232, 328
National Family Health Survey (2005–6), 30
National Maternity Benefit Scheme (NMBS), 83, 96, 220
National Population Register (NPR), 267, 342, 344, 345
National Rural Employment Guarantee Act (NREGA) (2005), 97, 230
National Rural Health Mission (NRHM), 34, 96, 327
National Rural Livelihoods Mission; *see* *Swarnajayanti Gram Swarozgar Yojana*
National Sample Survey Organisation (NSSO), 185
National Social Assistance Programme (NSAP), 34
National Statistical Commission, 152, 155, 179, 195, 198, 199, 202, 244, 245, 252, 267, 344
Nirmal Gaon Seva, 220

Paani Parota Yojana, 82, 94, 331
Panchayat Samiti Act (1961), 79
Paturda, 180, 183
Planning Commission, 189, 294, 333
Potential Linked Credit Plan (PLCP), 52
Pradhan Mantri Gram Sadak Yojana (PMGSY), 34, 233, 335
Project on Agrarian Relations in India (PARI), 59
Protibedon, 212, 229, 278, 280, 284, 341
Provident Fund for Landless Agricultural Labourers (PROFLAL), 90, 96, 171, 229, 328
Pune, 108

Quran, 180

Raina (village and village panchayat), 7, 59,

62–5, 68, 69, 73, 85, 91, 96, 105, 111, 119, 154, 155, 157, 159, 160, 161, 163, 167, 168, 170–1, 172, 173, 177, 178, 181, 182, 187, 188, 193, 198, 199, 200, 201, 208, 209, 210, 211, 212, 215, 216, 224–36, 240, 243, 244, 246, 250, 251, 257, 269, 278, 279–80, 283, 284, 286, 287, 293, 294, 301, 306, 309, 312, 314, 317, 321, 325, 326, 327, 329, 332
Rajaraman, Indira, 42
Rajasthan, 306, 315
Rajiv Gandhi Gandhi Niwara Yojana, 109, 238
Rajiv Gandhi Grameen Vidyutikaran Yojana (RGGVY), 35
Ramachandran, V.K., 59
Rangarajan, C., 2
Rawal, Vikas, 59
Right to Education Act (2009), 238, 324
Right to Information Act (2005), 26
Rural Household Survey (2002), 27, 189, 190, 192, 194, 247, 250, 251, 258, 308, 342
Rural Household Survey (2005), 172, 193, 194
Rural Infrastructure Development Fund (RIDF), 103

Sajaldhara scheme, 87, 96, 212
Sample Registration System (SRS), 269
Sampoorna Grameen Rozgar Yojana (SGSY), 88, 96, 97, 98, 212, 213, 229, 273, 328
Sangli, 108
Sangrampur (tehsil), 59, 115, 183, 186, 212, 239, 285
Sanjay Gandhi Niradhar Anudhan Yojana (SGNY), 83, 94, 117, 221
Sarva Shiksha Abhiyan (SSA), 34, 49
Satara, 108
Saxena, N.C., 264
Second Administrative Reforms Commission, 35, 49, 55, 79, 92, 93, 121, 217
Self-Evaluation Schedule for Panchayats (West Bengal), 211, 241
Sen, Abhijit, 4
Seventy-Fourth Amendment, 121, 195
Seventy-Third Amendment (1992), 1, 2, 6, 7, 8, 12, 13, 15, 18, 19, 24, 32, 34, 39, 41, 43, 44, 50, 57, 58, 113, 114, 121, 122, 195, 215, 339, 343, 344
Shegaon, 180
Sikkim, 313
Shishu Shiksha Karmasuchi, 88
Sixth Economic Census (2012–3), 201
Socio-Economic and Caste Census (SECC)

(2011), 56, 195, 203, 235, 245, 247, 248, 249, 250, 251, 252, 264, 266, 295, 307, 308–9, 342, 344, 345
Solapur, 108
State Sanitation Programme (SSP), 96
"Strengthening Rural Decentralisation" (SRD) programme, 104
Swarnajayanti Gram Swarozgar Yojana, 54, 75, 93, 94, 226, 231, 299, 325, 326

Tamil Nadu, 42, 203, 306
Tenth Central Finance Commission, 43
Thakkar Bappa, 238
Third Economic Census (1990), 201, 202
Third State Finance Commission of West Bengal, 47, 53, 112, 113, 117, 118, 280, 283, 288, 289, 290, 291, 293
Thirteenth Central Finance Commission, 35, 39, 41, 44, 45, 46, 48, 109, 292, 337
Timely Reporting Scheme (TRS), 185–6
Trinamool Congress, 11
Tripura, 203
Twelfth Central Finance Commission, 39, 41, 42, 44, 45, 46, 47, 273

United Nations Children's Fund (UNICEF), 173
Urdu, 179, 180
Uttarakhand, 39, 306, 308, 315
Uttar Pradesh, 39

Vidarbha, 77
Village Schedule on Basic Statistics, 55, 56, 154, 155, 159, 161, 203–9, 206, 224, 226, 233, 235, 241, 243, 246, 292, 296, 321, 323, 325, 329, 330, 331, 332, 333, 334, 335, 341
V.P. Naik Committee, 65

Warwat Khanderao (village and village panchayat), 7, 9, 30, 59–62, 68, 72, 73, 75, 77,

80, 81, 83, 84, 93, 94, 95, 97, 98, 100, 101, 107, 110, 111, 116, 121, 154, 155, 156, 160, 162, 163, 165, 166, 170, 171, 172, 175, 176, 178, 179, 181, 183, 185, 192, 193, 198, 199, 200, 201, 202, 208, 210, 211, 212, 213, 215, 216, 218–3, 226, 237, 238, 239, 240, 243, 244, 246, 247, 250, 251, 254, 256, 257, 259, 260, 261, 265, 266, 268–9, 270, 273, 274, 275, 276, 285, 286, 288, 292, 294, 300, 306, 312, 314, 321, 323, 324, 325, 332, 333, 343
West Bengal, 7, 11, 15, 16, 20, 29, 40, 46, 62, 66–8, 70, 71, 72, 74, 75, 76, 77, 78, 82, 84, 85, 87, 91, 93, 95, 96, 98, 100, 101, 102, 103, 104, 106, 112, 114, 117, 118, 119, 120, 121, 122, 123, 128, 162, 166, 170, 172, 180, 182, 183, 185, 186, 188, 189, 199, 201, 202, 203, 214, 228, 248, 253, 278, 280, 283, 286, 290, 292, 293, 296, 312, 326, 327, 333, 335, 341, 343, 344
West Bengal Panchayat (Amendment) Act (1994), 85, 293
West Bengal Panchayat (Gram Panchayat Accounts, Audit and Budget) Rules (2007), 166, 168, 212, 234, 239, 278, 279, 283
West Bengal Panchayat (Gram Panchayat Administration) Rules (2004), 166, 216, 234, 286, 301
West Bengal Panchayat (Gram Panchayat Miscellaneous Accounts and Audit) Rules (1990), 279
West Bengal Panchayati Raj Act (1973), 20, 26, 85, 116, 118, 216, 217, 326, 330
West Bengal Rural Employment Guarantee Scheme (2006), 231
West Bengal Self-Evaluation Schedule for Panchayats, 20, 26, 216
World Bank, 173
World Census of Agriculture, 199

Ziya-ul-Quran *Madrassa*, 180, 262